- CREDITS -

Design: Graeme Davis

Additional Design: Scott Bennie (Soothsayer adventure)

Editing and Development: Spike Y Jones **Additional Development and Proofreading:** Robert J. Schwalb

Art Direction: Hal Mangold with Marc Schmalz **Graphic Design:** Marc Schmalz with Hal Mangold

Cover Art: David Leri **Cartography:** Hal Mangold

Interior Art: Kent Burles, David Griffiths, Joseph Wigfield, Marcio Fiorito, Richard Becker

Executive Producer: Chris Pramas

Green Ronin Staff: Steve Kenson, Nicole Lindroos, Hal Mangold, Chris Pramas, Evan Sass, Marc Schmalz, and Robert J. Schwalb

Playtesters: Keri Armstrong, KC Arnold, Joe Baker, Anthony J. Bernardi, Martin Chamberlain, Michael Consoletti, Chris Crawford, James Crawford, Thad Erickson, Brian Fallehy, Timm Ferree, Jan-Philipp Gürtler, Kristian Hartmann, Beth Hendrickson, Douglas Hendrickson, Kenny Hill, Joe Holsinger, Roo James, Zach Lint, Andrew McCool, Bruce Ripka, Clemens Schäfer, Conrad Schäfer, Bruce Shanks, Nancy Shanks, Chris Simpson, Christina Stiles, David Tufts Jr., Dave Vershaw, Aaron Wamsley, Jennifer Wamsley, Dave Weiner

GREEN RONIN PUBLISHING

P.O. Box 1723
Renton, WA 98057-1723

Email: custserv@greenronin.com
Web Site: www.greenronin.com

TABLE OF CONTENTS

Introduction 5

Chapter One: Characters 6
Eras 6
Nationalities 9

Chapter Two: Character Classes 15
Core Classes 15
   Barbarian 15
   Bard 16
   Cleric 17
   Druid 17
   Fighter 19
   Paladin 23
   Ranger 23
   Rogue 23
   Sorcerer and Wizard 23
New Class: The Gladiator 24
   Adventures 24
   Characteristics 24
   Alignment 24
   Background 24
   Game Rule Information 25
   Gladiator Types 28
Prestige Classes 29
   Arcane Archer 29
   Arcane Trickster 29
   Archmage 29
   Assassin 29
   Blackguard 30
   Duelist 30
   Dwarven Defender 30
   Eldritch Knight 30
   Hierophant 30
   Horizon Walker 30
   Loremaster 30
   Mystic Theurge 30
   Shadowdancer 30
   Thaumaturgist 30
New Prestige Class: Crime Boss 31
New Prestige Class: Orator 32
New Prestige Class: Pankretiast 35
New Prestige Class: Soothsayer 36
New Prestige Class: Vigil (Watchman) 38

Chapter Three: Skills and Feats 40
New Skill Uses 40
New Skills 41
New Feats 43

Chapter Four: Fame 49
Fame Points, Modifiers, and Checks 49
   Gaining and Losing Fame 49
   Negative Fame 49
   Fame Awards for Adventurers 50
Uses for Fame 51

Expectations of The Famous 54
Military Honors 55

Chapter Five: Equipment 56
   Gladiator Weapons 56
   Alternate Names 56
New Weapons 56
Armor 59
   New Armor 59
   Helmets 60
   Partial Armor 62
Equipment 62

Chapter Six: Roman Magic 64
Spells 64
   Druid Spells 65
New Spells 66
Magic Items 71
   New Wondrous Items 71
   Minor Artifacts 72
   Major Artifacts 73
The Evil Eye 74
   Casting the Evil Eye 74
   Countering the Evil Eye 75

Chapter Seven: Bestiary 77
Animals by Region 77
   New Animals 78
Standard Monsters 79
Variant Monsters 81
New Monsters 82
Legendary Races 86
Non-Human Races 87
   Dwarves and Gnomes 87
   Elves 88
   Halflings 88
   Half-Orcs 88
   Nymphs and Satyrs 88

Chapter Eight: The Empire 89
   Italy 89
   Sicily, Corsica, and Sardinia 90
   Spain 90
North Africa 90
   Mauretania 90
Africa 91
Cyrenaica 91
   Egypt 91
The Middle East 91
   Arabia 91
   Judea 92
   Syria 92
   Mesopotamia 93
Asia Minor 93
   Asia 93
   Cicilia, Pamphylia, and Lycia 94

TABLE OF CONTENTS

Cyprus 94
Galatia and Cappadocia....................94
Armenia 94
Bithynia and Pontus 94
Thrace and Macedonia 95
Greece **95**
Epirus and Achaea.............................95
Crete 96
Rhodes 96
The Danube Frontier **97**
Moesia 97
Dacia 97
Pannonia 97
Noricum 97
Rhaetia 97
Illyricum 97
Germania...97
Gaul and Belgica...............................98
Britannia..99

Chapter Nine: Roman History.....................100
Ancient Italy....................................100
The Founding of Rome....................100
The Kingdom of Rome (753–510 BC) **101**
The Early Republic (496–133 BC) **102**
The Gauls 102
The Conquest of Italy......................102
More Samnite Wars 103
The Pyrrhic War 103
The Punic Wars 104
Expansion of Roman Rule...............106
The Late Republic (133–27 BC) **106**
Further Expansion 108
More Trouble in Gaul......................108
The End of Marius 109
The Rise of Sulla 109
The First Triumvirate 110
The Second Triumvirate...................112
The Early Empire (27 BC–69 AD) **113**
Augustus 113
Tiberius 114
Gaius (Caligula) 114
Claudius...114
Nero...115
The Year of the Four Emperors (69 AD)...........115
The Middle Empire (69–235 AD) **115**
Vespasian 115
Titus 116
Domitian 116
Nerva 116
Trajan 116
Hadrian 116
Antoninus Pius 117
Marcus Aurelius 117
Commodus...118

Septimius Severus.............................118
Caracalla 119
Elegabalus and Alexander Severus 119
The Anarchy **119**
Diocletian and Maximian................120
Constantine 120
The End of Empire **121**
Roman Timeline **122**

Chapter Ten: Roman Culture 124
Roman Society.......................................**124**
Social Classes....................................124
Women **125**
Childhood **126**
Patrons and Clients **126**
Careers and Offices...........................126
The Calendar **128**
Days of the Week 128
Hours...128
Holy Days and Festivals 129
Housing **131**
Fashion 131
Money...**132**
Foreign Currency..............................132
Roman Names **132**
The Army..**133**
The Legions 133
Auxiliaries 133
The Fleet..134
Law Enforcement 134
Bread and Circuses **135**
Food 135
The Games...135
Literature and the Arts 137

Chapter Eleven: Roman Religion.....................138
Cosmology **138**
Olympus 138
The Underworld 138
The Gods **139**
Minor Gods and Spirits 142
Imported Gods 143

The Soothsayer...**145**
Junius Servilius Strabo......................146
The Errand 146
Strabo's Estate 146
The Road to Cumae..........................147
Cumae 149
Concluding Prophecies 153
Consequences 154

Bibliography..**155**
Ancient Sources................................155
Modern Sources 155
Games 156

INTRODUCTION

From city to empire to memory, the history of Rome spans over a thousand years, from the city's founding in 753 BC to the end of the reign of the last emperor of the Western Roman Empire in 476 AD.

In name, though, Rome and the Empire lasted much longer. Three centuries after the fall of the last emperor in the west, the Frankish king Charlemagne was crowned Holy Roman Emperor in 800 AD, and this title was retained by German and Austrian rulers until Francis II surrendered the title in 1806 AD, becoming merely the emperor of Austria. Meanwhile, the eastern half of the Empire continued to function until its last remnants were conquered by the Turks in 1453 AD.

At the height of its power, the Roman Empire governed territories from Britain to the Middle East, and from the forests of Germany to the sands of the Sahara. The Mediterranean (meaning "the sea at the center of the world" in Greek) was known to the Romans as *Mare Nostrum* ("our sea") and the rule of all the lands that surrounded it was seen as Rome's divinely-ordained right.

The effects of Roman rule continue to be felt today. Most of the European lands formerly occupied by the Romans speak languages that are derived from Latin. Until the early 20th century, titles such as kaiser and czar (both derived from the Roman family name Caesar) were current. Although the practice is growing less common, Latin is still taught in schools across Europe and throughout the English-speaking world. Roman literature remains in print, both in the original Latin and in translation. Although the calendar was adjusted in the Middle Ages, an ancient Roman would recognize the names of the months. Even the days of the week retain their Latin roots in French, Spanish, and Italian. The Roman numbering system is still used for kings and queens, and for blue-blooded offspring named after their ancestors.

Despite its historical remoteness, the Roman world continues to exercise a fascination over the modern mind. Millions visit Roman remains across Europe, North Africa, and the Middle East, either in person or via television and the Internet. Epic movies continue to be set in the Roman Empire, even if the original "cast of thousands" is now replaced by digital crowds and armies. And even those who profess no interest in millennia-old history still recognize names like Julius Caesar, Augustus, Cleopatra, Mark Anthony, Nero, and so on.

Eternal Rome is a complete guide to roleplaying in Rome and the Roman world, from the founding of the city, through the turbulent end of the Republic, the ups and downs of Empire, to the final barbarian incursions that brought an end to Roman civilization. GMs can use this book to run purely historical campaigns, recreating historical events or experimenting with the "What ifs" of a thousand years; or they can throw fantasy into the mix, reinforcing the Roman legions with Greek and Egyptian sorcerers to help them stand up to armies of Scythian centaurs.

DATES

Throughout this book we use the familiar BC/AD dating scheme.

Other dating systems could be used for an *Eternal Rome* campaign. For instance, Romans themselves counted years AUC (*ab urbe condita* – "from the founding of the city"), starting with the mythical founding of Rome in 753 BC. While conversions from BC/AD to AUC are relatively simple (add 753 to AD dates, or subtract BC dates from 754), and would add some Roman flavor to this book, for ease of use and understanding modern dating is used.

Romans also referred to individual years by the names of the two consuls elected for that year (*e.g.*, "The year of the consulate of Quintus Pompeius and Lucius Cornelius Sulla Felix" was 88 BC, while "The year of the consulate of Lucius Cornelius Sulla Felix and Metellus Pius" was 80 BC).

CHAPTER ONE: CHARACTERS

Character creation in *Eternal Rome* is identical to that in other *d20 System* settings, with two additional steps.

- Because the setting covers 1,200 years of history, the class options, equipment, and religions open to player characters change over time. Therefore, the GM must choose an era for the campaign at the outset.

- While the *Eternal Rome* setting is designed for use with only one race, humans, there is more variety in the many different peoples found within the Empire and on its borders than in many d20 System settings using traditional fantasy races. Each player can choose his PC's nationality.

ERAS

History in the *Eternal Rome* setting is divided into eras. An era specifies the time and place in which a campaign can be set, and the people who are the likely focus of the campaign. Also provided is a crucial point in the era at which a slight change of events (such as the intrusion of the PCs into history) could radically change the future of Rome; and there are, of course, many other crux points in Roman history. The eras are as follows.

THE KINGDOM OF ROME (753–510 BC)

When it was founded by the legendary Romulus, Rome was just another farming village. It quickly came under the influence of the nearby Etruscan civilization, and the last few kings of Rome were Etruscans or Etruscan puppets: Romans themselves were second-class citizens. Only with the expulsion of Tarquinius Superbus in 510 BC did Rome begin to chart its own course in the world.

From its founding, the new city-state had to be protected, its growth had to be fostered, and its influence extended among its neighbors. Raiding hill tribes had to be fought off, and expansionist influence from elsewhere had to be resisted. And all the while, the crops and herds had to be tended or Rome would starve. In a fantasy setting, legendary creatures like nymphs and satyrs could still roam the land, adding to the complications of a farmer's life.

At the start of this era, the PCs are farmer-warriors, working hard to make a living in a hostile world. Later in the era, the PCs are Roman farmers and craftspeople or Etruscan aristocrats. The Etruscans' main concern is to keep the population under control and the tribute and taxes flowing northward into Etruria; the Romans are smarting under foreign rule, and increasingly driven to seek their freedom. Assassinations and attempted revolts are answered with an iron fist by the Etruscans, who are determined to maintain their control over this fertile area.

WHAT IF?

If the first of the Etruscan kings of Rome had been kept from taking the throne through trickery, Romans might have developed a traditional hereditary monarchy, and the uniquely flexible, highly militaristic, and somewhat unstable forms of the Republic might never have developed. This could leave it vulnerable to Carthage or the barbarians who attacked in the coming centuries, with devastating effects on Rome, but more positive ones on the other people's of the ancient world.

THE EARLY REPUBLIC (510–133 BC)

The early days of the Roman Republic were perilous ones. The Etruscans did not take their expulsion lightly, and it was nearly 15 years before Tarquin and his allies were finally defeated. Even afterward, the Etruscans were a constant threat, as were Rome's other neighbors. The Samnites were defeated in a series of wars, but raiding Gauls and expanding Greek powers caused recurring problems. Almost without intending to, Rome found itself expanding its influence throughout Italy in order to secure itself from external threats. This brought Rome into conflict with the two major powers in the Mediterranean region of the time: Greece and Carthage. Rome defeated these older empires in time, but not with ease.

This period was the most formative in the development of the Roman character and values. It was a time of citizen-soldiers serving a term in the legions before returning home to tend their fields or to pursue a career in politics.

The PCs are farmers and fighters, priests and politicians, working to ensure Rome's security as the Republic becomes involved in the affairs of the Mediterranean powers.

WHAT IF?

The closest Rome came to complete destruction was during the 2nd Punic War, when a series of Roman generals faced the Carthaginian Hannibal (and his famous Alps-crossing elephants). Hannibal was never defeated while in Italy, and with a little more luck, Carthage could have remained the dominant power in the western Mediterranean; in a strong position to take on the weakening successor states to Alexander the Great's eastern Mediterranean empire.

THE LATE REPUBLIC (133–31 BC)

This period began with Rome in control of not only Italy, but also the Mediterranean coast from Spain to Asia Minor. By the end of the period, Rome dominated France, the east coast of the Mediterranean from Antioch to Jerusalem, the southern shores of the Black Sea, and much of North Africa.

Along with territorial expansion, this was a period of intrigue and dirty politics as various power blocs struggled for control of Rome. The power of the *Optimates* (the old-established families who controlled the Senate) was challenged again and again by the *Populares* (progressive politicians who championed the common people). Elections became violent affairs, and politicians on both sides hired criminal gangs to look after their interests when action needed to be taken outside the law. Generals tried to restore order with their troops, but set a dangerous precedent whereby anyone with an army at his back could make a bid for power.

Eventually, an unofficial alliance of three powerful individuals, Julius Caesar, Pompey the Great, and Crassus (later called the First Triumvirate), restored order, but the ideals of the Republic suffered greatly in the process. The First Triumvirate eventually collapsed because of individual ambitions and personal rivalries among its members, and the Roman world was plunged into a prolonged series of civil wars.

After the death of all three triumvirs, Caesar's heir Octavian assembled a Second Triumvirate (with Mark Anthony and Marcus Aemilius Lepidus), but this too fell apart due to internal rivalries. When the dust settled, Octavian was the last man standing. To avoid further civil wars, the Senate voted to give him a multitude of Republican offices that was to form the basis of the power of the Emperors. He took the name Augustus, and the Roman Republic gave way to the Roman Empire.

PCs in this era can be involved in a variety of activities. Soldiers protected Roman territory and often officers and war heroes returned to pursue political careers. Politicians jockeyed for power and took military appointments to gain fame and glory they could parlay into votes at home. The underworld was heavily involved in rigging elections, buying votes, and intimidating candidates. The priesthood had become another form of political appointment with both religious and civic duties. Merchants and traders exploited the wealth of Rome's provinces and, becoming rich, sought political power of their own. And behind it all there were still the farmers and ordinary soldiers, the common folk whose interests were exploited by the politicians.

WHAT IF?

If Julius Caesar had chosen to employ bodyguards when in Rome (as many other prominent citizens did), or if Anthony and Caesar's other supporters had entered the Senate at the right time, he may have survived the Ides of March, and accomplished his goal of conquering Parthia (modern Iraq, Iran, and Afghanistan), a rival empire that stubbornly resisted Rome for centuries to come.

At the same time, the Chinese Han Empire extended its borders west to Parthia's eastern fringes. If Caesar had taken Parthia, Rome and China, the two greatest empires of the time, would have been in direct contact, instead of being separated by as much as 2,500 miles of the Silk Road

THE EARLY EMPIRE (31 BC–69 AD)

The early Empire is the period that typifies Rome in the modern imagination. There were good Emperors who strengthened and expanded the Empire, bad Emperors who presided over reigns of terror, and mad Emperors whose unpredictability meant nobody felt safe. The brick city of Rome was rebuilt in marble, literature and the arts flourished, and wealth flowed in from the provinces. Apart from expansions into Germany, Central Europe, and Britain, and the appropriation of Egypt, border skirmishes, rebellions in some provinces, and palace infighting, the Empire was at peace for much of this period.

This era saw the great fire of Rome, the rise of Christianity (and the first persecutions of Christians), spectacular shows in the arena, and many of the other things without which no Roman epic is complete. It ended with revolt and civil war, Nero's suicide, and a four-way power struggle as armies from all over the Empire marched on Rome intending to put their leaders in the palace.

PCs in this era could be soldiers or officials charged with preventing or suppressing revolts in far-flung provinces, Republican conspirators trying to topple the Emperors, provincials struggling for freedom or flocking to Rome in search of a better life, gladiators trying to survive the arena and garner enough wealth and renown to buy their freedom and open their own gladiatorial schools, or members of the Imperial family jockeying for position and influence.

WHAT IF?

One turning point in Imperial history was the annihilation of three entire legions and the permanent loss of Germany to the barbarians in 9 AD. If the general Tiberius (or a competent PC) had remained on the German frontier, instead of leaving command to the less competent Varus while he quelled rebellion in the Balkans, not only might Germany have remained a part of the Empire, but Rome would have been in a much better position to push eastward through northern Europe, absorbing barbarian populations into the Empire instead of leaving them to threaten civilization for centuries to come.

THE MIDDLE EMPIRE (69–180 AD)

69 AD became known as the Year of Four Emperors. One after another, armies from various parts of the Empire arrived in Rome, deposed the incumbent Emperor, and placed their own generals on the throne. The frontiers were stripped of troops by this power struggle, and revolts broke out in various parts of the Empire. For the rest of this period, the Emperors' major concern was keeping peace within the Empire and reinforcing the frontiers. Although Trajan expanded the Empire to its greatest extent, with conquests in Arabia, Mesopotamia, and Romania, later Emperors adopted the defensive posture that would characterize Rome for the rest of its existence: In Britain, Hadrian's Wall was built to regulate trade and act as a barrier to cross-border raiding; along the Rhine and the Danube, fortifications were built and strengthened against the pressure of Germanic and other tribes.

PCs in this era could be charged with pacifying rebellious or newly-conquered provinces, or they could travel across the Empire trading and exploring new territories.

WHAT IF?

Although there had been Jewish unrest before, in this period full-blown revolts broke out in Judea in 66–73 AD and again in 131–134 AD. Rome brutally put down both revolts (as well as a revolt of the Jewish community of Cyrene (in North Africa) in 116 AD), destroying the Second Temple in Jerusalem in 70 AD and expelling all Jews from Judea in 134 AD, building a Roman city on the ruins of Jerusalem, including a temple to Jupiter on the ruins of the Second Temple. If the revolts had been successful, or the punishments for failure less severe, Judaism may have played a larger role in Roman religious politics in the coming centuries; conversely, Christianity would have had less impetus to distance itself from Judaism with the Temple still intact, and may have stayed a minority Jewish sect, instead of becoming the dominant religion of the Empire of the course of the next few centuries.

THE LATE EMPIRE (180–476 AD)

The last 300 years of the Roman Empire were an unending struggle against barbarian incursions from the north and northeast. The Empire was devastated by a series of plagues, which, together with other factors, led to a severe shortage of manpower, both for the army and for agricultural and industrial production. Provinces rebelled and had to be conquered again; in the reigns of weak Emperors, ambitious provincial governors routinely stripped their own provinces of frontier troops to support a bid for power in Rome itself.

PCs in this era may be trying to hold the Empire together, or they may be independent-minded provincials trying to throw off Roman domination and keep all the tax money and other resources at home. They could even be barbarians looking to divide the wealth and land of the Roman Empire between themselves.

WHAT IF?

The most significant event of this period was the war of succession fought after the abdication of Diocletian and Maximian in 305 AD. Diocletian had passed a number of edicts persecuting the growing Christian minority in the Empire, and the claimants to Imperial power in the decade following the abdication included the Christian-tolerant Licinius, the Christian convert Constantine, the pagan Maxentius, and Maximinus Daia, who had vowed to eradicate Christianity if he won control of the Empire. Maximinus was beaten by Licinius in a battle that by all rights he should have won, and Maxentius was defeated by Constantine in a battle that Maxentius could have won with just a bit better public relations to rally the people of Italy and Rome to his side. A few good soldiers or orators in the right place could have turned the tide for the traditional religions of the Empire.

NATIONALITIES

The Roman Empire included a wide range of nationalities, from Celtic to Egyptian and German to Berber. As in any culture, stereotypes came to be attached to different nationalities. For players, these stereotypes offer hooks for developing and roleplaying a character; for the GM, they can supplement the Influencing NPC Attitudes table accompanying the Diplomacy skill in the *PHB* when the PCs interact with NPCs of different nationalities than their own.

Because of almost universal prejudices, people from within the Empire receive a −3 to Charisma-based skill checks when dealing with the barbarians outside of its borders, and vice-versa.

As well as the classes that are specialties of each nation, people from all over the Empire, as well as the bordering barbarian states, served in the legions, often in areas far removed from their homelands. This integrated the Empire, as the soldiers would be forced to learn Latin and/or Greek during their service and would often retire in the provinces in which they'd served, rather than returning to their homelands.

AFRICA

The Roman knowledge of Africa was limited to the continent's north coast, from Morocco to Egypt, and when they spoke of Africans, Romans meant solely North Africans, not people from south of the Sahara. The appearance of Central and West Africans made them novel and sought after as slaves and gladiators, but they came to Rome (along with many exotic beasts) through North African intermediaries rather than through direct contact.

In Roman times, North Africa was a fertile land, known as the granary of the Empire; it provided Rome with quantities of wheat, rye, and barley. Africans were generally regarded as farmers; good solid stock, a little rough, honest and hardworking rather than brilliant, but

sound none the less. Occasionally (as in the case of the Emperor Septimius Severus or Pope Victor I) the African provinces would produce an individual of significant ability, but by and large they were not considered the equal of Italian Romans.

Large numbers of African recruits (mostly Caucasians descended from Roman, Greek, and Phoenician colonists) served in the legions from the later Republic onward, and they inherited a reputation as sailors from the Carthaginians, who had been the predominant power in North Africa and the western Mediterranean before being destroyed by Roman armies.

AFRICAN PCS

African PCs can be of any class. Fighters, other than those who served in the legions of the Empire, were usually light infantry, light cavalry, or archers. As cities such as Carthage and Cyrene originated as colonies of Phoenicia, not all of the population in African cities was dark-skinned.

AMAZONIA

While the Amazons may have been an entirely mythical people, the Greeks and Romans both regarded them as real. Said to live on the shores of the Black Sea, they were a female-dominated society, worshiping the goddess Diana. Their name is derived from Greek, and, rather gruesomely, refers to their reputed habit of cutting off their right breasts so that they would not interfere with their archery; however, they are seldom depicted in Classical art with such mutilations. At least in literary terms, the Amazons seem to be the origin of the fascination with women warriors that persists in fantasy to the present day.

Although the Romans never encountered Amazons directly, they had a definite attitude toward them. Women had a well-defined place in Roman society, and by taking up arms the Amazons stepped outside the bounds of decency. This made Romans uncomfortable, and a male Roman would treat an encountered Amazon with a mixture of fear and condescension. Roman women would be divided between those who took society's line and regarded female warriors as beyond the pale, and those who secretly admired them. Even so, female gladiators (sometimes billed as Amazons) were always a crowd-pleaser in the arena.

AMAZON PCS

Most Amazon PCs are fighters or rangers, with clerics of Diana as the next most popular class. Like Scythians, the Amazons were reputed to be very skilled horse-warriors. Amazon warriors were typically armed with longspears, shortbows, daggers, and a handaxe with a light pick on the back of the blade, which could be used as either type of weapon (see page 56). Some used short swords instead of axes. Armor ranged from padded to breastplate; most infantry and all cavalry were equipped with light wooden shields.

ASIA

To the Romans, Asia meant modern-day Asia Minor or Turkey. The Greeks heavily colonized the coasts, but the mountainous interior was regarded as good for raising sheep and olives and not much else. The coastal cities (the greatest of which was Ephesus) were polyglot trading centers with large populations for the time. In the north, the Bosporus was a vital trade artery linking the Aegean to the Black Sea and the lands of Thrace, Bithynia, and Armenia. It was during Roman times that Byzantium (later Constantinople, now Istanbul) became a major city; in the later Empire period, it was the capital of the Eastern Roman Empire, which survived as the Byzantine Empire long after Rome and the Western Empire had fallen to the Goths.

To the average Roman, Asians were a mixed bunch. The Greek cities were as cultured as their mainland counterparts, but the lands in between were rough, populated only by shepherds and bandits. In the Kingdom and early Republic periods, the many islands and inlets of the Asian coastline were home to numerous groups of pirates, who raided throughout the Mediterranean; it took a major campaign by Pompey the Great to put them out of business in the late Republic period.

ASIAN PCs

Asian PCs can be Greek colonists, as well as shepherds, traders, craftspeople, or other townsfolk. Up until the late Republic, they can be pirates, and in any period, they can be bandits or fiercely independent hill-folk.

EGYPT

By the time Rome began making its power known around the Mediterranean in mid-Republican times, Egypt was no longer ruled by its native pharaohs. Instead, it was ruled by the Ptolemies, a Greek dynasty that dated back to the conquests of Alexander the Great. But Egypt's 3,000-year-long history and even longer cultural tradition was a powerful force, and Egypt was never Hellenized in the way that Rome or Judea was; instead, the Greeks and Romans ruling the lands of the Nile ran the risk of becoming Egyptianized. Cleopatra VII, the last of the Ptolemies, saw herself as completely Egyptian, even though she spoke and wrote in Greek. And one of the charges leveled against Julius Caesar was that he'd been corrupted by Egyptian ways.

Like many people before and since, the Romans regarded Egypt and the Egyptians as mysterious and somewhat threatening. Egyptian wizards and sorcerers were held in high regard, and were automatically assumed to be masters of their dark arts. Kemet, the Egyptian name for Egypt, became the root of the word *alchemy*, and well-to-do young Romans traveled to Egypt to marvel at the pyramids and receive instruction in the mysteries.

EGYPTIAN PCs

Egyptian sailors were well regarded, but the military glory days of Ramesses II were centuries in the past. Nomads crisscrossed Roman Egypt and North Africa, and can be represented by rangers with desert specializations or as desert hermits (see Green Ronin's *Testament* page 35). Egyptian wizards were well respected across the Empire,

and various Egyptian cults had followings in Rome and other major cities.

GAUL

The Gauls were a Celtic people who occupied present-day France, Belgium, Luxemburg, Britain, Switzerland, and parts of Germany and northern Italy; there were also Celtic enclaves in northern Spain (the Celtiberians) and in Turkey (the Galatians of the New Testament). They lived by hunting, herding, and farming, and they were nearly always engaged in tribal wars and feuds (at least in Roman accounts; little is known of their own opinions of themselves as they relied on an oral tradition rather than written laws or history). Some believed that their wild nature put them in closer touch with the elements and the forces of nature.

When first Gaul and then Britain were conquered and pacified, the Celtic peoples largely became Romanized. However, beyond the frontiers in Britain, the Caledonians of modern Scotland (which they shared with the Picts) and the Hibernians of Ireland lived a traditional Celtic lifestyle, and were constantly either raiding their neighbors for slaves and livestock or becoming embroiled in their political disputes. Hadrian's Wall in northern Britain placed a barrier between the conquered but fractious Brigantes and the unconquered Selgovae, who frequently sent arms and warriors to help one faction or the other of their feuding neighbors.

GALLIC PCs

Most Romans saw Gauls as the very definition of the barbarian, but in game terms, druids and rangers could also fit the stereotype. Romans who had visited the Celtic lands might also be familiar with Celtic bards and soothsayers.

GERMANIA

If the Gauls were barbarians, the Germanic tribes (the Cimbri, Teutones, Goths (divided into Ostrogoths and Visigoths), Franks, Alemanni, Burgundians, Vandals, and so on) were outright savages. Wilder, fiercer, and even less civilized than the Gauls, the Germans drew shocked comments from Roman historians, deploring the simplicity of their lives and their habit of slaughtering their neighbors. The image of the Germans in Roman literature may owe something to the fact that the Romans never conquered them: By playing up their ferocity, Roman writers explained to their readers why the Empire never overcame them; by deploring their poverty, it was shown that the effort of conquering them would not be worthwhile.

GERMANIC PCs

Most PCs hailing from the Germanic tribes would be barbarians or fighters, also some might be clerics or sorcerers.

GREECE

Rome took a lot from the classical Greek culture; one Roman historian observed "captive Greece took Rome captive." From time to time Roman conservatives condemned the unhealthy effect that Hellenization (after Hellas, the Greek name for

Greece) had on the moral fiber of Rome's younger generation. Greece (and especially Athens) was seen as the birthplace of the world's greatest artists, scientists, and philosophers, and all educated Romans spoke and read Greek as well as Latin. In the eastern half of the Empire, Greek eventually supplanted Latin as the official language. The inhabitants of Greek colonies in the western Mediterranean (most notably Massalia (modern Marseilles) and the Greek colonies in Sicily) were also regarded as Greek.

To most Romans, Greeks were clever but soft, lacking the traditional virtues that were (in theory at least) bred into every Roman since the time of Romulus. Their cleverness could also shade into dishonesty, and their outspoken, democratic spirit could easily become impertinence. Greeks overall were seen as better educated and quicker-witted than Romans; many Romans never quite overcame this cultural inferiority complex.

Despite the fame of the Spartans and the Greek heritage of Alexander and his empire, the Romans never held the Greeks in high regard as soldiers. Greek sailors were respected for their skills (likely because of Rome's lack of a maritime tradition). It is as philosophers and educators that the Greeks were most highly valued. Every Roman boy from a good family was educated by a Greek tutor, and Augustus founded the Roman civil service using Greek slaves and freedmen almost exclusively. Greek merchants were regarded with caution, as they had a reputation for getting the better of honest Romans in business.

Greek PCs

Greek poets and musicians could be regarded as bards, while Greek soothsayers were sometimes seen as superior to the oracles of Rome itself. Many eastern magical traditions reached Rome through Greek wizards, even those that had originated in Egypt and Persia. And Greek experts in mathematics, siegecraft, history, and languages were prized throughout the Empire.

Hispania

Spain was one of Rome's earliest conquests, taken from the Carthaginians during the Punic Wars. In addition to the chain of Phoenician trading colonies that ran along the Mediterranean coast, there were numerous Spanish tribes in the interior and Lusitanians on the Atlantic coast (in modern-day Portugal). In the north were the Celtiberians, a Celtic people who had probably entered the region across the Pyrenees.

The early Republic period saw a number of wars before the Spanish tribes were finally subdued. Before Spain was conquered, its inhabitants were seen as yet more barbarians on the fringes of the Roman world, not to be trusted because of their long-standing connection with Carthage. Afterward, Spain became one of the most Roman of the provinces, and Spaniards were generally regarded in much the same light as Italians.

Hispanian PCs

PCs from Spain can be of any class. Spain provided large numbers of auxiliary troops, and the inhabitants of the Balearic Islands (Majorca, Minorca, and Ibiza) were widely regarded as excellent peltasts, skirmishing troops armed with slings and javelins to harass enemy forces without engaging in hand-to-hand combat.

The Huns

Roaming the central Asian steppes north and east of the regions occupied by the Scythians and Parthians were a number of nomadic peoples. The Turks and Mongols would invade Europe in later centuries, but during the late Empire period the Huns, who'd raided the Chinese empire for centuries, turned westward to advance on Rome. The Scythians and Parthians were seen as great horsemen, but the Huns virtually lived on their horses, advancing unstoppably and terrifying Roman communities as they approached.

Hun PCs

Whether fighters or rangers, Hun PCs would have excellent survival and horse-based combat abilities.

Illyria

Illyrians occupied the lands north of Macedonia, across the Adriatic Sea from Italy. These lands were conquered in the late Republic and early Empire periods to safeguard a land route to Greece, establish the Danube as a defensible northeastern frontier, and put down piracy in the Adriatic. There is little documentary evidence of the Roman view of Illyrians, but they were probably regarded as little different from other provincials: more civilized than the Gauls, but less cultured than the Greeks.

Illyrian PCs

Illyria was best known for its sailors, who flourished among the islands of the Dalmatian coast.

Italy

To be Italian was a very different thing from being Roman. Italy beyond Rome's walls was a Roman province, most of it having been conquered during the early days of the Republic. Romans saw other Italians as being less valiant and less reliable than themselves; although Italians fought alongside Roman forces in the conquest of the Empire (and, in the early days, fought so well against the Romans some of their equipment and tactics were adopted by their conquerors), they were always regarded as yokels. Throughout most of Roman history, only Roman citizens were admitted to the legions, and although Roman citizenship was gradually extended throughout Italy and across the Empire, the Roman who was born in Rome of a Roman family always felt superior.

Italian PCs

Italian provincials were mostly farmers and hunters. Beginning in the Late Republic, they could enter any class that was open to Romans themselves, although they always suffered a degree of prejudice. However, most Romans would value an Italian above any other kind of provincial, or any foreigner.

Judea

Up until the middle Empire period, Jews were mainly found in their homeland of Judea, although there were significant Jewish communities in Babylon, Alexandria, and even Rome. Because of their blunt refusal to compromise in religious matters, and a history of rebellions beginning

centuries before Roman rule, they were a troublesome people to rule, and most Romans regarded them as unreasonable and unappreciative of the benefits of Roman civilization. Most Jewish revolts and separatist movements had a strong religious component, because of prophecies of a messiah who would come and lead the Jewish people to glory and freedom. At the start of the middle Empire period, Roman troops sacked Jerusalem and razed the Temple of Solomon; two generations later the Jews themselves were banned from Judea, making the Jews throughout the Empire a people without a homeland.

JUDEAN PCs

In the Roman mind, the Judean population was divided between rural shepherds and urban merchants and craftspeople. All were regarded as potential rebels and fanatics. The biblical tradition of wonder-working prophets and holy warriors fits well with the cleric and paladin classes (as well as core and prestige classes taken from *Testament*; see sidebars on pages 22 and 30 and also famous in the early Empire period were the *Sicarii* ("dagger-men"), a group of assassins devoted to ousting Roman rulers and punishing those who supported Rome.

The medieval stereotype of Jews as businessmen and moneylenders did not apply during the Roman period, since it wasn't until the introduction of Christian laws banning the lending of money for interest by one Christian to another during the Middle Ages that Jews began to fill this role in society.

Green Ronin's *Testament: Roleplaying in the Biblical Era* deals mostly with earlier ages, but provides useful background information to a GM planning a campaign based in Roman Judea.

MACEDONIA

Every educated Roman knew Macedonia was the birthplace of Alexander the Great, but in general little more was known about it, even after it was conquered. Its proximity to Greece (and the fact that Alexander and his father Philip had conquered almost the entire Greek world between them) made it culturally similar to Greece, if somewhat wilder.

MACEDONIAN PCs

Macedonian PCs are more likely to be fighters and rangers than poets and philosophers. Although not warlike in an expansionist sense, they were individually touchy about their honor and quick to take offense. Some of the more remote hill tribes might be regarded as barbarians.

PARTHIA

Parthia was never part of the Roman Empire, but it inflicted several telling defeats on Roman forces and left a great mark on the Roman psyche. Occupying an area from modern-day Iraq to Pakistan, the Parthians were renowned horse-warriors, most famous for the so-called "Parthian shot," turning in the saddle to fire arrows backward at pursuers.

PARTHIAN PCs

Most Parthians would be expected to be fighters or rangers, with very high Ride skill and feats including Ride-By Attack and Shot on the Run.

PHOENICIA

Based in the port cities of Tyre and Sidon, the Phoenicians controlled a long, thin strip of the eastern Mediterranean coastline (modern-day Lebanon and northern Israel). They were a seagoing, mercantile people. Carthage started out as a Phoenician trading colony, but eclipsed its homeland politically and militarily by the Roman era.

To most Romans, the Phoenicians were traders who brought exotic goods from the mysterious East. They were renowned as sailors and merchants, and no-one thought of them doing much else.

PHOENICIAN PCs

Phoenician PCs would most likely be merchant adventurers of various classes, including fighters and rangers (possibly with ranks in Professions such as merchant or sailor). Members of other classes, including clerics and wizards, seldom left their homelands. During the Punic Wars, they might have been seen as likely spies.

THE PICTS

Their name derived from the Latin for "painted people," the Picts were famous for their tattoos. A small, swarthy, wiry people, they are thought to have been the original inhabitants of present-day Scotland; the Scots immigrated from Ireland in the late Imperial period, forcing the Picts out of most of their lands. The Romans regarded the Picts as barely human; lower in their estimation than even the Germans—if that's possible. They sometimes joined forces with the Scots to raid the northern frontier of Roman Britain, and they were renowned for their stealth and fieldcraft.

PICTISH PCs

Many Pictish characters might be rangers and druids; others could be barbarians, fighters, or rogues.

THE SAXONS

In the late Imperial period, Germanic peoples from northern Europe started to migrate, creating pressure on the northern frontiers of the Roman Empire. The Saxons originated in what is now northern Germany, and crossed the North Sea to raid and settle in the east of Britain; together with the Angles and the Jutes, two other Germanic peoples, they laid the foundations of Anglo-Saxon England after the collapse of Roman authority.

SAXON PCs

Saxon characters are mainly fighters, rangers, and barbarians. Saxon clerics followed the pagan Saxon pantheon, which was similar in many ways to that of the Vikings. Saxon mystics, such as village wise-women and seers, can be treated as sorcerers.

VIEWS OF THE ROMANS

Throughout the Republic and most of the Empire, Romans considered the ideal Roman to be a perfect blend of martial and intellectual prowess. If in doubt, it was advisable to err on the side of the martial, for those who took too cerebral or artistic a path risked being branded as Greeks or would-be Greeks. But even so, a Roman of culture was expected to be able to appreciate art, music, and poetry, and to converse (in both Greek and Latin) knowledgeably on a range of subjects from philosophy and politics to engineering.

Romans were also expected to have strong wills, and strong stomachs, to enjoy the entertainments of the arena rather than being disgusted by them, and to have their nerves steeled for battle. A level-headed and practical approach was regarded almost as highly as courage or education: where the Greeks pondered philosophical questions to develop their minds, the Romans tackled practical problems in order to solve them. In Roman minds, they had created not an ideal society, but a practical one, capable of tackling the problems of the real world.

Other peoples (especially those conquered by the Romans) saw them a little differently. To most provincials, Romans were arrogant conquerors, at least until those provincials bought into the concept of *romanitas* (Roman civilization) and sought to adopt Roman virtues for themselves.

To the Celts and Germans, when they first encountered them, the Romans were cowards, fighting in close ranks behind tall shields in heavy armor rather than settling things in individual combat like true warriors.

To the Greeks and Egyptians, they were barbarians with more military muscle than culture or history.

To the Judeans, they were pushy, unrepentant pagans, given to worshiping all kinds of unsavory gods (and trying to force that worship onto other peoples) and not to be numbered among the righteous.

To the Spanish and Italians, they had an over-inflated idea of their own superiority.

To all their provincials at one time or another, the Romans were heavy-handed rulers who took too much in taxes, gave too little in return, and were somehow surprised that the provincials were dissatisfied.

THE SCOTS

In the later Imperial period, Picts and Scots made numerous raids across the northern frontier in Britain, often in cooperation. The Scots originated in Ireland, and migrated to present-day Scotland as Roman power in Britain began to decline. They were a Celtic race, and in ethnic and cultural terms, they were similar to Gauls.

SCOTTISH PCs

Barbarian, ranger, and druid would be the most common Scottish PC classes. Scottish bards could also be found.

SCYTHIA

The Scythians occupied an area in the Central Asian steppes running from what is now the southern Ukraine to Siberia. They were nomadic herders; one of the many horse cultures that have peopled the steppes. In Roman times, they were regarded as great horsemen and fierce warriors; barbarians (not being Greek or Roman) but somehow nobler than the barbarians of northern and western Europe. They occasionally raided Greek and Roman outposts along the shores of the Black Sea.

SCYTHIAN PCs

Scythian characters would most likely be fighters and rangers, with skills and feats reflecting their great horsemanship.

SYRIA

The Syrians were a Canaanite people like the Phoenicians, but less active in sea-travel. Antioch was one of the great cities of the eastern Empire, and its inhabitants included all classes, as well as visitors from all over the eastern Mediterranean. To most Romans, though, Syrians blended into the undifferentiated mass of "Easterners."

SYRIAN PCs

PCs from Syria would most likely be merchant adventurers. Unlike Phoenicians, they'd be more likely to travel on land than by sea. Clerics of various Eastern religions would usually stay within Syria.

THRACE

Thrace occupied the area between Greece and the Black Sea (what is now Bulgaria). The Thracians were widely renowned for their fighting prowess (Thracian was a popular gladiatorial style throughout the Empire) and there were constant skirmishes with Thracian tribes until the province was conquered in the middle Empire period. The Romans regarded Thracians in a very similar way to Macedonians: good fighters, but hot-tempered and lacking discipline.

THRACIAN PCs

Thracians in Rome would mainly be fighters, drafted into the auxiliaries or put to work in the arena.

CHAPTER TWO: CHARACTER CLASSES

The *Eternal Rome* setting uses most of the standard d20 System core and prestige character classes, although some are modified to fit the setting. It also adds a new base class and a number of new prestige classes.

- CORE CLASSES -

BARBARIAN

The word "barbarian" originated in ancient Greece, and was applied to anyone who didn't speak Greek (and therefore, according to Greek standards, could not be considered civilized). The Romans use the term much more widely, to cover just about everyone who wasn't in the Empire. According to the times, they were regarded with outr-ight hatred (when they are invading hordes or rebellious provincials) or patronizing contempt (when they are provincial bumpkins visiting Rome or being "civilized" by provincial governors). Their strength and ferocity made them favorites in the arena.

The Celtic or Germanic barbarian uses all the characteristics of the barbarian class described in the *PHB*.

STEPPE BARBARIAN

The Amazons, the Scythians, and the Huns were all regarded as barbarians, but these highly skilled horse-warriors from the Asian steppes are significantly different from the Celtic and Germanic barbarians.

The steppe barbarian uses all the characteristics of the barbarian class described in the *PHB*, except as follows.

NO RAGE

Steppe barbarians do not have the rage ability (nor do they have the greater rage, indomitable will, tireless rage, or mighty rage class features).

BONUS FEATS

At 1st level, a steppe barbarian gets a bonus feat in addition to the feat any 1st-level character gets and the bonus feat granted to a human character. The steppe barbarian gains an additional bonus feat at 4th, 8th, 11th, 14th, 17th, and 20th level. These bonus feats must be drawn from the following: Far Shot, Improved Mounted Archery*, Improved Precise Shot, Manyshot, Mounted Archery, Mounted Combat, Mounted Dodge*, Point Blank Shot, Precise Shot, Rapid Shot, Ride-By Attack, Shot on the Run, and Trample (*see **Chapter Three: Skills & Feats** for details on these new feats). A steppe barbarian must still meet all prerequisites for a bonus feat, including ability score and base attack bonus minimums. These bonus feats are in addition to the feat a character of any class gets from advancing levels. A steppe barbarian is not limited to the listed bonus feats when choosing these feats.

ETERNAL ROME CHARACTER CLASSES

Base Classes: barbarian, *steppe barbarian, Celtic bard, Orphic bard,* cleric, druid, *Celtic druid,* fighter, **gladiator,** paladin, ranger, rogue, sorcerer, wizard.

Prestige Classes: *arcane archer,* arcane trickster, archmage, assassin, blackguard, **crime boss,** duelist, dwarven defender, eldritch knight, hierophant, *horizon walker,* loremaster, mystic theurge, **orator, pankretiast,** shadowdancer, **soothsayer,** *thaumaturgist,* **vigil.**

Italics indicates a standard class modified for use in *Eternal Rome.*

Bold indicates a new class described in this chapter.

BARD

The original bards were a caste of minstrels and story-tellers in Celtic society, charged with preserving oral tradition and recording the deeds of the great and good in their own day. However, this is not the only kind of bard found in the Roman world.

Over centuries, Greece had built up a substantial body of epic poetry, which was studied and imitated by the Romans from the time of the early Empire. The legendary Orpheus was said to have made music so powerful even the gods were

moved by it, and songs and poetry were often said to be magical by way of a compliment. In a setting where magic is real, the minstrels and poets of this Orphic tradition would be bards, although they might not recognize any kinship with their Celtic counterparts.

Egypt's reputation as a land of magic and mystery goes back far before Roman times, and is another credible place of origin for musicians with magical powers.

CELTIC BARD

The standard bard character class requires only minimal changes to represent the Roman view of a Celtic bard. The bard must be Celtic (Gallic, including British). The Celtic bard uses all the characteristics of the bard class described in the *PHB*, except as follows.

WEAPON PROFICIENCY

Celtic bards are proficient with all simple weapons plus longsword, short sword, and shortbow, and with light armor and light shields.

ILLITERACY

Celtic bards do not automatically know how to read and write. Celtic bard spells are never found in written form, such as on scrolls or in spellbooks.

SATIRES

Many Celtic bards were so skilled that a barbed verse from them could cause a person physical harm as well as public ridicule. To reflect this, Celtic bards of 2nd level and above can use *bane* as a spell-like ability up to three times per day (no more than one per day against a single target). At 5th level, the power of a satire increases to the equivalent of a *bestow curse* spell. A Celtic bard may remove the effects of a satire produced by any bard of a lower level.

SOCIAL POSITION

Bards were highly respected members of Celtic society, closely associated with the druidic priesthood and protected by the same laws that shielded them. A Celtic bard gains a +2 bonus to all Charisma-based skill checks when dealing with other Celts.

ORPHIC BARD

Poets and musicians of the Orphic tradition (followers of the demigod Orpheus) are also bards. The Orphic bard uses all the characteristics of the bard class described in the *PHB*, except as follows.

DIVINATION

Orphic bards were sometimes inspired with prophecies. Add *augury* to the bard list of 2nd-level spells and *divination* to the bard list of 4th-level spells.

MULTICLASSING

It wasn't uncommon for Orphic bards to multiclass as clerics of Orpheus.

CLERIC

Rome's original religion was very similar to that of the Etruscans: a combination of ancestor veneration and worship of a number of nature spirits and mostly agricultural deities. As the Roman sphere of influence expanded, rather than imposing their own religion on conquered peoples to the exclusion of the native religion, the Romans absorbed all kinds of deities and cults from the provinces, combining them into a tolerant, pantheistic religion. Greek myth and religion had a great and lasting impact on Rome, but many other foreign religions enjoyed a brief vogue before lapsing into obscurity. Christianity and the Persian cult of Mithras came to dominate Roman religion in the Empire's last centuries.

This means clerics of many different religions were found throughout the Empire (including in Rome itself) and for the most part their diversity was tolerated. During the Kingdom, they mainly followed the Etruscan and Roman gods, but during the Republic, Greek influences pervaded religion along with the rest of Roman culture, and the Roman pantheon became basically the same as the Greek gods of Olympus with different names. As other foreign influences came to Rome during the late Republic and into the Empire, religions came with them. See **Chapter Eleven: Roman Religion** for information on the major religions of the Roman world.

DRUID

The Celtic druids the Romans encountered in Gaul and Britain were different in many ways from the nature priest presented in the *PHB*. In some ways, they were more like clerics of the Celtic religion. However, in the wilder parts of the Empire, nature-based shamanic practices that still remained are a reasonably good fit with the druid character class. Their ties to the land and the natural world mean druids will seldom, if ever, be encountered outside their homelands, but their abilities can be invaluable when adventuring in the wilds. They also make natural leaders for independence movements in the wilder provinces.

CELTIC DRUIDS

The druid in the *PHB* needs a few changes to bring it into line with the historical druids of both Roman and Celtic sources. Historical druids acted as more than priests of nature; they held the oral tradition of Celtic culture, and were both judges and advisors to kings. They must have been born and raised within the Celtic culture, since the oral tradition entrusted to them was not revealed to outsiders.

RELIGION

In *Eternal Rome*, most Celtic druids follow Cernunnos, the Horned God. Some, from areas occupied by Rome for at least two generations, may follow Silvanus, regarding him as an aspect of the Horned God. Both these deities are described in **Chapter Eleven: Roman Religion**.

CLASS SKILLS

Celtic druids add the following to their list of class skills: Knowledge (history), Knowledge (nobility and royalty), and Knowledge (religion).

ILLITERACY

Druids do not automatically know how to read and write. Druid spells are never found in written form, such as on scrolls or in spellbooks.

BARRED CLASS FEATURES

Celtic druids lose access to Animal Companion, Nature Sense, Wild Empathy, Trackless Step, Wild Shape, A Thousand Faces, and Timeless Body.

BARDIC KNOWLEDGE

Celtic druids have the same knowledge of legend and lore as bards, and a Celtic druid can use the ability as a bard of the same level; see the **Bard** in **Chapter Three: Classes** in the *PHB* for details.

BONUS FEATS

In lieu of class features normally granted to druids, Celtic druids gain bonus feats at 1st, 4th, 8th, 12th, 16th, and 20th levels. The bonus feat can be any feat for which the druid can qualify. These bonus feats are in addition to the feat a character of any class gets from advancing levels.

GEAS

Every Celtic druid is subject to a lifetime geas, similar to that of the spell of the same name. It takes the form of a prohibition that varies from druid to druid. Violating one's geas leads to loss of all spells, class features, and other druidic abilities, and a cumulative −2 penalty to each of his ability scores for every 24 hours that he willfully violates the geas (up to a total of −8, and no ability score can be reduced to less than 1 by this effect). If the druid resumes obedience to the geas, the ability score penalties are removed after 24 hours, but an *atonement* spell is required to restore the other lost abilities. Nothing short of abandoning the Celtic druid class (becoming an ex-druid) can get rid of the geas. Use the following tables to generate gessae (the Celtic language plural of geas).

SACROSANCT PERSONAGE

Druids were highly respected in Celtic society, and it was forbidden to raise one's hand against them; stories are told of druids who ended wars merely by standing between the massing armies. Druids gain a +4 bonus to all Charisma checks and Charisma-based skill checks when dealing with other Celts. In addition, a Celtic character who sees a Celtic druid being attacked or mistreated must make a Will saving throw (DC equals druid's Charisma score +4) or be compelled to go to his aid as if affected by a *charm person* spell.

If a druid abuses this status to gain personal power or wealth at the expense of other Celts, he may (at the GM's option) suffer the same effects as breaking his geas.

SPELLS

Celtic druids use druid spells as described in the *PHB*. At 5th level and every fifth level thereafter a Celtic druid chooses a cleric domain, gaining its granted power and access to its domain spells in the same manner as a cleric. Domains available to Celtic druids include Air, Animal, Earth, Fire,

TABLE 2-1: CELTIC DRUID GESSAE

Roll	Druid is forbidden to:
1–3	eat certain foods (see **Food**)
4–6	use certain weapons (see **Weapons**)
7–9	harm certain types of creature (see **Creatures**)
10–11	help certain types of creature (see **Creatures**)
12–13	help certain types of character (see **Characters**)
14–15	refuse help to certain types of character if asked (see **Characters**)
16–17	cast certain types of spells (see **Spells**)
18–19	ride certain types of mount (see **Mounts**)
20	GM's choice

FOOD

Roll	Food
1	Any meat
2–5	Meat of wild creatures
6–9	Meat of domesticated creatures
10–13	Fish
14–17	Fowl
18–19	Alcohol
20	GM's choice

WEAPONS

Roll	Weapon
1–2	Slashing weapons
3–4	Bludgeoning weapons
5–6	Piercing weapons
7–9	Ranged weapons
10	Magic weapons
11–13	Metal weapons
14–16	Wooden weapons
17–19	Martial weapons
20	Exotic weapons

CREATURES

Roll	Creature
1–2	Animals
3–4	Dragons
5–6	Fey
7–8	Humanoids
9–10	Giants
11–12	Magical beasts
13–14	Monstrous humanoids
15–16	Outsiders
17–18	Plants
19–20	Vermin

CHARACTERS

Roll	Character
1–5	Nationality (see **Nationalities**)
6–10	Class (see **Classes**)*
11–15	Gender (see **Genders**)
16–20	Race (see **Races**)**

NATIONALITIES

Roll	Nationality
1–4	Eastern (Asian, Jewish, Phoenician, Syrian)
5–6	Southern (African, Egyptian)
7	Gallic
8–9	Germanic
10–11	Greek and Macedonian
12–13	Illyrian and Italian
14	Pictish
15–16	Roman
17	Scythian
18–19	Spaniard
20	Thracian

CLASSES

Roll	Class
1–3	Barbarian
4–5	Bard
6–7	Druid
8–10	Fighter
11–13	Ranger
14–16	Rogue
17–18	Soothsayer
19–20	Sorcerer

GENDERS

Roll	Gender
1–10	Male
11–20	Female

RACES

Roll	Race
1–4	Human
5–6	Dwarf/Gnome
7–8	Elf
9–11	Half-Orc
12–13	Halfling***
14–15	Nymph
16–17	Satyr
18–20	Any halfbreed

SPELLS

Roll	Spell Type
1–2	Spells with the air descriptor
3–4	Spells with the earth descriptor
5–6	Spells with the fire descriptor
7–8	Spells with the water descriptor
9–10	Conjuration (healing) spells
11–12	Spells affecting animals (*i.e., calm animals* or *dominate animal*)
13–14	Spells affecting plants (*i.e., entangle* or *control plants*)
15–16	Evocation spells
17–18	Transmutation spells
19–20	Conjuration spells

MOUNTS

Roll	Mount Type
1–4	Horse
5–7	Mule
8–10	Donkey
11–12	Male animal
13–14	Female animal
15–16	Gelding
17–19	Chariot
20	Fantastic creature****

*Including multiclassed characters with levels in the prohibited class.
**Only in campaigns using fantasy races; in an all-human campaign, reroll.

***Reroll if the campaign does not include halflings.
****Reroll if the riding of such creatures in the campaign is rare.

Healing, Knowledge, Luck, Magic, Plant, Protection, Sun, Travel, Trickery, and Water. No matter how many domains he has, the druid has only one domain spell slot per day.

Non-Celtic Druids

Although the word "druid" originates in Celtic culture, there are several other kinds of nature priests in the Roman world considered druids in game terms.

Priests of Silvanus

Silvanus, the god of nature, is described on page 142. Some of his priesthood might be druids rather than clerics.

Priests of Diana

Diana (see page 140) is another deity with close ties to nature, and her priesthood might well include druids as well as clerics.

Barbarian Shamans

Many of the races considered barbarians by the Romans (the Picts, for example) are known for their closeness to nature. Although archaeologists and historians have not been able to discover any firm details about the religion of the historical Picts, their shamans may be treated as druids. Alternatively, if you use Green Ronin's *The Shaman's Handbook,* the shaman works equally well.

Fighter

The fighter class is usable in *Eternal Rome* without any changes. However, to convey the feel of various different fighter types NPC fighters and warriors (and preferably PCs as well) should usually be armed and equipped to match one of the following types, with skills and feats reflecting their capabilities.

Roman Troops

The armored legionary is the quintessential fighter of the Roman world, but by no means the only one. In addition to the legions, Roman armies included contingents of cavalry, archers, siege engineers, and auxiliary troops.

Legionary Infantry

The Roman legions featured the finest heavy infantry of their day. Trained to fight in a unit rather than individually, legionaries were equipped with large shields and short swords. The pilum (see page 58) was replaced by a shortspear in the later Empire period.

Recommended Skills: Craft (fortifications), Craft (smithing, leatherworking), Profession (cook).

Recommended Feats: Close Order Fighting, Improved Close Order Fighting (see pages 43 and 45 respectively).

Equipment: Short sword; dagger; pilum; banded mail, chain shirt, or scale mail; tower shield; helmet. Officers (centurions and up) may have breastplate.

A standard-bearer carried his unit's standard instead of a shield and often wore an animal skin over his helmet and body armor.

Notes: Only Roman citizens can become legionaries. A legionary's duty to his unit may prevent independent

adventuring, but retired (usually middle-aged) legionaries can be adventurers.

Legionary Cavalry

The role of the legionary cavalry changed over the centuries. In early periods, it was used for scouting on the march and protecting the flanks of the army in battle. Toward the end of the middle Republic period, legionary cavalry disappeared altogether, and provincial auxiliaries provided all the cavalry of the Roman army. Augustus revived the legionary cavalry in the early Empire period, but there were only 120 cavalry troopers attached to each 5,000-man infantry legion; for the most part used as messengers and escorts for mounted generals.

In the later Empire period, Emperor Gallienus reorganized the cavalry into a more potent and heavily-armored force to combat the continuing pressure on the northern frontiers.

Fighter Bonus Feats

Along with those listed in the *PHB*, fighters in *Eternal Rome* can choose from the following fighter bonus feats, described in **Chapter Three: Skills & Feats**: Canny Charge, Chariot Attack, Chariot Fighting, Chariot Shield, Chariot Specialization, Close Order Fighting, Drive-By Attack, Improved Close Order Fighting, Improved Mounted Archery, Mounted Dodge, Outlandish Weapon Finesse, Retaliatory Strike, Showy Fighting, Superior Trip, and Wrestler.

Over time these armored cavalry units developed into the cataphract heavy cavalry (see page 22).

Recommended Skills: Craft (fortifications), Craft (smithing, leatherworking), Profession (cook).

Recommended Feat: Spirited Charge.

Equipment: Longsword or short sword; dagger; shortspear; chainmail shirt or scale mail; heavy wooden shield; helmet; horse.

When mounted and using the charge action, a legionary cavalry trooper with the Spirited Charge feat causes triple damage when using a shortspear.

Notes: Only Roman citizens can become legionaries. During the Republic, a cavalryman had to provide his own horse, so only the wealthy joined this arm of the legions. A legionary's duty to his unit may prevent independent adventuring, but retired (usually middle-aged) legionaries can be adventurers.

AUXILIARY INFANTRY

As soon as Rome began extending its influence throughout Italy, auxiliary troops from the provinces began to be used in support of Roman armies. In the beginning, these units were often armed and equipped in their native style (see **Enemy Troops**, page 22), but by the later Republic period there was some standardization of equipment. Roman officers normally commanded auxiliaries but their own countrymen commanded some elite (and trusted) units.

Recommended Skills: Craft (fortifications), Craft (smithing, leatherworking), Profession (cook), Speak Language; Latin was a second language for most auxiliaries.

Recommended Feats: Close Order Fighting (see page 43).

Equipment: Short sword or longsword; dagger; shortspear; chain shirt, or scale mail; heavy wooden shield; helmet Officers (centurions and up) may have breastplate.

Notes: An auxiliary's duty to his unit may prevent independent adventuring, but retired (usually middle-aged) auxiliaries can be adventurers.

Auxiliaries were recruited as units, not individually, and every member of a unit was from the same province. Most auxiliary infantry were recruited in the western provinces, as well as Africa, Egypt, and Greece.

AUXILIARY CAVALRY

The legions placed more emphasis on infantry than they did on cavalry, and the overwhelming bulk of cavalry support for Roman armies came from mounted auxiliaries. Like other auxiliary units, they were usually commanded by Roman officers.

Recommended Skills: Craft (fortifications), Craft (smithing, leatherworking), Profession (cook), Speak Language; Latin was a second language for most auxiliaries.

Recommended Feat: Spirited Charge.

Equipment: Longsword or short sword; dagger; shortspear; light wooden shield or buckler; helmet; horse.

When mounted and using the charge action, an auxiliary cavalry trooper with the Spirited Charge feat causes triple damage when using a shortspear.

Notes: An auxiliary's duty to his unit may prevent independent adventuring, but retired (usually middle-aged) auxiliaries can be adventurers.

Auxiliaries were recruited as units, not individually, and every member of a unit was from the same province. Most

TERMS OF SERVICE

Historically, most people in the Roman world weren't as free as *Eternal Rome* PCs are to change careers from month to month, taking a level in gladiator, then switching to wizard, then becoming a ranger, then returning to the arena for another level. For instance, legionaries and vigiles signed up for multi-decade terms of service, and most gladiators were slaves whose owners could keep them in the profession for their entire lives. Even those at the upper end of society were obligated to serve in the legions or in public office, and could suffer if they followed careers that weren't in keeping with their station.

But a GM strictly enforcing such cultural rules won't win the hearts of the players.

Instead, the GM should remember that the PCs are supposed to be exceptional characters—the central part of the campaign's storyline even if there are more famous and powerful people surrounding them.

To enhance the Roman flavor, though, he should enforce those rules, but only for the NPCs in the campaign. If a PC gladiator changes class and leaves the arena (using a plot justification like having an NPC senator buy the gladiator from his current master and then free him afterwards), the GM can occasionally drop the names of NPC gladiators he met while in the profession, mentioning that they are still fighting in the arena, working toward the day they'll win their freedom—or that they've died still slaves.

Or the rules can be bent, but not broken, for the player characters. A PC vigil may leave the Cohorts Vigilum upon achieving citizenship after six years of service, but could find himself in a sort of reserve status: prepared to be called back to duty in the event of major calamity, but free to enjoy other activities in the meantime.

When in doubt, the GM would be wise to err on the side of making the players happy, not on the side of historical accuracy.

auxiliary cavalry were recruited in the western provinces, as well as Africa, Egypt, and Greece.

AUXILIARY ARCHER

The legions specialized in close combat, and throughout Roman history archers were recruited from the provinces. Unlike the auxiliary infantry and cavalry, which developed standardized equipment, auxiliary archers were often dressed and equipped in the style of their native land. Like other types of auxiliaries, they were usually commanded by Roman officers.

Archers were also encountered in the armies of many of Rome's enemies, especially in the east. After their home provinces were conquered, they were recruited into the Roman army with few changes.

Recommended Skills: Craft (fortifications), Craft (smithing, leatherworking), Profession (cook), Speak Language; Latin was a second language for most auxiliaries.

Equipment: Shortbow or composite shortbow; short sword; dagger; chain shirt or scale mail; helmet.

Notes: An auxiliary's duty to his unit may prevent independent adventuring, but retired (usually middle-aged) auxiliaries can be adventurers.

Auxiliaries were recruited as units, not individually, and every member of a unit was from the same province. Auxiliary archers were mostly recruited from the eastern provinces.

AUXILIARY SLINGER

Slingers, possibly the least expensive type of soldier to field, were encountered in the armies of many of Rome's enemies.

Recommended Skills: Craft (fortifications), Craft (smithing, leatherworking), Profession (cook), Speak Language; Latin was a second language for most auxiliaries.

Equipment: Sling; dagger; large wooden shield.

LEGIONARY AND AUXILIARY SKILLS

If a Roman army on the march found itself outside of existing fortifications when night fell, instead of commandeering houses and farms in the area, it built a new fortified camp on a defensible piece of land. While the average legionary didn't have to know how to *design* such a camp, he did have to know how to build the ditches, palisades, and other defenses of a camp, quickly and efficiently. While the camp (both fortifications and tents and other internal structures) were being built, half the troops did the work, while the other half remained under arms to guard the legion during the few hours that it was vulnerable.

While skill in cooking, smithing, and the like wasn't mandatory, those legionaries were able to occupy their time in these ways were often excused from latrine-digging, nighttime sentry duty, *etc.*

TESTAMENT AND TROJAN WAR BASE CLASSES

Some core classes in two other Green Ronin Mythic Vistas books are particularly useful in an *Eternal Rome* campaign to represent various peoples in parts of the Empire other than Italy.

From *Testament*, the Levite priest (only until the destruction of the Temple in 70 AD), the khery-heb, and the magus of the starry host are all usable without alteration. The qedeshot class can be used to represent the priestesses of secretive mystery cults found throughout the Roman world; the specific worship of the Canaanite goddess Asherah had died out. The spy class would be active throughout the Empire, not just in the *Testament* setting lands.

Trojan War's charioteer (for Celts and in the arena), dedicated warrior, and magician can all be added to the *Eternal Rome* setting.

Notes: An auxiliary's duty to his unit may prevent independent adventuring, but retired (usually middle-aged) auxiliaries can be adventurers.

Auxiliaries were recruited as units, not individually, and every member of a unit was from the same province. Auxiliary slingers were recruited from across the Empire. Those from the Balearic Islands (southeast of Hispania) were particularly renowned.

AUXILIARY PELTAST

These skirmishing troops were originally employed by the Greeks and other peoples who were subsequently conquered; they were then recruited into the Roman army with minimal changes to their equipment or tactics. They were a very mobile light infantry, used to pelt enemy formations with missiles and withdraw as heavier infantry moved to attack.

Recommended Skills: Craft (fortifications), Craft (smithing, leatherworking), Profession (cook), Speak Language; Latin was a second language for most auxiliaries.

Equipment: 1d4+1 javelins or 2d4 darts; dagger; large wooden shield.

Notes: An auxiliary's duty to his unit may prevent independent adventuring, but retired (usually middle-aged) auxiliaries can be adventurers.

Auxiliaries were recruited as units, not individually, and every member of a unit was from the same province. Auxiliary peltasts were recruited from across the Empire.

CATAPHRACT

The cataphract was a type of heavy cavalry trooper developed in the later Empire period. They were more heavily armored than any cavalry seen before them, and rode warhorses barded with chain or scale mail.

Recommended Skills: Craft (fortifications), Craft (smithing, leatherworking), Profession (cook).

Recommended Feat: Spirited Charge.

Equipment: Longsword; dagger; shortspear; chainmail or scale mail with mail coif; heavy wooden shield; horse; horse barding.

When mounted and using the charge action, a cataphract with the Spirited Charge feat causes triple damage when using a shortspear.

Notes: A cataphract's duty to his unit may prevent independent adventuring, but retired (usually middle-aged) troopers can be adventurers.

Auxiliaries were recruited as units, not individually, and every member of a unit was from the same province. Most cataphracts were recruited in the eastern provinces.

ENEMY TROOPS

GREEK HOPLITE

The hoplite was the classic Greek troop type. Armed with longspears and round shields, they were especially formidable in the phalanx, a wedge formation that allowed the front five ranks to level their spears for combat. The phalanx was almost impregnable to frontal attack.

Recommended Feats: Close Order Fighting, Improved Close Order Fighting (see pages 43 and 45 respectively).

Equipment: Longspear; short sword; dagger; breastplate; heavy wooden shield; ocreae, helmet.

Note: Hoplites were of Greek or Macedonian origin.

BARBARIC WARRIOR

Despite local differences in culture and language, the equipment and combat style of Celtic, Germanic, Pictish and other tribesmen was quite similar. The elite troops of these tribes could be barbarians or rangers, but were generally equipped similarly to the regular warriors. Celtic and Germanic armies were often supported by slingers (see **Auxiliary Slinger**, page 21), who were mostly boys and others considered unready for close combat.

Equipment: Longsword, shortspear, or axe; dagger; large wooden shield; either no armor or chain shirt, leather, or studded leather; helmet.

Note: This type covers British, Gallic, Germanic, Celtic, and Pictish "barbarians."

STEPPE HORSE WARRIOR

The lands to the north and east of the Roman Empire were peopled by several horse-riding steppe cultures (including the legendary Amazons). Wealthy steppe horsemen could wear full chain or scale mail, but they didn't wear heavier armor or put barding on their horses because of their reliance upon speed and surprise. Their battle tactics consisted of rapid advances into arrow range followed by equally rapid withdrawals, using the open spaces of the steppes to their advantage. The Parthians were famous for their tactic of turning around in their saddles to fire arrows at pursuers during a withdrawal.

Equipment: Composite shortbow; longsword or short sword; dagger; padded armor or chain shirt; helmet.

Note: This type includes Amazons, Huns, Parthians, Sarmatians, and Scythians, among others.

PALADIN

The Romans didn't regard spellcasting as compatible with the virtues of the warrior, so a paladin is likely to be a provincial, especially from the eastern half of the Empire, where magic was more widely accepted.

RANGER

Army scouts, as well as some tribal warriors, may be rangers rather than fighters. Rangers may also serve among the auxiliary units attached to an army, hunting and foraging for food as most armies lived off the land while they were on the march.

The Picts (see page 13) were famed for their stealth and woodcraft, and so rangers are as common among the Picts as fighters are among other peoples.

Experienced hunters were also employed to find and capture beasts for the arena, although these rangers may fall out of favor with their patron gods and lose their spellcasting abilities; few nature deities look kindly on the capture of beasts for slaughter in Rome.

ROGUE

Rome was an urban culture, and all towns and cities of any size house some number who make their living by means ranging from the shady to the downright illegal. In Rome and in some of the Empire's larger cities, organized criminal gangs made the streets dangerous and contributed in their own way to the political process (see **Crime and Politics**

sidebar). Rogues could also be found in rural areas, from individual poachers to small groups of rustlers and large outlaw bands (often made up of demobilized soldiers). Pirates haunted Mediterranean waters up until the end of the Republic, and made occasional resurgences after that.

SORCERER AND WIZARD

In *Eternal Rome*, the differences between sorcerers and wizards are cultural as well as magical. Some cultures (*e.g.*, the Celts and Germans) regard magic as a gift rather than a learned skill, while others (*e.g.*, Greece and Egypt) take the opposite view. This is not to say that there are no such things as Celtic wizards or Egyptian sorcerers: such individuals, while rare, can certainly exist, and may be disproportionately common among the adventuring population.

CRIME AND POLITICS

The final years of the Republic (see pages 106–113) were notorious for political corruption. As well as staging lavish games and giving food handouts to wins the votes of the urban poor, candidates made increasing use of violence and intimidation to win elections.

The time of the First Triumvirate saw this activity reach its peak. At that time, the streets of Rome were controlled by two rival gangs; one run by the aedile Clodius and the other by the tribune Milo. Julius Caesar hired Clodius to "look after things" while he was away in Gaul, and his rival Pompey tried to use Milo's gang to counter Clodius. Pitched battles on the streets became commonplace whenever members of the two factions met. Political rallies were disrupted by armed gangs, and candidates and voters alike were intimidated and even killed.

Clodius was eventually killed by Milo, and Clodius' funeral got out of hand, resulting in the Senate house being burnt to the ground. In 49 BC, when Caesar took control of Rome from Pompey, Milo was tried and exiled.

Egyptian wizards were more highly regarded than spellcasters from less exotic places. The other eastern provinces, and areas like Persia that lay just beyond the Imperial frontier for much of Roman history, were also regarded as potent sources of magic. Organized schools of magic existed in Rome, mostly drawing upon Greek, rather than indigenous Roman, traditions.

- NEW CLASS: THE GLADIATOR -

Some of the most skilled fighters in the Roman world weren't necessarily warriors, they were entertainers: gladiators. Almost all were slaves or prisoners of war, trained and equipped to kill each other in the arena for the enjoyment of the urban masses. Many specialized in particular sets of equipment and stylized styles of combat, and their matches were decided as much by the types of gladiator involved as by the skill of the participants.

Retired gladiators—those who survived the arena and either won enough to buy their freedom or achieved enough glory to be freed or bought by a wealthy freeman—were held in awe by most of the populace, and were much in demand as bodyguards and enforcers. Sometimes the owner of a gladiator school would supplement his income by hiring fighters out to political factions or organized crime syndicates.

ADVENTURES

A professional gladiator may only fight in the arena a few times each year, and so much of his time is taken up by other pursuits, from training to improve his chances in the games, to earning money to buy his freedom, to protecting his master (most gladiators were slaves) as the master pursued his own adventures.

Attempted escapes were frequent but almost never success, but a gladiator who had learned skills other than how to wield weapons (*e.g.*, one who learns lock picking or a bit of magic from a fellow prisoner) may prove the exception to the rule. An escaped gladiator was considered more dangerous than any other fugitive, though, so even a successful escapee might find himself pursued for years.

CHARACTERISTICS

Gladiators are accomplished fighters in the arena, but lose some of their prowess when forced to fight in less stylized combats against conventionally armed opponents.

ALIGNMENT

As gladiators come from many different backgrounds and quite frequently aren't voluntary members of the profession, they can be of any alignment.

BACKGROUND

Whether prisoners of war, criminals, members of heretical religions, or slaves performing at the pleasure of their masters, all successful gladiators share the will to survive the many years it might take to win their freedom.

Outside of the arena, gladiators are considered the social equals of slaves, even if they are freedmen. Still, some free Roman citizens voluntarily enter the arena, either to gain celebrity or to discharge debts (monetary or social). These gladiators are less likely to make a career out of the games,

	Base Attack	Fort	Ref	Will	
Level	Bonus	Save	Save	Save	Special
1st	+0	+2	+2	+0	Bonus feat, combat style +1, reputation
2nd	+1	+3	+3	+0	Dirty fighting +1d4, preferred opponent
3rd	+2	+3	+3	+1	Combat style +2
4th	+3	+4	+4	+1	Dramatic attack +1
5th	+3	+4	+4	+1	Bonus feat, combat style +3, uncanny dodge
6th	+4	+5	+5	+2	Dirty fighting +2d4
7th	+5	+5	+5	+2	Combat style +4
8th	+6/+1	+6	+6	+2	Dramatic attack +2, preferred opponent
9th	+6/+1	+6	+6	+3	Bonus feat, combat style +5
10th	+7/+2	+7	+7	+3	Dirty fighting +3d4, evasion
11th	+8/+3	+7	+7	+3	Combat style +6
12th	+9/+4	+8	+8	+4	Dramatic attack +3
13th	+9/+4	+8	+8	+4	Bonus feat, combat style +7
14th	+10/+5	+9	+9	+4	Dirty fighting +4d4, preferred opponent
15th	+11/+6/+1	+9	+9	+5	Combat style +8, defensive roll
16th	+12/+7/+2	+10	+10	+5	Dramatic attack +4
17th	+12/+7/+2	+10	+10	+5	Bonus feat, combat style +9
18th	+13/+8/+3	+11	+11	+6	Dirty fighting +5d4
19th	+14/+9/+4	+11	+11	+6	Combat style +10
20th	+15/+10/+5	+12	+12	+6	Bonus feat, dramatic attack +5, preferred opponent

TABLE 2-12: THE GLADIATOR

but their desperation to survive is as strong as that of those compelled to fight.

GAME RULE INFORMATION

Abilities: While the physical attributes are important to all gladiators, certain abilities are favored by those specializing in certain styles: a lightly armored retiarius or a missile-wielding sagittarius benefits greatly from a high Dexterity, a double-weaponed dimachaerius is much more dangerous if he has a high Strength, and a mirmillo with a high Constitution can afford to sustain a few minor wounds while he closes with his opponent. As gladiators are performers, and the decision of whether to allow a defeated gladiator to live or die rests on how good a show he put on before falling, Charisma can be of use. A retired gladiator with a high Wisdom is less likely to squander his fame, fortune, and freedom than the average veteran of the arena.

Alignment: Any.
Hit Dice: d10.
Starting Gold: 4d4 × 10 (100 gp).
Starting Age: As fighter.

CLASS SKILLS

The class skills of the gladiator (and the key ability for each skill) are Balance (Dex), Bluff (Cha), Climb (Str), Craft (Int), Handle Animal (Cha), Intimidate (Cha), Jump (Str), Knowledge (the games) (Int), Perform (gladiatorial combat) (Cha), Ride (chariot) (Dex), Swim (Str), and Tumble (Dex). See **Chapter Four: Skills** in the *PHB* and **Chapter Three: Skills & Feats** in this book for skill descriptions.

Skill Points at 1st Level: (4 + Int modifier) × 4.
Skill Points at Each Additional Level: 4 + Int modifier.

CLASS FEATURES

The following are the class features of the gladiator.

WEAPON AND ARMOR PROFICIENCY

A gladiator is proficient with all simple and gladiator weapons (lasso, net, scimitar, shortbow, shortspear, short sword, spear, and trident) and with gladiator armor (fasciae, galerus, helmet, breastplate, manicus, ocreae, shield, including tower shields).

BONUS FEATS

At 1st level, a gladiator gets a bonus feat in addition to the feat that any 1st-level character gets and the bonus feat granted to a human character. The gladiator gains an additional bonus feat at 5th level and again at 9th, 13th, 17th, and 20th levels. These bonus feats must be drawn from the following feats:

Blind Fight, Canny Charge*, Chariot Attack*, Combat Expertise, Dodge, Gladiator Trainer*, Improved Bull Rush, Improved Disarm, Improved Feint, Improved Grapple, Improved Shield Bash, Improved Sunder, Improved Trip, Improved Unarmed Strike, Outlandish Weapon Finesse*, Retaliatory Strike*, Showy Fighting*, Sprinter*, Stunt Driving*, Superior Trip*, Two-Weapon Fighting, Two-Weapon Defense, Weapon Focus, Weapon Specialization (*see **Chapter Three: Skills & Feats** for details on these new feats).

A gladiator must still meet all prerequisites for a bonus feat, including ability score and base attack bonus minimums. These bonus feats are in addition to the feat that a character of any class gets from advancing levels. A gladiator is not limited to the list of bonus feats when choosing these feats.

STYLE BONUS

As a result of his intimate knowledge of his equipment and its use, beginning at 1st level a gladiator gains a +1 bonus to either Armor Class, attack rolls, or damage rolls—which of the three it applies to must be selected when the ability is first gained and once the bonus is dedicated to one of the three categories it cannot be changed. This bonus is only conferred while the gladiator is armed and armored in the style of a particular type of gladiator (see **Gladiator Types** starting on page 26). The type must also be selected when the ability is first gained.

Thus a 1st-level gladiator could decide to give himself a +1 bonus to AC when fighting as a Samnite, wearing a helmet, ocreae, cingulum, manicus, and a large wooden shield, and wielding a short sword. If he deliberately wears the armor or arms himself with a weapon suited to a different gladiator type, he loses this bonus; changes to his equipment as a result of a sundering attack against his shield or picking up a stray dagger to use as a weapon after being disarmed do not cause the gladiator to lose his bonus, but once an opportunity presents itself to restore his armor or weapon he must take it or forfeit the style bonus.

At each odd-numbered level above 1st, the gladiator gains an additional +1 bonus he can apply to his AC, attack rolls, or damage rolls. Again, he must designate what type of bonus it is to be, and the bonus must be linked to a gladiatorial style. If he picks both the same style and bonus type, the bonuses stack, but he can choose to vary either style, type, or both each time he gains a new bonus.

Thus when that same gladiator reaches 3rd level, he can choose to: take the same type of bonus again (the two bonuses stacking to +2 AC when fighting as a Samnite); take a different bonus but with the same style (*e.g.*, +1 damage when fighting as a Samnite); take the same type of bonus but a different gladiator style (*e.g.*, +1 to AC when fighting as a retiarius); of take a different bonus and different style (*e.g.*, +1 to attack rolls as a retiarius).

None of these bonuses apply if the character is fighting in non-gladiatorial armor or with a non-gladiatorial weapon (except as noted above) or if fighting in a gladiatorial style he hasn't designated for a bonus, but they *do* apply regardless of what the gladiator's *opponent* is wearing or wielding.

Note: Careful record-keeping is required when using this ability, because by the time a gladiator character reaches 19th level, he will have a total of +10 in bonuses that can all be the same type and applied to a single style of gladiatorial combat, or they could be divided among the three different bonus types and a dozen different gladiatorial styles. Add in the bonuses for preferred opponents (see below) and things can get complicated.

REPUTATION (EX)

Gladiators occupied a unique position in Roman society. Like professional athletes today, some gladiators became stars, but outside the games attitudes changed and they were looked upon with disgust. Many gladiators were slaves or prisoners of war, and all were regarded by the Roman public as only fit to die for their entertainment.

When dealing with Roman citizens within the context of the games (including when attempting to arrange matches or performances), gladiators receive a +3 bonus to their Fame modifiers. This bonus also applies when using their status as gladiators to improve Intimidate checks. When dealing with Roman citizens outside the context of the games gladiators receive a −3 to their Fame modifiers.

These modifiers apply even to retired gladiators, but if a gladiator successfully disguises himself as another person, neither his gladiator class levels nor his gladiator reputation contributes to his Fame score for that encounter.

DIRTY FIGHTING

Beginning at 2nd level, if a gladiator can catch an opponent when he is unable to defend himself effectively from his attack, he can strike a vital spot for extra damage. The gladiator's attack deals extra damage any time his target would be denied a Dexterity bonus to AC (whether the target actually has a Dexterity bonus or not), or when the gladiator flanks his target. This extra damage is 1d4 at 2nd level, and it increases by +1d4 every four gladiator levels thereafter. Should the gladiator score a critical hit with dirty infighting, this extra damage is not multiplied. Ranged attacks can count as dirty infighting only if the target is within 30 ft.

This ability can only be used when attacking with gladiator weapons (see page 56). Unlike a rogue's sneak attack, a gladiator can use a weapon that normally deals lethal damage to deal nonlethal damage with dirty infighting by taking a −4 penalty to the attack roll.

A gladiator can use dirty fighting only against living creatures with discernible anatomies—undead, constructs, oozes, plants, and incorporeal creatures lack vital areas to

FEMALE GLADIATORS

Historically, while women could become gladiators, they were often restricted in the roles they could play: sometimes taking part in bloodless fights as comic relief or wearing fanciful Amazon costumes that revealed a breast (if not more) to the audience. In an *Eternal Rome* campaign, the GM is free to dispense with these restrictions, especially if they would cause embarrassment to players.

attack. Any creature that is immune to critical hits is not vulnerable to dirty infighting. The gladiator must be able to see the target well enough to pick out a vital spot and must be able to reach such a spot. A gladiator cannot dirty infighting while striking a creature with concealment or striking the limbs of a creature whose vitals are beyond reach.

Extra damage from dirty fighting stacks with similar types of extra damage, including sneak attack damage.

Preferred Opponent (Ex)

At 2nd level, a gladiator may select a type of gladiator that he has studied so well that he gets a +2 bonus on weapon damage rolls against such opponents. At 8th, 14th, and 20th levels, the gladiator may either select another gladiator type to receive a +2 weapon damage bonus against, or he can select a type that is already a preferred opponent, stacking the bonuses against that gladiator type; *e.g.*, if a gladiator picks Thracian as his preferred opponent at 2nd level, when he reaches 8th level he can either pick Thracian again (increasing his weapon damage bonus to +4) or pick a different gladiator type to receive a +2 bonus against.

This ability only applies when the character wears gladiator armor and uses gladiator weapons. In addition, if the gladiator faces an opponent armed and armored in a style he hasn't selected (including all non-gladiators), this ability provides no combat bonuses.

A gladiator may take "animal" or "bull" as his preferred opponent, in which case this ability only applies when he is fighting equipped as a venator or taurarius respectively. Selecting "animal" gives the venator a bonus against any typical arena animal, but not against oddities that the gladiator has never before encountered. Selecting "bull" gives the taurarius a +3 bonus on weapon damage rolls against bulls and aurochs, but not against any other animal species.

Dramatic Attack (Ex)

An experienced gladiator knows how to make the most of his attacks to instill a sense of drama and excitement in his audience. At 4th level, if the gladiator scores a threat when attacking with a gladiator weapon, he may choose not to roll for a critical, instead declaring to the GM that the attack was made with particular flair in order to please the audience. This gives the gladiator a +1 competence bonus on his Perform (gladiatorial combat) roll at the end of the bout (see page 40). The Perform bonuses from multiple threats turned into dramatic attacks stack.

The bonus received for a threat turned into a dramatic attack increases by +1 for every four gladiator levels above 4th level, to a maximum of a +5 bonus per dramatic attack at 20th level.

Uncanny Dodge (Ex)

At 5th level and higher, a gladiator can react to danger before his senses would normally allow him to do so. He retains his Dexterity bonus to AC (if any) even if caught flat-footed or struck by an invisible attacker. However, he still loses his Dexterity bonus to AC if immobilized.

If a gladiator already has uncanny dodge from a different class he automatically gains improved uncanny dodge (see the **Rogue** as described in the *PHB*) instead.

Evasion (Ex)

At 10th level and higher, a gladiator can avoid even magical and unusual attacks with great agility. If he makes a successful Reflex saving throw against an attack that normally deals half damage on a successful save, he instead takes no damage.

Evasion can be used only if the gladiator is wearing light gladiator armor (see page 59) or no armor. A helpless gladiator does not gain the benefit of evasion.

If a gladiator already has evasion from a different class he automatically gains improved evasion (see the **Rogue** as described in the *PHB*) instead.

Defensive Roll (Ex)

At 15th level, the gladiator can roll with a potentially lethal blow to take less damage from it than he otherwise would. Once per day, when he would be reduced to 0 or fewer hit points by damage in combat (from a weapon or other blow, not a spell or special ability), the gladiator can attempt to roll with the damage. To use this ability, the gladiator must attempt a Reflex saving throw (DC equals damage dealt). If the save succeeds, he takes only half damage from the blow; if it fails, he takes full damage. He must be aware of the attack and able to react to it in order to execute his defensive roll—if he is denied his Dexterity bonus to AC, he can't use this ability.

Since this effect would not normally allow a character to make a Reflex save for half damage, the gladiator's evasion ability does not apply to the defensive roll.

GLADIATOR TYPES

The earliest gladiator types fought in the style and with the equipment of Rome's conquered neighbors. In many cases, they were prisoners of war from those peoples, but centuries after those wars had been forgotten gladiators with different origins would still be trained to fight as Thracians Gauls, *etc.* As gladiatorial games became more frequent, those staging them invented new and interesting gladiatorial styles to bring novelty to the entertainments.

The different types of gladiator are presented here roughly in chronological order of their introduction to the games. Some are almost indistinguishable from each other now, but fans of the sport avidly debated even the finest points of differentiation.

SAMNITE

The Samnites, a hill people to the southeast of Rome, were one of Rome's first conquests. Their equipment and fighting style did much to influence the equipment of the first legions.

A gladiator fighting in the Samnite style (who needn't be a Samnite by birth) was equipped with a large rectangular shield, a short sword, and a visored helmet. Armor varied, but could include a manicus on his weapon arm, a cingulum covering his midsection, and one or two ocreae to protect his shins.

Weapon: Short sword.
Armor: Enclosed helmet, ocreae, cingulum, medium manicus, heavy wooden shield.

THRACIAN

In contrast to the heavily-equipped Samnites, Thracians fought wearing little armor, using a small round shield and a curved sword, in the traditional manner of the warriors of Thrace.

Weapon: Scimitar.
Armor: Light manicus, light wooden shield.

MIRMILLO

Known at first as the Gallic style, the mirmillo was equipped similarly to the Samnite. The main distinction was a fish-shaped crest on his helmet, and the fact that a mirmillo (whose name derives from *mormylos*, a kind of fish) was often pitted against a retiarius (a stylized fisherman).

Weapon: Short sword.
Armor: Enclosed helmet, manicus, fasciae, ocreae, heavy wooden shield.

RETIARIUS

Another lightly equipped style, a retiarius was armed with a weighted net and a trident. His armor consisted of a galerus protecting the shoulder of his weapon arm and one side of his neck, and infrequently a leather manicus as well.

Matching a retiarius against a mirmillo pitted the former's reach versus the latter's armor and close-combat ability; a retiarius often had to give ground or flee to create fighting room if his opponent got past his trident and closed with him. This undignified necessity led to retiarii being among the lower types of gladiator, and some retiarii trained in other styles as well.

Weapon: Trident, net.
Armor: Galerus, occasionally a light manicus.

AMAZON

Female gladiators were always a popular novelty act in the arena, armed as female variants of the male gladiator types or in "Amazon" attire. During the Republic, women's bouts were bloodless mock fights, but early in the Empire, the field was opened to proper female gladiators.

Weapon: Shortbow, shortspear, Amazon axe.
Armor: Helmet, light metal shield.

SECUTOR

The secutor ("chaser") style may have developed from the mirmillo, who often had to chase a retreating retiarius around the arena. A secutor's equipment was very similar to a mirmillo's, although the secutor's helmet normally lacked the distinctive fish crest.

Weapon: Short sword.
Armor: Enclosed helmet, manicus, galerus, ocreae, tower shield.

HOPLOMACHUS

Hoplomachi were the most heavily armored gladiators, and they fought with the same short sword and large rectangular shield as Samnites.

Weapon: Short sword.
Armor: Lorica (various types), manicus, galerus, fasciae, ocreae, heavy wooden shield.

ESSEDARIUS

The essedarius was a gladiator who fought from a chariot. Originally based on the chariot warfare that Julius Caesar encountered on his expeditions to Britain in 55 and 54 BC, these fighters used spears as their main weapons, the gladiator making drive-by attacks against his opponent. The chariot was controlled by a noncombatant driver, leaving the essedarius free to concentrate on fighting.

Weapon: Spear, chariot.
Armor: None.

DIMACHAERIUS

Another light style, the dimachaerius was armed with a short sword in each hand, and armored with either a manicus on each arm and a cingulum, or nothing at all. This style focused entirely on offense, at the expense of defense.

Weapon: Two short swords.
Armor: Cingulum and pair of manica, or none.

Laquearius

The laquearius was a variant on the retiarius, and was almost identically equipped except that his net was replaced with a lasso. Rules for lassos can be found on page 56.

Weapon: Trident, lasso.
Armor: Galerus.

Venator

Also known as the bestiarius, the venator ("hunter") fought wild beasts rather than fellow gladiators. Sometimes groups of these gladiators chased down various beasts, while in other matches a solitary venator was sent out to face a single dangerous creature such as a bear, bull, lion, or tiger.

The venator was typically unarmored and armed with a shortspear. Some individuals wore the skins of animals they'd killed as hooded cloaks, giving them some protection to their head and back.

While venators were popular with audiences, they were held in even lower esteem than retiarii by their fellow gladiators.

Weapon: Shortspear.
Armor: Usually none, but occasionally hide.

Taurarius

A specialist venator, a taurarius fought bulls with a shortspear or a longspear.

Weapon: Shortspear or longspear.
Armor: Usually none, but occasionally hide.

Sagittarius

The sagittarius was an unarmored archer, often pitted against more heavily armed and armored gladiators.

Weapon: Shortbow.
Armor: None.

Andabate

An andabate was heavily armored and his helmet was fully enclosed, without a visor or eye-holes; he had to fight blind, often on horseback.

Andabates were regarded as comic relief from the more serious combats, even though the combats were just as deadly.

Weapon: Shortspear.
Armor: Eyeless helmet, lorica (various types), ocreae.

- Prestige Classes -

The standard prestige classes described below are suitable for use in *Eternal Rome*, some with a few rules adjustments.

Arcane Archer

In a humans-only *Eternal Rome* campaign, some humans can become arcane archers, but access to this class is restricted to certain nationalities. Amazons were famed for their archery, as were other steppe races. The Amazons were also followers of Diana, who was a patroness of archers. At the GM's option, human followers of Diana (or any other patron deity of archers, such as the Egyptian goddess Neith) may become arcane archers if the deity permits; their powers are treated as divine rather than arcane in origin, and like a paladin's special abilities they may be withdrawn if the character offends the deity in any way.

Even in an *Eternal Rome* campaign allowing nonhuman races, elves are not a major race, while nymphs and satyrs are not famed for their archery skill. While elven arcane archers are possible in a fantasy *Eternal Rome*, they should be *much* rarer than in typical fantasy campaigns.

Arcane Trickster

Arcane tricksters are ideally suited to the *Eternal Rome* setting. Rogues with real or pretended magical powers roamed the Empire, providing magical services for a price.

Perhaps the best-known of these are the freelance miracle-workers mentioned in the New Testament, who appeared throughout the urbanized areas of the eastern Empire, as well as in Rome itself. There's less evidence for similar individuals operating in the western half of the Empire, but it seems likely that they were just as common. These individuals would heal the sick and cast out demons (which were blamed for a variety of ailments) for a price. In the *Eternal Rome* setting, such miracle-workers rely on spells such as *bestow curse* and *remove curse* rather than divine healing magic, sometimes causing ailments magically before offering to cure them.

Some clients would prefer their services to those of temple priests, because they only cared about payment and didn't ask potentially embarrassing questions about one's relationship with the gods. They might also be cheaper than the temples, which normally expected a hefty donation in exchange for supernatural services.

Arcane tricksters can also find employment in the criminal underworld, serving gang bosses and helping criminal enterprises from burglaries to fixing fights and races.

Archmage

Although Rome was not itself a highly magical culture, more than one province within the Empire was famed for its magicians. Both Egypt and Mesopotamia were renowned for their magical traditions, some of which had passed to Greece to form the basis of the Hermetic tradition that would underpin most academic magic in medieval and later Europe. An archmage could be a student of any of these magical traditions.

Assassin

From the late Republic onward, assassins for hire found almost constant employment in Rome. From the Imperial family on down, it seems that there was always someone who needed obstacles to their ambitions removed. The most sophisticated assassins used undetectable, incurable poisons; less subtle ones opted for the dagger in a dark alley.

While assassins ran the gamut from hired thugs to expert professionals, the most skilled individuals were thought to come from the east.

BLACKGUARD

From the middle Empire period onward, there were any number of foreign cults active in Rome, some of which engaged in extremely bloody rites. An NPC blackguard would make an ideal leader or champion for such a group.

DUELIST

Several types of gladiators fought in a light, unencumbered style, and the duelist is a logical prestige class for such characters to take.

DWARVEN DEFENDER

In a version of the *Eternal Rome* setting using nonhuman races, dwarven defenders can be found in their mountain fastnesses but never outside of them. Unlike arcane archers, no humans can become dwarven defenders, even in a humans-only campaign.

ELDRITCH KNIGHT

Romans favored pure strength and skill at arms, so combining magic with combat ability was seen as dishonorable.

In the eastern half of the Empire, magic was much more widely accepted, and an eldritch knight could be a powerful Egyptian or Mesopotamian warrior who studied magic in conjunction with combat. Celtic and Germanic tradition included sorcerer-warriors with magical abilities that are either inborn (often as a result of mixed human and nonhuman blood) or acquired through the favor of the gods.

TESTAMENT AND TROJAN WAR PRESTIGE CLASSES

Some prestige classes in two other Green Ronin Mythic Vistas books are particularly useful in an *Eternal Rome* campaign to represent various peoples in parts of the Empire other than Italy.

From *Testament*, the champion of Israel and prophet classes could be used to represent the charismatic Judean leaders who fought against Rome in the late Republic and early Empire periods. The ren-hekau, desert hermit, master charioteer, and royal astrologer are usable without alteration. The idol-maker prestige class (as opposed to just a craftsman who makes idols) would be a rare character.

Trojan War's runner class can be added for use either as a fighter option or by a gladiator of the secutor style hoping to gain a bit of an advantage in the arena.

HIEROPHANT

The favored servants of the gods are powerful individuals in the *Eternal Rome* setting.

HORIZON WALKER

As Roman cosmology doesn't include the multitude of planes found in other settings, the horizon walker's planar terrain mastery abilities can be replaced with improved versions of the mundane terrain mastery abilities that raise his insight bonus on attack and damage rolls versus native creatures to +3 and the competence bonus on relevant skills (if any) to +6.

LOREMASTER

Greek and Egyptian scholars were especially renowned in the Roman world, with Aristotle, Archimedes, and Pythagoras becoming almost legendary, and the cult of the Egyptian Imhotep and Amenhotep, son of Hapu, spreading to Rome following the conquest of Egypt. A character of any race or nationality may become a loremaster, although in the case of NPC loremasters, their native culture will likely have some effect on their areas of study.

MYSTIC THEURGE

In most of the Empire, divine and arcane magic were kept separate by cultural forces, but exceptionally gifted individuals could study both. The exception was in Egypt, where for thousands of years the priesthood held a virtual monopoly on all magic, both divine and arcane and mystic theurges were almost commonplace among spellcasters.

SHADOWDANCER

The eastern provinces (especially Egypt and Mesopotamia) were renowned for their spellcasters and assassins. The exotic east was also famed for its dancers, and many troupes traveled to Rome to entertain the great and the wealthy from the early Empire period onwards. Such troupes could include shadowdancers, perhaps employed by a rival of their audience to act as spies or assassins. And while the Canaanites and their religion had disappeared from the world stage by the Roman era, later mystery cults could revive elements of the Canaanite qedeshot priesthood, with its combination of dance, magic, and spirituality reworked for a Roman audience.

THAUMATURGIST

The thaumaturgist prestige class should only be used in the *Eternal Rome* campaign setting if the GM further develops the Roman cosmology summarized in **Chapter Eleven: Religion**.

The Roman view of the planes of existence was different from that set forth in the core rulebooks, and the population of outsiders was less well defined than those described in the *MM*. In addition, thaumaturgists tend to deal only with beings from the cosmology of their native lands.

- NEW PRESTIGE CLASS: CRIME BOSS -

Unlike adventurers who roam the Empire seeking fame, fortune, and excitement, a crime boss knows that there's money to be made at home. He's a leader of organized crime, powerful on his home turf and likely to stay there. He runs rackets, protection scams, cutpurse gangs, and the like and is the real power behind neighborhoods or even entire cities.

Hit Die: d8.

REQUIREMENTS

To qualify to become a crime boss, a character must fulfill the following criteria.

Alignment: Any non-lawful.
Feats: Leadership.
Skills: Gather Information 8 ranks, Intimidate 5 ranks, Knowledge (local) 4 ranks.
Special: Every crime boss needs a territory to control: a street, a neighborhood, a town, or even a city. To become a crime boss, a character must first take over a territory (likely by taking out the previous crime boss) or garner a suitable promotion from an existing criminal organization (thieves' guild, *etc.*).

CLASS SKILLS

The crime boss's class skills (and the key abilities for each skill) are: Appraise (Int), Bluff (Cha), Decipher Script (Int), Diplomacy (Cha), Disable Device (Dex), Disguise (Cha), Escape Artist (Dex), Forgery (Int), Gather Information (Cha), Hide (Dex), Innuendo (Wis), Intimidate (Cha), Knowledge (local) (Int), Listen (Wis), Move Silently (Dex), Open Lock (Dex), Pick Pockets (Dex), Read Lips (Int), Search (Int), Sense Motive (Wis), Speak Language (none), Spot (Wis), Tumble (Dex), and Use Magic Device (Cha). See **Chapter Four: Skills** in the *PHB* for skill descriptions.

Skill Points at Each Level: 8 + Int modifier.

CLASS FEATURES

The following are class features of the crime boss prestige class.

WEAPON AND ARMOR PROFICIENCY

Crime bosses do not engage in heavy combat; that's what bodyguards are for. Crime bosses tend to limit their equipment to weapons and armor that can be concealed easily or worn in cities without arousing suspicion. They are proficient with all simple weapons, as well as the sap, rapier, and shortbow. Crime bosses are proficient with light armor but not with shields.

LARCENOUS FOLLOWERS (EX)

At 1st level, a crime boss attracts criminal-minded individuals to his organization. This allows him to recruit rogues as followers (normally, the Leadership feat only allows followers from the warrior, expert, and commoner classes).

WEEKLY INCOME

A crime boss receives a base weekly income of (crime boss level + Cha modifier) × 100 gp. This represents normal profits from the crime boss's activities. Should the crime boss be away from his home territory for a given week, his profits are reduced by 1d100% due to non-payment, skimming, and other chicanery. Weekly income can also change based on events in the campaign, and the final amount is always subject to GM approval.

DAGGER

Many crime bosses favor the dagger, an easily concealable and poisonable weapon. At 2nd level, a crime boss gains Weapon Focus (dagger) as a bonus feat.

KILLER REPUTATION (EX)

At 3rd level, a crime boss's reputation is such that he gains a +2 bonus to his Leadership score. This increases to +4 at 6th level and +6 at 9th level.

SNEAK ATTACK (EX)

Stealth and ruthlessness are often required of a crime boss. At 4th level, a crime boss gains a +1d6 sneak attack as per the rogue class ability. This increases to +2d6 at 8th level. If a crime boss receives a sneak attack bonus from another source, the bonuses to damage stack.

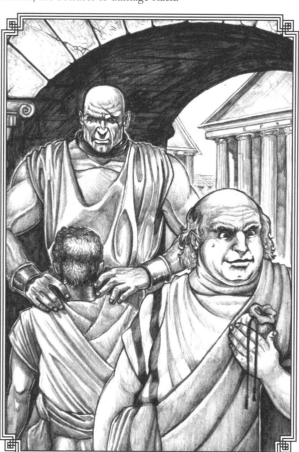

TABLE 2-13: THE CRIME BOSS

Level	Base Attack Bonus	Fort Save	Ref Save	Will Save	Special
1st	+0	+0	+2	+2	Larcenous followers, weekly income
2nd	+1	+0	+3	+3	Dagger
3rd	+2	+1	+3	+3	Killer reputation +2
4th	+3	+1	+4	+4	Sneak attack +1d6
5th	+3	+1	+4	+4	Infamy
6th	+4	+2	+5	+5	Killer reputation +4
7th	+5	+2	+5	+5	Fortuna's favor
8th	+6	+2	+6	+6	Sneak attack +2d6
9th	+6	+3	+6	+6	Killer reputation +6
10th	+7	+3	+7	+7	Untouchable

INFAMY (EX)

At 5th level, a crime boss is so powerful that even a negative Fame score isn't a problem for him. Whenever the crime boss makes a Fame check, he gets to decide whether his Fame modifier is applied as a bonus or a penalty to the roll.

FORTUNA'S FAVOR (EX)

Even the smartest crime boss needs a little luck to survive power grabs, assassination attempts, and other hazards of the criminal world. At 7th level, a crime boss can add his Charisma modifier as a luck bonus to his Armor Class. This bonus applies even when the crime boss is flat-footed and applies against touch attacks.

UNTOUCHABLE (EX)

By the time a crime boss reaches 10th level, his reputation is such that no sane person wants to cross him. No hirelings, assassins, mercenaries, or other paid toughs will take a contract on the crime boss; they know it would mean their death.

Similarly, such is the crime boss's power in his home territory that even the toughest opponents think twice before attacking him. As long as the crime boss is in his home territory, living, sentient opponents who are aware of his reputation must make a DC 20 Will save each round they want to attack, cast a spell at, or otherwise attempt to harm the crime boss. Those who fail must choose an alternate action.

- NEW PRESTIGE CLASS: ORATOR -

An orator is a character who can sway people's thoughts and emotions by making touching, rousing, and convincing speeches. Across Rome and throughout the Roman world political agitators on street corners harangue passers-by, military leaders make inspiring speeches before battle is joined, wily advocates argue points of law, and ambitious politicians campaign for votes. There's no guarantee that what an orator says is true, but whatever the content of his words, they are undeniably stirring.

Hit Die: d6.

REQUIREMENTS

To qualify to become an orator, a character must fulfill all the following criteria.

Skills: Bluff 4 ranks, Diplomacy 4 ranks, Perform (oratory) 4 ranks, Sense Motive 4 ranks.
Feats: Persuasive.

CLASS SKILLS

The orator's class skills (and the key ability for each skill) are Appraise (Int), Bluff (Cha), Concentration (Con), Diplomacy (Cha), Gather Information (Cha), Intimidate (Cha), Knowledge (any) (Int), Listen (Wis), Perform (oratory)(Cha), Profession (Wis), Sense Motive (Wis), and Spot (Wis). See **Chapter Four: Skills** in the *PHB* for skill descriptions.

Skill Points at Each Level: 4 + Int modifier.

CLASS FEATURES

The following are class features of the orator prestige class.

WEAPON AND ARMOR PROFICIENCY

Orators gain no proficiency with any weapon or armor.

CAPTIVE AUDIENCE (EX)

When a 1st-level or higher orator speaks to a gathered crowd or even a single individual, he may make a Perform (oratory) check against a DC determined by the crowd's general mood. DCs are as follows.

CAPTIVE AUDIENCE

Audience Attitude	DC
Hostile	50
Unfriendly	25
Indifferent	15
Friendly	10
Helpful	5
Fanatic	0

On a successful check, the orator holds the individual or group non-magically spellbound, as if under the effect of the *enthrall* spell. He can hold their attention for a number of hours equal to his Charisma modifier (minimum 1 hour), or as long as he continues to speak, whichever is shorter. The effects of this language-dependent, mind-affecting ability only apply to those who can both see and hear the orator.

ORATORY (EX)

An orator can use his eloquence and force of personality to create effects in the minds of a captive audience (see above). Each of these abilities can be used once per day per point of the orator's Charisma bonus (minimum 1/day).

The character's bard and orator levels are added to determine the *effects* of the abilities he's able to use based on his orator levels alone, but not to determine *which* abilities the orator can use. For example, a 5th-level bard who takes 7 levels of orator is treated as a 12th-level orator in order to determine the size of his Inspire Courage bonus (an ability usable by 6th-level orators), but he cannot Inspire Greatness, as he must be an *actual* 10th-level orator to first gain use of the ability. The reverse is not true: Orator levels are *not* added to bard levels in order to perform bardic music effects.

Starting an oratory effect is a standard action. Some oratory abilities require concentration, which means the orator must take a standard action each round to maintain the ability. Even while using oratory abilities that don't require concentration, the orator cannot cast spells, activate magic items by spell completion (such as scrolls), or activate magic items by magic word (such as wands).

All oratory abilities are language-dependant, mind-affecting abilities.

- *Inspire Complacency:* An orator with 4 or more ranks in Perform (oratory) skill can convince those in a captive audience to relax their vigilance or let down their guard. Subjects of inspire complacency take a −4 circumstance penalty to Listen and Spot checks. They are automatically flat-footed if attacked, but the captive audience effect ends when any member of the audience is attacked.

- *Inspire Trust:* An orator of 2nd level or higher with 5 or more ranks in Perform (oratory) skill can instill feelings of loyalty and trust in his audience. The orator can add a +20 to a Perform (oratory) check to improve the attitude of one NPC in a captive audience. The improved attitude remains for a number of hours equal to the orator's class level.

- *Inspire Anger:* An orator of 4th level or higher with 7 or more ranks in Perform (oratory) skill can instill feelings of anger in his audience. The effect lasts for as long as the audience hears the orator speak and for 1 round per effective orator level (adding orator and bard levels) thereafter.

  Once his audience is angry, the orator can attempt to direct that anger at a specific target or goal. This requires a Perform (oratory) check with a DC equal to the Will save of his audience (either that of each individual if the number of people is small, or the average of a large group

with the result applied to everyone in the audience). If the orator attempts to incite violence against the target (instead of just leaving the audience angry or, say, encouraging them to make noisy demonstrations against it), the DC increases by 5, and if the likelihood is high that the audience will face defeat and/or death in the ensuing violence, the DC increases by 15. ·

On a failed roll to steer the angry crowd toward a specific action, the crowd releases its anger at random. On a roll of a natural 1 on the Perform (oratory) check, the crowd's anger is directed at the orator (this is a special side effect of this ability; ordinarily a roll of a natural 1 is not an automatic failure).

- *Inspire Courage:* An orator of 6th level or higher with 9 or more ranks in Perform (oratory) skill can use a standard action to inspire courage in an individual or group with an impassioned speech. The effect lasts for as long as the ally hears the orator speak and for 5 rounds thereafter.

  An affected ally receives a +1 morale bonus on saving throws against charm and fear effects and a +1 morale bonus on attack and weapon damage rolls. At 12th level, and every six effective orator levels (adding orator and bard levels) thereafter, this bonus increases by +1 (+2 at 12th level, +3 at 18th, *etc.*).

- *Insinuate:* An orator of 8th level or higher with 11 or more ranks in Perform (oratory) skill can insinuate an idea into the mind of one member of his captive audience. The insinuation functions as a *suggestion* spell, but it isn't a magical effect. Using this ability does not break the orator's concentration on his captive audience, nor does it allow a second saving throw against the enthralling effect. The

TABLE 2–14: THE ORATOR

Level	Base Attack Bonus	Fort Save	Ref Save	Will Save	Special	Spells per Day 1st	2nd	3rd	4th
1st	+0	+0	+0	+2	Captive audience, inspire complacency, oratory	0	—	—	—
2nd	+1	+0	+0	+3	Glib, inspire trust	1	—	—	—
3rd	+1	+1	+1	+3	Resist persuasion +1	1	0	—	—
4th	+2	+1	+1	+4	Inspire anger	1	1	—	—
5th	+2	+1	+1	+4	Assess audience	1	1	0	—
6th	+3	+2	+2	+5	Inspire courage, resist persuasion +2	1	1	1	—
7th	+3	+2	+2	+5	Mass appeal ×2	2	1	1	0
8th	+4	+2	+2	+6	Insinuate	2	1	1	1
9th	+4	+3	+3	+6	Resist persuasion +3	2	2	1	1
10th	+5	+3	+3	+7	Inspire greatness, mass appeal ×4	2	2	2	1

target of this ability receives a Will save (DC 10 + ½ the orator's level + the orator's Cha modifier) to resist this effect.

- *Inspire Greatness:* A 10th-level orator with 13 or more ranks in Perform (oratory) skill can inspire greatness in a single willing member of a captive audience, granting him extra fighting capability. For every three effective orator levels (adding orator and bard levels) above 10th, he can target one additional ally with a single use of this ability (two at 13th level, three at 16th, *etc.*). The effect lasts for as long as the ally the hears orator's speech and for 5 rounds thereafter.

A creature inspired with greatness gains 2 bonus Hit Dice (d10s), the commensurate number of temporary hit points (apply the target's Constitution modifier, if any, to these bonus Hit Dice), a +2 competence bonus on attack rolls, and a +1 competence bonus on Fortitude saves. The bonus Hit Dice count as regular Hit Dice for determining the effect of spells that are Hit Dice-dependant.

SPELLS

An orator can cast a small number of arcane spells drawn from the orator spell list (see page 65). To cast a spell, the orator must have a Charisma score equal to at least 10 + the

spell level. The Difficulty Class for a saving throw against an orator's spell is 10 + the spell level + the orator's Charisma modifier.

An orator can cast only a certain number of spells of each spell level per day. His base daily spell allotment is given on **Table 2–14: The Orator**. In addition, he receives bonus spells each day if he has a high Charisma score. When **Table 2–14** indicates that the orator gets 0 spells per day of a given spell level, he gains only the bonus spells he would be entitled to based on his Charisma score for that spell level. An orator casts spells as a sorcerer does.

Upon reaching 6th level, and at 8th and 10th levels, an orator can choose to learn a new spell in place of one he already knows. The new spell's level must be the same as that of the spell being exchanged, and it must be at least two levels lower than the highest-level orator spell the orator can cast. An orator may swap only a single spell at any given level, and must choose whether to swap the spell at the same time that he gains new spells known for that level.

GLIB (EX)

Starting at 2nd level, if the orator has an opportunity to address his subject, he adds one-half his class level to all Fame checks and Charisma-based skill checks made to affect an audience.

RESIST PERSUASION (EX)

At 3rd level, an orator gains a +1 bonus to all saves against language-dependent mind-affecting magical effects, and a +2 bonus against non-magical language-dependent mind-affecting effects (including the oratory of other orators). At 6th level, this bonus rises to +2/+4. At 9th level, the bonus against magical effects increases to +3, and the orator becomes completely immune to non-magical mind-affecting effects.

ASSESS AUDIENCE (EX)

At 5th level, an orator learns to read his audience. To do so, he must succeed on a Sense Motive check opposed by the audience's attitude (see **Captive Audience** on page 32). If successful, the orator discerns what topics please his

TABLE 2–13: ORATOR SPELLS KNOWN

Level	1st	2nd	3rd	4th
1st	1	—	—	—
2nd	2	—	—	—
3rd	2	1	—	—
4th	2	2	—	—
5th	2	2	1	—
6th	3	2	2	—
7th	3	2	2	1
8th	3	3	2	2
9th	3	3	2	2
10th	3	3	3	2

listeners the most and what angers them. The orator gains a +4 bonus on Charisma-based skill checks used on the audience from that point onward. In addition, the listener takes a –4 penalty to all opposed rolls against any of the orator's class abilities, as the orator knows exactly how to affect him.

Mass Appeal (Ex)

Orators are at their best when dealing with large crowds. At 7th level, the orator can influence double the normal number of hearers with an oratory (*e.g.,* inspiring courage in the minds of two listeners instead of one). At 10th level, he can influence four times the usual number.

- New Prestige Class: Pankretiast -

The deadliest unarmed fighter in the Roman Empire was the pankretiast. Pankretion was a martial art developed in classical Greece. Its name can be translated as "by every means," and it started out as a no-holds-barred blend of boxing and wrestling. A minimal set of rules was developed to regulate the sport: The Spartans pulled their pankretion team out of one Olympic Games in protest when biting and eye-gouging were banned.

Most pankretiasts begin their careers as athletes, warriors, or gladiators. Many are devotees of martial gods. Some rogues train in the art of pankretion to enhance their streetfighting skills.

Hit Die: d10.

Requirements

To qualify to become a pankretiast, a character must fulfill all the following criteria.

Base Attack Bonus: +6.

Feats: Improved Grapple, Improved Unarmed Strike.

Class Skills

The pankretiast's class skills (and the key ability for each skill) are Balance (Dex), Escape Artist (Dex), Intimidate (Cha), Jump (Str), Sense Motive (Wis), and Tumble (Dex). See **Chapter Four: Skills** in the *PHB* for skill descriptions.

Skill Points at Each Level: 2 + Int modifier.

Class Features

The following are class features of the pankretiast prestige class.

Weapon and Armor Proficiency

Pankretiasts gain no proficiency with any weapon or armor.

Flurry of Blows (Ex)

When unarmored and unarmed (or armed with cesti), a pankretiast may make an extra attack each round at the expense of accuracy. The one additional attack each round is made at his highest base attack bonus, but all attacks he makes that round take a –2 penalty. This penalty applies for 1 round, so it also affects attacks of opportunity the pankretiast might make before his next action. When a pankretiast reaches 5th level, the penalty lessens to –1, and at 9th level, it disappears.

A pankretiast must use a full attack action to strike with a flurry of blows.

Unarmed Strike

A pankretiast deals more damage with an unarmed strike than a normal person would, as shown on **Table 2–15: The Pankretiast**. In both normal and grappling attacks, the pankretiast chooses whether to deal lethal or nonlethal damage with no penalty to his attack rolls.

The pankretiast's unarmed strike is treated both as a manufactured weapon and a natural weapon for the purpose of spells and effects that enhance or improve either manufactured weapons or natural weapons.

A pankretiast can wear leather or metal cesti and still gain the benefits of unarmed strikes, except he cannot choose to do nonlethal damage while using metal cesti.

Throw

At 2nd level, a pankretiast can throw a grappled opponent to the ground instead of dealing normal damage. The opponent takes 1d6 points of damage +1 point per class level. The pankretiast decides whether to inflict lethal or nonlethal damage before throwing the opponent. The opponent is

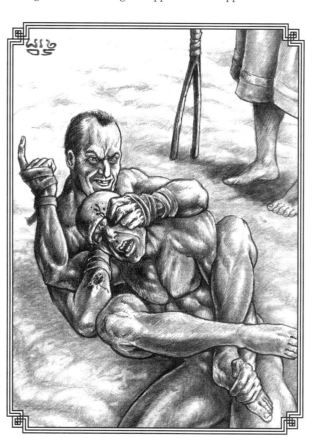

TABLE 2-15: THE PANKRETIAST

Level	Base Attack Bonus	Fort Save	Ref Save	Will Save	Special	Flurry of Blows Attack Bonus	Unarmed Damage
1st	+1	+2	+2	+0	Flurry of blows, unarmed strike	–1/–1	1d6
2nd	+2	+3	+3	+0	Throw	+0/+0	1d6
3rd	+3	+3	+3	+1	—	+1/+1	1d6
4th	+4	+4	+4	+1	Bonus feat	+2/+2	1d8
5th	+5	+4	+4	+1	—	+4/+4	1d8
6th	+6	+5	+5	+2	Crush	+5/+5	1d8
7th	+7	+5	+5	+2	Bonus feat	+6/+6	1d8
8th	+8	+6	+6	+2	—	+7/+7	1d10
9th	+9	+6	+6	+3	—	+9/+9	1d10
10th	+10	+7	+7	+3	Bonus feat	+10/+10	1d10

thrown to the ground in a square adjacent to the pankretiast, and is prone, taking a –4 AC modifier. A successful DC 15 Tumble check allows the thrown creature to reduce the damage suffered in the fall to just 1 point per class level.

BONUS FEAT

At 4th level, the pankretiast gains a bonus feat from the following: Combat Reflexes, Improved Disarm, Improved Trip, Superior Trip*, Stunning Fist (treating pankretiast levels as monk levels), or Wrestler* (*see **Chapter Three: Skills & Feats** for details on these new feats). A pankretiast need not have any of the prerequisites normally required for these feats to select them. Alternatively, he can choose any

other feat as a bonus feat, but he must meet the prerequisites for that feat. The pankretiast gains an additional bonus feat at 7th and 10th level.

CRUSH (EX)

At 6th level, the pankretiast can opt to cause automatic damage to a grappled opponent with a rib-cracking bear hug. For as long as the pankretiast chooses (or is able) to maintain the grapple, the opponent takes automatic damage each round equal to the pankretiast's unarmed damage without the pankretiast having to roll an additional grapple check. The pankretiast chooses whether to deal lethal or nonlethal damage.

- NEW PRESTIGE CLASS: SOOTHSAYER -

A soothsayer is a character with unusual insight into the future. Soothsayers specialize in divination spells, and have an array of skills that help them see the truth and predict what is to come. NPC soothsayers do not travel widely, relying instead on their reputations to bring questioners to them; some, like the Sybils of Cumae and the Oracle of Apollo at Delphi, were visited by kings and emperors. PC soothsayers may travel more widely, seeking further knowledge and insight.

Hit Die: d4.

REQUIREMENTS

To qualify to become a soothsayer, a character must fulfill all the following criteria.

Skills: Knowledge (arcana) 6 ranks.
Spells: Able to cast 2nd-level spells and at least three divination spells.

CLASS SKILLS

The soothsayer's class skills (and the key ability for each skill) are Appraise (Int), Concentration (Con), Decipher Script (Int), Knowledge (all) (Int), Sense Motive (Wis), Spellcraft (Int), Spot (Wis), and Use Magic Device (Cha). See **Chapter Four: Skills** in the *PHB* for skill descriptions.

Skill Points at Each Level: 2 + Int modifier.

CLASS FEATURES

The following are features of the soothsayer prestige class.

WEAPON AND ARMOR PROFICIENCY

Soothsayers gain no proficiency with any weapon or armor.

ORACLE (SU)

A soothsayer casts all divination spells at +1 caster level, and can learn divination spells that are not normally available to spellcasters of his class. For example, a wizard soothsayer can learn the *commune* spell, even though it is normally only available to divine spellcasters.

He also gains a +5 bonus to all Use Magic Device checks involving items with at least one divination function.

CLEAR SIGHT (EX)

Starting at 2nd level, a soothsayer may add one-half his class level to all Search and Spot checks.

SPELLS PER DAY

Starting at 2nd level, with a new soothsayer level is gained, the character gains new spells per day (and spells known, if applicable) as if he had also gained a level in a spellcasting class he belonged to before he added the prestige class. He does not, however, gain any other benefit a character of that class would have gained. This essentially means that he adds the level of soothsayer to the level of some other spellcasting class the character has, then determines spells per day, spells known, and caster level accordingly. If the character had more than one spellcasting class before he became a soothsayer, the player must decide to which class he adds each level of soothsayer for the purpose of determining spells per day.

ACCURATE SIGHT (SU)

Soothsayers of 4th level or higher can discern the nationality, class, and Fame score of anyone they meet. If the subject is disguised (mundanely or through magic), the soothsayer is allowed a Spot check to penetrate the disguise; if he's unsuccessful, he can only determine the nationality, class, and Fame score that the subject is trying to exhibit.

OMENS (SU)

A soothsayer of 6th or higher level is able to ask the gods for hints of unspecified future event. The soothsayer must prepare himself for the omen by entering a contemplative state (but not necessarily a trance) requiring a DC 10 Concentration check (DC 15 if there are significant distractions), opening himself up to the revelation to come. An omen is then presented to either the soothsayer or the client who commissioned the omen within the next 24 hours (although the omen could pertain to an event days, weeks, or even years in the future).

The omen is out of the ordinary enough to be obviously a response to the request, but the interpretation of the omen's meaning is left up to the soothsayer or to the client. A DC 10 bardic knowledge or Knowledge (religion) check must be made to correctly identify the context of the omen, and a DC 15 check (bardic knowledge, or a specific Knowledge skill pertaining to the subject matter: religion, arcana, nobility and royalty, *etc.*) must then be made to decipher the exact meaning. Some guesses can be made as to the nature of the omen from the nature of the god petitioned by the soothsayer: a fertility goddess is unlikely to send omens concerning war, while a god of war is unlikely to predict the coming harvest.

Categories of omens and how they may be presented, include:

The god promises victory in an upcoming battle: A two-headed snake slithers up to the soothsayer, but instead of attacking him, each head attacks the other. The client finds the helmet of an enemy warrior, split in two.

The god warns of defeat in an upcoming battle: The client encounter an ancient battlefield, littered with the bleached bones of the dead. The soothsayer cuts himself with his dagger as he's sharpening it.

The god counsels a peaceful approach: A hawk attacks a dove, but is struck by a lightning and slain. A cache of swords is found rusted from disuse.

The god recommends a belligerent stance: The soothsayer misplaces his knife and it's found skewering an olive branch to a table. The client's armor is polished and oiled even though he hasn't tended it in days.

TABLE 2–16: THE SOOTHSAYER

Level	Base Attack Bonus	Fort Save	Ref Save	Will Save	Special	Spells per Day
1st	+0	+0	+0	+2	Oracle	—
2nd	+1	+0	+0	+3	Clear sight	+1 level of existing spellcasting class
3rd	+1	+1	+1	+3	—	+1 level of existing spellcasting class
4th	+2	+1	+1	+4	Accurate sight	+1 level of existing spellcasting class
5th	+2	+1	+1	+4	—	+1 level of existing spellcasting class
6th	+3	+2	+2	+5	Omens	+1 level of existing spellcasting class
7th	+3	+2	+2	+5	—	+1 level of existing spellcasting class
8th	+4	+2	+2	+6	Defensive vision	+1 level of existing spellcasting class
9th	+4	+3	+3	+6	—	+1 level of existing spellcasting class
10th	+5	+3	+3	+7	Greater lore	+1 level of existing spellcasting class

The god warns of treachery: The client comes across a skeleton is found with a dagger sticking out of its back. The soothsayer witnesses one scorpion stinging another to death as they fight over a morsel of food.

(*Note:* The omens revealed have to walk the line between the obvious and the obscure, but it's better to be too obvious than it is to be too obscure. If the players figure out the omen's meaning without rolling skill checks, that's not a bad thing.)

DEFENSIVE VISION (SU)

At 8th level and higher, a soothsayer adds his Wisdom bonus (if any) to his Armor Class. The Wisdom bonus represents a preternatural awareness of danger due to waking visions of impending attacks; the visions aren't clear and early enough to enable him to avoid the situations depicted, but they allow him to modify his immediate circumstances enough to help guard his person. A soothsayer doesn't lose the bonus even in situations when he loses his Dexterity modifier due to being unprepared, ambushed, stunned, and so on. He does lose his bonus when immobilized.

Defensive visions only apply to the soothsayer himself; he never receives visions he can share with others to give them similar AC bonuses.

GREATER LORE (SU)

At 10th level, a soothsayer gains the ability to comprehend an object's significance. Whenever a soothsayer touches a magic item, he automatically learns all of the item's magical properties as though he had cast an *identify* spell. As with the spell, the soothsayer learns nothing when touching artifacts or items of similar power.

- NEW PRESTIGE CLASS: VIGIL (WATCHMAN) -

From 6 AD until the end of the Empire, the vigiles served the city of Rome as firefighters and watchmen. Heroic do-gooders, reformed thieves, and those with a special sense of duty to the city of Rome (as opposed to the Empire as a whole) all found a place within the Cohorts Vigilum. Using a mix of skills, equipment, and spells to protect the city from fire and crime, a vigil could find himself rescuing children from a burning tenement one day, breaking up a crime ring the next, and hunting escaped slaves the day after. Many learned either mundane or magical healing techniques to help the victims of fires and muggings. Their commanders even served as judges for minor offences encountered during their patrols.

While the force was organized along military lines, the vigiles weren't a branch of the army. Joining the Cohorts Vigilum was a way for a freedman to achieve Roman citizenship, but it took over a century for the group to become respected enough that plebeians could join without losing status (and −1 point of Fame).

Alignment: Any non-evil.
Hit Die: d8.
Starting Gold: 5d4 × 10 (125 gp).

REQUIREMENTS

To become a member of the vigiles a character must fulfil the following criteria.

Skills: Gather Information 4 ranks, Search 4 ranks, Sense Motive 4 ranks, and Spot 4 ranks.
Feats: Alertness and either Investigator or Skill Focus (Gather Information, Search, Sense Motive, or Spot).

CLASS SKILLS

The watchman's class skills (and the key ability for each skill) are: Balance (Dex), Bluff (Cha), Climb (Str), Concentration (Con), Decipher Script (Int), Diplomacy (Cha), Disable Device (Int), Escape Artist (Dex), Forgery (Int), Gather Information (Cha), Heal (Wis), Intimidate (Cha), Jump (Str), Listen (Wis), Open Lock (Dex), Search (Int), Sense Motive (Wis), Spot (Int), and Use Rope (Dex). See **Chapter Four: Skills** in the *PHB* for skill descriptions.

Skill Points at Each Level: 4 + Int modifier.

CLASS FEATURES

All of the following are class features of the vigil prestige class.

WEAPON AND ARMOR PROFICIENCY

Watchmen are proficient with the ballista, battleaxe, club, dagger, firehook (see page 56), quarterstaff, sap, and short sword. They are proficient with light armor but not with shields.

TABLE 2–17: THE VIGIL

Level	Base Attack Bonus	Fort Save	Ref Save	Will Save	Special	Nonlethal Attack/ Damage	Disarm Bonus	—Spells per Day—			
								1st	2nd	3rd	4th
1st	+0	+0	+2	+0	Fire resistance, nonlethal attacks	+0/+0	+0	0	—	—	—
2nd	+1	+0	+3	+0	Bonus feat	+0/+0	+0	1	—	—	—
3rd	+2	+1	+3	+1	Nonlethal attack bonus +1	+0/+1	+0	1	0	—	—
4th	+3	+1	+4	+1	Disarm bonus	+0/+1	+2	1	1	—	—
5th	+3	+1	+4	+1	Bonus feat	+0/+1	+2	1	1	0	—
6th	+4	+2	+5	+2	—	+1/+2	+2	1	1	1	—
7th	+5	+2	+5	+2	—	+1/+2	+4	2	1	1	0
8th	+6	+2	+6	+2	Bonus feat	+1/+2	+4	2	1	1	1
9th	+6	+3	+6	+3	—	+2/+3	+4	2	2	1	1
10th	+7	+3	+7	+3	—	+2/+3	+6	2	2	2	1

FIRE RESISTANCE

Beginning at 1st level, a vigil gains fire resistance equal to his class level.

NONLETHAL ATTACKS

At 1st level, a watchman is trained to be able to use a club or a quarterstaff as a nonlethal weapon without taking the normal –4 penalty on attack rolls.

Beginning at 3rd level, when making an attack to deal nonlethal damage, he gains a +1 bonus on nonlethal damage rolls. This extra damage increases to +2 at 6th level and +3 at 9th level.

At 6th level, a watchman gains a +1 insight bonus on nonlethal attacks, whether with lethal or nonlethal weapons (although lethal weapons other than the club or quarterstaff still suffer the normal –4 penalty, resulting in an overall –3 penalty). This increases to +2 at 9th level (overall –2 penalty for nonlethal attacks made with lethal weapons other than the club or quarterstaff).

BONUS FEATS

At 2nd level, a vigil gets a bonus feat drawn from the following: Elusive*, Endurance, Fearless*, Improved Balance*, Improved Disarm, Improved Grapple, Improved Nonlethal Attack*, Self-Sufficient, Shadow*, Smoke Survival*, Stunning Fist, Track, Voice of Command* (*see Chapter Three: Skills & Feats for details on these new feats). The vigil gains an additional bonus feat at 5th and 8th level. A vigil must still meet all prerequisites for a bonus feat, including ability score and base attack bonus minimums.

These bonus feats are in addition to the feat that a character of any class gets from advancing levels. A vigil is not limited to the list of bonus feats when choosing these feats.

SPELLS

A vigil can cast a small number of arcane spells drawn from the vigil spell list (see page 66). To cast a spell, the vigil must have an Intelligence score equal to at least 10 + the spell level. The Difficulty Class for a saving throw against a vigil's spell is 10 + the spell level + the vigil's Intelligence modifier.

A vigil can cast only a certain number of spells of each spell level per day. His base daily spell allotment is given on Table 2–17: The Vigil. In addition, he receives bonus spells each day if he has a high Intelligence score. When Table 2–17 indicates that the vigil gets 0 spells per day of a given spell level, he gains only the bonus spells he would be entitled to based on his Intelligence score for that spell level. A vigil casts spells as a sorcerer does.

Upon reaching 6th level, and at 8th and 10th levels, a vigil can choose to learn a new spell in place of one he already knows. The new spell's level must be the same as that of the spell being exchanged, and it must be at least two levels lower than the highest-level vigil spell the vigil can cast. A vigil may swap only a single spell at any given level, and must choose whether to swap the spell at the same time that he gains new spells known for that level.

DISARM BONUS

Beginning at 4th level, a vigil receives a +2 bonus to any disarm attempts. This bonus increases by +2 every third level thereafter (+4 at 7th level, +6 at 10th). The bonus stacks with any other disarming bonuses (such as having a larger weapon than the defender).

TABLE 2–18: VIGIL SPELLS KNOWN

Level	1st	2nd	3rd	4th
1st	1	—	—	—
2nd	2	—	—	—
3rd	2	1	—	—
4th	3	2	—	—
5th	3	2	1	—
6th	4	3	2	—
7th	4	3	2	1
8th	4	4	3	2
9th	4	4	3	2
10th	4	4	4	3

Chapter Three: Skills and Feats

In addition to all the skills found in the *PHB*, *Eternal Rome* presents one new skill and several new uses for existing skills.

- New Skill Uses -

Eternal Rome offers some new uses for existing skills.

Handle Animal: New Tricks

Voice (DC 20): With one week of work and a successful Handle Animal check, you can train your chariot horses to respond to voice commands, as well as the whip and reins. You take a –2 penalty to AC, attack rolls, and Dexterity-based skill checks while working a chariot by voice.

Tandem (DC 15): With one week of work and a successful Handle Animal check, you can train animals (such as chariot horses or plough oxen) in tandem. Each untrained animal forced to work in a team causes a –5 penalty to all work-related checks.

Perform (Gladiatorial Combat)

Benefit: During an arena match, if a gladiator surrenders or is unable to continue fighting, his life is at the mercy of the game's sponsor or the emperor (if he was in attendance). The decision takes the form of an attempt to influence an NPC's attitude (see the Diplomacy skill in the *PHB*), with an Indifferent result sparing the gladiator's life, a Friendly result adding +1 to his Fame score, and a Helpful result leading to rewards or honors (but not usually freedom) and +2 Fame. An Unfriendly result leads to the gladiator's death and a Hostile result gives his opponent +1 Fame in addition to the gladiator's death.

Instead of Diplomacy, though, a Perform (gladiatorial combat) skill check is made. The character's Fame bonus or penalty and his gladiator reputation modifies this roll. If a gladiator has built up a Perform bonus through use of the dramatic attack ability or the Showy Fighting feat (see pages 27 and 47 respectively), that bonus applies to this roll.

Any Perform bonus from Showy Fighting and dramatic attacks by his opponent is subtracted from the fallen gladiator's bonuses before the Perform check is made. If his opponent has a positive Fame modifier, it's subtracted as well. If his opponent's Fame modifier is negative, it's *added* to the gladiator's Perform bonus; the fans don't like to see villains win.

While this use of Perform is entirely appropriate for NPCs, GMs should be very careful about letting the life of a PC rest on a single attitude roll. At the GM's discretion, he can rule the PC gladiator's life spared for story reasons without making a roll, or after making a roll in secret, taking the hero's Perform bonus into consideration but fudging the result to further the storyline and the enjoyment of the players.

Perform (Oratory)

Special: If you have 5 or more ranks in Diplomacy or Bluff, you get a +2 bonus on Perform (oratory) checks.

- NEW SKILLS -

Eternal Rome offers the following new skill for PCs to acquire.

DRIVE (CHARIOT)

You can drive an animal-drawn chariot.

Check: You can hitch up a team, drive, steer, and stop a chariot under routine conditions without making Drive (chariot) checks. Make a check only when some unusual circumstance exists (such as inclement weather or an icy surface), or when driving during a dramatic situation (you are being chased or attacked, for example, or trying to reach a destination by chariot in a limited amount of time). In addition, any of the tasks on **Table 3–1: Chariot Driving** require checks.

- *Avoid Obstacle:* You can react quickly to steer around an obstacle such as a fallen tree or the wreckage of another chariot while driving at speed. A failure on the check means the chariot has failed to avoid the obstacle, possibly suffering damage. You must make a recover check to regain control.

- *Break Axle:* When alongside an enemy chariot, if both chariots are traveling at half walking speed or more, you can attempt to strike your opponent's axle with the iron rim on your wheel, resulting in loss of his wheel on a successful Drive (chariot) check. The driver of the wheel-less chariot must make a DC 20 Drive (chariot) check to avoid rolling the chariot, which causes damage as a collision (the amount based on the losing chariot's speed at the time of the axle break).

    If your opponent attempts to break your axle at the same time, your Drive (chariot) checks oppose each other: the loser loses a wheel.

    The successful driver's chariot takes 1d6 points of damage from this maneuver and must make a recover check to maintain control of the chariot.

- *Driving in Combat:* If this check is failed, all other checks made by occupants of the chariot (including yourself) take a −2 circumstance penalty. A recover check eliminates the penalty.

- *Fight While Driving:* You can use a weapon with one hand while driving. If this check is failed, the attack is made with a −4 circumstance penalty.

- *Guide Chariot through Narrow Space:* If your chariot is moving at walk speed or faster, attempting to move through a space less than double the chariot's width requires a Drive (chariot) check. If the roll is failed by less than 5 the chariot makes it through the opening but takes 1d6 points of damage. If the roll is failed by more than 5 the chariot doesn't pass through the opening, and suffers collision damage.

- *Jump from a Moving Chariot:* You can jump from a moving chariot (even one that is out of control) and take no damage. If you fail the check, you take damage as per a fall from a height equal to the chariot's speed when you jumped.

- *Jump into a Moving Chariot:* You can leap into a moving chariot, either from the ground or from another moving chariot. You must be within 5 ft. of the chariot to

TABLE 3–1: CHARIOT DRIVING

Task	Drive DC
Avoid obstacle	10
Make break axle attack	25
Drive in combat	15
Drive while fighting	20
Guide chariot through narrow space	15
Jump from moving chariot	15
Jump into moving chariot	20
Make tight turn	20
Make trample attack	target's AC
Make wheel-blade attack	14
Recover	15
Sideswipe chariot	20
Sideswipe person on ground	target's AC
Stop chariot quickly	14
Whip team	15

Situation Modifiers	Check Modifiers
Extra team of horses	+2
Fatigued horse	+5
Unfamiliar chariot	+3
Unfamiliar team of horses	+3

(All modifiers are cumulative.)

CHARIOTS AND WARFARE

In the Roman world, chariots were an expensive and showy form of personal transportation and chariot races drew huge crowds. They had largely gone out of use in war; the Egyptians and other ancient peoples had used them in earlier times, but the Romans encountered war chariots only in the arena and in some fringe lands.

Julius Caesar faced Celtic war chariots during his two expeditions to Britain in 55 and 54 BC, but these were no longer in use at the time of Claudius's conquest of Britain a century later. War chariots continued to be used in Ireland until about the 1st century AD.

attempt this maneuver. Failing the roll by more than 5 but less than 15 indicates you missed the chariot completely, but managed to avoid being trampled by the horses. Failing by more than 15 requires you to succeed on a DC 15 Reflex save or be trampled by the horses and chariot.

- *Recover:* This check is made to retain or regain control of a chariot after some other specific maneuvers are attempted. If the check is successful, you regain full control of the chariot and suffer no penalties; if it's failed and the chariot remains out of control, you may do nothing except repeat the recover check every round until you succeed.

- *Sideswipe:* You can hit another chariot or a person on the ground with your own chariot. If the check is successful, the attack deals 1d6 points of damage to the target. If it's failed, make a second check against DC 15: If the second check is successful, you have hit the target but must make a recover check to regain control; if the second check is failed, you haven't hit the target but must still make a recover check to regain control.

The target must be within 5 feet of the chariot (anywhere along its route, not just as its starting point). A sideswipe is a move action and may be used as part of a chariot's movement.

- *Stop Quickly:* Chariots are not known for their ability to stop on a denarius. It normally takes 1 round to slow a chariot from run or higher speed down to hustle, 1 round to slow from hustle down to walk, and another to slow from walk to a complete stop. Attempting to decelerate a chariot any faster requires a Drive (chariot) check; on a failure, a recover check is required.

- *Tight Turn:* A chariot moving at walk speed or less doesn't have to make Drive (chariot) checks for any turns. One moving at up to hustle speed requires a check for a turn of more than 90°. A chariot moving faster than a hustle must make a check in order to turn more than 45° in a single round. On a failed roll, the chariot can still turn up to the maximum turn that *wouldn't* have required a check, but you lose control and must make a recover check to regain control. If a natural 1 is rolled on the recover check, the chariot topples (see **Chariot Collisions**).

- *Trample:* You can trample opponents under your chariot's pounding hooves and spinning wheels. On a successful attack, you must succeed on a recover check (DC 15 + damage dealt) to keep the chariot from toppling (see **Chariot Collisions**).

CHARIOT COLLISIONS

When a chariot strikes a solid object (including another chariot) or when it is toppled, collision damage is suffered by the chariot, each of its occupants, the horses pulling it, and by whatever it hits. Damage depends on the chariot's speed at the time of the collision.

CHARIOT COLLISIONS

Speed	Damage
Up to walking speed	—
Walking to hustle speed	1d8
Hustle to running speed	2d8
Over running speed	3d8

- *Whip Team:* A chariot team can be made to run at up to four times its normal walking speed for a number of rounds equal to the Constitution of the weakest horse without a Drive (chariot) check. A chariot driver can use the reins, a whip, or spoken commands to push his horses beyond their normal limits.

A successful Drive (chariot) check either forces the horses to run at *five* times their normal walking speed for 1 round, or to run at four times their walking speed for 1 round past the limit of their Constitution. The driver can continue to whip the team in subsequent rounds, but the DC increases by +1 each round.

On the first round that the driver pushes the team past the limit, each horse in the team takes 1 point of nonlethal damage. Each subsequent round that he continues to push them the damage done is twice that of the previous round (2 points in the second round, 4 points in the third, 8 points in the fourth, and so on).

When the driver either stops pushing the horses or fails a whip team check, the horses immediately begin to slow down of their own accord, taking 3 rounds to slow from run to a complete stop. The horses must then rest 10 minutes for each round they exerted themselves. If the driver uses another whip team check to force the horses to pull the chariot again before resting fully, including if he tries to push them after they've started decelerating from a run, each horse must make a Fortitude check (DC 15 +1/round pushed). If it succeeds, it takes 2d6 points of nonlethal damage and its walking speed (and therefore its hustling and running speeds) is halved—whipping a team at this point cannot increase the horses' speed. A failed check, however, indicates the horse takes 4d6 points of nonlethal damage and collapses, useless for 1d4 days.

Action: A Drive (chariot) check is a move action.

Try Again: Yes. If a failed check doesn't mandate a recover check, a character who fails a Drive (chariot) check can try again after one round, but at a −2 penalty. The penalty increases by −2 each time he fails the check.

Special: The team of animals (usually horses) pulling a chariot must be trained to work together. You suffer a cumulative −5 penalty to checks for each animal that has not been trained.

If you have 5 or more ranks in Handle Animal, you get a +2 bonus on Drive (chariot) checks. If you have the Animal Affinity feat, you gain a +2 bonus on Drive (chariot) checks. These bonuses stack with each other.

- New Feats -

The following new feats are suitable for *Eternal Rome*.

Canny Charge [General]

You are less vulnerable when charging.

Prerequisites: Dex 13, Int 13, Combat Expertise, Dodge.

Benefit: When the character charges, he takes no penalty to Armor Class.

Normal: Without this feat, charging characters take a –2 penalty to AC until the beginning of their next turn.

A fighter may select Canny Charge as one of his fighter bonus feats.

Chariot Attack [General]

You can very effectively use your chariot as a weapon.

Prerequisite: Drive (chariot) 7 ranks.

Benefit: A chariot's driver doesn't need to make a recover check to keep his chariot from toppling after making a trample attack.

When attempting a sideswipe, he only needs to make a recover check if he misses both sideswipe rolls and his target is a chariot or a Larger or bigger creature.

When making a successful break axle attack, he doesn't need to make a recover check.

A fighter may select Chariot Attack as one of his fighter bonus feats.

Chariot Fighting [General]

You can use a ranged weapon or cast a spell from a moving chariot effectively.

Prerequisites: Dex 13, Drive (chariot) 5 ranks.

Benefit: A character with this feat can use a ranged weapon from a moving chariot without incurring any circumstance penalties for the motion of the chariot. He also receives a +2 bonus to Concentration checks to cast spells in a moving chariot.

Driving a chariot at the same times as shooting or throwing a ranged weapon or casting a spell with material or somatic components is impossible unless the horses have learned the Voice trick (see page 40).

Normal: A character attempting to use a ranged weapon from a chariot moving above walk up to hustle speed takes a –2 penalty to attack rolls because of the movement and jolting ride; in a chariot moving at more than a hustle, the penalty is –4. A spellcaster must make a DC 10 Concentration check to cast a spell in a chariot moving at above walk speed, and a DC 15 check to cast a spell in a chariot moving above a hustle.

A fighter may select Chariot Fighting as one of his fighter bonus feats.

Chariot Shield [General]

You know how to use your chariot defensively, gaining more protection than normal.

Prerequisites: Dex 13, Drive (chariot) 4 ranks.

Benefit: When mounted in a chariot, the character gains a +4 AC and +2 Reflex save bonus. If he takes the total defense action while in the chariot these bonuses are doubled.

Normal: Chariots provide a +2 bonus to AC and a +1 bonus to Reflex saves.

A fighter may select Chariot Shield as one of his fighter bonus feats.

Chariot Specialization [General]

When in a moving chariot, you can make devastating attacks.

Prerequisite: Drive (chariot) 9 ranks.

Benefit: When in a moving chariot moving at its walk speed or more, a character with this feat gains a +2 bonus to weapon damage rolls from any melee weapon or thrown weapon he wields. If the chariot moves at hustle speed or faster, the bonus increases to +3.

Special: If the character chooses to add this bonus to weapon damage rolls, he takes a –2 penalty to AC and may not use the benefits of Chariot Shield.

A fighter may select Chariot Specialization as one of his fighter bonus feats.

Close Order Fighting [General]

You are trained to fight with other soldiers in formation.

Prerequisite: Shield proficiency.

TABLE 3–2: NEW FEATS

Feat	Prerequisites
Canny Charge [1]	Dex 13, Int 12, Combat Expertise, Dodge
Chariot Attack [1]	Drive (chariot) 7 ranks
Chariot Fighting [1]	Dex 13, Drive (chariot) 5 ranks
Chariot Shield [1]	Dex 13, Drive (chariot) 4 ranks
Chariot Specialization [1]	Drive (chariot) 9 ranks
Close Order Fighting [1]	Shield Proficiency
Improved Close Order Fighting [1]	Close Order Fighting, Shield Proficiency
Drive-By Attack [1]	Drive (chariot) 4 ranks
Elusive	Hide 8 ranks
Fearless	—
Improved Balance	—
Improved Mounted Archery [1]	Ride 4 ranks, Mounted Archery, Mounted Combat
Improved Nonlethal Attack [1]	—
Mounted Dodge [1]	Ride 4 ranks, Dodge, Mounted Combat
Multiple Patrons [1]	A patron
Outlandish Weapon Finesse [1,2]	Weapon Focus (any melee weapon)
Polyglot	Int 13
Renowned	—
Retaliatory Strike [1]	Weapon Finesse, base attack bonus +1
Shadow	—
Showy Fighting [1]	Combat Expertise, Weapon Finesse, base attack bonus +6
Side-Step [1]	Dex 13, Dodge, Mobility, Spring Attack, base attack bonus +4
Smoke-Survival	—
Smooth Talker	Cha 13
Sprinter	Run
Stunt Driving	Dex 15, Drive (chariot) 2 ranks
Superior Trip [1]	Combat Expertise, Improved Trip
Unknown	—
Voice of Command	—
Wrestler [1]	Weapon Focus (grapple), base attack bonus +1

1 A fighter may select this feat as one of his fighter bonus feats.
2 The feat can be taken multiple times; its effects do not stack.

Benefit: The character gains a +2 AC bonus if another character with this feat is fighting immediately beside him. This goes up to +4 if he has a character with Close Order Fighting on each side.

If a multi-rank formation of soldiers armed with reach weapons and all possessing this feat is charged, and a person in the front rank who has set his weapon against the charge scores makes a successful attack against his charging opponent, the similarly situated soldier in the next rank may attack the same opponent with a +3 circumstance bonus to hit. If the soldier in the first rank misses, the soldier behind him can still attack, but without the bonus.

These bonuses do not stack with any bonuses from the aid another combat maneuver. The bonuses are lost if the formation is broken, even if all combatants remain in the same relative positions.

A fighter may select Close-Order Fighting as one of his fighter bonus feats.

DRIVE-BY ATTACK [GENERAL]

You can use the chariot's momentum to add power to your attack.

Prerequisite: Drive 4 ranks.

Benefit: When in a chariot and using the charge action, the character may move and attack as if with a standard charge and then move again (continuing the straight line of the charge). His total movement for the round cannot exceed double his chariot's walking speed. This doesn't provoke an attack of opportunity from the opponent attacked.

A fighter may select Drive-By Attack as one of his fighter bonus feats.

Elusive [General]

You are difficult to pick out of a crowd.

Prerequisite: Hide 8 ranks.

Benefit: The character may use a crowd as concealment for Hide checks. In addition, he may add his assassin, rogue, and vigil class levels to his Hide check to blend in.

Evil Eye Projector [General]

You're able to intentionally cast the evil eye on those you envy.

Benefit: If someone with Evil Eye Projector (sometimes called simply a projector) is both envious of another person (as with normal, involuntary casting of the evil eye) and consciously wishes to cause harm to the spell's subject, he can voluntarily cast the evil eye at a person. The voluntary projection of the evil eye follows all the same rules as for an accidental evil eye curse, except that the DC of the subject's Fortitude save is 30, not the usual 20.

The caster of a voluntary evil eye curse can remove it at will, but must make eye contact with the possibly wary subject to do so. For more information on the evil eye, see page 74.

Fearless [General]

You show no fear, even in the most terrifying of circumstances.

Benefit: The Fearless character gains a +4 morale bonus to all saving throws versus fear effects, and even if he fails a saving throw the effects are reduced by one category.

Improved Balance [General]

You can walk on precarious surfaces, such as tree limbs or fire-weakened rooftops, as though you were walking on a normal surface.

Benefit: If he makes a successful Balance check when walking on unsafe surfaces, the character can move at his normal speed for 1 round. A failure by 4 or less means he moves at half speed. A failure by 5 to 10 means he cannot move for 1 round. A failure by 11 or more means he falls.

Improved Close Order Fighting [General]

You are trained exceptionally well to fight with other soldiers in formation.

Prerequisites: Close Order Fighting, Shield proficiency.

Benefit: The character gains a +1 bonus to attack rolls if he and another character with this feat and in formation with him are both threatening the same target.

This bonus does not stack with any bonuses from the aid another combat maneuver. The bonus is lost if the formation is broken, even if all combatants remain in the same relative positions.

A fighter may select Improved Close Order Fighting as one of his fighter bonus feats.

Improved Mounted Archery [General]

You are highly skilled at using ranged weapons while mounted.

Prerequisites: Ride 4 ranks, Mounted Archery, Mounted Combat.

Benefit: The character never takes a penalty for using a ranged weapon while mounted.

Normal: A rider takes a −4 penalty to ranged attacks when his mount is taking a double move and −8 penalty when the mount is running.

A fighter may select Improved Mounted Archery as one of his fighter bonus feats.

Improved Nonlethal Attack [General]

You know how to subdue opponents with any weapon.

Benefit: This feat grants the character a +2 bonus to nonlethal attack rolls. A fighter may select Improved Nonlethal Attack as one of his fighter bonus feats.

Mal'occhio [General]

Your appearance can be off-putting, and your envy can be projected at others.

Prerequisite: A visible deformity of some sort (*e.g.*, prominent scars, withered limb, missing eye or ear).

Benefit: Evil eyes (either voluntarily or otherwise) cast by a person with Mal'occhio are more intense than usual. The save DC against these evil eyes increases by +3. This +3 bonus also applies to the check DC on attempts to remove an evil eye using *dispel magic*.

Special: While a character with Mal'occhio is under the effect of a *gravitas* spell, this feat has no effect on the save DCs of evil eyes he casts accidentally. *Gravitas* has no effect on the casting of voluntary evil eyes, nor does it provide any protection from either sort of evil eye.

Mal'occhio cannot be taken multiple times, even if the character has multiple disfigurements. For more information on the evil eye, see page 74.

Mounted Dodge [General]

You can dodge while in the saddle as well as you do on the ground.

Prerequisites: Ride 4 ranks, Dodge, Mounted Combat.

Benefit: The character may use the Dodge feat while mounted and may apply the benefits of this feat to either himself or his mount.

A fighter may select Mounted Dodge as one of his fighter bonus feats.

Multiple Patrons [General]

Whether because of inherited family ties, an almost unnaturally charming personality, or a unique set of events in your personal relationship with other Romans, you have more than a single patron—and you manage to get away with it.

Prerequisite: A patron.

Benefit: The character has a second patron and gains all the benefits of patronage (a monthly income, occasional favors, *etc.*; see page 53 for details) from each of his patrons equally. He's also equally beholden to both patrons, required to fulfill his duties to each of them except when duty to one would conflict with duty to the other, in which case he is excused from *both* duties.

Normal: While any person can become the client of multiple patrons, doing so without this feat is a dangerous affair. Such a character must keep his relationship to one patron secret from the other, and if he's caught out, not only will he lose both patronage but the patrons and their more loyal clients may seek to punish him for his double-dealing. During the Republic and the early years of the Empire having two patrons would be seen as a breach of contract, punishable by law.

Special: This feat can be gained multiple times, adding a new patron each time.

OUTLANDISH WEAPON FINESSE [GENERAL]

You are able to wield a weapon with a finesse that is far from usual for a weapon of that type.

Prerequisite: Weapon Focus (weapon type).

Benefits: Select any one weapon with which he has the Weapon Focus feat and which normally does not qualify as a finesse weapon; the character may use his Dexterity modifier instead of his Strength modifier on attack rolls with that weapon. If he carries a shield, its armor check penalty applies to attack rolls.

Special: This feat can be gained multiple times. Each time this feat is taken, the benefit applies to a new weapon.

A fighter may select Outlandish Weapon Finesse as one of his fighter bonus feats.

POLYGLOT [GENERAL]

You have a special knack for learning languages.

Prerequisite: Int 13.

Benefit: Speak Language is always a class skill for the character. For every skill point spent on the Speak Language skill, he gains two languages. In addition, he can declare an unused language slot as a reserve slot. When he encounters a language he doesn't know, he may attempt a DC 15 Concentration check. If he succeeds, he may learn that language in 1d4 days, filling the reserve slot.

Normal: Each skill point applied to Speak Language grants fluency in one language.

RENOWNED [GENERAL]

You are more widely known than are others of your status and accomplishments.

Benefit: The character's Fame score is increased by 4 points away from 0; *i.e.*, if he has a positive Fame score it is increased by +4; if he has a negative Fame score it is reduced by −4. If his Fame score without the bonus is exactly 0, he gets to decide whether the Renowned bonus is positive or negative. Because his Fame score is likely to change over time, the points gained or lost by being Renowned should be accounted for separately; *e.g.*, if his Fame is +5 without this feat, it should be recorded as +5 (+4 Renowned = +9).

If his Fame score *without* the bonus from the Renowned feat ever switches from positive to negative or vice-versa, the value of the bonus from the feat changes as well; *e.g.*, if a general with a Fame score of +2 (+4 Renowned = +6) loses −3 points for losing a battle, his new score wouldn't be +3 (+2 Fame −3 from battle loss +4 from Renowned), it would be −5 (+2 Fame −3 from battle loss = −1, then −4 from Renowned = −5).

Unfortunately, being Renowned gives a person trying to see through any disguise the character wears a +4 bonus to his Spot check, instead of the +2 bonus he'd normally receive.

Special: The Renowned and Unknown feats can't both be taken by the same character.

RETALIATORY STRIKE [GENERAL]

You can make one retaliatory strike with a light weapon.

Prerequisites: Weapon Finesse, base attack bonus +1.

Benefit: When using a light weapon, if the character's struck in melee and is neither flat-footed nor flanked, he may make one free strike per round as a retaliatory strike at his full attack bonus, but only with one-half his Strength bonus (if any) added to the damage.

A fighter may select Retaliatory Strike as one of his fighter bonus feats.

SHADOW [GENERAL]

While in urban areas, you can follow a visible target through the twisting alleys of a city, ideally without the subject knowing he is being followed. You can find someone and keep him in sight as he goes about his business.

Benefit: The character can make a Survival check when following some quarry. If the check is successful, he may follow the subject at a distance up to 60 ft. An additional check must be made each hour to keep the quarry in sight.

The DC depends on the population density and other conditions.

FILL IN TABLE TITLE

Population Density	DC
Abandoned area	5
Lightly populated area	10
Normal population density	15
Crowded	20
Very crowded	25

These base DCs reflect the ease with which the subject can hide or be lost in a crowd.

FILL IN TABLE TITLE

General Conditions	DC Modifier
Very clean	+5
Average	+0
Cluttered	−5

These modifiers to the base DC reflect the physical trail the subject leaves behind.

PHYSICAL TRAIL MODIFIERS

Other Modifiers	DC Modifier
Every three subjects in the group being shadowed	−1
Each hour of shadowing	+2
Subject is of a different race than most inhabitants	−2 to −5
Poor visibility*	
Overcast or moonless night	+6
Moonlight	+3
Fog or precipitation	+3
Shadowed individuals hides trail (and moves at half speed)	+5
Size of creature or creatures being tracked**	
Fine	+8
Diminutive	+4
Tiny	+2
Small	+1
Medium	+0
Large	−1
Huge	−2
Gargantuan	−4
Colossal	−8

* Apply only the largest modifier from this category. Good illumination in the city reduces visibility penalties.

** For a group of mixed races, apply the modifier for the largest size category.

If he fails a Survival check, the subject is lost.

If the quarry becomes suspicious, he can make a Spot check (opposed by the character's Hide check) to try pick him out of the background. If the character is moving at greater than one-half but less than his normal speed, he takes a −5 penalty to the Hide check. If he is running, he takes a −20 penalty to the check unless he is part of a crowd that is also running.

SHOWY FIGHTING [GENERAL]

You are able to use flashy moves in melee combat to cow an opponent or entertain a crowd.

Prerequisites: Combat Expertise, Weapon Finesse, base attack bonus +6.

Benefit: If the character takes the full-attack option in melee combat against a non-gladiator, he can attempt to impress an opponent by twirling, spinning, and weaving his weapon about in such a manner that he convinces the opponent that he is much more skillful. The character makes one fewer attacks in the round (the attack with the lowest base attack bonus is lost), but he can roll an Intimidate check, and if it's successful his other attacks gain an attack bonus that round equal to the amount by which the check was made (minimum +1). If the character doesn't have any ranks in Intimidate, his Charisma is used. This ability only works on creatures who are intelligent enough to be impressed by the difficulty of such a display.

Trying to intimidate a gladiator with a flashy display doesn't work, but the character can affect the reaction of the audience. Once again, he can make a full attack, and take one fewer attack in the round in order to make a Perform (gladiatorial combat) check. If he beats a DC of 15, he gains a +1 bonus on his Perform (gladiatorial combat) roll at the end of the bout (see page 40); beating a DC of 20 gives him a +2 bonus; a DC of 25 gives him a +3 bonus; DC 30, a +4 bonus. If he has no ranks in Perform (gladiatorial combat), his Charisma is used.

Special: Characters with any levels in the gladiator class are immune to the effects of Showy Fighting.

A fighter may select Showy Fighting as one of his fighter bonus feats.

SIDE STEP [GENERAL]

You are adept at avoiding attacks.

Prerequisites: Dex 13, Dodge, Mobility, Spring Attack, base attack bonus +4.

Benefit: Unless trapped or immobilized, the character can't be bull rushed.

SMOKE SURVIVAL [GENERAL]

You can function effectively in smoke—at least for a while.

Benefit: In a smoky environment, the character can hold his breath for a number of rounds equal to twice his Constitution score, but only if he does nothing other than take move actions or free actions. If he takes a standard action or a full-round action (such as attempting to break down a door), the remainder of the duration for which he

can hold his breath is reduced by 1 round. After that period, he must make a DC 10 Constitution check every round to continue holding his breath. Each round, the DC for that check increases by 1. If he fails the Constitution check, he begins to inhale the smoke.

Each round after he stops holding his breath the character must make a Fortitude save (DC 12 +1 per previous choking check) or spend a round choking. If he chokes for two consecutive rounds, he takes 1d6 points of nonlethal damage.

Normal: A character without this feat can hold his breath for a number of rounds equal to his Constitution score. The DC for Fortitude saves against choking is normally DC 15 +1 per previous choking check).

SMOOTH TALKER [GENERAL]

You excel at using your wits and honeyed tongue.

Prerequisite: Cha 13.

Benefit: The character gains a +1 bonus on all Bluff, Diplomacy, Gather Information, and Perform checks.

SPRINTER [GENERAL]

You are faster than a typical member of your race.

Prerequisite: Run.

Benefit: When the character takes a double move action or a run action, his base land speed increases as follows.

SPRINTER SPEED

Base Land Speed	New Land Speed
20 ft.	25 ft.
30 ft.	40 ft.
40 ft.	55 ft.
50 ft.	70 ft.
60 ft.	85 ft.

This speed increase stacks with other forms of speed increases, including the fast movement barbarian class feature, and the monk's unarmored speed bonus.

STUNT DRIVING [GENERAL]

You are able to control a chariot and its team with phenomenal expertise.

Prerequisites: Dex 15, Drive (chariot) 2 ranks.

Benefit: If at any time the character fails a recover check, he's allowed to immediately reroll, using the better of the two results (allowing him to try riskier maneuvers than other chariot-drivers).

In addition, he can jump a chariot over obstacles no more than 3 ft. high and/or 5 ft. wide (such as fallen comrades, the wreckage of other chariots, or narrow ditches) with a successful DC 15 Drive (chariot) check when moving at speed. A clear, straight approach of at least 50 ft. is required, and the check suffers a -3 penalty for every character in the chariot apart from the driver.

SUPERIOR TRIP [GENERAL]

You are especially adept at tripping opponents in battle, and you are able to avoid retaliatory trip attempts.

Prerequisites: Combat Expertise, Improved Trip.

Benefit: If the character fails on a trip attempt, his opponent doesn't get a chance to trip him in return, nor does he have to drop his weapon (if using one to attempt a trip) to avoid a retaliatory trip attempt. The character also gains a +2 bonus on all trip attempts. This bonus stacks with the one from Improved Trip.

A fighter may select Superior Trip as one of his fighter bonus feats.

UNKNOWN [GENERAL]

Despite your status and accomplishments, you have managed to maintain a low public profile.

Benefit: The character's Fame score is reduced by up to 4 points towards 0; *i.e.*, if he has a positive Fame score of +4 or more, it is reduced by −4, but if he has a positive Fame score of +1 to +3, it is only reduced to 0, not to −1 to −3; if he has a negative Fame score of −4 or more, it is reduced by 4, but if he has a negative Fame score of −3 to −1, it is only reduced to 0, not into positive numbers.

Because his Fame score is likely to change over time, the points gained or lost by being Unknown should be accounted for separately; *e.g.*, if the character's Fame is +5 without this feat, it should be recorded as +5 (−4 Unknown = +1).

Conversely, being Unknown gives a person trying to see through any disguise the character wears a −4 penalty to his Spot check, instead of the −2 penalty he'd normally receive.

Special: The Renowned and Unknown feats can't both be taken by the same character.

VOICE OF COMMAND [GENERAL]

You can project orders in an authoritative voice that grabs attention.

Benefit: The character's shouted orders can be understood up to 120 feet away.

Anyone suffering from the effects of fear who hears his order immediately rolls a Will save against the effect.

Normal: Under normal conditions a shout is understandable up to a range of 60 feet.

WRESTLER [GENERAL]

You know how to grapple exceptionally well.

Prerequisites: Weapon Focus (grapple), base attack bonus +1.

Benefit: The character receives a +3 bonus to all grapple checks, and deals +1 point of damage on a hold. In addition, when he gets a critical hit, his opponent must make a Fort save (DC 10 + character's level + character's Strength modifier) or one of his limbs is crippled. If one of the target's arms is crippled, he takes a −4 penalty to all Climb, Escape Artist, Sleight of Hands, Swim, Tumble, and Use Rope checks. If one of the target's legs is crippled, he takes a −5 ft. enhancement penalty to his speed and a −4 penalty to all Jump, Move Silently, Swim, and Tumble checks. A *heal* spell removes this penalty. Penalties are cumulative.

A fighter may select Wrestler as one of his fighter bonus feats.

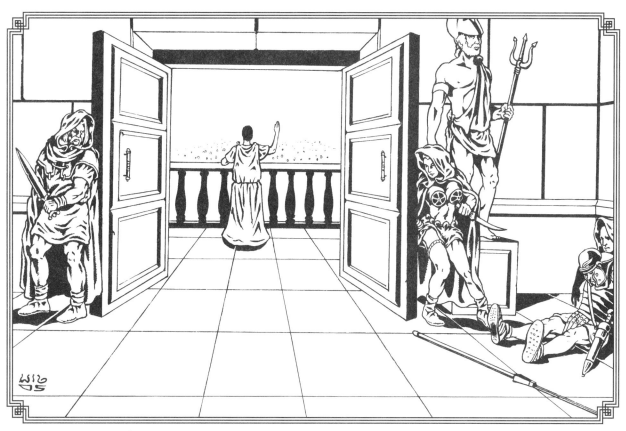

Chapter Four: Fame

Both Green Ronin's *Testament* and *Trojan War* feature an optional Piety mechanism measuring a character's obedience to his deities and respect for this society's norms. While Romans were certainly pious a people, they were also a very practical one. The gods of Rome played a less direct role in Roman life than the Greek gods during the Trojan War or the gods of Israel and its neighbors in their history, providing omens and lucky breaks but few blatant miracles. More important to a Roman than what he thought about the gods and what they thought about him was what his fellow citizens thought about him.

In the Roman world, a person's abilities and accomplishments are important, but how many people *know* about those traits and deeds is paramount. Good deeds performed anonymously can give someone a good feeling, but a person's career can be built on a foundation of a few successes and a lot of promotion and public relations.

As a recommended option, each character in an *Eternal Rome* campaign has a Fame score, representing how well known and how respected he is in Rome and throughout the Empire. A low Fame score provides benefits on its own and can serve as a springboard to gain public office and more Fame. A high Fame score provides greater opportunities but also responsibilities. And while a *negative* Fame score has its obvious drawbacks, even infamy can have its benefits.

- Fame Points, Modifiers, and Checks -

With rare exceptions (*e.g.*, the child of the emperor), every person is born with a Fame score of 0, and newly created PCs also have this score. There is no upper limit to a person's Fame, nor lower limit to a person's infamy.

When interacting with other Romans, a character is sometimes called upon to make a Fame check. This is 1d20 roll +/– his Fame modifier, which is one-half of his current Fame score. A positive modifier is a bonus in most circumstances, a negative modifier is usually a penalty, but there are times when this does not hold true (*e.g.*, both positive and negative Fame modifiers act as a bonus to another person trying to Spot a famous or infamous character in disguise).

Gaining and Losing Fame

There are many different ways for a Roman to gain Fame. These are listed on **Table 4–1: Gaining Fame**.

Negative Fame

There are two ways for a person's Fame to become negative. The first is to commit acts that result in an incremental drop in Fame, as shown on **Table 4–2: Losing Fame**.

But more drastically, a person's fame can be changed into infamy in an instant, swapping a positive score for the

TABLE 4–1: GAINING FAME

Act	One-Time Fame Award
Participate in Military Victory (soldier)	1
Battle honor (*corona*)	1
Battle honor (*imperator*)	2
Battle honor (*spolia opima*)	3
Command Military Victory (battle)	2
Command Military Victory (campaign)	3
Voted a Triumph	4
Become Senator (through election or inheritance)	1
Elected to Minor Office (*e.g.*, interrex)	0
Elected to High Office (assemblyman)	1
Elected to High Office (vigintivirates)	0
Elected to High Office (quaestor)	1
Elected to High Office (tribune)	3
Elected to High Office (aedile)	1
Elected to High Office (curator)	1
Elected to High Office (procurator)	0
Elected to High Office (praetor)	2
Elected to High Office (propraetor)	1
Elected to High Office (augur)	3
Elected to High Office (consul)	4
Elected to High Office (proconsul)	2
Elected to High Office (censor)	4
Elected to High Office (prefect)	5
Elected to High Office (pontifex maximus)	3
Elected to High Office (dictator)	6
Elected to High Office (augustus)	10
Elevation in Social Rank (*e.g.*, plebeian to equites)	2
Hold Games*	1d4
Pay Public Bath Fees for All Romans for a Month	1
Make Grain Donation for All Romans for a Month	2
Make Public Sacrifice to the Gods	1
Dedicate Temple	2
Dedicate Public Building	2
Found City	5
Associate with the Famous	1
Patron of the Famous	2
Related to the Famous (including *via* adoption)	1
Take Something from a Rival (*e.g.*, office, command, wife)	2

*With some exceptions, in the Empire period only the Emperor was allowed to stage games; a measure taken to eliminate a source of popularity for potential rivals.

equivalent negative score as a result of a single particularly heinous act; *e.g.*, the assassination of the emperor or the betrayal of a Roman army to the enemy. The character is still as well known as before (and probably more so since the commission of his atrocity), but those he meets are less likely to be positively disposed toward him.

Similarly, an infamous person's status can change overnight (say, when an emperor's assassin is declared emperor himself), again switching his negative Fame score to a positive one.

Incremental Fame loss can be handled mechanically, using the entries on **Table 4–2** as a guide, but a radical switch from positive to negative Fame (or back) must be at the discretion of the GM.

A negative Fame modifier is generally a penalty on Fame checks, except when the check involves relations between two people who both have negative Fame (*e.g.*, an infamous character trying to recruit another such person as a client or patron).

FAME AWARDS FOR ADVENTURERS

Along with the various acts one can perform to gain Fame (see **Table 4–1: Gaining Fame**), the day-to-day exploits of

TABLE 4–2: LOSING FAME

Act	One-Time Fame Award
Command Military Defeat (battle)	–3
Command Military Defeat (campaign)	–4
Fail to be Voted a Triumph	–2
Failed Election	a
Implicated in Scandal (*e.g.*, failed assassination plot, foreign or cross-class lover, impious behavior)	–2/–4*
Avoiding Public Service (military or civil)	–4/–8*
Failure to Observe Major Religious Rite	–1/–2*
Commit a Crime	–2
Commit a Crime Against Someone of Higher Social Station	–3/–6*
Patron Failing to Honor Client Request	–1/–2*
Client Failing to Honor Patron Request	b
Patron Found Asking Clients for Loans	c
Associate with the Infamous	–2
Related to the Infamous (including *via* adoption)	–2
Year Spent Out of the Public Eye	d

* The figure after the slash is for those with Fame scores above 24.
a Lose Fame equal to amount Fame check missed by
b No Fame loss, but legal repercussions
c Patron's Fame score halved
d Lose 1/10 Fame score (see page 54)

adventurers also lead to celebrity. So long as the character's adventures aren't kept secret from the general public, every time he gains a character level above 1st he receives 1 Fame point.

The GM should also award bonus Fame points during play if a player character does something spectacular (*e.g.*, slaying a monster that should have been beyond his capabilities) or something impressive in the public interest (*e.g.*, predicting a volcanic eruption in time for the population of a city to flee) even if the act doesn't appear on **Table 4–1**.

- USES FOR FAME -

A character can use his fame or infamy in a variety of ways.

BATTLEFIELD ORATORY

Before any battles, a character can use his Fame and speaking ability to inspire an army. If he succeeds at a DC 20 Fame check, his Side/Force receives a bonus on melee damage and morale checks equal to his Fame bonus that lasts for one battlefield round per 5 points of Fame of the speaker (minimum one round). The character may add one-half his orator class levels to the Fame check.

If the character attempts to rouse the troops in the middle of an ongoing battle, the DC is increased by 4. The oratory takes the place of one attack the character would otherwise be able to make in the round.

If the character has a negative Fame modifier, it acts as a penalty to his check unless the majority of those he is addressing have either 0 or negative Fame scores themselves.

Note: If the GM isn't using the Biblical or Homeric Battlefield Resolution System, battlefield oratory's effects apply to 10 soldiers per point of the character's Fame total.

CLIENTS

Most Roman equites and patricians (and even some plebeians) have a retinue of clients to whom they give daily gifts in exchange for flattery and favors (see page 53). Each month, the character has to pay out at least twice his Fame bonus in copper if he's a plebeian with clients, twice his Fame bonus in silver if he's an equites, and twice his Fame bonus in gold if he's a patrician. The number of clients his character has is up to the player, but the maximum number is equal to his Fame score.

If the player wants his character to have a client of a specific type (*e.g.*, a retired gladiator) or a specific person (*e.g.*, the son of a general) he must make a DC 20 Fame check. If the desired client is particularly noteworthy or powerful (*e.g.*, a senator or a high-level adventurer) the DC can rise to 25 or beyond. If the Fame check is failed, the PC loses −1 Fame point and cannot attempt to recruit that particular person until the PC gains a new level.

When a character is away from his home and in need of help, there's always a chance that one of his clients is nearby. He must make a DC 20 Fame check if in Rome or a regional capital, DC 25 in a small city, DC 30 in a town, or DC 35 in a rural setting. If he's in a place he's never been before, the DC of the check increases by +10. If he's trying to find a *specific* client in a distant locale, the DC is increased by +5 to +15, depending on the likelihood that that person would be in that place (*e.g.*, a trader client could easily find his way into any port, but a simple farmer is unlikely to be found hundreds of miles from his land). If this Fame check is failed, the character cannot attempt to find one of his clients again until he enters a different city or province.

DISGUISE

A character's Fame works against him if he's trying to conceal his identity. Along with any other bonuses someone attempting to penetrate the character's concealment may receive (see the Disguise skill in the *PHB*), he also receives a bonus to his Spot check equal to the magnitude of the character's Fame modifier; *i.e.*, a +5 bonus to his Spot check if the disguised character has a Fame score of 10 or 11 (+5 Fame modifier), *and* a +5 bonus if the character has a Fame score of −10 or −11.

FAME AND SECRET IDENTITIES

If someone wears a disguise on a one-off basis, his Fame can have an effect on the ruse, giving others an improved chance to see through the disguise. The disguise also affects his Fame: any exploits he makes while in disguise gain (or lose) him no Fame points unless his identity is later revealed, allowing others to properly associate the deeds with the man.

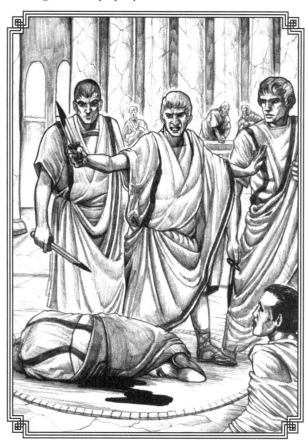

Fame and Alignment

Unlike the Piety system in *Testament* and *Trojan War*, this optional Fame system isn't meant to be substituted for the conventional alignment system; a Roman is as likely to be good and famous as evil and famous.

But if he takes to wearing the disguise on a regular basis, performing exploits without revealing his true identity, then (at the GM's option) his alternate identity can begin to develop a reputation of its own, resulting in the character having a dual Fame score: one score for his real self and one for his alternate persona.

The false identity starts with a Fame score of 0, and gains points for those actions the character performs in that guise, and for any background details he can firmly establish (DC 25 Bluff check) as part of his alternate identity, such as claiming to be a veteran of a successful military campaign.

If the person's alternate identity is ever permanently revealed to the general public, one-half of all Fame points the alternate persona gained for actual deeds (not faked background stories) are added to the character's true identity's Fame score.

Divination

If a character has a positive Fame score, once per game session he can use his Fame modifier as a bonus to an attempt at divination, through the *augury* or *divination* spells or astrology and other fortune-telling skills. For those divination methods that require a percentage roll, the character's Fame modifier is applied as a bonus to the roll. For those methods that use a d20 roll, 1/5 the character's Fame modifier is applied as a bonus to the roll.

Election

Once per month of game time, a character can attempt to use his Fame to win election to public office. This requires a vote in the Senate or other like body: a Fame check with a DC that varies with the office (see **Table 4–3**). On a successful check, the character gains the new office (and any related Fame; see **Table 4–1**). On a failed check, the character loses a number of Fame points equal to the amount by which he failed the check—a natural 1 on the check roll is always a failure. In most cases, a candidate can lose more Fame in a failed election bid than he stood to gain if he won, so a decision to run for office is usually made only after careful consideration.

An election can be opposed by another PC or an NPC, and almost all elections are opposed. If the opposing character is vying for the same office, each of the candidates makes a Fame check and the candidate who wins by the largest amount gains the office *and* the loser loses a number of Fame points equal to the amount by which he was defeated. If the opposing character is not himself a candidate for the office (he merely attempts to persuade the voters not to back the candidate), his Fame modifier is subtracted from the candidate's before the Fame check is made.

Most candidates for public office are patrons with a number of clients they can order to accompany them during the election. Every member of the appropriate voting body the character can count among his clientele (*e.g.*, senators for those offices voted on by the Senate, plebeians for the office of tribune that's voted on by the Popular Assembly) gives him a +1 bonus on his Fame check, and he receives another +1 for every 10 other clients who raise their voices in support of him. If an office is granted (directly or indirectly) by the emperor, the candidate receives no bonus from his clientele; in fact, being too popular can work against him if the emperor sees him as a potential claimant for the Empire's highest office.

Note: Some elected offices have a number of prerequisites (see page 126). A character who doesn't meet the prerequisites for an office can still seek it, but the DC is increased by +5 for each prerequisite he fails to meet.

Fame And Elected Office

Rolling a Fame check isn't the only way to gain elected office. A GM can always decide to give a PC an office as a reward for exemplary service to the Empire, as a recognition of a character's rising status, or as a plot device leading to political adventure.

Table 4–3: Elected Office

Office	Fame DC	Voting Body
Minor office (*e.g.*, interrex)	5	varies
Vigintivirates	5	Senate or aediles
Assemblyman	10	Popular Assembly
Senator	10	Senate
Quaestor	15	Senate
Tribune	20	Popular Assembly
Aedile	15	Senate
Curator	15	Senate
Procurator	12	Senate
Praetor	20	Senate
Propraetor	15	Senate
Augur	25	Senate
Consul	25	Senate
Proconsul	20	Senate
Censor	30	Senate
Prefect	30	Emperor
Pontifex maximus	30	Popular Assembly
Dictator	50	Senate
Augustus	75	Senate

If a PC is granted an office by the GM instead of rolling for it, he still gains Fame points from the new office without the risk of losing Fame. On the other hand, being elected to an office you weren't actively seeking is sometimes less than good fortune.

Even if a GM allows the optional Fame system to be used in his campaign, he can still rule that PCs cannot roll for elected office as one of the used of their Fame points. Public office, especially high offices like consul or emperor, can be central to the course of the campaign, and a GM may want to reserve those plot details in order to further an ongoing storyline.

New Patron

There are many ways for a Roman to gain a patron: through associations formed during military service, through family connections, as a result of a slave being freed, *etc.* And character who is a free Roman citizen (and many that aren't) is automatically entitled to a patron during character creation or at the moment the PC becomes a citizen.

If the player has no preference for the type of patron his character receives, the GM can simply assign one. But if he wants his PC to be bound to a specific patron (either a type, such as a senator or general, or a specific personage), he can make a Fame check with a DC equal to the magnitude of the Fame score of the desired patron. If the check is failed, the player can retry at a later date, but each subsequent attempt suffers a –1 cumulative penalty on the roll as the intended patron becomes increasingly annoyed.

Gaining Patrons and Clients

The mechanics in this chapter for gaining clients and patrons only apply to player characters. The GM can assign NPC patrons and clients to each other at will, and with the exception of clients or patrons specifically rolled for by the player the assigned of all other patrons and clients is at the GM's discretion. A GM cannot assign a second patron to a PC unless the player requests it (with or without taking the Multiple Patrons feat, see page 45).

Note: Even if a player gains a specific client or patron through a Fame check, the patron or client is still an NPC in the control of the GM. He may invite the player to participate in the creation of the NPC, although the players shouldn't know *everything* about the patron/client.

NPC Attitudes

A person's Fame modifier is applied as a bonus or penalty to checks made to influence the attitudes of NPCs. Animals and those in places or situations where they couldn't possibly have heard even rumors about the character's Fame aren't affected.

Patronage

With few exceptions, every Roman citizen is the client of a patron with a higher social standing (see page 49). So long as he fulfills his obligations as a client, the character receives a monthly income equal to twice his Fame bonus in copper pieces if he's a plebeian, silver pieces if an equites, or gold pieces if a patrician.

As well as his regular gifts from his patron, once per day a character can see if he can quickly come up with a small amount of extra money from his patron or other sources. If the character succeeds on a DC 10 Fame check, he receives a number of copper, silver, or gold pieces (as above) equal to half his check result.

If he fails this Fame check he isn't able to wheedle any extra money from his patron on this day, but he can try on another day without any penalty.

The character can also try to receive a non-monetary favor from his patron. The DC of this Fame check depends on the nature of the request; see **Table 4–4**.

Triumph

After a military victory, the commanding general can attempt to use his Fame to win public recognition of his feat in the form of a triumph. This requires a vote in the Senate (a DC 25 Fame check). Every senator the character

Table 4–4: Client Requests

Task	DC
Trivial request	>1*
Simple request	10
Complicated or expensive request	20
Dangerous to reputation (e.g., possible Fame loss)	30
Dangerous to person (e.g., possible injury or death)	40

Condition	Check Modifier
Client convinces patron that client will suffer Fame loss if request not granted	+1
Client convinces patron that patron will suffer Fame loss if request not granted	+2
First time client has made special request of patron	+5
Exceptionally close and positive relationship between client and patron	+5
Exceptionally distant or negative relationship between client and patron	–5
Request against the plans or interests of patron	–5

* Anything less would causes the patron to berate the client for the annoyance.

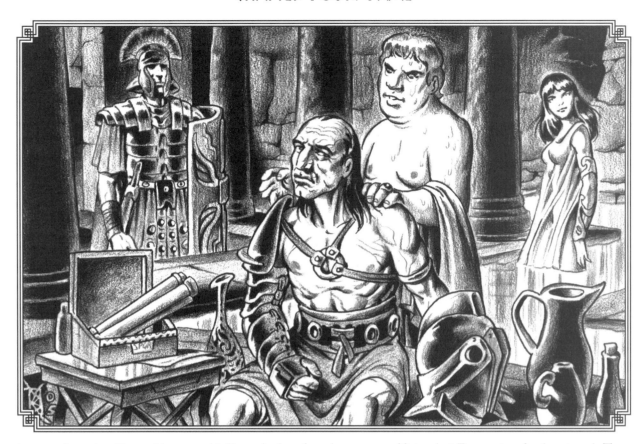

has as a client gives him a +1 bonus on his Fame check, and he receives another +1 for every 10 other permanent clients who raise their voices in support of him; a general may be supported by entire legions, but only his actual clients have an effect on the vote. If the vote is successful, the character is allowed to parade into Rome and is heaped with honors, resulting in an increase of +4 to his Fame score.

The triumphator is expected to distribute gifts to his troops during the celebrations, and if he distributes an equal amount of money to the public (either in cash or grain, or in the form of donations to temples or public institutions)

he earns an additional +2 Fame points for the triumph. The cost of the triumph (1,000-10,000 gp) is assumed by the triumphator, although the booty from his military victory would usually more than cover this expense.

If the character's attempt to be voted a triumph fails, he loses −2 Fame points.

Note: A triumph can only legally be awarded to someone in public office. If the character isn't an office holder at the same time as the Senate votes him a triumph, they'll also elect him (on an extremely temporary basis) to some available office.

- Expectations of The Famous -

Along with its many benefits, Fame comes with a price: increased expectations.

Inactivity

The first of these expectations is that a famous person will continue to work to increase his renown. If he fails to perform any activities to increase his Fame in a year (public sacrifices, (re)election to office, gaining a level), the character loses 1/10 of his Fame score (minimum loss of 1 Fame), continuing until his Fame reaches 0, but not into negative numbers.

His Fame score doesn't have to end the year higher than it began, it just must have experienced at least one increase over the course of the past 12 months. For example, if a character starts with a Fame of 5, then is implicated in a political scandal (−2 Fame) early on in the year, but toward the end of the year is elected **quaestor** (+1 Fame), he doesn't

lose Fame due to inactivity, because he did have one addition to his total even though his final Fame score (4) is 1 point lower than his score at the start of the year.

Table 4-1 shows that election to minor office, to a procuratorship, or to a vigintivirate results in a +0 increase to the character's Fame score. This isn't the same thing as inactivity leading to a lose of Fame. These offices can be considered placeholders, maintaining the character's Fame score without change while he works to find a way to increase it.

Note: A Roman with a negative Fame score doesn't lose Fame as a result of inactivity. While fame can be fleeting, infamy tends to survive even time.

Propriety

Another expectation of Roman society is that a famous person be held to a higher standard than a less public

THE NUMBERS GAME

Some GMs may fear that players will play the numbers instead of roleplaying their PCs; *e.g.*, making a public sacrifice and recruiting a couple senators as clients merely to get the extra Fame needed for a try at election to a consulship. Fortunately, this isn't a problem—it's actually a very Roman way of looking at things. The worried GM should just take care to roleplay the Fame-related events; *e.g.*, playing out the public sacrifice, instead of letting the player simply mark off some gold from his character sheet and boost his Fame score.

figures; a moral offense that could be ignored if performed by a social nobody would be scandalous if a senator or other official did it.

On **Table 4–2: Losing Fame** (see page 50), some ways to lose Fame have two entries separated by a slash. The lower number before the slash is for those with Fame scores of 24 or less, the higher number after the slash is for those with 25 Fame or more.

In addition, those with a high Fame score usually face increased scrutiny from the censors of Rome. Among the duties of the censors is the maintenance of the senatorial rolls—and they have the power to remove any senator from office if they determine that he is morally unfit to serve in the Senate. They can also permit or forbid an upwardly mobile citizen entrance into the equites or patrician classes on the same moral grounds.

- MILITARY HONORS -

The Romans had a number of honors they could bestow on members of the legions for valorous acts. Unlike triumphs, player characters can't use their Fame to campaign for these honors. They have to be earned by actual deeds, notthrough political machinations. The GM should use his discretion when it comes to awarding them to PCs.

CORONA AUREA

This golden laurel wreath was given to a Roman soldier who held his ground to the end of a battle.

CORONA CIVICA

A wreath of oak leaves, this award was given for saving a Roman citizen's life in combat.

CORONA GRAMINEA

Bestowed for the breaking of an enemy siege, this wreath was made from grass gathered at the site where the honoree performed his deed.

PATRON AND CLIENT REQUESTS

And finally, as a character's Fame increases, the sorts of favors that his clients and patrons ask of him grow larger. At a minimum, the value of the gifts he has to give to his clients increases directly as his Fame bonus increases. But in addition, the more powerful the character becomes, the more his patron and clients think he can accomplish for them, and naturally the requests they make of him reflect that, becoming more expensive, complicated, demanding, or dangerous (in more ways than one).

A player character can always decide not to grant a client's request, but if that refusal becomes public knowledge, he loses Fame—the public doesn't like breaks with the patron/client system. If a PC decides not to acquiesce to his *patron's* demands, he doesn't lose Fame but can be brought up on breach of contract charges.

CORONA MURALIS

Gold wreath in the form of fortifications bestowed on the first man over the wall of an enemy city during an attack.

IMPERATOR

Although this sounds like a title for an Emperor, it's actually an honor that could be granted by soldiers to a general who led them to victory; while being voted a triumph served as public recognition for a general's actions, being voted imperator was often more meaningful to a military man. Not all Emperors received this accolade, while others received it multiple times (some before they became Emperor). After Vespasian, Emperors took the title "Imperator" without actually being voted the honor by the legions.

SPOLIA OPIMA

Only awarded four times in Roman history, this honor was bestowed on one who defeated an enemy commander in single combat.

Chapter Five: Equipment

This chapter presents new equipment for use in the *Eternal Rome* setting.

Table 5–1: Roman Weapons lists weapons available in the *Eternal Rome* setting.

Gladiator Weapons

The following are the weapons used by the standard gladiator types:

> lasso, longspear, net, scimitar, shortbow, shortspear, short sword, spear, trident.

Alternate Names

Although they have the same stats as standard weapons, the GM might want to substitute Latin names for the arms of the Empire to add Roman flavor.

- *Fuxina* (trident): Used by laquearius and retiarius gladiators.
- *Gladius* (short sword): The standard weapon of the legions until the late Empire.
- *Iaculum* (net): Used by retiarius gladiators.
- *Plumbata* (dart): Named for the lead weights that gave them heft.
- *Pugio* (dagger): The secondary weapon on most Roman troops.
- *Sica* (scimitar): The chosen weapon of Thracian gladiators.
- *Spatha* (longsword): Originally favored by Celtic and German auxiliaries, it became a popular cavalry weapon in the middle Empire period, and by the late Empire it was standard for infantry as well.

- New Weapons -

This section presents new weapons for use in the *Eternal Rome* setting.

Amazon Axe

A handaxe with a light pick on the back of the blade, which could be used as either type of weapon. The first damage given is for the axe blade; the second for the pick.

Ballista

The ballista is a very heavy weapon, essentially an oversized crossbow that fires a dart the size of a javelin. It is used by the army in siege warfare, by the navy on warships, and by the Cohorts Vigilum in firefighting. A character must have a Strength of at least 25 to fire a ballista without a tripod or some other kind of mount. Regardless of Strength, a wielder takes a –4 penalty to attack rolls when wielding this weapon in addition to the normal –2 non-proficient penalty. Loading a ballista takes 2 full-round actions, and provokes attacks of opportunity.

Cestus

The cestus is a piece of leather or metal bound to the fist to enhance the damage caused by punches—an ancient version of brass knuckles. Participants in some boxing matches fought with cesti rather than bare-knuckles. Because it is bound to the hand, it is not subject to disarming. Damage done by a cestus wearer increases the unarmed strike's damage as if the wielder had also increased one Size category (see **Chapter 4: Improving Monsters** in the *MM*). For instance, a normal unarmed strike for a Medium creature deals 1d3 points of nonlethal damage. While wearing cesti, the damage increases by one step to 1d4 points of nonlethal damage. Leather cesti deal nonlethal damage (although a pankretiast can choose to cause lethal damage with them); metal cesti deal lethal damage.

A cestus makes it difficult for the wearer to use the hand for anything except punching, imposing a –6 penalty to any rolls requiring any degree of manual dexterity (including grapple rolls), and a 30% arcane spell failure chance for spells with somatic components or material components that have to be handled by hand.

Chariot-Spikes

Chariot-spikes were rarely necessary in combat, as showy attempts to board moving chariots were rare on the battlefield. But in the arena they were more useful. Chariot-spikes are a defensive weapon, intended to stop enemies from climbing aboard the chariot. Chariot-spikes add +2 to the DC of an attempt to board a chariot, and the boarder suffers damage from the spikes only if his boarding attempt fails.

Firehook

Consisting of a sturdy 6-8 ft. pole with a large metal hook on one end, the firehook allowed a vigil to clear debris or pull down fire-weakened structures from a (hopefully) safe distance. In addition to this noble purpose, it can also be used as a weapon. It has reach, and can be used against opponents 10 feet away but not against adjacent foes. Its curved hook can also be used to make trip attacks. If the wielder is tripped during his own trip attempt, he can drop the firehook to avoid being tripped.

Lasso

A lasso is a length of rope, 10 to 25 feet long, with a noose at one end. It was used by the laquearius class of gladiator to trap and entangle enemies.

Throwing a lasso is a ranged touch attack. If it hits, it partially entangles the target, imposing a –1 penalty to

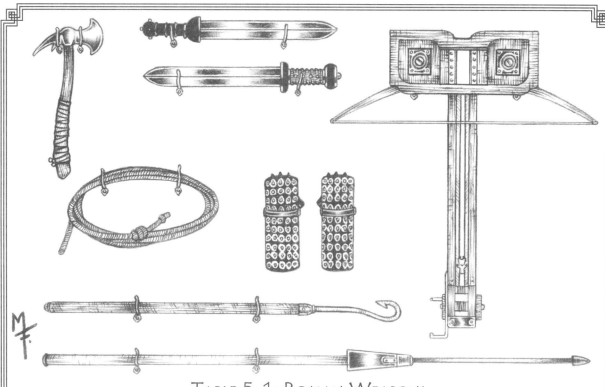

TABLE 5-1: ROMAN WEAPONS

Simple Weapons	Cost	Dmg (S)	Dmg (M)	Critical	Range Increment	Weight	Type
Unarmed Attacks							
Unarmed Strike	—	1d2 1	1d3 1	×2	—	—	Bludgeoning
Cestus	1 gp	1d3 2	1d4 2	×2	—	1 lb.	Bludgeoning
Light Melee Weapons							
Dagger	2 gp	1d3	1d4	19-20/×2	10 ft.	1 lb.	Piercing or slashing
Mace, light	5 gp	1d4	1d6	×2	—	4 lb.	Bludgeoning
Sickle	6 gp	1d4	1d6	×2	—	2 lb.	Slashing
One-Handed Melee Weapons							
Club	—	1d4	1d6	×2	10 ft.	3 lb.	Bludgeoning
Mace, heavy	12 gp	1d6	1d8	×2	—	8 lb.	Bludgeoning
Shortspear	1 gp	1d4	1d6	×2	20 ft.	3 lb.	Piercing
Two-Handed Melee Weapons							
Longspear 3	5 gp	1d6	1d8	×3	—	9 lb.	Piercing
Quarterstaff 4	—	1d4/1d4	1d6/1d6	×2	—	4 lb.	Bludgeoning
Ranged Weapons							
Dart	5 sp	1d3	1d4	×2	20 ft.	½ lb.	Piercing
Javelin	1 gp	1d4	1d6	×2	30 ft.	2 lb.	Piercing
Pilum 2	2 gp	1d4	1d6	×2	30 ft.	2 lb.	Piercing
Sling	—	1d3	1d4	×2	50 ft.	0 lb.	Bludgeoning
Bullets, sling (10)	1 sp	—	—	—	—	5 lb.	—

1 This weapon does nonlethal damage   3 Reach weapon

2 See weapon description for special rules   4 Double weapon

attack rolls and a −2 penalty to the target's Dexterity score. He can move at normal speed, but cannot charge or run. He must make a DC 15 Concentration check in order to cast a spell.

The lassoed creature can use a full-round action to free himself from coils of the lasso with a DC 15.

The user of the lasso can attempt to restrict the movement of the lassoed creature to within the limits that the rope allows by making an opposed Strength check modified by the Size modifier to grapple checks for both targets (Small creatures take a −4 penalty while Large creatures gain a +4 bonus). A lasso is only useful against creatures within one size category of the wielder.

PILUM

The pilum is the throwing spear of the legions. Its broad point and long, thin metal neck were designed so that even if the pilum didn't harm its target, the point would lodge in an enemy's shield and then the neck would bend, making the spear difficult to remove and the shield awkward to use, forcing the shield's user to throw away his shield or fight encumbered by the heavy spear shaft.

If a pilum attack misses its target but would have hit if not for the opponent's shield bonus (*e.g.*, if the target is carrying a heavy wooden shield, +2 shield bonus, and the attack misses by 2 or less), roll damage for the pilum; if the damage exceeds the hardness of the shield (typically 5 for a wooden shield, 10 for a metal one), the pilum is lodged in it and the shield's user

takes a –2 penalty to attack rolls and loses any Dexterity bonus to Armor Class until the shield is thrown away or the pilum is removed. Removing a pilum from a shield is a full-round action, and provokes attacks of opportunity.

In the late Empire, lead weights were added to pila in order to increase their penetrating power. A weighted pilum receives a +1 bonus to attack rolls, but its range increment is reduced to 20 feet.

WHEEL-BLADE

Although rarely used on war chariots, wheel-bladed chariots were sometimes used in the arena, and they sometimes featured in Celtic myths and other fantasy sources. Wheel-blades are scythe-like projections mounted on a chariot's wheel-hubs. They cannot be used against

TABLE 5–1: ROMAN WEAPONS (CON'T)

Martial Weapons	Cost	Dmg (S)	Dmg (M)	Critical	Range Increment	Weight	Type
Light Melee Weapons							
Amazon axe [2]	7 gp	1d4/1d3	1d6/1d4	×3/×4	—	6 lb.	Slashing or piercing
Axe, throwing	8 gp	1d4	1d6	×2	10 ft.	2 lb.	Slashing
Handaxe	6 gp	1d4	1d6	×3	—	3 lb.	Slashing
Sap	1 gp	1d4 [1]	1d6 [1]	×2	—	2 lb.	Bludgeoning
Shield, any	special	1d2	1d3	×2	—	special	Bludgeoning
Sword, short	10 gp	1d4	1d6	19-20/×2	—	2 lb.	Piercing
One-Handed Melee Weapons							
Battleaxe	10 gp	1d6	1d8	×3	—	6 lb.	Slashing
Longsword	15 gp	1d6	1d8	19-20/×2	—	4 lb.	Slashing
Scimitar	15 gp	1d4	1d6	18-20/×2	—	4 lb.	Slashing
Trident	15 gp	1d6	1d8	×2	10 ft.	4 lb.	Piercing
Warhammer	12 gp	1d6	1d6	×3	—	5 lb.	Bludgeoning
Two-Handed Melee Weapons							
Firehook [3]	8 gp	1d6	2d4	×2	—	10 lb.	Piercing
Greatsword	50 gp	1d10	2d6	19-20/×2	—	8 lb.	Slashing
Ranged Weapons							
Longbow	75 gp	1d6	1d8	×3	100 ft.	3 lb.	Piercing
Arrows (20)	1 gp	—	—	—	—	3 lb.	—
Longbow, composite	100 gp	1d6	1d8	×3	110 ft.	3 lb.	Piercing
Arrows (20)	1 gp	—	—	—	—	3 lb.	—
Shortbow	30 gp	1d4	1d6	×3	60 ft.	2 lb.	Piercing
Arrows (20)	1 gp	—	—	—	—	3 lb.	—
Shortbow, composite	75 gp	1d4	1d6	×3	70 ft.	2 lb.	Piercing
Arrows (20)	1 gp	—	—	—	—	3 lb.	—
Exotic Weapons							
One-Handed Melee Weapons							
Lasso [2]	1 gp	—	—	—	10 ft.	5 lb.	—
Whip [2]	1 gp	1d2 [1]	1d3 [1]	×2	—	2 lb.	Slashing
Ranged Weapons							
Ballista	500 gp	2d8	3d8	19-20/×2	120 ft.	200 lb.	Piercing
Bolt, ballista	1 gp	—	—	—	—	2 lb.	—
Net	20 gp	—	—	—	10 ft.	6 lb.	—
Chariot Weapons							
Chariot-spikes	2 gp	1	1d2	×2	—	2 lb.	Piercing
Wheel-blade	3 gp	1d6	2d4	×4	—	4 lb.	Slashing

1 This weapon does nonlethal damage

2 See weapon description for special rules

3 Reach weapon

opponents directly in front of a chariot or against anyone actually on the chariot; the driver must drive toward his opponent but miss him by just enough to bring him into the path of the blades, requiring a DC 14 Drive (chariot) check. If the chariot is moving at less than its walking speed, damage is halved.

- ARMOR -

Table 5-2: Roman Armor lists armor available in the *Eternal Rome* setting. Other types of armor (a full suit of chain, scale, or plate mail, for example) can be made on request but are not available off the shelf. Custom-making armor requires the services of a skilled armorer, takes two to three months, and costs five times as much as the amounts given in the *PHB*.

GLADIATOR ARMOR

The following pieces of armor are used by gladiators fighting in the traditional styles:

fasciae, galerus, helmet, lorica, manicus, ocreae, shield (including tower shields).

While most styles allowed the gladiator some form of armor, few provided any chest protection, forcing gladiators to place extra reliance on their shields to protect their most vital organs.

NEW ARMOR

This section presents new armor for the *Eternal Rome* setting.

CINGULUM

A studded leather belt up to a foot wide, covering the belly and groin area.

FASCIAE

Bands of leather armor wrapped around the thighs.

GALERUS

A metal shoulder guard usually worn only on the right (or weapon-side) shoulder; the shield (if any) was counted on to protect the other.

MANICUS

An arm guard worn usually only on the weapon arm. It could be light (leather or studded leather) or medium (banded, chain, or scale) armor.

OCREAE

Metal greaves covering the lower leg from knee to ankle.

Note: Some types of Roman armor (chain shirt, scale mail, banded mail, and breastplate) left arms and legs exposed. These areas could be protected with additional armor pieces: fasciae (thighs), manica (forearms), ocreae (shins), and galerus (shoulder). Padded, leather, studded leather, or hide armor could only add the galerus. Banded mail included its own shoulder guards, and thus wouldn't benefit from the addition of a galerus. The cingulum couldn't be worn with any armor that protected the torso.

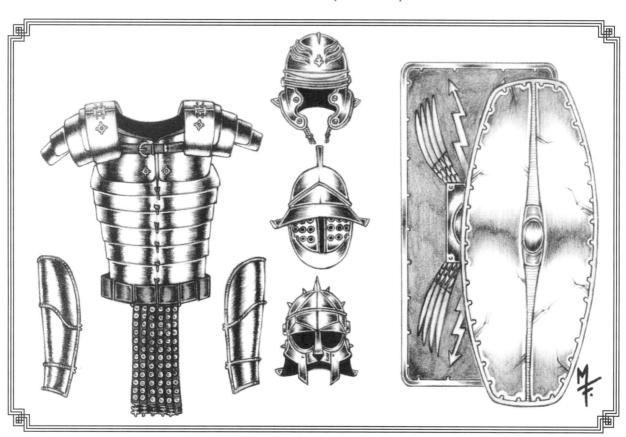

Table 5–2: Armor

Armor	Cost	Armor/Shield Bonus	Max Dex Bonus	Armor Check Penalty	Arcane Spell Failure Chance	Speed (30 ft.)	Speed (20 ft.)	Weight [1]
Light armor								
Cingulum	3 gp	+1	–2	0	5%	30 ft.	20 ft.	3 lb.
Padded	5 gp	+1	–0	0	5%	30 ft.	20 ft.	10 lb.
Fascia	4 gp/leg	+1[4]	–1/2	–1	5%	30 ft.	20 ft.	2 lb.
Manicus, light	4 gp/arm	+1[4]	–1/2	–2	5%	30 ft.	20 ft.	2 lb.
Leather	10 gp	+2	–2	0	10%	30 ft.	20 ft.	15 lb.
Studded leather	25 gp	+3	–3	–1	15%	30 ft.	20 ft.	20 lb.
Chain shirt	100 gp	+4	–4	–2	20%	30 ft.	20 ft.	25 lb.
Medium armor								
Ocreae	6 gp/leg	+1[4]	–1/2	–1	5%	30 ft.	20 ft.	5 lb.
Galerus	10 gp/side	+1[4]	–1/2	–1	5%	30 ft.	20 ft.	7 lb.
Manicus, medium	6 gp/arm	+2[4]	–1/2	–2	5%	30 ft.	20 ft.	5 lb.
Scale mail	25 gp	+3	–3	–2	20%	20 ft.	15 ft.	25 lb.
Hide	15 gp	+3	–4	–3	20%	20 ft.	15 ft.	25 lb.
Breastplate	175 gp	+5	–3	–2	20%	30 ft.	20 ft.	15 lb.
Heavy armor								
Banded mail	120 gp	+5	–5	–3	20%	20 ft. [2]	15 ft. [2]	30 lb.
Shields								
Buckler	15 gp	+1	—	–1	5%	—	—	5 lb.
Shield, light wooden	3 gp	+1	—	–1	5%	—	—	5 lb.
Shield, light metal	9 gp	+1	—	–1	5%	—	—	6 lb.
Shield, heavy wooden	7 gp	+2	—	–2	15%	—	—	10 lb.
Shield, heavy metal	20 gp	+2	—	–2	15%	—	—	15 lb.
Shield, tower	30 gp	+4[3]	+2	–10	50%	—	—	45 lb.
Extras								
Helmet	10 gp	+2	—	–2[5]	5%	—	—	6 lb.
Enclosed helmet	20 gp	+3	—	–4[5]	10%	—	—	8 lb.
Eyeless helmet	25 gp	+4	—	–4/–8[5,6]	10%[6]	—	—	9 lb.
Masked helmet	30 gp	+3	—	–4[5]	10%	—	—	8 lb.

1 Weight figures are for armor sized to fit Medium characters. Armor fitted for Small characters weigh half as much, and armor fitted for Large characters weighs twice as much.

2 When running in heavy armor, you move only triple your speed, not quadruple.

3 A tower shield can instead grant you cover. See description in **Chapter Seven: Equipment** in the *PHB*.

4 If this armor type is worn on one side only, the AC bonus only applies to attacks from the front and from the protected side.

5 This penalty applies to Spot, Listen, and Search checks while wearing a helmet.

6 See helmet description for special rules.

Helmets

The standard Roman legionary helmet changed little through the centuries. It was an open-faced helm with metal cheek-flaps, a flared neck-guard at the back, and no visor. There were other types of helmets with different properties.

Enclosed Helmet

Some gladiators wore fully-enclosed helmets with pierced visors. The visors allowed them to see forward, but severely hampered peripheral vision, and interfered with hearing; the loudest thing inside an enclosed helmet is often the sound of the wearer's own breath, especially in the exertion of combat.

An enclosed helmet interferes with vision and hearing (as described on **Table 5–2: Roman Armor**), but provides more armor protection than a standard helmet. It also hides the wearer's face and muffles his voice, adding +4 to Disguise checks where applicable.

Eyeless Helmet

A certain type of gladiator, the andabate (see page 29), fought wearing a helmet with no eye-holes at all. This was never intended to be a practical item of equipment; the audience at the arena enjoyed the spectacle of two armed men blindly trying to fight each other: Often they were mounted on horses, pointed at each other, and their horses charged.

An eyeless helmet completely hides the wearer's face, adding +8 to Disguise checks where applicable. It also renders the wearer completely unable to see by normal means (including low-light vision and darkvision). The

A LEGIONARY'S PACK

During the Republican era, members of the Roman legions provided their own equipment, but after the reforms of Marius in the late Republic and then through all the Empire period soldiers were issued armor, weapons, and other equipment necessary for their job for free; they only had to pay to replace lost or irreparably damaged gear. Player characters becoming legionaries should be given this gear without charge, but a PC who becomes a legionary at 1st level should receive only 1/10 the usual random starting gold.

Along with the weapons and armor appropriate to his fighting role (*i.e.*, longsword or short sword, dagger, shortspear, chain shirt or lorica squamata, heavy wooden shield, helmet, and horse for a legionary cavalryman; shortbow or composite shortbow, short sword, dagger, chain shirt or lorica squamata, helmet for an auxiliary archer), each legionary had the following equipment: cloak, bathing and shaving kit, weapon polishing kit, repair kit (with needle, thread, spare leather cords, *etc.*), tin bowl, cooking pot, bag of food rations, knapsack, wineskin or water canteen, hobnail boots, and a forked, 6-ft. pole to carry much of the gear with when marching. With armor and weapons, a legionary's marching gear could weigh more than 60 lb.

Equipment used by an eight-man contubernium of legionaries (including the tent they slept in as a group, saws, shovels, pickaxes, mattocks, a portable mill to grind wheat, and large wooden stakes for protecting camp sites) were carried on a pack mule assigned to the squad.

character is blinded (see Darkness in the *DMG*) while the helmet is on. Non-visual senses, such as blindsight and blindsense, are unaffected by an eyeless helmet.

The wearer cannot cast spells requiring a line of sight from the caster to the target, and the arcane spell failure chance for this helmet is 20% (instead of its normal 10%) when attempts are made to cast spells with material components.

Clairvoyance and similar magic may be used to counter the effects of an eyeless helmet, although *clairvoyance* shifts the character's point of view—he is effectively watching himself rather than seeing through his own eyes resulting in a –2 penalty to all rolls for tasks where sight is a factor. Search and Spot checks take a –8 penalty, but Listen checks take only a –4 penalty.

MASKED HELMET

For parades, games, and some formal occasions, cavalrymen sometimes wore ornate helmets with lifelike metal masks. These were also worn by the standard-bearers in some cavalry units. Masked helmets require very skilled craftsmanship (DC 25 on relevant Craft checks) and cost a minimum of 50 gp—more if they're gilded or silver plated.

A masked helmet interferes with vision and hearing (as described on **Table 5–2: Roman Armor**), but provides more armor protection than a standard helmet. It also hides the wearer's face and muffles his voice, adding +4 to Disguise checks where applicable.

PARTIAL ARMOR

Many fighter types in the Roman world (especially gladiators) wore pieces of armor rather than full suits. To calculate the value of a set of mismatched armor pieces, use the following rules:

ARMOR CLASS

A character's Armor Class is the sum of the AC of all the pieces of armor he is wearing, plus Dexterity and other modifiers as usual.

If a piece of armor is worn on one side only (arm or leg armor, for example), it only contributes to the wearer's armor class when dealing with attacks coming from the front or from the protected side. If a pair of such items is worn (e.g., a galerus on each shoulder), the AC value of the armor piece is only added once to the character's overall AC, but that AC applies to attacks from all directions.

No more than one piece of armor may be worn on a single location. It is not possible, for example, for a legionary to add a cingulum to his chainmail lorica hamata in order to improve his armor class.

Therefore, a legionary wearing a helmet (+2), banded mail lorica segmentata (+5), and a pair of ocreae (+1), and carrying a heavy shield (+2) has an overall Armor Class of 10.

If some or all of the armor has magical bonuses, only the highest protective bonus is added to the wearer's armor class; thus, if the legionary had *+1 banded mail*, a *+2 helmet* and *+3 ocreae*, this would add +3 to his AC, not +6. A magic shield's bonus would be added to that of the armor.

MAXIMUM DEXTERITY BONUS

A person wearing no armor has no limit to his Dexterity bonus. If he wears any armor at all, his maximum Dexterity bonus begins at +8, and each piece of armor reduces that maximum bonus by the indicated amount. Fractional penalties are added together, with any remaining fraction rounded down at the end of the calculation. If a pair of items can also be worn individually (e.g., galerus or ocreae), the maximum Dexterity bonus of that item is the same.

For example, if a legionary is equipped with banded lorica segmentata (-5), a pair of ocreae (-1/2), a heavy shield, and a helmet, the total penalty is -5.5 (as shields and helmets have no effect on maximum Dex bonus), which is rounded down to a maximum Dexterity bonus of +8-5=+3 while so armored. If he adds a manicus on his sword arm (-1/2 whether one or two are worn), the total becomes -6, for a maximum Dex bonus of +8-6=+2.

Note: The maximum Dexterity bonuses for some types of armor in the *Eternal Rome* setting are better than those for the equivalent armors in the standard d20 System setting. This is because Roman armor usually only covers the torso, and even if a character adds extra pieces to cover his thighs, shins, and forearms, these leave the joints exposed but unencumbered.

ARMOR CHECK PENALTY

A character's armor check penalty is the sum of the modifiers for all pieces of armor worn. If a pair of items can also be worn individually (e.g., galerus or ocreae), the armor check penalty of each item of the pair is counted.

Therefore, a legionary wearing a helmet, banded lorica segmentata (−3), and a pair of ocreae (−1 × 2), and carrying a heavy shield (−2) has an armor check penalty of −7. The helmet gives him a −2 penalty to Spot, Listen, and Search checks, but it doesn't affect his armor check penalty.

ARCANE SPELL FAILURE CHANCE

A character's arcane spell failure chance is the sum of the values for all pieces of armor worn. If a pair of items can also be worn individually (e.g., galerus or ocreae), the arcane spell failure chance of each item of the pair is counted.

Therefore, a legionary equipped with banded lorica segmentata (20%), a heavy shield (15%), a helmet (5%), and a pair of ocreae (5% × 2) has an arcane spell failure chance of 50%.

SPEED

A character uses the lowest speed value for any piece of armor worn. Therefore, the legionary in the previous examples has a speed of 20 ft. (assuming his base speed is 30 ft.), because of the encumbrance of his banded mail.

- EQUIPMENT -

The majority of the items on the Goods and Services list of the *PHB* are available in the *Eternal Rome* setting at standard prices, although sometimes there are minor differences; e.g., small mirrors are made of bronze, not steel, parchment or papyrus sheets (or wax tablets for non-permanent writing) are substituted for paper, "noble's outfit" can be renamed "senator's toga", and so on. Some comparatively high-tech items (spyglasses, magnifying glasses, and military saddles) are not available in a Roman setting, unless the campaign features an advanced technology timeline. Additionally, each GM must decide if the magical and alchemical arts are advanced enough in his version of *Eternal Rome* to allow for cheap and easily available acid, alchemist's fire, antitoxin, everburning torches, smokesticks, sunrods, tindertwigs, thunderstones, and tanglefoot bags; in the default *Eternal Rome* setting these items cost 10 times the *PHB* prices, if they're available at all.

Type	Hit Points	Hardness	Drive Check Modifier	Speed	Trample Damage	Weight	Cost
Light (including racing chariots)	60	6	--	60 ft.	1d6	75-100 lb.	100 gp[1]
Heavy (including war chariots)	125	12	-3	50 ft.	2d6	200 lb.	150 gp[1]

TABLE 5–3: CHARIOTS

1 This price does not include horses.

ROMAN CHARIOTS

The Roman chariot was of fairly light metal construction, with a semi-enclosed body and spoked wheels set at the back for tight turns; it was built for speed and agility rather than durability. Teams of two or four horses were used; a four-horse chariot was used for racing or as a status symbol. Roman chariots were not used for warfare: Their light construction and easily-damaged wheels were unsuited to travel across open ground, and required roads or a similar fairly smooth surface. They were, however, used for combat in the arena; the essedarius (see page 28) style of gladiator always fought from a chariot.

Light horses were most often used to pull Roman chariots. Racing chariots were stripped down to reduce weight, and were at the lighter end of the range.

CELTIC CHARIOTS

Although Celtic war chariots went out of use by the end of the first century of the Empire, they continued to be used in the arena, especially in contests that pit groups of "civilized" fighters, armed and equipped in the Greek or Roman styles, against groups of "barbarians," dressed in skins and armed in the Celtic and Germanic styles.

Celtic chariots were of simpler construction than Roman models. They were plank-built, with a yoke-pole attached to the center plank. Their wheels were solid and capable of movement across uneven ground. The front and back of these chariots were open, but the sides were protected with semicircles of wickerwork or hide on wood frames. A Celtic chariot was normally drawn by a pair of war ponies.

Celtic charioteers were not warriors in their own right; their job was to carry their noble masters into battle and to be on hand in case a withdrawal or redeployment was necessary. The warriors dismounted and fought on foot.

MASTERWORK CHARIOT

A masterwork chariot provides a +1 bonus to its Drive (chariot) checks and +1 to its

Hardness, and costs an additional 700 gp.

ADDITIONAL TEAMS

A standard chariot is pulled by a pair of horses. Doubling the number of horses adds +10 feet to the chariot's speed, but adds +2 to the DC of Drive (chariot) rolls. Doubling the number again to eight horses adds an additional +10 ft. to the speed, but adds another +2 to the Drive (chariot) DC.

CHARIOT CREW

War chariots have two or three riders: a driver and a warrior (armed with javelins or bow) and sometimes a shieldbearer (who increases the +2 AC, +1 Reflex save bonus the chariot provides to +4 AC, +2 Reflex save bonus against attacks originating on his side of the chariot). If a chariot driver is killed, the warrior or shieldbearer may perform a move

CHAPTER SIX: ROMAN MAGIC

In *Eternal Rome*, while not everyone can *cast* spells, magic is a part of the everyday experience of average Romans. This chapter contains new spells, clerical domains, and magic items.

- SPELLS -

All spells marked with an "*" are described following the spell lists starting on page 66.

BARD SPELLS

0-LEVEL BARD SPELLS

Celebrity*: Increase subject's Fame in the eyes of one person

2ND-LEVEL BARD SPELLS

Dying Curse*: Curses whoever kills the caster.

CLERIC SPELLS

1ST-LEVEL CLERIC SPELLS

Dying Curse*: Curses whoever kills the caster.
Protection from Spirits*: Grants +2 to AC and saves vs. spirit creatures, counters mind control, hedges out spirits.

2ND-LEVEL CLERIC SPELLS

Deathly Sight*: Detects ghosts or spirits.
Protection from Poison*: Confers +4 resistance bonus *vs.* poisons.
Refresh*: Sunject gets benefits of a full night's sleep in two hours.

3RD-LEVEL CLERIC SPELLS

Mantle of Leadership*: The subject is made to seem more noble and commanding.

4TH-LEVEL CLERIC SPELLS

Increase Fertility*: Improves chances of a pregnancy.
Zone of Peace*: Creates an area where a truce is enforced.

CLERIC DOMAINS

CHARM DOMAIN

Granted Power: Add Bluff, Intimidate, and Perform to your list of cleric class skills. You cast enchantment (charm) spells at +1 caster level.

CHARM DOMAIN SPELLS

1 **Charm Person:** Makes one person your friend.
2 **Mantle of Leadership*:** The subject is made to seem more noble and commanding.
3 **Suggestion:** Compels subject to follow stated course of action.
4 **Charm Monster:** Makes monster believe it is your ally.

5 **Dominate Person:** Controls humanoid telepathically.
6 **Suggestion, Mass:** As *suggestion*, plus one subject/level.
7 **Charm Monster, Mass:** As *charm monster*, but all within 30 ft.
8 **Sympathy M:** Object or location attracts certain creatures.
9 **Dominate Monster:** As *dominate person*, but any creature.

Hearth Domain

Granted Power: You can cast *hold portal* once per day at your caster level.

Hearth Domain Spells

1 **Create Food and Water:** Feeds three humans (or one horse)/level.
2 **Refresh*:** Gives subject the benefits of a full night's sleep in two hours.
3 **Helping Hand:** Ghostly hand leads subject to you.
4 **Everlasting Hearth*:** Creates a flame that burns without consuming fuel.
5 **Secure Shelter:** Creates sturdy cottage.
6 **Heroes' Feast:** Food for one creature/level cures and grants combat bonuses.
7 **Forbiddance M:** Blocks planar travel, damages creatures of different alignment.
8 **Antipathy:** Object or location affected by spell repels certain creatures.
9 **Mage's Magnificent Mansion F:** Door leads to extradimensional mansion.

Weather Domain

Granted Power: You can cast *endure elements* once per day on yourself at your caster level. Add Knowledge (nature) to your list of cleric class skills.

Weather Domain Spells

1 **Obscuring Mist:** Fog surrounds you.
2 **Gust of Wind:** Blows away or knocks down smaller creatures.
3 **Call Lightning:** Calls down lightning bolts (3d6 per bolt) from sky.
4 **Ice Storm:** Hail deals 5d6 damage in cylinder 40 ft. across.
5 **Control Winds:** Change wind direction and speed.
6 **Call Lightning Storm:** As *call lightning*, but 5d6 damage per bolt.
7 **Control Weather:** Changes weather in local area.
8 **Whirlwind:** Cyclone deals damage and can pick up creatures.
9 **Storm of Vengeance:** Storm rains acid, lightning, and hail.

Druid Spells

1st-Level Druid Spells

Dampen Flames*: Halves damage of fires or one magic item.
Protection from Poison*: Confers +4 resistance bonus *vs.* poisons.

2nd-Level Druid Spells

Dying Curse*: Curses whoever kills the caster.

Orator Spells

1st-Level Orator Spells

Celebrity*: Increase subject's Fame in the eyes of one person
Charm Person: Makes one person your friend.
Daze: Humanoid creature of 4 HD or less loses next action.
Hypnotism: Fascinates 2d4 HD of creatures.
Sleep: Puts 4 HD of creatures into magical slumber.

2nd-Level Orator Spells

Daze Monster: Living creature of 6 HD or less loses next action.
Hideous Laughter: Subject loses actions for 1 round/level.
Hold Person: Paralyzes one humanoid for 1 round/level.
Touch of Idiocy: Subject takes 1d6 points of Int, Wis, and Cha damage.

3rd-Level Orator Spells

Deep Slumber: Puts 10 HD of creatures to sleep.
Gravitas*: Grants immunity to emotion-altering spells.
Heroism: Gives +2 bonus on attack rolls, saves, skill checks.
Rage: Subjects gains +2 to Str and Con, +1 on Will saves, –2 to AC.
Suggestion: Compels subject to follow stated course of action.

4th-Level Orator Spells

Charm Monster: Makes monster believe it is your ally.
Confusion: Subjects behave oddly for 1 round/level.
Crushing Despair: Subjects take –2 on attack rolls, damage rolls, saves, and checks.
Geas, Lesser: Commands subject of 7 HD or less.

Sorcerer/Wizard Spells

0-Level Sorcerer/Wizard Spells

Celebrity*: Increase subject's Fame in the eyes of one person

1st-Level Sorcerer/Wizard Spells

Dying Curse*: Curses whoever kills the caster.
Hydrokinesis*: Moves (including hurling) up to 20 gallons of water.
Protection from Spirits*: Grants +2 to AC and saves vs. spirit creatures, counters mind control, hedges out spirits.
Water Spray*: Water jet deals 1d4 damage/level.

2nd-Level Sorcerer/Wizard Spells

Deathly Sight*: Detects ghosts or spirits.
Determine Allegiance*: Reveals Fame, patrons and clients of subjects
Hide Allegiance*: Misleads *determine allegiance* for one creature
Infant's Augury*: Reveal's a child's future.
Protection from Poison*: Confers +4 resistance bonus *vs.* poisons.

3rd-Level Sorcerer/Wizard Spells

False Omen*: Creates what appears to be a divine omen.
Gravitas*: Grants immunity to emotion-altering spells.
Greater Hydrokinesis*: Moves (including hurling) up to 200 gallons of water.
Smoke Sight*: Allows sight 5 ft./caster level through smoke.

4TH-LEVEL SORCERER/WIZARD SPELLS

Hasty Defense*: Allows fortifications to be constructed in 1/4 their normal time.

5TH-LEVEL SORCERER/WIZARD SPELLS

Mass Disorder*: Subjects think allies are enemies, and enemies allies

8TH-LEVEL SORCERER/WIZARD SPELLS

Treacherous Phantasm*: Lures the victim into danger by way of a phantasmal companion.

VIGIL SPELLS

1ST-LEVEL VIGIL SPELLS

Alarm: Wards an area for 2 hours/level.
Animate Rope: Makes a rope move at caster's command.
Calm Animals: Calms 2d4+level HD of animals.
Create Water: Creates 2 gallons/level of pure water.
Detect Secret Doors: Reveals hidden doors within 60 ft.
Endure Elements: Allows subject to exist comfortably in hot or cold environments.
Feather Fall: Makes objects or creatures fall slowly.
Floating Disk: Creates 3-ft.-diameter horizontal disk that holds 100 lb./level.
Hydrokinesis*: Moves up to 20 gallons of water.
Jump: Subject gets bonus on Jump checks.
Open/Close: Opens or closes small or light things.
Water Spray*: Water jet deals 1d4 damage/level.

2ND-LEVEL VIGIL SPELLS

Continual Flame: Makes a permanent, heatless torch.
Cure Light Wounds: Cures 1d8 damage +1/level (max +5).

Dampen Flames*: Halves damage of fires or one magic item.
Darkvision: Allows subject to see 60 ft. in total darkness.
Gust of Wind: Blows away or knocks down smaller creatures.
Knock: Opens locked or magically sealed door.
Levitate: Subject moves up or down at caster's direction.
Locate Object: Senses direction toward a a specific or particular type of object.
Resist Energy: Ignores first 10 (or more) points of damage/attack from specified energy type.
Smoke Sight*: Allows subject to see 5 ft./caster level through smoke.

3RD-LEVEL VIGIL SPELLS

Cure Moderate Wounds: Cures 2d8 damage +1/level (maximum +10).
Daylight: Creates 60-ft. radius of bright light.
Greater Hydrokinesis*: Moves (including hurling) up to 200 gallons of water.
Hold Person: Paralyzes one humanoid for 1 round/level.
Protection from Energy: Absorbs 12 points/level of damage from one kind of energy.
Slow: One subject/level takes only one action/round, -2 to AC, -2 on attacks rolls.
Tiny Hut: Creates shelter for 10 creatures.

4TH-LEVEL VIGIL SPELLS

Cure Serious Wounds: Cures 3d8 damage +1/level (maximum +15).
Dimensional Anchor: Bars extradimensional movement.
Dimension Door: Teleports caster a short distance.
Locate Creature: Indicates the direction to a familiar creature.
Quench: Extinguishes nonmagical fires or one magic item.

- NEW SPELLS -

The following new spells for *Eternal Rome* are presented in alphabetical order.

BESTOW CURSE

Necromancy

Range: Close (25 ft. + 5 ft./2 levels)
Target: One creature

In the *Eternal Rome* setting, the *bestow curse* spell is the same as that in the *PHB*, except that the caster must first make eye contact with his target and the caster can choose a curse to bestow from the following list:

- The accursed physically ages by one age category (see Vital Statistics, Age in the *PHB*), suffering all negative effects of aging, but none of the positive effects.

- The accursed is unable to produce or bear offspring. This is a touchy subject, and the effects of the affliction might be entirely unimportant in some campaigns. *Increase fertility* cannot break this curse.

- The accursed suffers a −4 luck penalty on attack rolls, saving throws, ability checks, and skill checks.

- One of the accursed's ability scores is decreased by −6 (min. 1).

- At least once per day an ill omen (*e.g.*, a dog howling, domesticated animals refusing to eat, a servant breaking an expensive item, finding a dead animal in the road) occurs in the vicinity of the accursed. All who witness the omen recognize it as linked to the accursed.

- The accursed's breast milk dries up. Obviously, this curse is only effective against lactating women, and may also be a subject best avoided in certain gaming groups.

CELEBRITY

Enchantment (Charm) [Mind-Affecting]

Level: Bard 0, Orator 1, Sorcerer/Wizard 0
Components: V, S
Casting Time: 1 standard action
Range: Close (25 ft. + 5 ft./two levels)
Target: One humanoid
Duration: 1 minute/level (D)
Saving Throw: Will negates (harmless)
Spell Resistance: Yes (harmless)

Select one person. That person gains +1 bonus/ three levels of the caster (at least +1, maximum +6) to its Fame score. The Fame bonus only applies to the first person the subject encounters after being affected by *celebrity*.

DAMPEN FLAMES

Transmutation

Level: Druid 1, Vigil 2
Components: V, S
Casting Time: 1 standard action
Range: Close (25 ft. + 5 ft./2 levels)
Area or Target: One 10-ft. cube/level (S) or one fire-based magic item
Duration: 1 minute/level
Saving Throw: None or Will negates (object)
Spell Resistance: No or Yes (object)

Dampen flames is used to slow the growth and reduce the damage of fires. It halves the intensity of all nonmagical fires in its area, causing them to do half their normal damage to creatures and objects exposed to them and to grow at only half normal speed. The spell halves the damage of fire spells in its area, but only if the caster of *dampen flames* succeeds at a dampen check (1d20 +1 per caster level, maximum +10) against each spell to be affected, with a DC of 11 + the caster level of the fire spell. When the spell's duration ends, the flames (mundane or magical) return to full intensity within a round.

Each elemental (fire) creature within the area of a *dampen flames* spell takes 1d3 points of nonlethal damage per caster level (maximum 15d3, no save allowed). When the spell's duration expires, the damage is healed at a rate of 1 hp/ minute/Hit Die of the elemental.

The spell can also target a single magic item that is burning with magical flames at the time *dampen flames* is cast, but not one that isn't afire at the time of casting even if the item does begin burning during the spell's duration. The intensity of the item's magical flames are halved for the spell's duration unless it succeeds on a Will save. (Artifacts are immune to this effect.) When the spell's duration expires, the item's flames return to full intensity immediately.

DEATHLY SIGHT

Necromancy

Level: Cleric 2, Sorcerer/Wizard 2
Components: V, S, M, F
Casting Time: 1 standard action
Range: Personal
Target: You
Duration: 1 minute/level (D)

The caster can see any ghosts or spirits within his visual range.

Material Component: A drop of blood.

Focus: Two copper pieces (placed over the eyes)

DETECT EVIL EYE

Divination

Level: Cleric 2, Sorcerer/Wizard 2
Components: V, S, DF
Casting Time: 1 standard action

Range: Touch
Target: Creature touched
Duration: 24 hours
Saving Throw: None
Spell Resistance: No

The subject immediately becomes aware of any evil eye cast on him. The subject can sense the direction from which the evil eye was cast, but not the identity of the caster, nor whether or not the curse was cast voluntarily.

This spell provides no protection from the evil eye.

DETERMINE ALLEGIANCE

Divination [Mind-Affecting]

Level: Sorcerer/Wizard 2
Components: V, S, F/DF
Casting Time: 1 standard action
Range: Close (25 ft. + 5 ft./two levels)
Target: One humanoid
Duration: Concentration, up to 1 round/level (D)
Saving Throw: Will negates; see text
Spell Resistance: No

The caster can determine the patronage and clientele of one person. The amount of information revealed depends on how long he studies a particular subject.

- *1st Round:* The subject's Fame score. If the subject has two Fame scores (*e.g.*, if he has a dual identity), only the most obvious Fame score is revealed.

- *2nd Round:* The subject's most important patron and client. If there's any question as to which patron or client is the most important, the one with the highest Fame score is revealed. If the subject has two Fame scores, his second score is revealed.

- *3rd Round:* All the subject's patrons and clients.

The caster must be able to see clearly the subject throughout the duration of the spell, and the magic cannot penetrate any opaque barrier. Each round he can turn to determine the allegiances of a different subject, so long as none of the subjects make any of their saving throws.

Each round that the spell is in effect, the subject attempts a Will save to negate its effects. The magnitude of his Fame modifier (ignoring positive or negative sign) is applied as a penalty to the roll. If the subject makes a save, the spell immediately ceases.

Arcane Focus: A small piece of glass.

DYING CURSE

Necromancy3

Level: Bard 2, Cleric 1, Druid 2, Sorcerer/Wizard 1
Components: V
Casting Time: 1 immediate action
Range: Close (25 ft. + 5 ft./two levels)
Target: One creature
Duration: 1 hour/level (D) or until discharged
Saving Throw: See text
Spell Resistance: See text

If the caster is mortally wounded in battle, he may cast this spell (or have already cast it at some time within the spell's duration) and speak a dying curse (pick a suitable curse from the *bestow curse* list). The target must make a Will save or fall victim to the curse at the moment the caster dies. The caster can willingly forego the curse and die in peace.

Casting this spell is an immediate action (which means the caster may cast it even when it is not his turn), like casting a quickened spell, and it counts toward the normal limit of one swift action per round.

EVERLASTING HEARTH

Evocation [Fire]

Level: Hearth 4
Components: V, S, M
Casting Time: 1 minute
Range: Touch
Effect: Illusory flame
Duration: Permanent
Saving Throw: None
Spell Resistance: No

A flame, equivalent to a cooking fire, springs forth from an object the caster touches. The flame looks like a regular flame, creating both heat and light, but it doesn't consume fuel or air. The heat from the fire deals 2d4 points of fire damage if touched, but the flame cannot start additional fires or be transferred to a different object (including a victim touching the fire). The flames can be covered and hidden, but not smothered or quenched.

Material Component: Ruby dust (worth 50 gp) and sulfur sprinkled on the item that is to carry the flame

FALSE OMEN

Illusion (Phantasm) [Mind-Affecting]

Level: Sorcerer/Wizard 3
Components: V, S
Casting Time: 1 standard action
Range: Medium (100 ft. + 10 ft./level)
Target: One creature/level
Duration: 1 round/level
Saving Throw: Will disbelief
Spell Resistance: No

The caster creates what appears to be a divine omen, determining the appearance of the omen when casting. Anyone who fails the saving throw believes it to be genuine. If such a person tries to interpret the image, with a successful check he deciphers the message the caster intended the omen to convey.

GRAVITAS

Enchantment [Mind-Affecting]

Level: Orator 3, Sorcerer/Wizard 3
Components: V, S
Casting Time: 1 standard action
Range: Touch
Target: Humanoid touched
Duration: 10 minutes/level
Saving Throw: Will negates (harmless)

Spell Resistance: Yes (harmless)

The subject of this spell is able to control the outward expression of his emotions. He can maintain a neutral expression against any provocation (which is considered an important trait in the Roman world). He is immune to emotion-controlling spells (including *bane, calm emotions, cause fear, charm person,* and *doom*), but *gravitas* doesn't protect him from mind-affecting spells that aren't emotion-altering (such as *confusion, daze,* and *hideous laughter*).

Unlike *calm emotions, gravitas* doesn't erase a person's own emotions, not does it prevent him from acting in an emotional manner while subject to the spell's effects; for example, he can still attack someone as a result of passionate hatred, but he won't appear to be enraged unless he wants to, and the attack won't break the spell.

GREATER HYDROKINESIS

Transmutation [Water]

Level: Sorcerer/Wizard 3, Vigil 3
Components: V, S
Casting Time: 1 standard action
Range: Close (25 ft. + 5 ft./2 levels)
Target: 200 gallons of water
Duration: Concentration, 5 rounds/level, or instantaneous
Saving Throw: Will negates (object), Fortitude prevents knock down (see text)
Spell Resistance: Yes (object) (see text)

As *hydrokinesis,* except the caster can control up to 200 gallons of water (the amount in a small hot tub), and it can do up to 3d6 points of impact damage per foe by hurling it at foes in a spot 10 ft. in diameter—the caster can choose to use less water, and thus deal less damage.

Note: Two hundred gallons of water is about a volume of 25 cubic ft., and weighs three quarters of a ton.

HASTY DEFENSE

Transmutation

Level: Sorcerer/Wizard 4
Components: V, S, M
Casting Time: 1 standard action
Range: Medium (100 ft. + 10 ft./level)
Area: All creatures within a 400 ft. burst.
Duration: 1 hour/level (D)
Saving Throw: None
Spell Resistance: No

This spell hastens the construction of walls and other fortifications, such that they only take one-quarter of the normal time to erect by enhancing the abilities of those building them. It increases their building speed to supernatural levels by granting a +20 bonus to their Craft checks, but only for building fortifications.

Material Component: A sliver of wood and a chip of stone.

HIDE ALLEGIANCE

Illusion (Glamer)

Level: Sorcerer/Wizard 2
Components: V, S

Casting Time: 1 standard action
Range: Touch
Target: Humanoid touched
Duration: 1 hour/level
Saving Throw: Will negates
Spell Resistance: No

By means of this spell, the warded person is protected from the *determine allegiance* spell. Each round that a *determine allegiance* is directed at the warded person, *hide allegiance* deflects the spell to another target within 10 ft. per caster level, thus revealing another target's allegiances instead of the glamered subject.

If the caster of *determine allegiance* becomes suspicious due to the odd information his spell elicits, he's entitled to a Will save each round after the first to negate the *hide allegiance* spell's effects (without dispelling the spell).

Hide allegiance has no effect on other divination spells.

Hydrokinesis

Transmutation [Water]

Level: Sorcerer/Wizard 1, Vigil 1
Components: V, S
Casting Time: 1 standard action
Range: Close (25 ft. + 5 ft./2 levels)
Target: 20 gallons of water
Duration: Concentration, 1 round/level, or instantaneous
Saving Throw: Will negates (object), Fortitude prevents knock down (see text)
Spell Resistance: Yes (object) (see text)

With this spell, the caster can control up to 20 gallons of water (the amount in two standard fish tanks), moving it in any direction to the extent of the spell's range, for a duration of 1 round per level.

Or he can hurl it at a single opponent (after which the spell's duration immediately ends), using an attack roll (caster's base attack bonus + Int modifier) to hit for 1d4 points of damage; the target must also make a Fortitude save on a successful attack to keep from being knocked down. Other than the effect of this spell, the water manipulated by *hydrokinesis* has the consistency of normal water—creatures can pass through it with no damage other than getting wet.

A creature made of water can be affected by this spell, providing it is of a size that's within the spell's target limit, but it is allowed a Will save to negate the effect.

The spell ends if the distance between the caster and the water ever exceeds the spell's range.

Note: Twenty gallons of water is about a volume of 2.5 cubic ft., and weighs about 160 lb.

Increase Fertility

Transmutation

Level: Cleric 4
Components: V, S, DF
Casting Time: 1 hour
Range: Touch

Targets: Two willing targets of opposite sexes
Duration: Permanent
Saving Throw: None
Spell Resistance: No

This powerful spell allows two willing individuals (including animals) to improve their chances of producing offspring. After the ritual is performed, their next coupling has a 40% chance +1% per caster level of resulting in a pregnancy.

Furthermore, the pregnancy is relatively painless, free of complications, and has a lower chance than normal of resulting in stillbirth and/or the death of the mother.

If either partner is barren the spell has no effect.

Infant's Augury

Divination

Level: Sorcerer/Wizard 2
Components: V, S, M
Casting Time: 10 minutes
Range: Touch
Target: Creature touched
Duration: Instantaneous
Saving Throw: None
Spell Resistance: No

By listening to the babble of a newborn infant during the first day of its life, the caster can determine whether the infant will live to adulthood or die, whether he'll grow up to be good, neutral, or evil, and whether he's destined to achieve great things or live a humble life.

The base chance for receiving a meaningful reply is 50% + 1% per caster level; the GM makes the roll secretly. The words that the caster hears are often couched in riddles or metaphors. If the roll fails, the caster receives no impressions of the infant's destiny (but he may create a false augury to tell the child's parents anyway).

Note: This spell should be restricted to NPC use, both on the part of the caster and the target.

Mantle of Leadership

Enchantment [Fear, Mind-Affecting]

Level: Charm 2, Cleric 3
Components: V, S, DF
Casting Time: 1 standard action
Range: Close (25 ft. + 5 ft./level)
Target: One creature
Duration: 1 minute/level (D)
Saving Throw: Will negates (see text)
Spell Resistance: Yes (see text)

Mantle of leadership enhances the target's natural qualities of leadership, making him appear more noble and commanding. The subject gains a +2 bonus to all Charisma-based skill checks and all Morale checks of a Force/Side he's attached to. All foes within 30 feet of the subject must succeed on a Will save against the spell or become frightened. In addition, all allies within 30 feet gain a +4 morale bonus to Will saves.

Mass Disorder

Illusion (Glamer)

Level: Sorcerer/Wizard 5
Components: V, S, M
Casting Time: 1 standard action
Range: Medium (100 ft. + 10 ft./level)
Target: One creature/level
Duration: 1 round/level (D)
Saving Throw: Will negates
Spell Resistance: Yes

Affected creatures who fail their saving throw perceive their allies as enemies and their enemies as allies. They hear the shouts of their friends as threats, and the jeers of their enemies as encouragement from their allies. The subjects attacks their perceived enemies to the best of their ability.

Material Component: Scraps of cloth from the uniforms or clothing of men from both sides.

Protection from Evil Eye

Abjuration

Level: Cleric 1, Paladin 1, Sorcerer/Wizard 1
Components: V, S, DF
Casting Time: 1 standard action
Range: Touch
Target: Creature touched
Duration: 10 minutes/level
Saving Throw: Will negates (harmless)
Spell Resistance: Yes (harmless)

The subject gains a resistance bonus +1 bonus/ three levels of the caster (minimum +1) on saving throws against the evil eye.

This spell provides no protection against gaze attacks or other ocular effects.

Protection from Poison

Abjuration

Level: Cleric 2, Druid 1, Sorcerer/Wizard 2
Components: V, S, M/DF
Casting Time: 1 standard action
Range: Touch
Target: Creature touched
Duration: 1 minute/level (D)
Saving Throw: Will negates (harmless)
Spell Resistance: No

The subject gains a +4 resistance bonus on saving throws against poisons of all sorts (but not spells or supernatural effects that mimic poison, such as the *poison* spell).

Material Component: Snake, scorpion, or spider venom daubed on the subject's face.

Protection from Spirits

Abjuration [Spirit]

Level: Cleric 1, Sorcerer/Wizard 1
Components: V, S
Casting Time: 1 standard action
Range: Touch
Target: Creature touched

Duration: 1 minute/level (D)
Saving Throw: Will negates (harmless)
Spell Resistance: No (see text)

This spell works like *protection from evil*, except it only affects creatures classed as spirits and affects them regardless of alignment, preventing bodily contact with spirits (even incorporeal ones).

Refresh

Enchantment (Compulsion) [Mind-Affecting]

Level: Cleric 2, Hearth 2
Components: V, S
Casting Time: 1 round
Range: Touch
Target: Creature touched
Duration: 2 hours
Saving Throw: Will negates
Spell Resistance: Yes

The caster lowers the recipient into a deep sleep which lasts for two hours but grants the sleep the benefit of a full night's rest. The sleeper suffers no fatigue from sleeping in armor. Moreover, a wounded person heals naturally at an accelerated rate, recovering ½ hit point per character level after two hours' sleep. At the end of the duration, a wizard or sorcerer finds himself able to cast spells as if he'd had a full night's sleep, although a wizard still has to spend an hour studying his spell books (clerics and druids don't regain spells any faster under the effects of a *refresh* spell).

Waking up someone from this magical slumber is difficult. Normal noise won't awaken the sleeper before the end of the spell's duration. Shaking, slapping or wounding (1 point of damage) a sleeper immediately awakens him.

Smoke Sight

Divination

Level: Sorcerer/Wizard 3, Vigil 2
Components: V, S
Casting Time: 1 standard action
Range: Touch
Target: Creature touched
Duration: 1 minute/level
Saving Throw: Will negates (harmless)
Spell Resistance: Yes (harmless)

The subject gains the ability to see through smoke, fog, and mist. Smoke or fog normally reduces visibility to 5 feet, but the target of *smoke sight* can see 5 ft./level of the caster, up to the maximum range he'd be able to see if the smoke weren't present.

Smoke sight also negates the 20% concealment provided by normal smoke. If the caster of *smoke sight* succeeds at a check (1d20 +1 per caster level, maximum +10) against each spell to be affected, with a DC of 11 + the caster level of the opposing spell, the 50% concealment of spells such as *fog cloud* and *obscuring mist* is reduced to 20%. Success doesn't dispel the magical fog.

Smoke sight's effects cannot be further magically enhanced, so one cannot use the spell through a crystal ball or in conjunction with *darkvision*.

TREACHEROUS PHANTASM

Illusion (Mind-Affecting)

Level: Sorcerer/Wizard 8
Components: V, S
Casting Time: 1 action
Range: Long (400 ft. + 40 ft./level)
Target: One creature
Duration: See text
Saving Throw: None
Spell Resistance: No

This insidious spell creates an illusory image of someone close to the target or someone whom he trusts. This image is overlaid on his sense of reality and is accepted as real by all his senses; even magical effects such as *true seeing* fail to reveal the illusion to the victim. Statements or arguments by others that contradict the phantasm become altered or twisted to conform to the victim's perceptions. Any attempt by others to confine the victim of the spell is twisted to the illusion's advantage.

The illusory double does everything in its power to mislead the victim into eventually committing a tragic act (*e.g.,* killing himself or a loved one, or committing a sin of extreme heinousness). The illusion ends when the tragic act has been committed, leaving the spell's target to deal with the consequences.

The *treacherous phantasm* is a particularly subtle illusion, usually taking weeks or months to work its magic. A *dispel magic* or *break enchantment* dispels the illusion, but they take a −4 penalty against this powerful enchantment.

WATER SPRAY

Conjuration (Creation) [Water]

Level: Sorcerer/Wizard 1, Vigil 1
Components: V, S
Casting Time: 1 standard action
Range: Medium (100 ft. + 10 ft./level)
Effect: Shoots and arc of water
Duration: 1 round/level
Saving Throw: Fortitude negates
Spell Resistance: No

When *water spray* is cast, a jet of water shoots forth from the caster's palm. If it is aimed at a target, requiring a ranged

FAME AND SCRYING

Targets of *scrying* and *greater scrying* take a penalty to their Will saves equal to their Fame modifier (ignoring positive or negative sign).

touch attack, the jet deals 1d4 points of damage; the caster is free to change targets as long as the spell is in effect, but can only strike one target per round.

Although the volume is lower, the spray of water is as pressurized as water coming out of a fire hose, so targets must also make a DC 15 Balance check or fall prone. The target receives a +1 bonus to his save for every 10 feet he is away from the caster.

ZONE OF PEACE

Abjuration
Level: Cleric 4
Components: V, S, DF
Casting Time: 1 standard action
Range: Close (25 ft. + 5 ft./2 levels)
Area: 5-ft. radius/level emanation
Duration: 1 hour
Saving Throw: See text
Spell Resistance: No

The *zone of peace* is a special fortified *sanctuary*. When it is set up, anyone who enters it is compelled to proclaim whether he will respect the truce of the zone; this declaration is a free action. If he agrees to honor the truce, he is protected by a *sanctuary* spell until he leaves the zone, must make a Will save to make any attack (even in response to another's attacks on him) within the zone, and even if he succeeds, he takes 3d8 points of divine damage. He loses his *sanctuary* when he attempts to commit an act that violates the zone, but must continue to make saving throws when he attempts to commit further acts of violence and continues to take additional damage on successful saves.

The *zone of peace* is most commonly used during parlays in battle.

- MAGIC ITEMS -

While the magic items in the *DMG* can be found in the *Eternal Rome* setting, some may need some modification to fit the Roman world; *e.g.,* the invention of the *apparatus of the crab* could be attributed to a famous engineer, such as Archimedes or Hero of Alexandria, instead of some wizard.

In general, minor magic items (*e.g.,* scrolls, potions, minor amulets) should be as common in the Roman world as in standard fantasy campaigns, and artifacts should play a slightly more important role than in other campaigns, being presented in public displays, used in crucial battles, *etc.* Items between these two extremes of power should be somewhat rarer in an *Eternal Rome* campaign, although the average mid-level PC should still be armed with items like a *+1*

gladius and *+2 lorica hamata* instead of the *Club of Hercules* and the *Armor of Aeneas*.

NEW WONDROUS ITEMS

BULLA

A *bulla* is an amulet hung around a child's neck when it is first given a name. Those who could afford them always give their children magical *bullae*, but even the poor give their children nonmagical bullae in hopes that they'd still have *some* effect. A *bulla* only works for a child until he or she comes of age (usually around 14 years old), and many *bullae* are passed down from generation to generation within a family, with the first-born son in each family receiving the most potent *bulla* available.

A *lesser bulla* gives the wearer the benefits of a *resistance* spell. A *greater bulla* gives the wearer the benefits of a *protection from evil* and a *resistance* spell (the bonuses do not stack). If a person wears multiple *bullae*, only the most powerful one has an effect.

Faint abjuration; CL 3rd; Craft Wondrous Item, *resistance* (lesser) or *protection from evil, resistance* (greater); Price 1,000 gp (lesser), 13,000 gp (greater); Cost 500 gp + 40 XP (lesser), 6,500 gp + 520 XP (greater).

FASCINUM

A *fascinum* is an amulet that grants the wearer a resistance bonus of +2, +4 or +6 against the evil eye. It can be made in any form, but the most common are charms in the shape of a hand making a warding gesture, a twisted animal horn, a phallic symbol, or a piece of branching red coral, all designed to be hung on a cord or chain around the wearer's neck. They can be made of any material: coral, precious metals, or even plain iron.

Faint/Moderate/Strong abjuration; CL 4th/10th/15th; Craft Wondrous Item, *protection from evil eye*; Price 4,000 gp (+2), 16,000 gp (+4), 36,000 gp (+6); Cost 2,000 gp + 160 XP (+2), 8,000 gp + 640 XP (+4), 18,000 gp + 1,440 XP (+6).

SAFEGUARDING STYLUS

For non-permanent writing, Romans used a wax-covered wooden tablet and a stylus, a pointed metal, wood, or ivory wand about the size of a pencil; the stylus made marks in the wax that could be erased by heating and smoothing the wax. While an important Roman might walk the streets of the city unarmed, he (or his servant) would rarely be found without a tablet and stylus.

A *safeguarding stylus* has the special property that it can be used as a weapon by its wielder, functioning as a *+1 dagger* in melee and as a *+1 dart* when thrown; if Julius Caesar had been armed with a *safeguarding stylus* instead of a mundane one when he was assassinated, he might have been more successful at fighting off his attackers.

Faint transmutation; CL 3rd; Craft Magic Arms and Armor; Price 4,300 gp; Cost 2,300 gp + 92 XP.

SCYTHIAN SADDLE

These magic saddles aren't produced by or for Scythians; their name is derived from the way the saddle can magically enable a Roman to be as skillful on horseback as any of the steppe horsemen are normally.

When placed on a mount, a *Scythian saddle* grants the rider a +3 competence bonus to Handle Animal checks and a +5 competence bonus to Ride checks. The rider can never fall from the horse unless he chooses to or is killed. Riders who have the appropriate proficiency receive a +3 circumstance bonus to attack rolls with a lance or held (not thrown) spear.

Moderate enchantment; CL 9th; Craft Wondrous Item, *charm animal*; Price 14,400 gp; Cost 7,200 gp + 576 XP.

TINTINNABULUM

These charms are designed to ward a building or other enclosed area from the evil eye. Hung from the ceiling of the area to be protected, a *tintinnabulum* takes the form of a phallus, a statuette of the god Priapus (a minor god of abundance and fertility), or an oil lamp, each decorated with a number of small bells attached to it by short cords or chains.

If an evil eye is cast (whether or not the subject makes his saving throw) within the protected area, or a person under the effects of an evil eye enters the area, the bells begin to gently ring, continuing until either the affected person leaves the area, a command word is spoken, or (in the case of an evil eye that was cast on a victim who made his save) for one full minute. The bells are much quieter than an *alarm* spell, and while they can be heard throughout the warded area (even through doors and walls), their sound cannot be heard outside the area. A *silence* spell or continuous loud noises (such as those of combat or a raucous party) can overpower the sound of the bells. The bells do not ring if blown by the wind or if shaken by hand.

A single *tintinnabulum* protects a volume of 5,000 cubic feet; enough to protect a single shop or apartment. Romans with more property to protect either bought multiple *tintinnabula* or, if they couldn't afford that, placed a single one in the *vestibulum* ("entry hall"). A building could have multiple nonmagical tintinnabula hung as decoration and to give visitors the impression that the owner could afford that much magical protection.

Faint abjuration; CL 3rd; Craft Wondrous Item, *alarm, detect evil eye*; Price 12,000 gp; Cost 6,000 gp + 480 XP. Weight 1 lb.

MINOR ARTIFACTS

LEGION EAGLE

In the early days of the Republic, Roman legions had a variety of standards: poles surmounted with a variety of animals or symbols designed as group identifiers and rallying points. But after the First Punic War these were replaced with a single pattern found across the legions: the *aquilia*, or eagle. A legion's eagle was important as a symbol of its group honor: it was the center around which encampments were pitched, binding oaths would be sworn before the eagles, and on holy days it was decorated with garlands and battle honors and anointed with oils and spices: the equivalent of anointing every man in the legion. When losing battles, some commanders were known to cover the heads of their eagles so that they wouldn't witness the shame of defeat.

Each eagle also has two magical powers. The first is that it grants a +1 morale bonus (granting a +1 bonus to all saves) to all members of its legion so long as it is present where they can see it. Unfortunately, if the eagle is captured by the enemy, the morale of the legion is reduced by −2. (If using the Biblical Battlefield Resolution System or Homeric Battlefield Resolution System of Green Ronin's *Testament* and *Trojan War*, the morale bonus is applied to all members of the legion, even if they are divided into multiple Sides/Forces.)

The other power is the ability for the standard-bearer who carries it (called an *aquilifer*) to command the eagle to come to life up to three times per day to fight for the legion. The summoned eagle is in reality the result of a *greater shadow conjuration* spell that replaces the eagle statue on the standard with a phantasmal one in the air.

The bird can carry messages for battlefield commanders (although it must stay within sight of the standard or else it winks out of existence), fly patterns in the air to relay orders or serve as a rallying point, or fight as a normal eagle, usually targeting the commanders on the opposing side. The eagle has 3 hit points, AC 14, and attacks as a normal eagle. If the target of the eagle's attack succeeds on a DC 25 Will save, the eagle's damage is halved and its AC drops to 12.

The standard itself can be used as a makeshift heavy pick (−1 to attacks because of its unwieldiness), although an *aquilifer* would have to be in dire straits before he'd consider damaging the legion's standard.

While it would seem easy to make replacement eagles, for some reason the replacements never had the magical powers of the originals—no wonder both Emperors Tiberius and Claudius launched campaigns to recover the eagles lost by Varus and his annihilated legions in the Teutoberg Forest decades before, and four legions were disbanded after losing their eagles to the enemy in 70 AD.

Caster Level: 13th; *Weight:* 15 lbs.

Waters of the Lethe

The River Lethe, which flows through the Elysian Fields, causes forgetfulness in all who drink it, so that they can be reincarnated into a new life unburdened by memories of the past. A vial of this water has the same effect on a living person, unless he succeeds on a DC 35 Fortitude save. On a failed save, the imbiber loses all skills and experience, forgets how to talk or do anything else, and effectively has the mind of a newborn—he must learn *everything* over again through experience. This effect can only be negated by a *miracle* or *wish*.

Waters of the Styx

The waters of the River Styx that borders the underworld are a deadly poison to all living creatures and all undead. They have no effect upon constructs or outsiders. Because of their divine nature, the waters of the Styx are not affected by *neutralize poison* or similar spells cast by any spellcaster of less than 20th level.

According to Homer, the Greek hero Achilles was made invulnerable by being dipped in the Styx as a newborn. PCs who have heard this legend may be very eager to get their hands on some water from the Styx, but they will find that it does not have the effect they expect, unless the character in question is newborn and his parents have been advised by an oracle to dip him or her in the Styx. In this case, the character permanently gains the benefits of the *iron body* spell, without the associated weight gain; this is a divine protection and his skin isn't actually changed to iron.

The waters of the Styx are a contact poison. Those coming into contact with it must succeed on a DC 25 Fortitude save or take 3d6 points of Constitution damage as initial damage and 1d6 points of Constitution damage and 1d6 points of Charisma damage as secondary damage.

Price 10,000 gp.

Major Artifacts

The Armor of Aeneas

Forged by Vulcan at the request of Venus, this armor was worn by the hero Aeneas during his struggle to settle in Italy along with his fellow Trojan refugees. It consists of a Greek-style helmet, a breastplate, and a pair of ocreae, with a large, round, bronze-faced, wooden shield. Mysteriously, the shield bears an engraved scene of the great naval battle at Actium even though it was made many centuries before the battle was fought.

This divinely-forged armor gives +5 protection (for an overall AC of 13), and has spell resistance 17. Despite this formidable protection, it is as light as padded armor, and has an armor check penalty of 0, a maximum Dex bonus of +8, and an arcane spell failure chance of 5%.

The *Armor of Aeneas* was lost before Rome was founded, but probably rests in the hero's tomb along with his body and his sword (a *+1 short sword of speed*). The shade of Aeneas (and the goddess Venus, who gave him the armor) may object to a presumptuous mortal taking it unless Rome is in grave danger and the mortal can convince the shade that he is a true hero.

A character wearing the *Armor of Aeneas* and fighting hand-to-hand with the enemies of Rome gains a +10 Charisma bonus when dealing with Romans, and can inspire heroics in Romans fighting alongside him in battle as a 15th-level bard.

Cloak and Club of Hercules

Although his fabled bow and arrows were lost centuries before, the *Cloak* and *Club of Hercules* were still kept as holy artifacts in the god's temple in Greece until Greece was conquered and the artifacts were moved to a temple in Rome near the end of the early Republic era. The cult of Hercules grew in popularity during the late Republic and early Empire, with Mark Antony claiming descent from the demi-god, and Emperor Commodus (180-192 AD) declaring himself to actually *be* Hercules, liberating "his" cloak and club from the temple to parade through the streets of the city and then fight wild animals in the arena.

Hercules's cloak is made from the skin of the Nemean lion, a beast invulnerable to weapons. The cloak grants its wearer a +6 deflection bonus to AC and damage reduction 20/bludgeoning.

His club is an unadorned *+5 greatclub*, a two-handed weapon Hercules wielded one-handed with ease. Once per day, it can be used to automatically kill one creature struck as per an *implosion* spell (DC 35 Fortitude save negates).

Crown of Thorns

Before his crucifixion, one of the many tortures endured by Jesus of Nazareth was having a wreath of braided brambles placed on his head. Afterwards, the *Crown of Thorns* was taken and hidden away by Jesus's followers, for fear of its destruction

gifts to important Christian potentates (*e.g.*, the Emperors and powerful bishops), and become objects of veneration wherever they end up, even after their *resurrection* power is expended.

SPEAR OF LONGINUS

At the end of the crucifixion of Jesus of Nazareth, a centurion named Longinus checked to see if he was truly dead by piercing Jesus in the side with a longspear. Blood and water poured from the wound, but Jesus himself didn't react to the stabbing, and his followers were allowed to remove his dead body from the cross. As with other artifacts of the Crucifixion, the *Spear of Longinus* was taken by the early Christians and hidden away for centuries. It was brought forth after St. Helena, the mother of Emperor Constantine, made a pilgrimage to the Holy Land sometime after 324 AD and founded a number of churches to commemorate holy sites and house holy relics. Along with the wood and nails of the cross, the *Spear of Longinus* was put on display.

Although the *Spear* takes the form of a weapon of war (and it can be used as a mere *+1 longspear* if someone really wants to), it acts as a tool for peace. The wielder of the *Spear* is constantly under the protection of a *sanctuary* spell; if he decides to attack using another weapon, the *sanctuary* disappears, returning a full minute later; if he attacks using the *Spear* itself, the *sanctuary* disappears for a full day, or until a different person wields the *Spear*.

In addition, the wielder of the *Spear* can use it to cast *calm emotions*, *shield other*, and *zone of peace* three times each per day, as a 20th-level cleric.

STATUE OF VESTA

The cult statue of Vesta installed in her temple in Rome was one of the treasures brought from Troy to Rome by Aeneas. It provided the ultimate protection for the city for so long as it stood in its temple and the sacred fire before it continued to burn, while foreign armies might take control of part of the city, none would ever conquer it all—as demonstrated when the Gauls took the entire city in 390 BC, but failed to dislodge the final tiny garrison on the Capitoline Hill and left after an unsuccessful months-long siege.

It was destroyed in a citywide fire in 191 AD, and while it would be centuries before the city was finally taken by foreigners, some saw that end as inevitable after the loss of the statue.

or confiscation by the pagan authorities of the Empire only occasionally being brought forth so that its miraculous powers could be used. Following the reign of Julian the Apostate, the time was deemed ripe, and in the late 4th century AD the *Crown* was placed on display in a church in Jerusalem.

As is the case with many artifacts connected with the blood of Jesus, the *Crown of Thorns* is famed for its healing powers. Once per hour it can be used to cast *cure light wounds*, once per week it can cast *cure critical wounds*, once per month *heal* or *restoration*, and once per year *regeneration*, all cast as by a 20th-level cleric. The *Crown's* caretakers decide who has access to it, but they have no control over whom it decides to bestow its miraculous powers.

The individual thorns on the *Crown* can be removed from it, and each then becomes its own healing relic. Each of these can be used to cast *cure light wounds* once per day, and *resurrection* a single time. The thorns are sometimes given as

- THE EVIL EYE -

In ancient Rome, the rich, famous, handsome, and successful had to always be on guard against the envious glares of others, because in Rome envy could lead to bad luck through the power of the evil eye. Magic amulets and even non-magical actions designed to ward off the evil eye were almost universally known and used.

CASTING THE EVIL EYE

The evil eye is a spell-like effect that can be cast by anyone (usually unintentionally) in the *Eternal Rome* setting. All that's required is exceptional envy on the part of the caster,

with the GM deciding what counts as "exceptional": merely making note of a disparity in the fortunes of the caster and the curse's subject isn't sufficient; the caster has to seethe over the unfairness of the situation or express negative feelings about the subject (even if the caster would deny a desire that actual harm come to the subject).

To accidentally cast the evil eye, the caster and the subject must make eye contact (this is the GM's call; a blind man can neither cast nor be affected by the evil eye, nor can it be cast in conditions of zero visibility). If the subject then fails a DC 20 Fortitude save, he's cursed with bad luck, taking a

−2 luck penalty on all attack rolls, damage rolls, saves, skill checks, and ability checks made for the next 24 hours. The subject of an evil eye curse isn't automatically aware of the effect, but it can be detected by *detect evil eye* or *detect magic*.

There are many modifiers to the evil eye check, as listed on **Table 1**. Potentially the most significant are the Charisma and the Fame of the subject: beauty and fame breed envy, after all. It is the *difference* between the Charisma and Fame scores of the caster and the subject that determine the bonus to the evil eye check, though: If the subject's Charisma is higher than that of the caster, then he receives a penalty on his save equal to half the difference. But if the caster's Charisma is the higher, then the subject receives a +1 bonus on his save for *each* point of difference. The same rules apply to the Fame scores of the two.

The caster of an evil eye isn't automatically aware that he's done so, but if the subject accuses him of this the caster realizes what happened on a successful DC 20 Will check. The caster can remove the curse at will, but only if he first realizes that he is its cause.

(See also the Evil Eye Projector feat, on page 45, for the ability to *intentionally* cast the evil eye on another.)

Multiple Evil Eyes

While a person can cast an unlimited number of evil eyes (either accidentally, or, if he has the Evil Eye Projector feat, voluntarily), he can only cast it twice on the same person if something has happened between the two castings to increase the caster's jealousy towards the subject (*e.g.*, an increase in the subject's Fame, or the birth of a healthy heir). No matter what the circumstances, he can never cast the evil eye twice on the same person in the same day.

Multiple evil eyes (from different casters, or from the same caster, voluntarily and accidentally) aren't cumulative. The luck penalty from an evil eye does stack, however, with that of a *bestow curse* spell.

Countering the Evil Eye

Despite its relatively minor effects (a simple −2 luck penalty for a day that the victim might not even realize is in effect), a number of different ways have been developed to defend against the evil eye.

Bullae, Amulets, and Spells

The most effective defense against the evil eye is the *bulla*. In addition to the listed effects of this magical amulet (see *Eternal Rome*, page 71), a *greater bulla* renders its wearer completely immune to the evil eye, while a *lesser bulla* provides a +2 resistance bonus to saves against the evil eye. Even a nonmagical bulla provides a +1 resistance bonus on evil eye saves.

Unfortunately, all *bullae* become useless once the child reaches adulthood. Those who can afford them then buy a *fascinum* or a *tintinnabulum* (see page 72) or both.

The evil eye-related spells *detect evil eye* and *protection from evil eye* are found on page 67 and page 70.

Table 6-1: Evil Eye

Condition	Fortitude Save DC
Caster is female	+2
Caster is blue-eyed (The majority of people around the Mediterranean are brown-eyed.)	+1
Caster is a non-Roman	+1
Caster is a spellcaster	+1/spellcaster level
Caster's Charisma is lower than subject's	+1/2 per point of difference
Caster's Charisma is higher than subject's	-1 per point of difference
Caster's Fame is lower than subject's	+1/2 per point of difference
Caster's Fame is higher than subject's	-1 per point of difference
Subject grasps genitals (male) or iron	-5
Subject pronounces counter-charm within same round	-5

Counter-Charm

Another protection is the pronouncement of a counter-charm. If a person thinks an evil eye is being cast on him or on someone in his charge (*e.g.*, a baby or slave), as an immediate action he can utter a short prayer to a god (*e.g.*, "Hera, guard me," for most Romans, Isis for Egyptians, the god of Israel for Jews and Christians, *etc.*) that serves to give him a measure of protection from the evil eye (reducing the save DC by −5).

Those within hearing of the counter-charm usually recognize it as a counter to a suspected casting of the evil eye, and may reflexively take precautions themselves. It may also be seen as a hostile act by those around the person uttering the counter-charm; after all, by doing so, the person is accusing *someone* of attempting to cast an evil eye in his vicinity.

(*Note:* This counter-charm is unrelated to the counterspells described in the Magic chapter of the *PHB*.)

Grabbing "Iron"

The most common defense against the evil eye is one known throughout the Empire: grabbing something symbolically powerful. If a Roman man thinks the evil eye is being cast at him, or even *might* be cast on him (*e.g.*, he sees an old, ugly, blue-eyed, foreign woman look his way), he'll surreptitiously slip his hand under his tunic or toga to cup his genitals. If there's no time to be subtle, he'll grab at his genitals through the cloth, likely causing all men around him to do the same—instead of being embarrassed by his action, the others will be thankful for the warning. But grabbing iron may also be seen as a hostile act, because it implies that the subject thinks someone is attempting to cast the evil eye on him.

INDISCRIMINATE EVIL EYES

Because it's the GM who decides when a character (a PC or an NPC) involuntarily casts an evil eye on someone else, he must take care not to abuse this authority. Every instance of jealousy shouldn't lead to an evil eye, just the most noteworthy—especially those that are significant to an ongoing plotline.

Thus, if a PC is trying to convince the Senate to vote him an honor he doesn't really deserve, the jealousy of those who really do deserve the honor is part of the plot, and the possibility of an evil eye affecting the vote is justified. On the other hand, if a PC is merely walking down a city street on his way to the baths, there's no plot value to be gained in the GM assessing the envy level of every beggar, delivery boy, and vegetable seller he passes on the trip to see if he's accidentally cursed along the way.

And since the evil eye can happen with the victim unaware that it's occurred, saddling a character with a luck penalty that he doesn't even know about adds little to any plot. So the GM has to make the existence of the penalty known to the PC, by playing up his bad fortune when he fails a roll, mentioning that he's feeling unlucky, or having animals and soothsayers feel uneasy about him because of something they can't quite identify that just seems *wrong* about him.

But while actual instances of accidental evil eyes should be rare, accusations of the casting of this inobvious curse can be more commonplace. Thus, if a PC expresses envious thoughts that are likely to cause an involuntary casting of the evil eye, a nearby NPC (possibly the subject of the envy) should warn the PC to be more careful how he expresses himself in future. If the players know that the evil eye can be cast merely by a careless phrase, they'll be better at adopting a cautious Roman attitude towards public expressions of jealousy, and they'll be appropriately wary when the GM has NPCs speak enviously of their characters.

Women have to substitute another potent substance, grabbing at iron, in the form or weapons, tools, or even amulets worn for that purpose (some *fascina*, see page 72, are made of iron for just this purpose; the save bonuses for the *fascinum* and for grabbing iron stack).

Grabbing iron reduces the DC of a person's save against an evil eye by –5.

CHARITABLE ACTS

A nonmagical means of removing the evil eye if a person believes he is already under its curse is to perform a charitable act in public in an effort to lower the envy that can be associated with fame and success.

The act has to involve a minimum of 1% of the person's accessible wealth (*i.e.*, his ready cash; he doesn't have to sell his house and slaves in order to liquidate all his assets), it has to be a true act of charity (*i.e.*, he can't make a public show of generosity and then secretly take the money back), and it has to be witnessed by a number of people (not including his relatives, employees, slaves, or clients) at least equal to his Fame modifier (but it doesn't have to be witnessed by the person who originally cast the evil eye on him). If all these requirements are met, then the act of charity automatically breaks any existing evil eye curse on the subject, and protects him from the evil eye for the rest of that day.

Typically, a Roman wouldn't make donations of this sort on a daily basis, but would consider making such a charitable act if he had a string of unfortunate events that could be attributed to the presence of the evil eye, if he had the curse confirmed through magical means, or if he was about to undertake a major project and didn't want to risk being magically hampered.

MAGIC SPELLS

An evil eye curse can be removed by a *dispel magic* with a dispel check DC of 11 + the evil eye's caster level (regardless of whether the casting was voluntary or involuntary) +3 if the caster has the Mal'occhio feat (see page 45). It can also be removed by a *break enchantment, limited wish, miracle, remove curse,* or *wish* spell.

FOLK REMEDIES

Throughout the Empire, there are folk remedies for the evil eye. For a few copper or silver pieces, folk magicians (not necessarily of spell-casting classes) will, with enthusiastic ritual, draw the curse from the subject and place it into an ordinary egg which can then be buried underground (taking the curse with it); or sweep him from head to toe with a specially crafted and decorated soft brush or with an ordinary straw broom; or fumigate him with incense and secret herbs; or throw consecrated salt at him.

All these cures are effective at breaking the curse of the evil eye, but only because no matter what one does the evil eye's curse wears off in a day anyway. This doesn't make these healers con-artists (although some surely are): the exact details of how the evil eye functions is knowledge at the level of the GM and the players, not something that's completely understood and widely known among the PCs and NPCs within the *Eternal Rome* setting.

And even if the treatments are bogus, the average Roman believes in them, so a PC who's being shunned by NPCs who believe him to be under an evil eye curse can change their attitudes by being seen having locally accepted anti-evil eye rituals performed over him. It's cheaper than a *dispel magic*, and almost as effective.

CHAPTER SEVEN: BESTIARY

This chapter describes the types of creatures that existed, or were thought to exist, in the Roman world. The Roman Empire stretched from the North Sea to North Africa, from the Atlantic Ocean to the Arabian Desert, and thus a wide range of beasts could be found within its borders.

- ANIMALS BY REGION -

The following animals from the *MM* were found in the Roman world. Aggressive creatures were used in the arena, while others were kept as exotic pets by the wealthy. Emperor Augustus had an extensive menagerie, and many others followed his example. Most were originally founded to provide beasts for the arena shows that their owners sponsored, but over time they became wider collections of exotic creatures. Of course, PCs traveling in the wilder parts of the Empire and its neighboring lands can encounter local wildlife.

AFRICA

Ape (from central Africa), baboon, camel, cheetah (from central African), crocodile, elephant, hyena (from central Africa), leopard (from central Africa), lion, monitor lizard, monkey, rhinoceros (from central Africa), snake (constrictor), vermin (monstrous scorpions).

ARABIA

Camel, lion, vermin (monstrous scorpions).

ASIA

Tiger (through trade via Mesopotamia).

CENTRAL EUROPE

Bear (black), bison (forest-dwelling, herds of 4-12).

EMPIRE-WIDE

Bat, boar, cat, cattle (use stats for the Auroch, following), dog (large hunting dogs use wolf stats), donkey, eagle (the golden eagle was a symbol of Rome), hawk, horse (light or heavy horses, and light warhorses), lizard (warm climes), mule, owl, pony, rat, raven, snake (viper), toad, vermin (giant ant, beetle, wasp; monstrous bee, centipede, spider), weasel, wolf.

MEDITERRANEAN SEA

Giant octopus (remote parts of Mediterranean and Black Seas, Atlantic Ocean), octopus, porpoise, squid (small squid are widespread; larger squid are restricted to remote waters or might be pets of supernatural beings or the creations of evil magic), whale (small toothed whales are found in the Mediterranean; they can be treated as orcas, although less aggressive).

Northern Europe

Bear (black and brown), bison (forest-dwelling, herds of 4-12).

Western Europe

Badger (less aggressive than its American cousin), war pony (northern Britain).

New Animals

Auroch

Large Animal

Hit Dice: 4d8+8 (26 hp)
Initiative: +2
Speed: 30 ft. (6 squares), swim 10 ft.
Armor Class: 14 (−1 size, +2 Dex, +3 natural), touch 11, flat-footed 12
Base Attack/Grapple: +3/+11
Attack: Gore +6 melee (1d6+6)
Full Attack: Gore +6 melee (1d6+6)
Space/Reach: 10 ft./5 ft.
Special Attacks: —
Special Qualities: —
Saves: Fort +6, Ref +6, Will +1
Abilities: Str 18, Dex 14, Con 15, Int 2, Wis 10, Cha 7
Skills: Listen +6, Spot +5
Feats: Alertness, Run

Environment: Temperate and warm plains and forests
Organization: Solitary or herd (2–12)
Challenge Rating: 1
Treasure: —
Alignment: Always neutral
Advancement: 5–8 HD (Large)
Level Adjustment: —

A long-horned beast lows in the plains.

The auroch was a species of large, long-horned wild cattle. They were found from Mesopotamia to Gaul in the earliest Roman times, but by the beginning of the Republic they were extinct except in the forests of central and western Europe in Roman times.

Deer

Small Animal

Hit Dice: 1d8+1 (5 hp)
Initiative: +3
Speed: 50 ft. (10 squares)
Armor Class: 14 (+1 Size, +2 Dex, +1 natural), touch 13, flat-footed 12
Base Attack/Grapple: +1/−2
Attack: Gore +1 melee (1d4+1)
Full Attack: Gore +1 melee (1d4+1), 2 hooves -4 melee (1d3)
Space/Reach: 5 ft./5 ft.
Special Attacks: —
Special Qualities: Low-light vision
Saves: Fort +3, Ref +2, Will −1
Abilities: Str 12, Dex 14, Con 12, Int 2, Wis 12, Cha 6
Skills: Listen +5, Spot +5
Feats: Alertness

Environment: Temperate and warm forests and plains
Organization: Herd (6-25)
Challenge Rating: 1
Treasure: None
Alignment: Always neutral
Advancement: Medium (2 HD), Large (3 HD)
Level Adjustment: —

Deer of various sizes were found throughout the Roman world. Groups generally consist of one dominant male, 3-6 juvenile males, 12-20 females, and a number of young depending on the time of year. Size varies from small (fallow deer) through medium (red deer) to large (Irish elk).

Giraffe

Huge (Tall) Animal

Hit Dice: 3d8 (13 hp)
Initiative: +0
Speed: 40 ft. (8 squares)
Armor Class: 12 (−2 size, +2 Dex, +2 natural), touch 10, flat-footed 10
Base Attack/Grapple: +1/+13
Attack: Hoof +5 melee (1d6+4)
Full Attack: 2 hooves +5 melee (1d6+4), gore +0 (1d4+2; males only)
Space/Reach: 10 ft./10 ft.
Special Attacks: —
Special Qualities: Low-light vision
Saves: Fort +3, Ref +5, Will −1
Abilities: Str 18, Dex 14, Con 10, Int 2, Wis 7, Cha 6
Skills: Listen +6, Spot +4
Feats: Alertness, Run

Environment: Temperate and warm forests and plains
Organization: Herd (6-25)
Challenge Rating: 2
Treasure: None
Alignment: Always neutral
Advancement: —
Level Adjustment: —

Giraffes are popular in menageries and animal shows (and occasionally in the arena) because of their distinctive appearance.

Combat

Giraffes are not usually aggressive usually kicking only toward the rear at pursuers. If cornered, male giraffes butt with their horns.

Ostrich

Medium Animal

Hit Dice: 2d8+2 (11 hp)
Initiative: +3

Speed: 40 ft. (8 squares)
Armor Class: 14 (+3 Dex, +1 natural), touch 13, flat-footed 11
Base Attack/Grapple: +2/+4
Attack: Kick +4 melee (1d4+3)
Full Attack: 2 kicks +4 melee (1d4+3), bite +0 melee (1d2+1)
Space/Reach: 5 ft./5 ft.
Special Attacks: —
Special Qualities: Low-light vision
Saves: Fort +3, Ref +3, Will −2
Abilities: Str 14, Dex 16, Con 12, Int 2, Wis 6, Cha 5
Skills: Hide +4, Listen +2, Spot +3
Feats: Run

Environment: Warm plains
Organization: Solitary, pair, or flock (2-12)
Challenge Rating: 2
Treasure: None
Alignment: Always neutral
Advancement: —
Level Adjustment: —

These aggressive, flightless birds were imported from Africa as a novelty. Some were used in mock hunts in the arena or even trained to pull small chariots.

Carrying Capacity: A light load for an ostrich is up to 75 lb.; a medium load, 76-150 lb.; and a heavy load, 151-225 lb. An ostrich can drag 500 lb.

- STANDARD MONSTERS -

The following creatures from the *MM* are particularly appropriate for use in the *Eternal Rome* setting. Creatures not listed here can also be used, but should be rare and may require some explanation for their presence in the Roman world.

Allip: Some of the first ghost stories ever written come from the Roman world.

Animated Object: These constructs can be animated by a powerful magician, or by the gods themselves.

Assassin Vine: This plant can be found in remote forests and jungles.

Athach: Originating in Celtic lore, the athach may be found among remote areas of Britain and Ireland.

Barghest: Found in Gaul, Britain, and other Celtic areas, they are traditionally treated as a magical beast rather than an outsider.

Chimera: Originally a unique creature slain by the Greek hero Bellerophon in antiquity, in the *Eternal Rome* setting, some of its children survive on remote Greek islands and in other deserted places.

Cockatrice: These monsters lurk in the plains and forests of central Europe.

Constrictor Snake, Giant: Constrictors large enough to swallow children are found in Italy as late as the early Empire.

Dinosaur, Elasmosaurus: Large lakes and inland seas in the northern half of the Empire might house such sea serpents.

Dire Animals: Dire forms of any animals in this chapter might be found in similar circumstances to their normal-sized kin. Dire animals fetch a high price if they can be captured for the arena.

Dragon: Dragons are very rare in classical lore, but are known to exist. Red and metallic dragons are the most common, but all types are possible.

Dragon Turtle: Sea monsters of various types are thought to haunt the waters of the great Ocean beyond the Mediterranean Sea, and dragon turtles could be among them.

Dragonne: Although not represented in classical lore, the dragonne is a typical crossbred magical creature. It might be found in the deserts beyond the eastern frontier of the Empire.

Dryad: All ancient forests are home to at least one dryad.

Eagle, Giant: Giant eagles aren't common, but can be found in mountainous regions of the Empire. During the Empire periods, they are potent symbols of Rome herself and no-one but the Emperor is allowed to own them.

Elemental: The concept of four elements comes from Greek and Roman philosophy. Most elementals may be summoned by spellcasters with the appropriate spells. The largest and most powerful serve only the gods.

Ettin: Ettins may be found in remote mountainous areas and on deserted islands. Typically they try to eat any mortals who cross their path.

Genie: Although genies belong to later Arabic tradition, they might be found serving powerful Mesopotamian spellcasters or living free in the deserts of the southeast.

Ghost: Ghosts of all types are found in the Roman world. The restless spirit of a Roman who died but didn't have the proper burial rites performed for it could haunt not only the place where it died or its own families, but also any Roman who came across its body but didn't either bury it or at least throw a token handful of dirt over the body.

Ghoul: Ghouls belong to Indian and Arabian traditions. As their homelands border the southeastern part of the Roman Empire, they might occasionally be found in the Roman world.

Giant: Cloud giants, hill giants, stone giants, and storm giants may be found in remote parts of the Empire. Frost giants are found mainly in the lands of the Hyperboreans (see page 87). Some fire giants serve Vulcan in his forge.

Girallion: Girallions may be used in the *Eternal Rome* setting as divinely-created apes that live among their two-armed kin, usually as leaders. A captured girallion would fetch a very high price from a promoter of animal shows in the arena.

Goblin: Orculli (singular: orcullo) remained in the wilder and more mountainous parts of Italy and the Alps until the Middle Ages. Goblins can be used to represent the smaller creatures.

Golem: Clay golems come from medieval Jewish tradition, although a powerful Jewish spellcaster might known how to make them in the Roman period. Stone and iron golems could be created by powerful spellcasters of any background; around the Mediterranean, most would take the form of animated statues, while in the wilder lands of the north and west, stone golems in particular might be created from ancient standing stones and similar objects. Stone and iron golems are also used by the gods to guard their treasures. The Roman world does not have the level of surgical skill necessary to create flesh golems.

Gorgon: In the *Eternal Rome* setting, this magical beast is called a *bos ferrus* ("iron bull").

Griffon: Griffons are found in remote hilly regions of Thrace and Scythia, and beyond the northeastern frontiers of the Empire.

Hag: The annis is native to northern Europe, but green hags and sea hags are comparatively widespread.

Harpy: Harpies are found in wilder parts of Greece and on the northeastern fringes of the Empire. The majority of them do not have the captivating song ability, and are thus CR 3 with a level adjustment of +2.

Hippogriff: Hippogriffs are found in the wilder parts of Greece and the northeastern fringes of the Empire.

Homunculus: Homunculi may be created by any spellcaster with the requisite abilities. They are more common in parts of the Empire with a long-established magical tradition, such as Egypt.

Hydra: The original hydra lived in the Peloponnese region of Greece. It was killed by Hercules. Hydras in the *Eternal Rome* setting are descendants of the original. Pyrohydrae and cryohydrae are unknown.

Lamia: Lamiae are a race of half-beasts native to the deserts of North Africa.

Lammasu: Lammasus come from Mesopotamian mythology and may be encountered in those eastern lands.

Lich: A lich can be from any background, although areas with long-established magical traditions, such as Egypt, are ideal for them. An Egyptian lich may be impossible to distinguish by sight from a mummy.

Lycanthrope: Werewolves and werebears originated in the Germanic traditions. Both types may be encountered north of the Danube and east of the Rhine. Other kinds of lycanthropes may be encountered wherever their animal species are common.

Manticore: Manticores roam the dismal marshes, deserts, and wastelands beyond the eastern fringes of the Roman Empire. Their physiology varies wildly: some are wingless, and a few have the tail of a monstrous scorpion, substituting a poison attack (injury DC 17, initial damage 1d6 Str, secondary damage 1d6 Str, 200 gp) for the spikes.

Medusa: Medusa was one of three monstrous sisters called the gorgons; she was slain by the Greek hero Perseus in distant antiquity, but the surviving medusae may be her descendants and those of her sisters.

Mephit: Earth, air, fire, and water mephits are appropriate in the *Eternal Rome* setting.

Merfolk: Merfolk are found in many parts of the Mediterranean, although they tend to stay away from ports and shipping routes, preferring privacy. Some groups of merfolk are actively hostile towards humans.

Minotaur: The Minotaur was a unique creature that lived in a labyrinth in the palace of King Minos of Crete. It was killed by the Greek hero Theseus. Surviving minotaurs might be the creature's monstrous offspring, or they might have been created by the gods for reasons of their own.

Mummy and Mummy Lord: Mummies and mummy lords may be found in remote tombs and other setting across Egypt, and sometimes they find their way to Greece or Rome.

Nymph: Nymphs are found in all kinds of natural settings throughout Greece and Italy. Under different names, they were known in other parts of the world as well. Nymphs are discussed as a player character race on page 88.

Ogre: Ugly, man-eating giants called gigans are found in remote places all across the Roman world. The smaller ones may be treated as ogres, and the larger as ettins or hill giants.

Orc: Orchi (singular: orcho) and orculli (literally "little orchi") are found throughout the wild and remote parts of Italy and in the southern foothills of the Alps. Small individuals may be treated as goblins, larger individuals are orcs, and the largest are almost as big as ogres.

Owl, Giant: Giant owls may be found in the wilder lands of the Empire. Because of their size, they tend to favor thin woodlands over close-growing forests, where they would have trouble flying between the trees.

Owlbear: Although the owlbear is not a creature from classical myth, its composite nature is in keeping with the classical tradition. At the GM's option, owlbears may be found in deep forests beyond the northern and northeastern frontiers of the Empire.

Pegasus: Pegasus was a unique creature, captured and tamed by the Greek hero Bellerophon. In the *Eternal Rome* setting, surviving pegasi might be his offspring. Such creatures would be in great demand as mounts.

Satyr: Satyrs are found in forested areas throughout Greece, Italy, and adjoining regions. Satyrs as player characters are discussed on page 88.

Sea Cat: Sea cats may be found in less-traveled waters throughout the Roman world. They are sometimes used as mounts and war-beasts by merfolk.

Shadow: Shadows are found throughout the world of *Eternal Rome*.

Shield Guardian: Like golems, shield guardians can be created by any spellcaster who has the ability to do so.

Skeleton: Skeletons are found throughout the world of *Eternal Rome*.

Spectre: Spectres are found throughout the Empire.

Sphinx: Sphinxes of all kinds are found in Egypt, and gynosphinxes (and, more rarely, androsphinxes) are also found in the more remote parts of Greece, Macedonia, and Thrace.

Sprite: Nixies are found in water throughout the lands north of the Mediterranean. In Greece, Italy, and surrounding areas, they are often found in the company of nymphs. Grigs and pixies are only normally found in

Gaul, Germany, and the British Isles.

Stirge: Stirges are found in marshes and deep forests throughout Italy, Greece, and lands to the north.

Swarm: Swarms of all kinds (except hellwasps) are encountered throughout the Roman world. Locust and rat swarms are the most common.

Titan: The titans were the ancestors of the gods of Olympus. The titan as described in the *MM* represents merely the largest type of giant.

Treant: The deepest, darkest forests of Gaul and Germany hold many secrets, and traditions of sentient, mobile trees are widespread.

Triton: The tritons are servants of Neptune, the god of the sea. They are found throughout the Mediterranean.

Unicorn: Unicorns can be found in the forests of Gaul and Germany. Celestial chargers are of divine origin, but may be found occasionally.

Vampires: Vampires are found throughout the Roman world. The traditional vampire heartland of Transylvania is in the province of Dacia.

Wight: Gaul, Germany, and Britain abound with ancient burial mounds where wights may be found.

Will-O'-Wisp: Will-o'-wisps are found in marshes throughout the Roman world.

Worg: Worgs may be found in the dark, forbidding forests beyond the northern frontiers of the Empire, often in association with wolves and dire wolves.

Wraith: Wraiths may be encountered throughout the Roman world.

Wyvern: Like dragons, wyverns are rare in the Roman world. They are most often found in remote hills and mountains beyond the Empire's northern frontier.

Zombie: Zombies can be found throughout the Roman world. In Egypt, some animated corpses may be zombies rather than mummies; both are bandaged, however, and it is difficult to tell them apart by sight alone.

- VARIANT MONSTERS -

Some monsters familiar from the *MM* require slight adjustments to work in a Roman setting.

ANGEL

Angels were quite active in the Middle East and Rome according to the New Testament, but those presented in the *MM* are more combat-oriented. If you have *Testament: Roleplaying in the Biblical Era*, the malachim and mazzalim are more appropriate for this role. Other excellent examples can be found in *The Avatar's Handbook*.

BASILISK

The basilisks found in deserts on the eastern fringes of the Empire are no more than a foot long; rather smaller than the standard. What they lack in size, they make up in the virulence of their poison. A basilisk's touch and breath scorch

grass, kill bushes, and split rocks; Pliny wrote that a man on horseback once speared a basilisk, and the creature's venom traveled up the shaft of the spear, killing both horse and rider.

These basilisks have the statistics of a lizard, with the following special attacks:

Petrifying Gaze (Su): Turn to stone permanently, range 30 ft., DC 13 Fortitude save negates. The save DC is Charisma-based.

Poison (Ex): The basilisk continually secretes a potent acid, which drips from its jaws, coats its skin, and is carried on its breath up to 6 inches away. This is a contact poison, DC 18, initial and secondary damage 2d6 Con.

Venom Transference (Su): The basilisk's venom is so potent that it can travel up hand-held weapons that wound the creature. The weapon takes 1d10 points of damage. The attacker holding it and any other creature in physical contact with the attacker must save against the poison as if they had touched the creature. Gauntlets are no protection in handling a basilisk; only objects that are specifically enchanted to protect against poison are immune to this effect.

DEMON, SUCCUBUS

Also known as the empusa (plural: empusae), the succubus was well documented in the Classical world. The Greek philosopher and magician Apollonius of Tyana, who lived in the early Empire period, confronted an empusa who, disguised as a Phoenician noblewoman, preyed upon one of his students.

In the *Eternal Rome* setting, succubi are independent demons rather than being part of a hierarchy; they are not able to summon other demons (although some may be sorcerers, and able to do so by casting spells), but they have the ability to *polymorph* into human form in order to disguise their true nature.

DEVIL, ERINYES

Classical sources sometimes use the name erinyes to mean the furies (see page 83), and sometimes to mean a separate type of creature altogether.

Erinyes are not part of a devil hierarchy. Instead, they work for the gods (sometimes for Dis Pater, and sometimes for other deities) to punish and frighten mortals who have angered them. In this, they are similar to both the furies and the harpies, and it could be that these three types of creature form a hierarchy of their own as divine punishers. Harpies might be sent to punish less powerful sinners or minor transgressions, while erinyes take the middle ground in both respects and the furies are only sent to punish the most horrible crimes against the gods, committed by the most powerful mortals or demons.

In the *Eternal Rome* setting, erinyes are lawful neutral (which does not make them one jot more merciful toward their victims). They do not have *unholy blight* or the ability to summon other devils, but once per day an erinyes can attempt to summon 1d4 harpies with a 50% chance of success. This ability is the equivalent of a 3rd-level spell.

DEVIL, LEMURE

In Rome, lemures were the spirits of the dead rather than devils. The lost souls stranded on the banks of the Styx (see page 139) are sometimes called lemures. They have the same alignment as they had during life, and lack the damage reduction of lemures described in the *MM*.

GIANT ANT

According to Pliny the Elder (23–79 AD), in the Dardae region of India there are tawny ants the size of wolves that dig gold out of the earth and are fast enough to catch up with a robber on a camel if their gold has been stolen. These are identical to giant soldier ants, except that their hoard of gold counts as standard treasure; note that whatever its value, it consists entirely of gold nuggets.

HYENA

Pliny wrote that the hyena found in the southern reaches of the Empire can imitate the human voice, and sometimes lures shepherds to their doom by pretending to be a human in distress. It also has a weak gaze weapon that only works on animals: Any creature a hyena looks at three times is paralyzed.

Paralyzing Gaze (Su): Effective only against animals. DC 12 Fortitude save. The first and second uses in a day have no effect even if the save is failed; the third use causes paralysis. The save DC is Charisma-based.

These hyenas are CR 2.

SNAKE, AMPHISBAENA

Along with normal snake types, the Roman world included the amphisbaena, with a head at each end of its body, giving it two bite attacks. It is otherwise identical to a small or medium viper.

- NEW MONSTERS -

There are some monsters in the *Eternal Rome* setting that are wholly new or completely different from the standard version. These are presented in the following pages.

BONASUS

This is a bull-like creature found in Paeonia (modern Bulgaria and Romania). Its horns curve inwards and are useless for fighting, so it has developed a highly unusual defensive strategy. It turns its back on its enemies and expels a great stream of liquid dung that burns everything it touches.

The bonasus has the same statistics as a bison in the *MM* but without the gore attack. It is CR 3.

Corrosive Dung (Ex): The bonasus can squirt liquid dung in a ray up to 80 ft. Damage 6d4 acid, DC 21 Reflex save halves.

CATOBLEPAS

This bull-like creature lives near a spring in Ethiopia, and spends its life with its head down, munching aquatic plants. Its head is large and very heavy, and it cannot lift its head by itself. This is a good thing, because its eyes instantly kill anyone who looks into them. Because the plants upon which it feeds are poisonous, the catoblepas also has foul and dangerous breath.

The catoblepas has the same statistics as a bison, but no gore attack. It is CR 4.

Deadly Gaze (Su): Death, 30 ft., DC 15 Fortitude save negates. The save DC is Charisma-based.

Poisonous Breath (Su): Cloud 10 ft. high, 10 ft. wide and 20 ft. long, poison contact DC 15, initial damage 1d6 hp, secondary damage 1d4 Con.

FURY

Medium Outsider (Extraplanar, Evil, Lawful)

Hit Dice: 17d8+102 (178 hp)
Initiative: +7
Speed: 30 ft. (6 squares), fly 60 ft. (average)
Armor Class: 30 (+3 Dex, +17 natural), touch 13, flat-footed 27
Base Attack/Grapple: +17/+25
Attack: +1 *flaming longsword* +26 melee (1d8+13 plus 1d6 fire)
Full Attack: +1 *flaming longsword* +26/+21/+16/+11 melee (1d8+13 plus 1d6 fire), 2 claws +20 melee (1d4+4)
Space/Reach: 5 ft./5 ft.
Special Attacks: Spell-like abilities
Special Qualities: Darkvision 60 ft., damage reduction 10/magic and chaos and good
Saves: Fort +21, Ref +15, Will +22
Abilities: Str 27, Dex 17, Con 23, Int 24, Wis 24, Cha 24
Skills: Balance +17, Climb +8 (+10 ropes), Concentration +20, Decipher Script +21, Diplomacy +11, Disable Device +21, Escape Artist +3 (+5 ropes), Hide +17, Intimidate +30, Knowledge (arcana) +21, Knowledge (geography) +21, Knowledge (history) +21, Knowledge (nobility and royalty) +21, Knowledge (religion) +21, Knowledge (the planes) +21, Listen +29, Move Silently +17, Search +21, Sense Motive +21, Spellcraft +23 (+25 decipher scrolls), Spot +29, Survival +21 (+23 avoid getting lost and hazards, on other planes, and when following tracks), Use Magic Device +21 (+25 scrolls), Use Rope +17
Feats: Flyby Attack, Hover, Improved Initiative, Skill Focus (Intimidate), Track, Wingover

Environment: Tartarus
Organization: Solitary or trio
Challenge Rating: 17
Treasure: Standard
Alignment: Always lawful evil
Advancement: —
Level Adjustment: —

This creature has a bird's lower body and a woman's upper body, but it exudes an aura of power that indicates that it is more than just a harpy. You see great intelligence in its eyes, but no mercy.

A fury is very similar in appearance to a harpy, but is much more powerful. The furies were servants of the gods, sent to punish those who had displeased them. In classical myth, there were three of them, Tisiphone, Allecto, and Megaera; in *Eternal Rome*, there could well be more.

COMBAT

Furies enjoy tormenting their victims, and prefer to use their magical abilities instead of entering combat directly. A typical punishment by the furies might consist of the victim being barraged with fear spells and pursued to the point of exhaustion, or until he unthinkingly runs off a cliff. Other victims are tormented until they are hopelessly insane.

If the need arises, the furies are formidable fighters. When dispatched to bring a damned soul down to Tartarus, for example, they carry out their task with ruthless efficiency.

For the purpose of overcoming damage reduction, a fury's natural attacks and attacks made with weapons count as magical, lawful, and evil.

Spell-Like Abilities: At will—*cause fear* (DC 18), *daze* (DC 17), *daze monster* (DC 19), *hypnotism* (DC 18), *scare* (DC 19); 3/day: *bestow curse* (DC 21), *confusion* (DC 21), *crushing despair* (DC 21), *contagion* (DC 21), *enervation* (DC 21), *fear* (DC 21); 1/day—*binding* (DC 25), *eyebite* (DC 23), *feeblemind* (DC 22), *insanity* (DC 23), *soul bind* (DC 26). Caster level 17th. The save DCs are Charisma-based.

True Seeing (Su): Furies have continuous *true seeing* ability as per the spell cast by a 17th-level spellcaster.

Skills: Furies have a +8 racial bonus to Listen and Spot checks.

HERCYNIA

This bird lives in the Hercynian Forest in Germany. It is a perfectly ordinary songbird, except for the fact that its feathers glow brightly, each casting an amount of light equal to a candle. The hercynia has the same statistics as a hawk, except that it does not have a talon attack. Hercynia feathers continue to glow after the bird has been killed, as if they were affected by a *continual flame* spell. Alchemists will pay up to 1 gp per feather.

HIPPOCAMPUS

Large Magical Beast

Hit Dice: 2d10+10 (21 hp)
Initiative: +2
Speed: 5 ft. (1 square), swim 80 ft.
Armor Class: 16 (−1 size, +3 Dex, +4 natural), touch 12, flat-footed 13
Base Attack/Grapple: +2/+10
Attack: Bite +2 melee (1d4+4)
Full Attack: Bite +2 melee (1d4+4), plus tail slap +2 melee (1d8+4)
Space/Reach: 10 ft./5 ft.
Special Attacks: —
Special Qualities: Darkvision 60 ft.
Saves: Fort +8, Ref +3, Will +1
Abilities: Str 18, Dex 16, Con 20, Int 3, Wis 13, Cha 8
Skills: Listen +4, Spot +3, Swim +8
Feats: Run

Environment: Temperate and warm seas
Organization: Domesticated or herd (6-30)
Challenge Rating: 2
Treasure: None
Alignment: Always neutral
Advancement: —
Level Adjustment: —

This creature's front half looks very much like a horse, but instead of back legs, it has a long, fish-like tail. Its mane is a webbed membrane like the dorsal fin of a fish, and its front legs end in fins instead of hooves. Its fur and scales are white, with a blue-green sheen.

Hippocampi are domesticated and used as mounts by merfolk and tritons. Neptune himself has a chariot shaped like a great sea-shell, and drawn by a team of four magnificent hippocampi. In the wild, they swim in herds just like terrestrial horses, and their temperament is very similar.

COMBAT

Skills: A hippocampus has a +8 racial bonus on any Swim check to perform some special action or avoid a hazard. It can always choose to take 10 on a Swim check, even if distracted or endangered. It can use the run action while swimming, provided it swims in a straight line.

Carrying Capacity: A light load for a hippocampus is up to 230 pounds; a medium load, 231-460 pounds, a heavy load, 461-690 pounds. A hippocampus can drag 3,450 pounds. Loads that float are treated as half their actual weight.

LEUCROTTA

The leucrotta is the size of a donkey, and has the neck, tail,

and chest of a lion, the haunches of a stag, cloven hooves, a badger's head, and a mouth that opens from ear to ear, with ridges of bone instead of teeth. It is the swiftest of wild animals, and is able to imitate the human voice to lure unsuspecting humans into traps.

The leucrotta has the same statistics as a donkey, except that its move is 60 feet and it has a bite attack is +7 melee that deals 1d8 points of damage. It is CR 1.

SIREN

Medium Monstrous Humanoid (Aquatic, Shapeshifter)

Hit Dice: 3d8+3 (16 hp)
Initiative: +1
Speed: 30 ft. (6 squares), swim 50 ft.
Armor Class: 11 (+1 Dex), touch 11, flat-footed 10
Base Attack/Grapple: +3/+4
Attack: Dagger +4 melee (1d4+1)
Full Attack: Dagger +4 melee (1d4+1)
Space/Reach: 5 ft./5 ft.
Special Attacks: Paralyzing beauty, song of longing, spell-like abilities
Special Qualities: Alter self, darkvision 60 ft.
Saves: Fort +2, Ref +4, Will +7
Abilities: Str 12, Dex 13, Con 12, Int 13, Wis 14, Cha 18
Skills: Bluff +11, Diplomacy +6, Disguise +10 (+12 acting)*, Intimidate +6, Listen +7, Perform +7, Sense Motive +6,

Spot +7

Feats: Alertness, Iron Will

Environment: Any temperate aquatic
Organization: Solitary, pair, or gang (3–6)
Challenge Rating: 4
Treasure: Standard
Alignment: Usually neutral
Advancement: By character class
Level Adjustment: —

When you first glanced at the rocks, you thought you saw a woman with a fish's tail, but after a second look it's obvious you were mistaken: She's all woman—and a looker at that.

Sirens are cousins to the merfolk, with the same outlook on life. They are quite varied in appearance, but always fair, having the form of beautiful humanoid women from the waist up. From the waist down, they sometimes appear human, and other times have the tails and fins of great fish.

They live in colonies on rocky islands, whiling away their days tending each other's hair or sunning on the rocks. They decorate themselves with shells and coral, and jewelry from ships that are wrecked on their coasts.

There are no male sirens; although sirens can make with merfolk, they prefer human partners, mostly out of fear that interbreeding too frequently with other fish-folk will remove whatever humanity they have and cause their daughters to be born wholly fish. They use their beauty and song to lure men to them, slipping into the water to help those they find pleasing to shore, leaving the less comely to drown. Women are ignored unless they pose a threat to the siren or her chosen "husband." Even if men survive to reach the arms of the sirens, they may not survive for long; many are driven mad by constant exposure to the sirens' beauty, or die from lack of water and shelter, or from the constant attentions of their new "wives."

Combat

Sirens strike first with their song. The only physical weapons they carry are daggers, and if engaged in battle on land they try to avoid combat until their can trick their opponents into the sea, where several sisters can attack at once, pulling the victim under the waves to drown.

Paralyzing Beauty (Su): This ability operates continuously, affecting all male humanoids within 60 feet. Those who gaze directly at the siren must succeed on a DC 15 Fort save or become paralyzed with desire for 1d4 rounds. The siren can suppress and resume this ability as a free action. The save DC is Charisma-based.

Song of Longing (Su): Every man within a 300-foot radius who hears this song must succeed on a DC 15 Will save every two rounds of singing or make every attempt to reach the siren, either individually or even steering entire ships onto the rocks. Every woman within a 300-foot radius who hears this song must succeed on a DC 15 Will save in the first round or become incapacitated by helpless weeping until the song ends. The save DC is Charisma-based.

Spell-like Abilities: 1/day—*wail of the banshee* (DC 23). Caster level 18th. The save DC is Charisma-based.

Alter Self (Su): A siren can assume human or merfolk form at will. This works like the *alter self* spell as cast by an 18th-level sorcerer, but the siren can remain in the form indefinitely. It can assume a new form as a standard action. Individual sirens can live to be hundreds of years old, and when a siren enters her third century she slowly begins to lose the ability to maintain human features, becoming more and more fish-like until finally she slips away to live permanently below the waves.

Skills: Sirens gain a +4 racial bonus to Bluff and Disguise checks. *When using *alter self*, a siren receives an additional +10 circumstance bonus to Disguise checks.

Stymphalian Bird

Small Magical Beast

Hit Dice: 1d10+1 (6 hp)
Initiative: +3
Speed: 20 ft. (4 squares), fly 60 ft. (average)
Armor Class: 18 (+1 Size, +3 Dex, +4 natural), touch 14, flat-footed 15
Base Attack/Grapple: +1/–3
Attack: Beak +1 melee (1d6)
Full Attack: Beak +1 melee (1d6)
Space/Reach: 5 ft./5 ft.
Special Attacks: —
Special Qualities: Darkvision 60 ft.
Saves: Fort +3, Ref +3, Will +1
Abilities: Str 10, Dex 17, Con 13, Int 3, Wis 12, Cha 4

Skills: Spot +4
Feats: Flyby Attack

Environment: Temperate marshes and lakes
Organization: Flock (6-25)
Challenge Rating: 1
Treasure: Standard
Alignment: Usually neutral evil
Advancement: Medium (2-3 HD)
Level Adjustment: —

This bird is about the same size and shape as a stork or heron, but its feathers and sharp beak are made of shining bronze.

Stymphalian birds get their name from a flock that lived by Lake Stymphalus in Greece before being destroyed by Hercules as one of his famous 12 Labors. They are found in marshes and by lakes in remote areas. Stymphalian birds stand about 3 feet tall, and weigh around 20 pounds.

Combat

Man-eating Stymphalian birds attack as a flock, overwhelming enemies with repeated fly-by attacks.

Swarm, Scorpion

Diminutive Vermin (Swarm)

Hit Dice: 7d8+7 (38 hp)
Initiative: +2
Speed: 20 ft. (4 squares), climb 20 ft.
Armor Class: 18 (+4 size, +2 Dex, +2 natural), touch 16, flat-footed 16
Base Attack/Grapple: +5/—
Attack: Swarm (2d6 plus poison)
Full Attack: Swarm (2d6 plus poison)
Space/Reach: 10 ft./0 ft.
Special Attacks: Distraction, poison
Special Qualities: Darkvision 60 ft., immune to weapon damage, swarm traits, tremorsense 30 ft., vermin traits
Saves: Fort +6, Ref +4, Will +3
Abilities: Str 1, Dex 14, Con 12, Int —, Wis 13, Cha 11
Skills: Climb +10, Survival +5
Feats: Track B

them forward or back, fighting with each horn alternately.

The yale has the same statistics as a bison. It deals 1d10+9 points of damage with its gore attack.

- Legendary Races -

Several legendary races are features of Roman folklore, and it;s quite possible that heroes might encounter them in the course of their adventures.

Arimaspi

The Arimaspi are a race of one-eyed humans living on the northern steppes of Scythia, bordering on the lands of the Hyperboreans. Little is recorded about them, except for the fact that in their lands is an immense hoard of gold, guarded by fierce griffons. The Arimaspi fight perpetually with the griffons, but are never able to take the gold, much to their frustration.

The single eye of an Arimaspi limits depth perception and

Environment: Desert, underground, or warm hills
Organization: Solitary, mass (2-4 swarms), or swathe (7-12 swarms)
Challenge Rating: 4
Treasure: None
Alignment: Always neutral
Advancement: None
Level Adjustment: —

A moving carpet of scorpions covers everything in front of you.

A scorpion swarm is a crawling mass of tiny scorpions that can climb over obstacles to get at prey. They are rare in nature, but may be summoned by certain spellcasters or in response to divine action. They have been the death of more than one treasure-seeker who attempted to violate the ancient tombs of the pharaohs in Egypt.

Combat

A scorpion swarm seeks to surround and attack any living being it encounters.

Distraction (Ex): Any living creature that begins its turn in the same space as a scorpion swarm must succeed on a DC 14 Fortitude save or be nauseated for 1 round. The save DC is Constitution-based.

Poison (Ex): Injury, DC 16 Fortitude save, initial and secondary damage 1 Con. Some species of scorpion have more powerful venom, ranging up to 1d4 Con. The power of the venom does not necessarily correspond to the size of the creatures. The save DC is Constitution-based and includes a +2 racial bonus.

Skills: A scorpion swarm has a +8 racial bonus on Climb checks, and uses its Dexterity modifier instead of its Strength modifier for Climb checks. A scorpion swarm can always choose to take 10 on a Climb check, even if rushed or threatened.

Yale

Found in Ethiopia, the yale is something like a bull, with a black or tawny body and a short tail like that of an elephant. It head looks like the head of a boar, but lacks tusks. The yale's horns are long and straight, and it has the ability to swivel

gives him a –2 penalty to all ranged attacks, although they otherwise function as humans.

Centaurs

In classical lore, centaurs lived in and around the wooded hills of Thessaly in northern Greece. By Roman times, they have been almost wiped out in wars with the Greeks, but a few isolated communities could still exist. They tend to be chaotic good or chaotic neutral rather than neutral good. The most famous centaur was Chiron, known for his skill at archery, music, and medicine, and as a tutor to the Greek hero Achilles.

Cyclopes

The cyclopes (singular: cyclops) are a race of a one-eyed

giants, mentioned in Homer's *Odyssey*. They live on a desolate island somewhere in the central or western Mediterranean. Some think the island is Sicily, but by Roman times there is no mention of them on the island. They may be encountered in the more remote parts of Sicily, or on other desolate islands in the western half of the Mediterranean Sea. They are identical to stone giants, except that their single eye limits depth perception and gives them a –2 penalty to all ranged attacks.

HYPERBOREANS

The name "Hyperboreans" translates as "the people beyond the north wind." Worshipers of Apollo, they live in a land of perpetual sunshine and plenty. The Greek historian Herodotus places them in southern Russia near the Arimaspi. Hyperboreans are humans.

LAESTRYGONIANS

A race of man-eating giants living on an island somewhere in the western Mediterranean, thought by some to be Corsica. Use statistics for hill giants.

NEREIDS

The nereids are all daughters of Nereus, an ancient sea god. Neptune married a nereid named Amphitrite, and became the god of the sea. Classical sources disagree over how many nereids there were; some say 50 and some 100. Nereids can be treated as nymphs, except that their preferred environment is temperate and warm seas.

- NON-HUMAN RACES -

While the *Eternal Rome* setting is designed on the assumption that human are the only race available for player characters, a GM wanting a campaign with a much more fantastic flavor can introduce some of the standard d20 non-human races for PC use, modified to fit the Roman world.

DWARVES AND GNOMES

Dwarves in the folklore of the people surrounding Rome usually look very much like shorter, stockier versions of local humans. One common theme is a hat or hood of a certain color that is a prized possession of every dwarf and that he will do anything to recover if it is lost or stolen. In some traditions, the hat is a spell focus, and the dwarf is magically powerless without it. Dwarfs can have a range of magical powers, the most common being the ability to become invisible at will.

Dwarves sometimes help travelers lost in bad weather in mountainous terrain, but seldom speak and generally have a grumpy demeanor. They guard their mines zealously, and humans who trespass usually receive a fatal punishment, usually as a result of mysterious rockslides and cave-ins instead of direct combat. Sometimes regular offerings of food can induce them to let humans work close to their mines.

In such cases, the sound of dwarven hammers and picks can lead human miners to rich deposits of ore and gems. They also throw pebbles and give other warnings of impending cave-ins.

Dwarves can come from any of the mountainous areas of the Empire. They are identical to those in the *PHB*, except that their racial bonus to saves against spells is replaced by the ability to cast *invisibility* (self only) once per day (caster level equal to the dwarf's character level).

In European folklore, there is no distinction made between dwarves and gnomes; treat gnomes as Small dwarves.

ELVES

Elves are part of a northwestern European tradition, and may be encountered in Gaul, Germania, Britain, and lands beyond the northern and western frontiers of the Empire. In Italy and Greece, however, nymphs and satyrs are more common (see below).

HALFLINGS

There are similarities between the Roman conception of the Picts (see page 13) and halflings as presented in the *PHB*. At the GM's option, Picts may be treated as halflings rather than humans.

HALF-ORCS

Half-orcs (as described in the *PHB*) in an *Eternal Rome* campaign can be from any of the wilder parts of the Empire, or from the barbarian lands beyond the frontiers. The orchi of folklore are renowned for smelling foul, and this trait may be passed on to their half-breed offspring.

NYMPHS AND SATYRS

In Classical myth and legend, nymphs and satyrs filled the same role occupied by elves in northwestern Europe: wild spirits of the woods. Nymphs are always female and satyrs are always male; they interbreed freely, and are treated as a single race with extreme sexual dimorphism. They are also fond of dalliances with good-looking humans, and more than one Roman family numbered nymphs among its ancestors.

NYMPHS

Nymph characters possess the following racial traits.

- Female only.
- +6 Dexterity, +2 Constitution, +6 Intelligence, +6 Wisdom, +8 Charisma.
- Medium size.
- A nymph's base land speed is 30 ft.
- Low-light vision.
- **Racial Hit Dice:** A nymph begins with 6 levels of fey, which provide 6d6 hit dice, a base attack bonus of +3, and base saving throw bonuses of Fort +1, Ref +4, and Will +4.
- **Racial Skills:** A nymph's fey levels give her skill points equal to 6 × (6 + Int modifier). The nymph's class skills are Bluff, Handle Animal, Hide, Knowledge (nature), Listen, Move Silently, Perform, and Spot. Nymphs have a +4 racial bonus on Bluff, Handle Animal, Hide, Knowledge (nature), Listen, Move Silently, Perform, and Spot checks.
- **Racial Feats:** A nymph's fey levels give her three feats. Combat Casting, Dodge, and Weapon Finesse are standard although the player may substitute others with the GM's agreement.
- **Special Attacks:** Blinding beauty, spells, spell-like abilities, stunning glance. See *MM* for details.
- **Special Qualities:** Damage reduction 10/cold iron, unearthly grace, wild empathy.
- **Automatic Languages:** Sylvan, Greek. Bonus Languages: Aquan, Celtic, Latin.
- **Favored Class:** Druid.
- **Level Adjustment:** +7.

SATYRS

Satyr characters possess the following racial traits.

- Male only.
- +2 Dexterity, +2 Constitution, +2 Intelligence, +2 Wisdom, +2 Charisma.
- Medium size.
- A satyr's base land speed is 40 ft.
- Low-light vision.
- **Racial Hit Dice:** A satyr begins with five levels of fey, which provide 5d8 Hit Dice, a base attack bonus of +2, and base saving throw bonuses of Fort +1, Ref +4, and Will +4.
- **Racial Skills:** A satyr's fey levels give it skill points equal to 8 × (6 + Int modifier). Its class skills are Bluff, Hide, Knowledge (nature), Listen, Move Silently, Perform, and Spot. Satyrs have a +4 racial bonus on Hide, Listen, Move Silently, Perform, and Spot checks.
- **Racial Feats:** A satyr's fey levels give it two feats. A satyr receives Alertness as a bonus feat.
- +4 natural armor bonus.
- **Natural Weapons:** Head butt (1d6).
- **Special Attacks (see above):** Pipes. See *MM* for details.
- **Special Qualities (see above):** Damage reduction 5/cold iron.
- **Automatic Languages:** Sylvan. Bonus Languages: Greek, Latin.
- **Favored Class:** Orphic bard.
- **Level Adjustment:** +2.

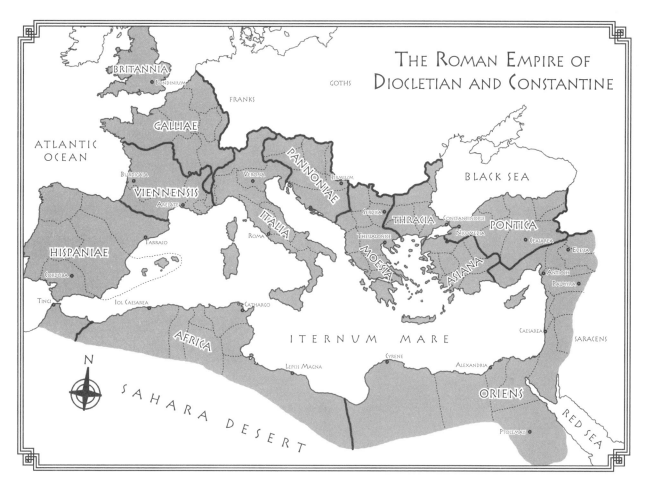

The Roman Empire of Diocletian and Constantine

CHAPTER EIGHT: THE EMPIRE

The Roman Empire reached its greatest extent during the reign of Trajan (see page 116). His successor, Hadrian, reorganized the frontiers, letting go of some land in the interests of defensibility. For most of the next 300 years, the borders of the Empire were constant. This chapter gives brief descriptions of the provinces that Hadrian and his successors ruled; GMs intending to run a campaign set before 100 AD or after about 400 AD should refer to **Chapter Nine** for information on the extent of the Empire in those times.

ITALY

Rome's first steps towards greatness involved throwing off Etruscan rule, and then expanding its own rulership over the rest of Italy. Campaigns set in the period of the Kingdom and the early Republic focus on action in Italy, with the PCs as farmer-warriors of Rome or a neighboring people.

For most of Roman history, Italy was a tranquil province, providing taxes, materials, and manpower vital to Roman expansion. But when the situation changed, the changes were dramatic. In 309 BC, a large force of Gauls crossed the Alps, devastating Italy and even sacking Rome, which was forced to pay a heavy tribute before the Gauls withdrew.

In 218 BC, the Carthaginian general Hannibal made his famous crossing of the Alps with elephants and all and rampaged around Italy for 15 years, coming right up to the walls of Rome on one occasion, and throwing a spear inside the city, although he did not mount an actual attack. Many Italian cities deserted Rome and either accepted Hannibal's rule or struck out for independence, and when the war was over these communities paid a high price for their lack of loyalty.

In 73 BC, a revolt headed by the Thracian gladiator Spartacus led to a powerful army of escaped gladiators and runaway slaves moving through Italy, plundering towns and driving off the forces sent against them for two years, until they were finally defeated by a Roman army under Crassus in 71 BC.

The final battles of the Roman Empire in the west were fought against invading Visigoths, over 500 years later.

ADVENTURES IN ITALY

Any of the more dramatic periods in Italy's history could form a good backdrop for adventure. In more peaceful times, Italy was largely rural, and people with ambition (including would-be adventurers) went to Rome to seek their fortunes. The turbulent politics of the late Republic and the Imperial court offer great opportunities for intrigues, while those seeking action and adventure gravitate toward the frontier provinces or seek a career in the arena.

Sicily, Corsica, and Sardinia

As Rome was expanding its influence beyond Italy, these three islands featured an assortment of native farming communities dotted with Greek and Carthaginian trading colonies. By the end of the Punic Wars in the 2nd century BC, all three islands were in Roman hands, and remained so until the final collapse of the Empire in the West.

Adventures in the Western Mediterranean

There's good money to be made transporting grain from North Africa to Italy throughout Roman history, and early on hazards like pirates add to the challenges. In a fantasy version of the *Eternal Rome* setting, sea monsters and other fantastic problem would also have to be overcome. Many of the hazards encountered by the Greek hero Odysseus in the *Odyssey* (such as the island lairs of the sirens and the enchantress Circe) were in the western half of the Mediterranean, offering many opportunities for monster hunts and similar adventures to early Romans.

Spain

The Mediterranean coast of Spain was controlled by Carthage at the start of the Punic Wars, with a chain of ports running all the way to the south of France. While Hannibal was campaigning in Italy, Roman general Scipio attacked the Carthaginian possessions in Spain before crossing to North Africa, forcing Hannibal to leave Italy and return to defend his homeland. After the Punic Wars, the Roman conquest of Spain moved northward and westward, until the whole peninsula was in Roman hands. Spain became a staunchly Roman territory; as thoroughly Romanized as Italy itself.

For administrative purposes, Spain was divided into three provinces: Tarraconensis in the north and east, Baetica in the south, and Lusitania extending from the center to what is now Portugal.

Adventures in Spain

Spain was vital to the Carthaginian supply lines during the Punic Wars, and was an ideal location for commando-style raids against Carthaginian ports. In the conquest that followed the Punic Wars, adventure opportunities existed on both sides.

Some of the fiercest fighting took place in northwestern Spain against the Celtiberians, an ethnically Celtic people with distinctive weapons and equipment, including a machete-like slashing sword called the falcata (the equivalent of a scimitar).

- North Africa -

The Roman Empire controlled the coast of North Africa as far south as the start of the Sahara Desert. Most of Africa was taken from the Carthaginians during the Punic Wars (see page 104). In Roman times, North Africa was a major source of grain for the Empire; later climate shifts and the northward spread of the desert have made it less fertile today.

Mauretania

In Trajan's time, Mauretania (present-day Morocco and Algeria, north of the Sahara) was divided into two provinces: Mauretania Tingitana in the west and Mauretania Caesariensis in the east. The main city in Mauretania Tingitana was Tingis (modern Tangiers), and the capital of Mauretania Caesariensis was Caesarea, one of several cities of that name throughout the Empire.

Adventures in Mauretania

During the Punic Wars, Mauretania was a strategically important province because it offered the shortest passage between Africa and Europe, across the Pillars of Hercules (now called the Straits of Gibraltar) to Spain. Action-oriented adventures could include commando-style raids to neutralize strategic forts and other installations; if

Rome had seized control of the straits in time, Hannibal would have been stuck in Africa and never got the chance to march his elephants across the Alps. The Carthaginian navy was more powerful than the Roman fleet early in the Punic Wars, so raids against naval ports, aimed at destroying ships or stealing plans for the latest type of trireme, would also be potentially history-changing.

The Roman Empire began with Emperor Augustus's conquest of Egypt and the death of Cleopatra VII. But Cleopatra's daughter, Cleopatra Selene, was queen of Mauretania at the time. Could the nascent Empire have survived if Cleopatra Selene's son Ptolemy had sailed at the head of a mercenary fleet to seat himself on the throne of his grandfather? Would the people of Egypt have rallied to the cause of Pharaoh Ptolemy XVI? Historically, Emperor Caligula had Ptolemy assassinated, to prevent those questions from being answered.

In all time periods, Mauretania's position on the northwest tip of Africa made it an ideal jumping-off point for expeditions down the west African coast, and an important link in the supply chain of exotic African beasts for the arena. All kinds of fantastic creatures lived in the jungles of sub-Saharan Africa, but bringing them back alive would be a challenge.

- AFRICA -

The Roman province of Africa occupied an area corresponding roughly to modern-day Tunisia and the western two-thirds of Libya. The site of Carthage is just outside modern-day Tunis; destroyed by the Romans at the end of the Punic Wars, Carthage was later rebuilt as a Roman colony.

ADVENTURES IN AFRICA

Following the Punic Wars, Carthage was razed to the ground, the site was ritually cursed, and it even had salt plowed into the ground in hopes that nothing would ever grow there again. A few years later, Rome decided to build a new colony on the same site. Trouble with undead was almost sure to follow, as the spirits of the defeated Carthaginians found a new supply of Romans close at hand; or perhaps a crazed survivor of the wars who studied necromancy in Egypt could rebuild Carthage in all its glory—even if the citizens are all undead.

- CYRENAICA -

The province of Cyrenaica corresponded roughly to the eastern third of modern Libya and the western third of Egypt. It was one of the more fertile African provinces, and its capital was at Cyrene, north of modern Benghazi. It was originally ruled by Egypt, and entered the Roman Empire with the death of Cleopatra.

ADVENTURES IN CYRENAICA

During the Punic Wars, Cyrenaica was a border area between the independent Egyptian and Carthaginian Empires. If Rome could gain a foothold in neutral Cyrenaica, it would be able to put pressure on the Carthaginians from two directions. Roman spies and diplomats could converge on Cyrene, with instructions to find out what the Egyptian governor is thinking, and, if necessary, organize a revolt.

EGYPT

Egypt had several thousand years of history before Rome arrived on the scene, and was once the greatest power in the eastern Mediterranean. Conquered by Alexander the Great, Egypt became a Greek kingdom, ruled by the dynasty of the Ptolemies from their new capital of Alexandria. Roman Egypt occupied approximately the eastern two-thirds of the modern country, along with parts of northern Sudan. In Trajan's time, it was a major grain-producing province and, with the rebuilding of a canal from the Nile to the Red Sea, the gateway to Arabia and India.

ADVENTURES IN EGYPT

During the Punic Wars, Egypt was a strategic neighbor of Carthage, and the outcome of the war (and the future history of the Mediterranean) could depend on whether or not Egypt could be drawn into the war on one side or another. The PCs might find themselves disguised as Carthaginians, and mounting attacks on Egyptian shipping and ports intended to provoke Egypt into entering the war on Rome's side.

Conquered by Greeks, and then by Romans, Egypt was reduced from a great power to a provider of grain and a historical theme park for wealthy Greek and Roman tourists. A proud Egyptian (perhaps an ancient lich or mummy lord who remembers first-hand the glory of the old days) might raise an army of mummies and other creatures and try to kick the foreigners out.

On a smaller scale, one of Egypt's many claims to fame was the Library of Alexandria, the greatest collection of learning in the ancient world. Who knows what tomes of lost power and forbidden lore may be found on its shelves? The keepers of the library took extensive security measures (both magical and mundane) to prevent thefts, but that just makes the task of finding a lost manuscript there more challenging. Or if a tome of forbidden lore fell into the wrong hands, a group of heroes could be hired to somehow prevent the earth-shattering spells in the book from being voiced and return the tome to the library.

Nearby Judea was the center of many revolts against the Romans, culminating in the razing of Herod's Temple by Roman forces. At the height of one of these revolts, a separatist Jewish mage might travel to Egypt to revisit the biblical plagues on Rome's largest provider of grain. Locusts alone could weaken Rome's economy and the supply lines of the Roman forces in Judea quite severely, but what effect might all 12 plagues have?

- THE MIDDLE EAST -

At its greatest extent, the height of its powers, the Roman Empire controlled the eastern coast of the Mediterranean inland to the start of the Arabian Desert, as well as Assyria and Mesopotamia down to the Persian Gulf. This did not last forever, but it represented the the peak of the Roman conquest of the world.

ARABIA

The Roman province of Arabia corresponds roughly to the western part of present-day Jordan and the Sinai Peninsula. Its greatest wonder was the city of Petra, cut out of solid rock. The Sinai was known from biblical times for its copper,

and the addition of some land on the east bank of the Jordan River. Its largest city was Jerusalem (renamed Aelia Capitolina after the suppression of the revolt of 134 AD).

ADVENTURES IN JUDEA

Before the destruction of the Temple in 70 AD, Judea was a turbulent province, with various political factions within the Jewish population taking different approaches to Roman rule and rebellions breaking out from time to time. The PCs could very easily be caught up in one of these rebellions, either taking an active role on one side or the other, or simply trying to survive. Many Jews were waiting for a warlike messiah who would deliver them from Roman rule. If a messiah arose with divine powers to sweep the Romans from the Holy Land, the Roman administration would face a revolt like no other.

For a few years around 30 AD, religious movements led by John the Baptist, Jesus of Nazareth, and others infuriated the Jewish establishment and the Roman administration. Having the PCs caught up in the events of the New Testament could make for a memorable and challenging roleplaying campaign, although the GM must take great care not to offend the religious sensibilities of the players.

Just as recovering the lost eagles of the XVII, XVIII, and XIX Legions in the German forests is a possible PC quest during the reigns from Augustus to Claudius (see page 113), the eagle of the XII Legion was taken by the Jewish rebels in 66 AD, but it had been regained by 136 AD. History doesn't record how the eagle was recovered—an opportunity perfect for PC intervention.

SYRIA

The Roman province of Syria corresponds roughly to Lebanon and the modern country of Syria, extending northward into the mountains of eastern Turkey. The south of Syria was the homeland of the Phoenicians, based around the port cities of Tyre and Sidon, cities that achieved a near-monopoly on sea trade in the eastern Mediterranean early in the Roman period. The greatest city in the northern part of Syria was the port of Antioch (called Antioch in Syria in the New Testament, to distinguish it from the nearby city of Antioch in Pisidia).

ADVENTURES IN SYRIA

Carthage started out as a Phoenician colony in the western Mediterranean, but quickly eclipsed its homeland. The Phoenicians played no active part in the Punic Wars, because Carthage was too far away and too independent for them to care about. However, if they had thought otherwise, they might have been able to establish a Mediterranean empire to rival Rome. With the wealth they'd gained from trade, the Phoenicians could have hired large numbers of mercenaries from Greece, Egypt, and elsewhere in the eastern Mediterranean, and either sent them to aid Carthage directly or mounted an attack through Greece and Illyricum that would force Rome to fight a war on two fronts. The PCs could be involved on either side, mounting raids on key

turquoise, and other mineral wealth, and during periods when the provinces of Mesopotamia and Assyria were out of Roman hands, and Trajan's canal to the Red Sea was inoperable, the most direct route for gems and luxury goods from India to reach the Roman Empire was by caravan across the Arabian Desert.

ADVENTURES IN ARABIA

Petra makes an interesting site for an adventure, since it's essentially a city that takes the form of a dungeon. Who knows what secret passages link some of the buildings, and what unspeakable rites were conducted in hidden, rock-hewn temples to ancient Eastern gods?

The Arabian desert held secrets of its own. It was here, for example, that the legendary phoenix was said to fly into the hottest part of the desert to die in a flaming pyre and be reborn from the ashes. Many wealthy Romans, the Emperor included, would pay a fortune for a live phoenix. A wizard or alchemist might be able to study a phoenix and discover the secret of immortality.

JUDEA

During the late Republic, Judea had managed to wrest independence from the Seleucid Empire, but after only a century Pompey the Great conquered the nation for Rome. It was to be ruled by client kings (beginning with Herod the Great) for another century before the last king of Judea was replaced by a Roman governor.

The province of Judea corresponds roughly to modern Israel and Palestine, with the exception of the Negev Desert fortresses, rescuing prisoners, escorting shipments of gold to pay mercenaries, or taking various other roles.

The gods of the Phoenicians were reviled as demons by their Jewish neighbors, inspiring accusations of child sacrifice and ritual sex, among other atrocities. High-level PCs might be Roman or Jewish demon-hunters, members of a secret and esoteric order, sent to confront the demons and wipe their followers from the face of the Earth.

Mesopotamia

The Roman province of Mesopotamia correspond roughly to modern Iraq and western Iran. In pre-Roman times, this area was the homeland of the Persian Empire, but it had been conquered by Alexander the Great and overlaid with a veneer of Greek culture by the time Roman rule extended to it. Mesopotamia was short-lived as a Roman province, largely because it was difficult to defend from raiding Parthians; it was added to the Empire by Trajan in 114 AD, and quickly abandoned by his successor Hadrian by 120 AD. It was retaken by Septimius Severus in 197 AD, and then fought over for the next two centuries, changing hands multiple times.

Adventures in Mesopotamia

The Parthian Empire was a constant threat on the Roman Empire's eastern frontier, and a number of inconclusive wars were fought against these renowned horse-warriors. The PCs could be involved as scouts or spies, or in a number of other capacities.

One of the most important benefits of ruling Mesopotamia is that it gave access to the Persian Gulf, and tha meant access to the riches of India and the other lands further east. The PCs could find themselves sent to India in search of fabled treasures, or to find the lost cities founded by Alexander the Great. India is also a source of tigers and elephants for the arena, and Indian elephants are much easier to train for war and other purposes than their African relatives; animal-hunters could easily make a fortune there.

Within Mesopotamia lie the remains of more than one lost empire, whose treasures and secrets are simply waiting to be discovered. Lost cities in the desert, legendary creatures like the lammasu, and powerful, immortal Babylonian magi may await western heroes here.

- Asia Minor -

The region of Asia Minor corresponds roughly to modern Turkey and Armenia. In Roman times, it was divided into a number of provinces, and it was also divided culturally. The western part was a conglomeration of Greek-speaking states descended from Greek trading colonies, while the east and the mountains of the interior were home to fiercely independent tribes.

Asia

The province of Asia consisted of a coastal fringe, extending from the southern shores of the Sea of Marmara to the southwestern edge of the Turkish peninsula, along with the mountains that lay behind. Lying on the sea-route between Greece and the Middle East, it derived most of its wealth from trade, although the hills and mountains of the interior had some mineral wealth. Its largest city was Ephesus, which was a cosmopolitan port city and home to many different nationalities. The temple of Diana at Ephesus was famous throughout the world. A contemporary account of the city can be found in the Acts of the Apostles.

Adventures in Asia

Ephesus is the kind of large, polyglot trading city that is a standard in many roleplaying campaigns, and adventures can spring off from there in all directions. The PCs might head into the mountainous interior in search of wild beasts for the arena, or looking for fabled lost cities and legendary monsters.

In the northwestern part of Asia are the ruins of the fabled city of Troy, whose location was lost in antiquity and would not be recovered until the 19th century AD. An expedition to find the city and recover the famous Trojan Horse (or

other treasures, such as artifacts related to Aeneas, one of Rome's legendary founders) could run into hazards ranging from hostile ghosts to powerful demons, drawn to the ruined city because of the resonating aura of violence from the ancient war.

CICILIA, PAMPHYLIA, AND LYCIA

These three provinces took up most of the southern coast of what is now Turkey. The area was notorious for its pirates, who operated unchecked until Pompey mounted a huge campaign against them in the late Republic period. For the rest of the Roman period, the area was fairly peaceful.

ADVENTURES IN CICILIA, PAMPHYLIA AND LYCIA

The campaign against the pirates in 66 AD offers plenty of possibilities for adventure, with the PCs playing either the pirates or their Roman pursuers. In history, neither side was able to call upon supernatural resources and allied aquatic creatures, but in an *Eternal Rome* campaign, these advantages might tip the balance one way or the other.

Where there are pirates, there is bound to be treasure. It might be in sunken ships, beyond the reach of land-dwellers without magical assistance. It might be buried in secret locations, hidden inlets along the coast and on remote islands. Or it might be secured in abandoned pirate fortresses that were never found by the Romans. Many enterprising souls may be out searching for pirate treasure, and a few even more enterprising individuals might be making a fortune supplying them with fake treasure maps either just for a quick profit, or in league with a gang of slavers who have an ambush prepared where X marks the spot.

CYPRUS

The island of Cyprus was culturally a part of Greek Asia, although it sat between Asia and the Middle East in the eastern Mediterranean. It had its share of pirate bases before they were wiped out by Pompey, and was a major link in the sea route from the Middle East to Greece and Rome.

ADVENTURES IN CYPRUS

Cyprus is a crossroads, were people headed in all directions cross paths. Political exiles one step ahead of arrest and execution, provincial governors headed east to take up appointments or west to continue a political career in Rome (or, as often happened, to stand trial for the way they extorted money from their provinces to fund a continuing political career), smugglers, and small-time crooks; all might be found rubbing shoulders in the ports of Paphos and Salamis.

GALATIA AND CAPPADOCIA

When Rome was still a simple kingdom and its greatness lay far in the future, a Celtic people from eastern Europe made their way south across the Greek world and settled in the mountains of central Anatolia. Galatia was named for these Gauls, and for many centuries, it existed as an island of Celtic culture among its Asian neighbors. To the east, the mountains continued into the province of Cappadocia.

ADVENTURES IN GALATIA AND CAPPADOCIA

Adventures in Galatia might include the search for fabled lost mines in the Anatolian mountains, or enforcing the *pax romana* ("the peace of Rome") between the Galatians and their neighbors. Bears and other beasts wanted for the arena were also to be found in the mountains.

In the late Republic, Caesar's campaigns in Gaul might prompt the Celts in Galatia to stir up trouble, to draw Roman forces eastward from their cousins in the west. This never happened in history, but it might in a roleplaying campaign.

In remote antiquity, the Hittites built some of the world's first cities in Anatolia. Who knows what ancient treasures and forgotten secrets may be lying among the ruins, waiting to be discovered? Who knows what primordial spirits and other hazards might be guarding them?

ARMENIA

The province of Armenia lay across the southern end of the Caucasus Mountains between the Black and Caspian Seas, in what is now Armenia, Azerbaijan, and northern Iran. It was at the western end of the so-called Silk Road, a series of caravan routes that led eventually to China. And silk was not the only luxury item that reached Rome from the east through Armenia: spices, incense, exotic animals from the east, and all kinds of other goods came through, making their way west towards Greece or south to the Middle East. As with Mesopotamia to the south, Armenia was never a firm possession of the Empire.

ADVENTURES IN ARMENIA

Between Roman Armenia and the China of the Han Empire lay the Parthian Empire, the Kushan Dominions, and the Himalayas. All might be avoided by taking a northerly route across the Caspian Sea to the Aral Sea, and heading eastward to the Great Wall of China. There is no indication that the Roman and Han Empires were aware of each other's existence, even though their goods were traded back and forth along the Silk Road. An expedition by enterprising Roman merchants to China could pioneer a new overland trade route that would cut the Parthians out of the equation. Such an expedition would require adventurous souls with a wide array of skills, especially fighters and rangers.

BITHYNIA AND PONTUS

As Rome's influence spread to Greece, the Romans encountered the kingdom of Pontus, which sat on the southern shores of the Black Sea. Ruled by a series of kings all named Mithridates, this former Persian territory had been conquered, along with the rest of the Persian Empire, by Alexander the Great a few centuries earlier, but it had ambitions of its own, and was a constant thorn in Rome's side. So was neighboring Bithynia, which was ruled, more often than not, by in-laws of the kings of Pontus.

After subduing the pirates in the eastern Mediterranean, Pompey went on to subdue Bithynia and Pontus. Later, Rome's power extended along the entire southern Black Sea coast.

ADVENTURES IN BITHYNIA AND PONTUS

Across the Black Sea lay barbarian country every bit as wild as the hills of southern Scotland or the forests of Germany. Much of the northern coast was controlled by the Scythian horse nomads. The Sarmatians were also there, a people identified by some with the legendary Amazons. It was from Colchis, north of Roman Armenia in the foothills of the Caucasus Mountains in modern Georgia, that the Greek hero Jason had recovered the famous Golden Fleece. Scythia and the lands beyond were said to be home to all kinds of monsters and the most fabulous of treasures.

Pontus is a natural starting point for adventures across the Black Sea, with hazards varying from Scythian hordes to Amazons to rampaging griffons. If any of the region's fantastic beasts could be captured alive and sent back to Rome, any promoter of arena games would be prepared to pay a fortune for it. And who knows what treasures might be found to eclipse the Golden Fleece and make the PC more famous even than Jason and the Argonauts?

THRACE AND MACEDONIA

These wild, rugged lands to the north of Greece (modern-day Macedonia, southern Albania, and southern Bulgaria) were famous for the ferocity of their warriors; although they were not regarded as equal to their Greek neighbors in science and culture, nobody doubted their toughness and effectiveness on the battlefield. The Thracian was one of the most popular gladiator types, and the renowned Spartacus, who led the slave revolt in 73 BC, was a Thracian. Macedonia was famous as the birthplace of Alexander the Great.

Although Thrace and Macedonia were more or less inherited by Rome, among the other remnants of Alexander's conquests, they retained the air of wild frontier provinces in contrast to the more pliant and "civilized" lands of Greece.

Despite its wild reputation, Thrace was to become the center of the eastern Empire as power shifted away from Italy and the West. The city of Byzantium (later Constantinople; modern Istanbul) stood on the coast of Thrace facing Asia Minor across the Dardanelles, and it was here that the Byzantine Empire would endure for centuries after the fall of Rome.

ADVENTURES IN THRACE AND MACEDONIA

PCs might go to Macedonia to seek the birthplace of Alexander the Great, whose historical stature and mystique was as great in Roman times as was that of any of the Emperors. Perhaps some pretender has arisen in the eastern Mediterranean, claiming to be a descendant of Alexander, and thereform the leagl heir. Such a usurper could be stirring up rebellion. Or perhaps one of the PCs is told by a soothsayer that he or she is Alexander's kin, which would lead to great celebrity and perhaps some wealth—if it could be proven. In either case, the purported heir might head to Macedonia to look for clues that would prove the family link, and other parties would be just as interested in making sure this never happens.

Thrace, although it was within the boundaries of the Roman Empire, remained a wild place, about which wild stories were told. In an *Eternal Rome* campaign, Thrace offers a perfect hunting ground for PCs in search of fantastic beasts to slay, or to capture and sell for the arena.

Late in the Empire period, the PCs could be involved in the political and military maneuvering that saw power in the eastern half of the Empire devolve to Byzantium, and the struggle to keep the eastern Empire alive while the west crumbled.

- GREECE -

To the Romans, Greece was the acknowledged cradle of civilization, birthplace of democracy, science, and philosophy; a place of history and culture, degraded by time and fallen from its once-powerful place in the world, but still well worth visiting. An upper-class Roman's education wasn't complete without a visit to Greece.

The Romans divided Greece into two parts: Epirus in the west and Achaea in the east and south. The islands of Crete and Rhodes were governed separately.

EPIRUS AND ACHAEA

These two provinces encompassed the whole of mainland Greece, along with most of the Aegean islands and the Cyclades. In Achaea could be found the great cities of Athens, Sparta, and Corinth, Mount Olympus, the legendary home of the gods, and many other sites that resounded in the Roman imagination from history and legend. Epirus (modern Albania) was the lesser of the Greek provinces, culturally as well as in land area; its only claims to fame were as the birthplace of Alexander's mother, and as the site of a short-lived regional power in the 3rd century BC.

ADVENTURES IN EPIRUS AND ACHAEA

PCs visiting the sites of myth and legend in Greece might find all kinds of adventures. The ghost of Oedipus might want his side of the story told, and it might be very different from the version that has come down from the Greek playwright Sophocles. The gods might have decided to leave Olympus because of all the mortal tourists and pilgrims who have come looking for them. Or they might decide to reassert their old power and clear mortals away from the sacred mountain.

The sphinx (or one of its descendants) might still be haunting lonely mountain roads, eating anyone who cannot answer its riddle. It might have a tougher riddle this time, since every Greek and Roman with even a smattering of education knows how Oedipus solved the first one.

Descendants of winged Pegasus might still be found in some remote area, prompting business-minded PCs to capture a few and establish a breeding herd for profit. Somewhere, satyrs and centaurs might still exist in wooded enclaves, desperately resisting the pressure of human expansion, first from Greeks and now from Romans, that could leave them with nowhere to live, driving them to a nomadic lifestyle similar to that of the Gypsies a millennium later.

Also in Achaea is Delphi, home to a temple of Apollo, which held the most famous oracle in the ancient world. Generals and Emperors consulted the oracle regularly to learn the will of the gods; what might she tell the PCs?

In 280 BC, Pyrrhus of Epirus, a second-cousin of Alexander the Great, launched an invasion of Italy, barely defeating Roman armies in a number of engagements, but in the end being driven from the peninsula. At the same time, Rome was facing the Gauls and the Samnites; to many in the capitals of the Mediterranean nations, Epirus looked like the nation to back in the struggle, and a group of powerful or clever PC mercenaries could have turned the tide decisively against Rome.

CRETE

Crete lies to the south of the Greek mainland. In pre-Classical times it was the home of the Minoans, an advanced culture who traded with the ancient Egyptians, and were famous for their bull-dancing rituals where an unarmored dancer took the horns of a charging bull and somersaulted over its back. The legendary King Minos of Crete ruled here in the great palace of Knossos, and here he had the master architect and inventor Daedalus create the labyrinth to contain the terrible Minotaur. With the help of Minos' daughter Ariadne, the Greek hero Theseus penetrated the labyrinth and slew the creature.

The Minoan civilization apparently never recovered from the destruction wrought by the eruption of the volcano on the island of Thera (also known as Santorini), some 75 miles to the north, around 1650 BC. Some have suggested that the tidal waves and earthquakes that accompanied this massive eruption were the inspiration for the myth of the sinking of Atlantis.

ADVENTURES IN CRETE

The labyrinth of Minos, if it can be found, could contain all manner of other monsters, as well as some of Minos' famous wealth. After all, what safer place to put one's treasure than in a maze filled with monsters?

It could be, of course, that the great Minotaur of myth was not the only one of its kind. Perhaps its relatives and offspring stalk the mountains and hills of Crete, terrifying peasants and eluding military patrols from the local Roman garrison. Anyone who could capture a minotaur for the arena could become very rich as a result.

If there is a link between the Minoan civilization and Atlantis, then all kinds of wonders and lost knowledge might still lie buried in the ruins of Atlantean cities on the island of Crete.

RHODES

Lying off the coast of Greek Asia, Rhodes was most famous in ancient times as the home of the Colossus, a massive bronze statue of the sun god Helios (an aspect of Apollo) that towered above the harbor. It was one of the Seven Wonders of the World, and even after it fell to an earthquake in 226 BC, its shattered remains were still an object of wonder to those who came to the island. There were many offers to rebuild the Colossus, but all were declined after an oracle forbade it. The ruins remained in place for the rest of the Roman era.

ADVENTURES IN RHODES

History does not record why the oracle advised against rebuilding the fallen Colossus, beyond some vague fears of the displeasure of Helios. However, this is just the sort of project that might appeal to a megalomaniac Emperor like Nero or Caligula. When a mysterious curse or a series of inexplicable accidents begins to strike the reconstruction crew, the PCs might be sent to investigate. It is quite possible that Apollo is not at all displeased with the idea of rebuilding the Colossus; it's just that he objects to the great statue's face being replaced with a likeness of Nero or Caligula.

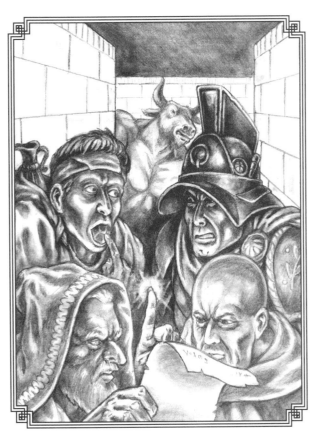

Alternatively, the PCs might be sent to recover the pieces of the fallen statue, and ship them back to Rome for reassembly as part of a lavish new Imperial palace. In that case, the PCs will have to deal with local resistance as well as the possible displeasure of the gods, and it may be difficult to tell the difference between the two.

- THE DANUBE FRONTIER -

For most of the history of the Roman Empire, the frontier in Europe followed the Rhine and Danube Rivers. It was from this direction that pressure mounted in the late Empire, leading to the incursions of the Goths and other Germanic peoples that triggered the collapse of the Empire in the west.

The establishment of the Danube frontier was the result of an ongoing military campaign that lasted over a century from the reign of Augustus to that of Trajan. The area was kept heavily garrisoned against barbarian from the north, and the Danube army was the largest single force in the Empire. For a while, the generals of the Danube took turns at being Emperor as though it were their right, and Rome could certainly not have resisted had they brought their troops to Italy to press their claim.

MOESIA

Moesia was north of Thrace and Macedonia, running from the border of Illyricum to the western shores of the Black Sea. It was divided into two parts, Moesia Superior in the west and Moesia Inferior in the east ("Superior" meant closer to Rome when used in province names), and occupied parts of modern-day Serbia and northern Bulgaria.

DACIA

Dacia was the only Roman province across the Danube, and occupied parts of modern Romania. Like Moesia, it was a frontier province, heavily garrisoned and the site of regular skirmishes with local tribes. It was first taken by Trajan in 106 AD, but was abandoned to the invading Goths in 272 AD. Many later Emperors would retake, and then lose again, parts of Dacia, but it was never wholly restored to the Empire.

PANNONIA

Pannonia lay between Illyricum and the Danube, including parts of modern-day Bosnia, Croatia, Slovenia, and Austria. Like Moesia, it was divided into two parts: Pannonia Superior and Pannonia Inferior.

NORICUM

Noricum was west of Pannonia, south of the upper Danube, in western Austria and southern Germany.

RHAETIA

Rhaetia was west of Noricum and south of the Danube's headwaters. The Danube itself formed the border between Rhaetia Inferior and Rhaetia Superior; the latter lay in the angle formed by the headwaters of the Rhine and the Danube, and was protected by a fortification called the *limes*

("frontier") built between the two rivers to create a shorter and more defensible frontier.

ADVENTURES ON THE DANUBE FRONTIER

The Danube provinces were heavily garrisoned frontier areas for most of their history, under the almost constant threat of attacks from across the river. PCs in this region could be special agents of the Empire (either Romans or recruited barbarians), sent on daring raids across the river to sow confusion and uncertainly among the massing barbarians, or they could be the barbarians themselves, constantly testing the strength of the Roman frontier and the resolve of the troops who manned it.

ILLYRICUM

The Roman province of Illyricum ran along the east coast of the Adriatic Sea, covering parts of present-day Slovenia, Croatia, Bosnia-Herzegovina, and Montenegro. It became a Roman province around 53 BC, but 20 years later Octavian (the future Emperor Augustus) was still campaigning to pacify the region. Illyricum was a vital land link to Greece, and in the early years of the Empire it was also a frontier province, threatened by unconquered tribes from Pannonia and Moesia.

ADVENTURES IN ILLYRICUM

Except for the period of its initial conquest and the final collapse of the northern frontier of the Roman Empire centuries later, Illyricum was mostly peaceful. In a campaign set in either of these periods, the PCs could fight on one side or the other, but in other periods, they are most likely to be passing through, either on their way from Rome to the Danube frontier or traveling between Italy and Greece.

GERMANIA

The Roman province of Germania consisted of more than modern-day Germany: Germania Superior included much of Switzerland and part of France, while Germania Inferior included parts of Belgium, the Netherlands and much of Germany.

Like the Danube frontier, Germania was heavily garrisoned, but it also included some considerable Roman cities.

ADVENTURES IN GERMANIA

According to Pliny the Elder, the forests of southern Germany were home to the hercynia, a rare bird whose feathers glowed in the dark (see page 83). They were also renowned for their larger animals, and supplied many bears, boars, and bison for the arena.

The other claim to fame of Germany's forests is that they are the last known resting place of three entire legions, which were slaughtered almost to a man in 6 AD. This defeat was the worst in Rome's history and halted Roman expansion into Germany. If the PCs had been with General Varus and his army, perhaps the disaster might have been averted. Or, later, perhaps the PCs are given the task of recovering the lost eagles of the XVII, XVIII, and XIX Legions in the Teutoberg Forest, the standards of the three destroyed legions (historically, two were recovered by Tiberius's adopted son Germanicus, and the third by Claudius's general Publius Gabinius Secundus Cauchius). As well as hostile tribesmen and dangerous wildlife, they may have to contend with the restless spirits of almost 15,000 dead legionaries. If the Germans find a necromancer capable of raising them and turning them against their former countrymen, the whole of the Rhine frontier could be in danger.

GAUL AND BELGICA

Gaul (modern France) was conquered by Julius Caesar in a series of campaigns from 58–51 BC, and was divided into three parts: Narbonensis in the south and southeast, Aquitania in the southwest, and Lugdunensis in the north and northwest. Most Romans, however, thought of Gaul as divided into two: *gallia togata* ("toga-ed Gaul"), which had adopted Roman culture, and *gallia comata* ("long-haired Gaul") which retained the traditional Celtic (in Roman eyes, uncivilized) culture and way of life.

The Roman province of Belgica encompassed Belgium, Luxemburg, and parts of France, Germany and the Netherlands, including Augusta Treverorum (modern Trier) and Colonia Agrippina (modern Cologne). The Belgae were very similar to the Gauls culturally.

ADVENTURES IN GAUL

The most famous Gauls today are Asterix and Obelix, the stars of a long-running French comic book series that has been translated into many languages including English. Thanks to a magic potion brewed by the druid, their village remains unconquered despite Rome's best efforts, and they travel to every corner of the Empire causing havoc and rewriting history. There is a lot of inspiration here for a roleplaying campaign with a humorous tone.

In a more serious vein, player characters may be involved in Caesar's conquest of Gaul on either side, playing a number of different roles. Caesar's victory was due in no small part to the fractious nature of the Gallic tribes, who failed to unite against this threat from without until it was too late, and were absorbed into the Roman Empire piecemeal. Gallic PCs could have the task of persuading the tribes to put aside generations of blood feuds and ancient grudges to unite against the common enemy; or they could be Roman agents sent to persuade the leaders of key tribes to give in without a fight, or to remove the more warlike leaders and establish pro-Roman chiefs in their place.

The last gasp of Gallic independence was the rebellion of Vercingetorix. This charismatic leader managed to hold together a powerful alliance of tribes in an ill-fated revolt that ended in a siege at Avaricum (modern Bourges). This dramatic episode offers opportunities for adventure to both Roman and Gallic characters.

It was in a forest in Gaul, according to Caesar's commentaries, that the druids of the entire Celtic world (or at least the whole of Gaul) held a great convocation. PCs who are Celtic druids (see page 17) or who have been charged with the task of escorting a local druid have an opportunity to witness great things, and perhaps advance in their own training. On the other side of the coin, Roman PCs might be sent to break up the meeting or to make sure that some of the most powerful and independence-minded druids never arrive.

More than 400 years later, as the Roman Empire crumbled in the west, there was a short-lived attempt to establish an independent Gallic Empire and stave off the flood of Germanic invaders from across the Rhine. Among those who took troops to help was a British warlord by the name of Artorius Riothamus, who would later be identified by some with the legendary King Arthur. Perhaps his remains do not lie on the fabled Isle of Avalon (or in the Abbey of Glastonbury) after all, but are somewhere in the countryside of Gaul. Perhaps the great sword Excalibur was never returned to the Lady of the Lake either, but awaits discovery by a new wielder. Or perhaps, the heroes accompanied Artorius in his expedition to Gaul, and became the prototypes for the Knights of the Round Table.

Britannia

Although Julius Caesar visited Britain twice during his campaigns in Gaul, it was not until almost a century later, in 43 AD, that the Roman conquest began with four legions sent across the English Channel by Emperor Claudius. At an early stage, the frontier was established along a diagonal line dividing modern England roughly in half from northeast to southwest. Over time, Wales was pinned down by forts along the coast and along the line of the later border with England.

In 61 AD, during the reign of Nero, the tribes of the southeast rebelled under the famous Queen Boudicca (also known as Boadicea), destroying one Roman colony and causing serious damage to Londinium (London) as well. During the reign of Domitian, the Roman general Agricola pushed northward, advancing the frontier at least to the line where Hadrian's Wall was later built. According to his biographer Tacitus, Agricola pushed to the very farthest reaches of the British mainland, and received the surrender of the farthest and most warlike tribes, but Tacitus was Agricola's son-in-law, and his account may not be entirely impartial.

Over time, the frontier settled along the line of Hadrian's Wall; the later Antonine Wall, built further north, proved to be too easy to circumvent by sea. It was overrun a few times by attacking Picts and Scots, most seriously during the so-called *barbarica conspiratio* ("barbarian conspiracy") of 367 AD, when the Saxons joined in from across the North Sea and the whole north of Britannia was overrun.

Increased raiding by the Saxons (anticipating what the Vikings would later do to Saxon England) led to various responses and reorganizations, none of which were entirely effective. Rome formally abandoned Britannia in 410 AD, withdrawing the legions to fight to protect the capital of the Empire.

Adventures in Britannia

The rebellion of Boudicca was squashed in history, but in an *Eternal Rome* campaign this needn't be the case. The player characters could fight on either side, or be busy trying to persuade neutral tribes to enter the fray on one side or the other.

Ireland was visible from England and Wales on a clear day, but the Romans never set foot there. According to Roman sources, Ireland was thought to be a wondrous country where gold was lying on the ground in great quantities, and various other marvels took place. There was even a rumor of a "bridge of sand": a causeway exposed at low tide by which it was possible to walk from Britain to Ireland, and there are unsubstantiated claims that detachments of Roman troops were sent to find it. In an *Eternal Rome* campaign, this might be a job for the PCs, and Ireland might be more full of wonders than even its own fantastic literature attests.

The period immediately after the withdrawal of Roman rule from Britain, as the invading Anglo-Saxons conquered the Celtic Romano-Britons, is the setting for the earliest stories of King Arthur, and many scholars believe that he was an actual person: a Christian Briton fighting to defend both his religion and Roman culture in Britain from the savage invading pagan Saxons, perhaps with the name Artorius Riothamus. PCs in this period could fight alongside him, or against him, and help form one of the greatest legends in the English language.

CHAPTER NINE: ROMAN HISTORY

According to tradition, the city of Rome was founded in 753 BC. The fall of the western half of the Roman Empire can be arbitrarily pinned to the year 476 AD—the date when the last Emperor was deposed, although the Western Empire had been a mere shell for decades before that date. To Romans living at the end of the Empire, the foundation of the city was as long ago as the beginning Viking age is to a 21st-century reader.

Both the city of Rome and Roman culture saw many changes over the centuries. Initially a kingdom, Rome became first a republic and then an empire; its influence spread from a single city-state to embrace most of the known world; and its religious life went from Etruscan-influenced paganism through liberal polytheism to Christianity. These changes were not without upheaval, and the Roman Empire endured a number of civil wars and periods of anarchy, along with barbarian invasions, plagues, and other disasters.

This chapter offers a brief outline of Roman history. The bibliography gives references to more detailed histories that the GM can use to research a particular period in more detail for campaign planning.

ANCIENT ITALY

Like most of Europe, Italy in the Bronze Age and early Iron Age was peopled by a collection of scattered tribes, with different cultures and languages. Out of these emerged the Etruscan civilization, which dominated central Italy from around 800 BC until its cities were conquered by the expanding Romans in the 4th and 3rd centuries BC. As the Etruscans expanded, they came across Greek colonies in Sicily and the south of the Italian peninsula: Rome grew up between these two powers, and ultimately conquered both of them.

The heartland of Etruscan civilization was in the region of Etruria, which lay west of the Appenines between the Arno and Tiber Rivers. To the east lay the Umbrians and Sabines, and to the south were the Aequi and the Latins. Together with the Samnites and Oscans further south, these Italic peoples were culturally and linguistically different from the Etruscans.

THE FOUNDING OF ROME

According to legend, Rome was founded by and named after Romulus, one of a pair of twins born to a princess of the nearby city of Alba Longa. Their mother, Rhea Silvia, was forced to become a Vestal Virgin after her father, King Numitor, was deposed by his brother. When she became pregnant, she claimed that the god Mars was the father of her children.

Rhea Silvia was imprisoned by her wicked uncle, and when she gave birth to twin boys they were thrown into the Tiber.

When a shepherd found them, they were being suckled by a she-wolf—a popular artistic theme in the early days of Rome. The shepherd took them home and reared them as his own sons, but they found out about their true heritage, restored their grandfather Numitor to the throne of Alba Longa, and set out to found their own city.

As the boundaries of the new city were being laid out on a hilltop above the Tiber, Romulus and Remus quarreled and Remus was killed. Romulus went on to rule Rome for 40 years. It is said that he disappeared in a whirlwind in the Campus Martius, but another tradition holds that the *lapis niger* ("black stone"), a slab in Rome's Forum inscribed with an early Latin law code, covers his tomb.

The early inhabitants of Rome were a mixed bag of fugitives and landless wanderers, farming the surrounding hills and plains. As they were predominantly male, a shortage of potential wives threatened the city's future. Romulus solved the problem by inviting the neighboring Sabines to a festival in the newly-founded city; at a given signal, the Romans kidnapped wives for themselves from among the attending Sabines. The "Rape of the Sabines" was a popular subject in art up until the 19th century AD, and led, understandably, to war with the Sabines. However, the war was short-lived (tradition credits the mothers of the stolen women with intervening to make peace), and the Romans intermarried with the Sabines.

Aeneas and Troy

Early traditions paint the founding fathers of Rome as a collection of bandits and outcasts, and later it was thought necessary to create a nobler heritage for a city that was fast becoming the ruler of the known world. During the reign of Augustus, the poet Virgil, perhaps drawing on an existing tradition, wrote the Aeneid, an epic poem in the style of Homer's *Odyssey*, which tells of the adventures of Aeneas, the son of a Trojan prince (or a shepherd, according to some

traditions) and the Greek goddess Aphrodite, who survived the destruction of Troy by the Greeks.

After escaping the fall of Troy, Aeneas made a long and eventful journey that ended with him and his men landing in Italy, where, after initial conflicts, he made peace with the native Latins and married a Latin princess. His son Ascanius (also known as Iulus) founded the city of Alba Longa, making Romulus and Remus descendants of Aeneas.

- The Kingdom of Rome (753–510 BC) -

The Roman monarchy was not hereditary. Instead, kings were elected by an assembly of the citizens; far from being absolute monarchs, they were advised by a council of landowning nobles (the predecessors of the Senate), who played an important part in deciding and implementing policy.

The original site of Rome was on the Palatine Hill, but the city spread out over the centuries to take in a total of seven hills (the Palatine, Esquiline, Capitoline, Aventine, Quirinal,

Viminal, and Caelian). The city's influence also expanded, leading it into occasional conflict with its neighbors. Tullus Hostilius, the third king of Rome, destroyed Alba Longa, the home of his predecessor Romulus. His successor Ancus Martius bridged the Tiber River and founded the port of Ostia, giving Rome access to the sea and enhancing its trade.

The last three kings of Rome were Etruscans. Lucius Tarquinius Priscus ("Tarquin the Elder") had a peaceful reign, but there is a story that he gained the throne through trickery, convincing the sons of Ancus Martius to leave the city immediately after their father's death, and then campaigning successfully for the crown in their absence.

Trade with Etruria grew during his reign, and a part of the city called the *Vicus Tuscus* ("Etruscan Quarter") housed Etruscan merchants and traders. Rome's wealth grew rapidly, partly from trade with the Etruscans, and partly because Rome stood on the route from Etruria to markets in southern Italy.

The sons of Ancus Martius eventually grew tired of waiting for Tarquin to die so one of them could inherit the throne, and they had him assassinated. But through the

The Kings of Rome

Romulus (Latin)	753–715 BC
Numa Popilius (Sabine)	715–673 BC
Tullus Hostilius (Latin)	673–641 BC
Ancus Martius (Latin)	641–616 BC
Tarquinius Priscus (Etruscan)	616–579 BC
Servius Tullius (Etruscan)	579–535 BC
Tarquinius Superbus (Etruscan)	535–510 BC

maneuverings of Tarquin's wife, rule passed to Tarquin's son-in-law, Servius Tullius, at first serving as regent and then as king in his own right. The sons of Ancus Martius went into exile and weren't heard from again.

By the time Servius Tullius took the throne, Rome had grown so much that he had to build a new city wall. Servius also built a temple to Diana on the Aventine Hill, as an expression of the city's growing status.

Servius reorganized the city's institutions, creating the foundations of the Roman army. Previously, the farmer citizens of Rome had taken up arms to deal with a threat when it materialized; Servius Tullius organized a tax to support the military, and divided the citizens into military classes, according to their wealth. At the top were the *equites* ("equestrians" or "knights"), who could afford to provide themselves with horses to serve in the cavalry. Those who could afford heavy armor served in the front ranks of the infantry, and those who could not afford armor served as light infantry and reserves.

The same organization was also applied to voting in the Assembly, which had previously been by *curiae* ("clans"). Now each class had a number of votes in proportion to the troops it provided. The wealthy provided more troops and had more votes; the poor, while more numerous, provided fewer troops and had correspondingly fewer votes.

The last king of Rome, Lucius Tarquinius Superbus ("Tarquin the Proud"), the son of Tarquin the Elder and the son-in-law of Servius Tullius, continued the work of expanding the city's influence, placing Rome (mostly by force) at the head of a confederation of city-states called the Latin League. He built a temple to Jupiter on the Capitoline Hill.

A ruthless and unpopular ruler, Tarquin had to be surrounded by armed bodyguards while in Rome. When his son Sextus raped a Roman lady named Lucretia, the entire family was expelled, and the Romans declared themselves a republic. Tarquin gathered Etruscan support and tried to reclaim the throne of Rome, but was unsuccessful. It was during the ensuing battles that Etruscans captured part of Rome, and were only prevented from conquering the city by the heroic defense of a narrow bridge by Horatius Cocles ("Cyclops," as he'd lost an eye in earlier campaigning): an event celebrated in poetry and paintings for centuries afterward. A decisive battle fought at Lake Regillus in 496 BC ended the Etruscan threat once and for all.

- THE EARLY REPUBLIC (496–133 BC) -

After the expulsion of Tarquin the Proud, *rex* ("king") became a hated word in Rome. Although the city was to see a number of dictators and dynasties of emperors over the following centuries, none of them adopted the title king, even though they wielded more power than the early monarchs.

In place of a king, the early Roman republic was ruled by two officials called consuls. They were elected annually, and no-one could be consul more than once in his life. The religious functions of the kings were vested in the *pontifex maximus* ("high priest"), who was appointed from among the nobility. The purpose of having two consuls and replacing them annually was to ensure that absolute power was never held by a single person. Although each consul could veto the acts of the other and cause a deadlock, this apparently seldom happened, and the system worked well.

In times of emergency, when a single unified command was needed, a *dictator* ("commander") could be appointed, normally for a period of six months. The position of the Senate was unchanged; it still sat as an advisory council to the consuls. As the consuls' workload grew, they were given subordinates called quaestors, who were primarily concerned with criminal justice and taxation.

During the early republic, Roman society was divided into two classes: the *patricians* (nobles), from whose ranks senators and consuls were drawn, and the *plebeians* (commoners). Since the magistrates and other officials of the republic were all patricians, the law favored the upper class, and the office of tribune was created to redress the balance. Tribunes were plebeians themselves, and could intervene in any legal proceeding (including the deliberations of the Senate) to redress injustice or oppression against the lower class.

THE GAULS

In 391 BC, a tribe of Gauls called the Senones, led by their chief, Brennus, attacked the Etruscan town of Clusium, and marched on Rome. They routed the Romans 11 miles outside the city, and Rome was left open. Most of the populace had fled, but a few held out on the citadel, and after a seven-month siege the Gauls accepted tribute and left.

This was the first major defeat in Roman history, and it had a profound effect in Rome and the region. The city was left in ruins, and the population level took years to recover. The Etruscans rebelled, and Rome's position within the Latin League was severely damaged. There was even talk of abandoning the city and relocating to nearby Veii. From being the preeminent power in the area, Rome fell to a city struggling to survive.

It was said that when the Romans were weighing out the gold to be given to the Gauls, they complained that the terms were too heavy. At this, Brennus threw his sword onto the scales, tipping them still further, saying "Woe to the conquered." It was not the first time that Romans and Gauls had been in conflict, and it wouldn't be the last, but this enduring image did much to shape the Roman attitude to the Gauls in the following centuries. It was only when Julius Caesar conquered Gaul almost 350 years later that the shame of this defeat was finally erased.

THE CONQUEST OF ITALY

Despite this setback, Rome recovered and its influence continued to spread. The Etruscans to the north and the Latins to the south were the first to be conquered, although they were not treated as conquered peoples. They were required to pay Roman taxes, but they were accorded most of the rights of Roman citizenship, including the right to hold office. In some areas, Rome founded colonies, establishing settlements where previously landless Romans and Latins could have their own farms. Since all citizens were required to serve in the army if needed, this effectively created garrisons in areas of doubtful loyalty.

THE SAMNITE WAR

Expansion to the east was not as easy. The Samnite hill tribes had overrun the plain of Campania and founded the city of Capua. The Samnites of the plains came to be known as Oscans, and in 343 BC they were attacked by the hill Samnites, and appealed to Rome for help. By 341 BC, a Roman garrison was left in Capua and Campania was under Roman protection. The hill Samnites, too, became Rome's allies under the terms of the peace treaty.

THE END OF THE LATIN LEAGUE

Roman expansion worried the other members of the Latin League. Although they were loyal to Rome, they worried that their cities had to share in the expense and risk of expansions by supplying taxes and troops while Rome reaped all the benefit. They demanded greater representation in the Senate and government of Rome, and when no compromise could be reached armed conflict broke out. Together with the hill Samnites, the Romans defeated the Latins and Campanians in a decisive battle near Mount Vesuvius.

Despite their rebellion, Rome granted generous terms to the defeated Latins and Campanians, giving them the privileges of citizenship, which allowed them access to representation in the Assembly and Senate, although not as much as they had demanded. However, each town gave up its right to conclude alliances with anyone except Rome, making it difficult for them to organize a rebellion in the future.

MORE SAMNITE WARS

Despite their treaty with Rome, further conflict with the Samnites was inevitable. When factional fighting broke out in the Greek colony of Naples in 327 BC, one side brought in Samnite mercenaries, so the other side naturally appealed to Rome for help. In 321 BC, a Roman army was trapped by the Samnites and forced to surrender. The Romans had fought using the Greek phalanx formation (which they'd learned from the Etruscans), which was effective on open ground but very badly suited to mountain warfare against the Samnites. Accordingly, the Roman army was re-equipped following the Samnite pattern; this marked the first use of the shield, short sword and throwing spear that became standard legionary equipment for much of later Roman history. In addition, the legions were organized into maniples of 120 men, giving them more tactical flexibility than the unwieldy multi-thousand-man phalanx.

Conflict with the Samnites resumed in 316 BC, and although Rome won a major victory in two years later the wars were costly. Rome itself was threatened, and only

saved by the firm allegiance of the Latins. In 310 BC, the Etruscans sensed weakness in the republic and declared war, supported by many tribes of the central Appenines. Rome was surrounded by enemies, but with careful strategy the Romans divided them and defeated them one at a time. In 304 BC, the Samnites agreed to a peace treaty and renounced all claims to Campania. Trouble flared up again in 299 BC when Rome was distracted by another influx of Gauls, who allied themselves with several Etruscan cities. At the battle of Stentium in 296 BC, the Samnites joined the Gauls and Etruscans, but were resoundingly defeated.

After the battle of Stentium, Samnite resistance collapsed, and Rome was left as the pre-eminent power in Italy. The countryside was stabilized by the planting of more colonies, and by the construction of roads to allow troops to reach any trouble spots quickly. The roads also had a beneficial effect on trade; all roads led to Rome, so a great deal of trade passed through the city, increasing its wealth. Further Gallic incursions in 289 BC gave Rome an excuse to annex several Etruscan cities under her control to prevent them from giving aid to the Gauls in the future.

THE PYRRHIC WAR

Southern Italy was home to a number of flourishing Greek colonies, which suffered occasional attacks from neighboring Italian hill tribes. The colonies normally hired Greek mercenaries to defend them, but on one occasion, the town of Thurii appealed to Rome for help. A Roman expedition was successful, but incited the jealousy of the Greek city of Tarentum, which was accustomed to acting as a protector for the colonies, and resented being usurped by

Roman "barbarians." Relations between Rome and Tarentum deteriorated, and after several incidents (including the sinking of four Roman ships in Tarentum's harbor and the pelting of Roman envoys with excrement) war was declared.

Although the Tarentines were capable of protecting the colonies from occasional hill tribe raids, they didn't feel they could stand up to Rome on their own. At this time, after the death of Alexander the Great and the breakup of his empire, the Greek world was flooded with mercenaries looking for work, and the Tarentines asked for help from Pyrrhus, the prince of Epirus and a relative of Alexander.

Pyrrhus was a skilled and ambitious military commander, and saw an opportunity to emulate in the west the successes that Alexander had enjoyed in the east. He brought 20,000 heavy infantry, a strong contingent of cavalry, and 20 elephants—the first the Romans would ever face in battle. The Romans were defeated near Heraclea in 280 BC, but at a heavy cost to Pyrrhus' forces. The following year, allied with some rebel Samnites and Lucanians, Pyrrhus won another victory at Asculum, again taking severe losses in the process. Pyrrhus said that another such victory would be the end of his army, and the term "Pyrrhic victory" was coined to describe a victory won at crippling cost.

While his army was licking its wounds in Tarentum, Pyrrhus received an appeal from the Greek colony of Syracuse in Sicily, a city under attack by the Carthaginians. Carthage had made several attempts to gain control of Sicily in the past. Pyrrhus defeated the attackers easily, and even considered invading Carthage for a while, but in the end, he decided to return to Italy.

The following years saw a number of inconclusive battles against the Romans, with Pyrrhus increasingly on the losing side. At last, in 275 BC, he withdrew his troops, having taken more than 60% losses in the campaign. When the last of Pyrrhus's garrison in Tarentum was withdrawn in 272 BC, the town was forced to surrender. As before, Rome's terms were generous. Tarentum and the other Greek colonies were free to govern themselves, but had to supply a quota of warships to Rome on demand.

The failure of Pyrrhus' expedition to Italy drew the attention of Ptolemy II, who ruled the Egyptian remnant of Alexander's empire and hoped to expand his domain. He sent an embassy to Rome, and Rome responded by sending ambassadors of its own to Ptolemy's court in Alexandria. Rome was now recognized as a player on the world stage.

The Punic Wars

Carthage was the major power in North Africa in the 3rd century BC, and the only power in the western Mediterranean to rival Rome; conflict was inevitable. Carthage had started out as a trading colony from the Phoenician city of Tyre. It had come to dominate North Africa, with colonies of its own in Spain, Sardinia, and Sicily. Carthage had the most powerful fleet in the western Mediterranean, and maintained a large mercenary army recruited from Africa and Spain. Commanding both sides of the Pillars of Hercules, Carthage had sole sea access from the Mediterranean to the Atlantic coast of Europe, including the profitable tin mines in Britain. Together with a near monopoly of maritime trade in the western Mediterranean, this made Carthage the richest city in the ancient world at this time.

The First Punic War

The Carthaginians made several attempts to take control of Sicily. Pyrrhus drove them back from Syracuse in 276 BC, but in the years following his withdrawal from Italy the Carthaginians occupied most of the island. Only Syracuse and the small town of Messana (which faced Italy across the Straits of Messina) remained in Greek hands. When war broke out between the Messana and Syracuse, the people of Messana appealed first to Carthage and then to Rome.

To the Romans, a Carthaginian garrison in Messana would effectively close the straits to trade. Ships bound for Rome would have to sail around the south of Sicily, risking conflict with the Carthaginian navy. In 264 BC, two legions (a comparatively small force) were sent south. Slipping across the straits at night, they occupied Messana (which had already ejected its Carthaginian garrison) and beat back an attack by the combined forces of Carthage and Syracuse.

It took time for Carthage to hire another mercenary army for a renewed attack on Messana, and the Romans put the time to good use. In 263 BC, they attacked Syracuse and forced it into an alliance against Carthage. In 262 BC, they attacked the Carthaginian-held town of Agrigentum, and defeated an army sent to relieve it.

By 260 BC, however, the Carthaginian war machine was in gear. The fleet sealed Sicily off from the Italian mainland, stranding the Roman forces on the island. The Carthaginian navy then mounted constant raids against the coastal cities. Unless the blockade could be broken, it was only a matter of time before Carthage could put enough troops on Sicily to destroy the Roman forces. Rome had always relied on its armies in the past, and had never organized an effective navy, but now it needed one desperately.

By good luck, a Carthaginian quinquereme, a massive warship powered by five banks of oars, had run aground off the Italian coast. The ship was seized, and Roman shipwrights built a hundred copies of it, while crews of rowers trained on banks of benches set up on shore.

But even with a navy, Rome's true advantage lay in the superior quality of its infantry, and to make use of this a way had to be found to put troops aboard enemy ships quickly and easily. To achieve this, each new ship was fitted with a moveable gangplank tipped with an iron spike, nicknamed *corvus* ("crow's beak"). The corvus dug into the timbers of an enemy ship, holding the far end of the ramp securely as Roman troops poured across it.

In 260 BC, the formerly invincible Carthaginian navy suffered its first defeat of the war off Mylae, not far from Messana. More victories followed, culminating in a huge sea battle off the southern coast of Sicily, involving more than 300 ships on each side.

Rome pressed its advantage by attacking Carthage directly rather than trying to reduce the Carthaginian strongholds in Sicily one by one. The Roman fleet headed for the African coast and started raiding and ravaging the countryside in preparation for an invasion the following spring. Over the winter, however, a contingent of Greek mercenaries arrived in Carthage; their commander, Xanthippus, trained the garrison and even the citizens of Carthage, and when spring came the Romans suffered a serious defeat. Further invasion attempts were hampered by bad weather and poor navigation, and more than one fleet was lost at sea. Carthage took advantage of Rome's misfortune and defeated the remnants of the Roman fleet in 249 BC.

Roman forces besieged the Carthaginian strongholds on Sicily, but little progress was made. Finally, the Carthaginians were defeated in a decisive sea battle off the west coast of Sicily in 241 BC. Under the terms of surrender, Carthage paid a heavy tribute, abandoned all its settlements in Sicily, and undertook to keep its ships out of Italian waters. Sicily became a Roman territory.

The Second Punic War

Carthage was quick to recover from the First Punic War. Some Spanish territories lost in the war were recovered in a brutal campaign known as the Truceless War. When the Carthaginian general Hannibal attacked and conquered Saguntum (an ally of Rome) in 219 BC, it was a challenge that couldn't be ignored.

Hannibal didn't wait for Rome to respond. In a bold move, he marched his army (elephants and all) across the Alps and attacked Italy. In 218 BC, reinforced by Gallic allies who resented the Roman subjugation of northern Italy, he inflicted a number of defeats on the Roman army. Moving south the following year, his successes continued. At Cannae in 216 BC, a Roman army was all but annihilated, leaving Rome almost defenseless.

Rome appointed Quintus Fabius dictator to deal with this emergency. Rather than raising an army and engaging Hannibal directly, as many people expected, Fabius used delaying tactics and raids on Hannibal's supply lines. Hannibal, for his part, relied on the damage he inflicted on Rome's credibility by his victories to weaken the loyalty of Roman allies in Italy and try to bring them over to his side. Although some Italian cities did defect, enough of Rome's allies stayed loyal. Cut off from reinforcements from home, Hannibal's forces slowly weakened, dogged at every step by Roman forces that mounted raids and ambushes, but refused to be drawn into a decisive battle.

Over the next few years, Carthage made several attempts to attack Sardinia and Sicily, but without any great success; the Roman fleet continued to rule the western Mediterranean. In the spring of 214 BC, a Roman army was sent into Spain, seizing the Carthaginian possessions there and dashing any hope of Hannibal receiving supplies from across the Alps. He came within sight of Rome—indeed, close enough in 212 BC to throw a spear into the city in a futile gesture—but he lacked the manpower to take Rome and his army was growing weaker all the time. Hannibal was forced to retreat.

As Hannibal retreated, Rome retook the rebel cities, executing some of their citizens and selling others into slavery as an example of what happened to faithless allies. Although Hannibal was forced into retreat, Carthage wasn't defeated; in the autumn of 208 BC, the news came that despite Rome's successes in Spain, another Carthaginian army, led by Hannibal's brother Hasdrubal, was preparing to cross the Alps.

Winter prevented any immediate action on either side, but the following spring Hasdrubal's army was wiped out, and his severed head was thrown into Hannibal's camp. Hannibal withdrew to the southern end of Italy, knowing that defeat was all but inevitable.

Meanwhile, Roman forces under Scipio had taken nearly all of Carthage's territories in southern and eastern Spain. In 205 BC, Scipio went to Sicily to prepare for an invasion of North Africa. When he landed the next year, the Carthaginians sued for peace, and then rejected the terms that he offered. While Scipio was fighting in Africa, Hannibal managed to escape from Italy by sea, returning to Carthage with the remnants of his army.

The final battle of the Second Punic War was fought at Zama in 202, and ended in a resounding defeat for Carthage. The terms of peace were harsher than those imposed at the end of the First Punic War.

AFTER THE WAR

As well as bringing more territory under Roman control, the Second Punic War changed Rome's attitude to the rest of Italy. Cities that had originally been allies were now treated as subjects. The Gauls in the north of Italy were overrun in a series of campaigns, and by 191 BC their territory was made into the Roman province *Gallia Cisalpina* ("Gaul on this side of the Alps").

Across Italy, a great deal of land had been laid waste, either by the invaders or through neglect while farmers were serving in the army. In addition, slaves (most of them prisoners of war) were abundant and cheap. Rich Romans were able to buy distressed properties at rock bottom prices, consolidating small family farms into large properties called *latifundia*, operated by absentee landlords and worked mainly by slaves. The displaced free farmers moved into the cities.

At the same time, there was a growing interest in Greek culture and literature. Contact with Syracuse and other Greek colonies in the war had brought the Romans their first major exposure to Greek culture, and many educated Romans felt that their city should have a culture and literature of its own, reflecting its position in the world. This was the first of several periods of Hellenization in Roman history.

EXPANSION OF ROMAN RULE

With the second defeat of Carthage, the Romans expected an era of peace, but they were to be disappointed. The new provinces in eastern and southern Spain were threatened by the tribes of the Spanish interior, and weren't subdued for another 60 years. In Greece, meanwhile, a number of warlords were squabbling over the remains of Alexander the Great's collapsed empire, and as a growing Mediterranean power Rome was inevitably sucked into the conflicts.

Kings Philip of Macedon and Antiochus of Syria were both expanding into Greece, and appeals for aid came to Rome from various Greek cities. Philip had sided with Hannibal during the Second Punic War, but Rome kept the Macedonians occupied by funding proxy wars in Greece and maintaining naval control of the Adriatic. After defeating Philip in the Second Macedonian War, Rome declared a policy of "freedom for the Greeks" and withdrew from the peninsula, but Roman troops were soon back in Greece fighting first Antiochus, and then Philip's son Perseus.

In the years that followed, Rome concluded that peace would have to be maintained in Greece by military force. In 148 BC, the Roman province of Macedonia was created, and two years later Roman troops sacked Corinth as an example to the other cities of Greece.

The same year, Carthage was finally destroyed after a three-year siege. For 50 years following the Second Punic War, Rome and Carthage had lived in peace. The kingdom of Numidia, to the west of Carthage, had become a Roman client state, keeping an eye on Roman interests in the area. But Massinissa, the king of Numidia, had ambitions to expand into Carthaginian territory, and finally Carthage was provoked to war. Rome took the Numidian side, and the result was inevitable. Carthage was razed, and Carthaginian territory became a new Roman province called Africa.

- THE LATE REPUBLIC (133–27 BC) -

Although Rome had not followed a deliberate policy of imperialist expansion, by the mid-2nd century BC it found itself the dominant power in the Mediterranean. In many ways, a system of government designed to serve a city-state was inadequate to control an empire, and the strain on the apparatus of the republic was showing: As Rome's external power grew its internal government became more and more unstable.

Despite the office of tribune, Rome was effectively ruled by the patrician class. The senators, consuls, and the holders of most other offices were drawn from the upper levels of Roman society. Within the patrician class, individuals and families had more or less influence, the more powerful acting as patrons and sponsors to the less powerful, and expecting their votes in return. In effect, the whole of Republican government lay in the hands of a comparative few individuals.

Within the Senate, there were two main parties. The *Optimates* were conservatives who favored the status quo and sought to perpetuate the oligarchy. Their name translates roughly as "the best men." Opposed to them were the *Populares*, or "popular party," who supported reform and greater democracy. Despite their name, the Populares were every bit as aristocratic as the Optimates; only patricians were ever elected to the Senate.

While the Optimates were a cohesive force, the Populares were less organized and more dominated by charismatic personalities. More than once, men in a hurry tried to use the popular platform as a route to personal power—Julius Caesar arguably the most successful of them.

The continuing migration of free farmers to the city, replaced by slaves working latifundia, was exacerbated by a fall in the price of grain as Rome's expanding empire provided cheap imports from across the Mediterranean. The influx of slaves from foreign wars made it extremely difficult for free people to find employment and the swelling ranks of the urban poor became a major factor in city politics, willing to sell their votes to whoever offered them an advantage. Out of this situation was born the policy of "bread and circuses" (handouts of food and free public entertainments to keep the restless poor quiet) which was to dominate the 1st century BC.

LAND REFORMS

Another effect of the drift from the countryside to the cities was, paradoxically, a reduction of the manpower available for the army. Under republican law, a citizen-soldier had to satisfy a minimum property qualification; those who owned no land weren't subject to conscription. In addition, retiring soldiers expected a grant of land (the equivalent of a pension) on the completion of their service. Failing this, they too would join the ranks of the discontented urban poor.

TIBERIUS GRACCHUS

The Optimates in the Senate, many of whom were major landowners, blocked attempts at land reform legislation. In 133 BC, a tribune named Tiberius Sempronius Gracchus drew up a bill that proposed a limit on private land holdings to make more land available for individual farmers. Resurrecting a century-old precedent, Gracchus took his bill to the Popular Assembly first; it was bound to receive overwhelming support there, and then the senators couldn't reject it without embarrassment. However, it was vetoed in the Assembly by another tribune, M. Octavius. Gracchus made several concessions in the hope of persuading Octavius to withdraw his veto, but without success. Finally, in frustration, he called the Assembly together and persuaded them to vote Octavius out of office. The bill was passed, but Gracchus had alienated the Senate; even the Populares would not support him after such a snub.

It was not completely unprecedented for a bill to be passed without ratification by the Senate (which, in theory, was still just an advisory council to the consuls) but it was a radical step. To implement the bill, Gracchus proposed a three-man commission independent of the Senate, which the Assembly passed. Securing funding to run the commission and to provide seed and livestock to get the allotments started was a major problem, as the Senate controlled the treasury. Then the news arrived that King Attalus of Pergamum had died without heirs and had made the Roman people his heirs. The Senate would normally deal with such things, but Gracchus declared that he would bring the matter before the Assembly, clearly hoping to use these funds to implement his land bill.

Elections were drawing near, and Gracchus took the unusual, but not entirely unprecedented, step of running for a second term as tribune. After some heated debate, a mob of anti-Gracchus senators and their supporters attacked the Assembly, clubbing and stoning to death nearly 300 of his supporters. Gracchus himself was murdered near the temple of Jupiter on the Capitoline Hill, and all the bodies were thrown into the Tiber.

The Senate closed ranks, punishing several of Gracchus' supporters with death or exile. A modified form of the land bill went forward, alienating the Italian allies who stood to lose some of their lands for the allotment program. One, named Fregellae, actually revolted, and was destroyed. The problem rumbled on for another 10 years.

GAIUS GRACCHUS

Tiberius's younger brother, Gaius Gracchus, became tribune in 123 BC, and unlike his brother, he was reelected to the post the next year. He introduced various small pieces of legislation that strengthened the position of the Assembly in different ways, as well as several measures that promoted the equites (now a middle class between the patricians and the plebeians) into various functions that had previously been reserved for senators. He reintroduced his brother's land reform bill, undoing various modifications made by the Senate after Tiberius's death, as well as a number of other economic measures. He also proposed the founding of a

colony, Junonia, near the site of Carthage, with further land allotments to those who chose to settle there. This was the first Roman colony outside Italy.

While he was away supervising the founding of Junonia, Gracchus' enemies worked to undermine his position in Rome. His absence from the city led to a drop in support from the fickle Roman mob, and he failed to be reelected in 121 BC. After a servant of one of the consuls was killed in a scuffle with Gracchus' supporters, the consul, Opimius, declared this an act of rebellion, and the Senate passed a measure urging the consuls to do whatever was necessary to preserve the republic. This measure was known as *senatus consultum ultimum* ("the ultimate decree of the Senate"— essentially declaring a state of emergency) and would be used and misused several more times as the Republic decayed. The senators took up arms; Gracchus and his supporters occupied the Aventine Hill, and after fruitless negotiations, they were surrounded and killed. In the days that followed, over 3,000 surviving supporters of Gracchus were rounded up and executed.

The Senate had re-established its supremacy in brutal fashion, but the Assembly had realized that it could take on the Senate, and Rome's poor had found their political voice. Perhaps more importantly, the equites of the middle class began to lay claim to a share of power, which would have far-reaching consequences.

Further Expansion

Although Rome was focused on its internal problems throughout this period, its foreign territories continued to expand. When King Attulus of Pergamum willed his kingdom to the Roman people, it became the province of Asia. He had intended to prevent civil strife in his realm by substituting the rule of Rome for squabbles between various pretenders, but it was only partially successful. It was four years later that the province was finally settled.

In 125 BC, Rome received an appeal for help from the Greek trading city of Massalia, which was having trouble with Gallic raiders. A Roman army pacified the local tribes, and annexed their lands as the new province of *Gallia Transalpina* ("Gaul beyond the Alps"), also known as Narbonensis. The Balearic Islands off the southeastern coast of Spain, previously a favorite base for pirates, were also taken over to secure the sea routes.

The Jugurthine War

There was also trouble in North Africa. With the death of King Micipsa in 118 BC, Numidia was torn between three candidates for the throne. This was quickly reduced to one, Jugurtha, by the murder of one rival and the defeat of another, Adherbal, who fled to Rome. In 116 BC, the Senate sent a commission to divide Numidia between the two claimants, but Jugurtha invaded Adherbal's part of the kingdom in 112 BC, besieged him in the city of Cirta, and then tortured him to death after he surrendered. Many Italian merchants were also killed in Cirta, although this was probably not deliberate on Jugurtha's part.

An army was sent to Numidia, and Jugurtha surrendered after a brief military campaign, on the condition that he retain the throne. He went to Rome under a safe-conduct from the Senate to explain his actions, and while there, he arranged for the murder of another rival, his cousin Massiva. There were widespread accusations that he had bribed certain officials, and on leaving Rome, he is said to have described it as "a city for sale."

The war continued, and a Roman army was subjected to a humiliating defeat in 110 BC. A new commander, Quintus Caecilius Metellus, was sent to Africa, and began to wear Jugurtha's forces down in a long campaign. His deputy, Gaius Marius, was a commoner who had long been associated with the Metellus family, and had won a number of offices thanks to their patronage. He proved himself an able lieutenant in Numidia, but was anxious to return to Rome to run for consul. He was finally allowed to do so, according to some sources, after he stirred up dissatisfaction in the army and accused Metellus of incompetence.

With the support of the common people and the equites, Marius was appointed consul in 107 BC. The Assembly ignored the Senate's decision to renew Metellus' command, and appointed Marius to take over in Africa. As consul, Marius carried out several reforms in the army, the most notable of which was his abolition of the property qualification, which opened recruitment to all classes of society. He also placed generals in charge of paying and provisioning their own armies, starting a dangerous trend of armies being more loyal to their general than they were to Rome itself.

Having raised a large army from the newly expanded pool of military manpower, Marius and his men then sailed for Africa and, after an initial period of training and some indecisive skirmishes, his forces set about taking the fortresses controlled by Jugurtha, one by one. He was joined by his quaestor, Lucius Cornelius Sulla, who had been initially left behind in Italy to raise additional cavalry for the campaign.

Marius made steady progress, and his command was extended into 106 BC. Jugurtha recruited Bocchus, the king of neighboring Mauretania, to his side with the promise of land, and the two risked a pitched battle. At first, things looked bleak for the Romans, but the tide of the battle turned—for different reasons according to different sources. The historian Livy mentions a sudden storm, while Sallust credits the arrival of Sulla with additional troops. Bocchus sued for peace, and betrayed Jugurtha to Sulla in 105 BC.

Rome did not annex any territory after the defeat of Jugurtha. Bocchus was given part of Numidia and allowed to stay on the throne of Mauretania in exchange for betraying his onetime ally. The remainder of Numidia was given to Jugurtha's half-brother Gauda.

The Jugurthine war further sharpened the rivalry between the Senate and the people. Suspicions of corruption and incompetence in high places fueled the fire, and while Marius was established as a champion of the *Populares*, Sulla became the favorite of the *Optimates*.

MORE TROUBLE IN GAUL

While the war in Numidia was going on, a new menace emerged north of the Alps. Celtic and Germanic tribes were on the move throughout Europe, displacing others from their homelands in a general southward movement. It was only a matter of time before the first ripples of this mass migration reached Rome.

The Cimbri and Teutones were two Germanic tribes that originally came from somewhere in what is now Denmark. They briefly threatened Rome's northern frontier, but an army was sent to head them off in 113 BC, and they turned west. On the way, several Celtic tribes joined their migration, and in 110 BC this conglomeration of people reached Cisalpine Gaul. They proposed to settle on the borders of the Roman province, but the Senate was nervous about having such a host of barbarians sitting right on the frontier. After defeating a Roman army sent against them, the alliance split apart, with the Cimbri turning northwards while the others carried on westward to threaten Rome's Spanish possessions. A series of battles culminated in a comprehensive Roman defeat at Aurasio (modern Orange) in 105 BC; the worst defeat since the disaster at Cannae.

Considering the situation an emergency, the Popular Assembly appointed Marius consul for 104 BC, ignoring both the Senate and the law that required a gap of 10 years between consulships. In fact, Marius was consul for every year from then until 100 BC. Bickering between the Optimates and the Populares continued, with both sides trying to bring its opponent's supporters to trial on various charges of corruption and incompetence. More than once, the trials were disrupted by partisan mobs storming in to support their patron.

The Celts and Germans didn't press their advantage after the battle at Aurasio, and Marius had plenty of time to raise and train an army. It was not until 102 BC that they planned a joint attack on Italy: the Teutones along the coast from the west, the Cimbri over the Brenner Pass from the north, and the Celtic Tigurini over the Alps from the northeast. Marius defeated the Teutones, but his subordinate Catulus (a Senate appointee) only just escaped from the Cimbri, leaving a large part of Cisalpine Gaul to the invaders. The following year, Marius and Catulus combined forces to defeat the Cimbri, while Sulla pushed the Tigurini back into the Alps.

THE END OF MARIUS

Marius followed up his victory by securing grants of land for his veterans in Gaul, Sicily, Africa, and elsewhere. His popularity was at its peak. Saturninus, a supporter of Marius who was a tribune in 103 and 100 BC, forced through the veterans' land grants, and may have played a part in securing Marius' appointment to a powerful command, aimed at reducing piracy in the eastern Mediterranean. Saturninus also alienated the Senate further, and was tried for insulting an embassy from the kingdom of Pontus, but was rescued by a violent mob. When senatorial opposition to Saturninus's measures boiled over into open conflict, he brought some

of Marius' veterans into the Forum (an open square in the center of Rome), routed his opponents, and saw his legislation passed.

The elections for 99 BC were accompanied by such violence that the Senate passed the *senatus consultum ultimum* and called upon Marius to restore order. His onetime allies had seized the Capitol, and he forced them to surrender by surrounding the Senate House and cutting off their water supply. However, he was unable to prevent an angry mob from breaking in through the roof of the Senate House and pelting the trapped senators to death with broken roof tiles. A more politically motivated commander might have seized power at this point, but Marius perhaps sensed that he had been discredited by the crimes of his followers, and in 98 BC he went off to Asia in obscurity.

THE RISE OF SULLA

In the years that followed Marius' withdrawal from politics, some semblance of order was restored. Alleged sympathizers of Saturninus were purged, and the Senate and the equites struck an uneasy peace. For almost 10 years, they maneuvered around each other, looking for political advantage.

Meanwhile, electoral legislation aimed at reinforcing the distinction between Roman citizens and other Italians who had settled in Rome led to strained relations with the allied cities of Italy. This boiled over into war in 90 BC; resentment against Rome's high-handed treatment of fellow Italians had been growing for generations, and a series of revolts developed into what became known as the Social War (the war of the *socii*, or allies).

Rome faced enemies to both the north and south. One consul was given charge of each front; Marius, returning from self-imposed exile, was on the staff of the northern command, and Sulla served in the south. Legislation was passed giving all Italian communities easier access to full Roman citizenship, which partly defused the situation, but it was only with great loss of life that the war was brought to an end.

Sulla was rewarded for his service in the Social War by being elected consul for 88 BC. Later, he was given the governorship of Asia and a military command against Mithridates of Pontus. Shortly after Sulla left, Marius raised troops and marched on Rome, ruling jointly with Lucius Cornelius Cinna until his death in 86 BC. Cinna ruled effectively alone until Sulla returned having subdued Mithridates in 83 BC. Over the next three years, Sulla reconquered Italy, and conducted purges designed to rid him of all political opposition.

Having taken control of Rome by force, Sulla then tried to repair the faults in the constitutional machinery that had led to more than 20 years of upheaval. Various measures were passed to strengthen the Senate and prevent tribunes from bypassing it as the Gracchus brothers had done, and then Sulla announced his retirement from public life. However, the military coups staged by Marius and Sulla had set a precedent for the future.

THE FIRST TRIUMVIRATE

There was no shortage of ambitious men in Rome. Gnaeus Pompeius, a onetime officer of Sulla's who had become Rome's greatest military hero, granted the title *Magnus* ("the Great") for his military exploits, and Marcus Licinius Crassus, another of Sulla's lieutenants, who had become rich as a land speculator, buying up cheaply the properties of those who fell victim to Sulla's purges. Rebellions (including a slave uprising led by a Thracian gladiator named Spartacus) were put down in Italy and Spain, and the Senate tried to play the most powerful men against each other until Pompey and Crassus joined forces, led their armies to Rome, and shared the consulship for 70 BC. After this, there was a lull as both men apparently retired from politics.

POMPEY IN THE EAST

Pompey took a far-reaching and powerful command in the eastern Mediterranean in 66 BC aimed at clearing out pirates who were again menacing trade among the islands. Crete became a Roman province, and Pompey was then appointed to deal with Mithridates of Pontus who was again a problem. Pompey defeated Mithridates (who committed suicide in 63 BC), attacked Armenia, conquered Syria and Judea, and then returned to Rome.

CATALINE

At the same time, Lucius Sergius Cataline began a plot against the rulers of Rome. A former governor of Africa, he wanted to run for consul in 65 BC, but his candidacy

was rejected due to a pending corruption case. The plot was to murder the two consuls for the year as they took office, and replace them with Cataline and one of his supporters. The conspiracy failed, but was successfully covered up. After being cleared of the corruption charges (largely through political influence), Cataline ran for the consulship in 63 BC, but was defeated by Cicero, who gave an eloquent speech hinting that there were secret powers behind Cataline. After trying again the next year and failing, Cataline returned to direct action, planning to murder Cicero and start an armed uprising. But Cicero was warned of the plot and Cataline and his followers were defeated.

THE RISE OF CAESAR

While Pompey was away in the east, Gaius Julius Caesar rose from being a successful minor official to a real force in Roman politics. Although he was of patrician birth, he espoused the cause of the plebeians. When Pompey returned, he asked the Senate to ratify his peace settlement in the east and to provide land for his veterans—neither of them unreasonable requests—but the Senate refused. Meanwhile, Crassus was fighting a losing battle with the Senate as he tried to get a tax contract approved. Caesar returned from Spain, where he had been governor in 61 BC, and sought the Senate's permission to run for consul for the following year. The three men decided to act together to ensure that each got what he wanted, and the result was the First Triumvirate.

Pompey, Caesar, and Crassus combined their power, wealth, and political influence, and dominated the Senate. Caesar became consul for 59 BC; Pompey's eastern settlement was ratified, and his veterans received their land grants, while Crassus's business contacts saw their tax-gathering contract successfully renegotiated.

After leaving the consulship, Caesar was given a five-year command in Gaul and Illyricum. To look after his affairs while he was away from Rome, he had Publius Clodius appointed tribune, and senatorial opponents (including Cicero) removed. However, Clodius was soon out of control, mounting attacks on Pompey that often turned violent. After spending several months virtually confined to his house, Pompey recruited a thug named Milo to lead a counter-force. Rome lacked a police force at that time, and there was nothing to stop the two gangs fighting for control of the streets. Pompey suspected (possibly without a valid basis) that Crassus lay behind these attacks, and even denounced him publicly; without Caesar's moderating influence, the old rivalry between the two was rising to the surface. The three were able to smooth things over at an emergency meeting, however, and Pompey and Crassus were joint consuls for 55 BC while Caesar returned to Gaul.

CAESAR IN GAUL

During his five-year command, Caesar conquered the rest of Gaul and even mounted two reconnaissance expeditions to Britain. His *Commentaries on the Gallic War*, not surprisingly, paint him in the best possible light, and gloss over some glaring military and logistical errors; they were probably written more as propaganda to keep him in the public eye at home while away on campaign than as painstaking reports.

Despite some setbacks, Caesar proved himself an able general, whose talent for getting out of tight situations was only matched by his talent for getting into them. He made the most of his gifts for oratory and politics, and seems to have been worshiped by his soldiers, especially the X Legion in which he took a particular interest. His strategy in Gaul consisted of turning the various tribes against each other by offering support first to one tribe and then to another; by exploiting their fractious Celtic nature, he was able to prevent them from uniting and using their considerable numerical superiority.

Caesar finally defeated a confederacy of Gallic tribes under the command of Vercingetorix at Avaricum (modern Bourges) in 52 BC.

MEANWHILE...

While Caesar was fighting in Gaul, Crassus decided that he wanted a military command so that he wouldn't be overshadowed by the military exploits of Caesar and Pompey. He was given a command against the Parthians after his term as consul. The result was disastrous. A gifted financier with no significant military experience, Crassus led his forces to a crushing defeat at Carrhae in 53 BC, in which he himself was killed; the Triumvirate was reduced to Pompey and Caesar.

The elections for 53 BC were abandoned in the face of increasing gang violence between Clodius and Milo. Milo's followers murdered Clodius, sparking riots in which his body was taken to the Senate House by his followers and cremated, burning down the building in the process. The Senate declared martial law, and gave Pompey command of a force to restore order. Milo was exiled, and Pompey began to prepare for Caesar's return from Gaul by passing a law obliging all candidates to appear in person; coupled with another that forbade a general bringing his forces into Italy south of the Rubicon River, this meant that Caesar had to give up the protection of his troops and enter a Rome controlled jointly by Pompey and the Senate if he wished to stand for election.

Another complication was the fact that various cases were pending against Caesar in Rome. As a provincial governor and military commander and, if he were elected, as consul, he could not be tried, but the moment he left his troops and resumed civilian life in order to run for election the cases would proceed.

THE CIVIL WAR

In 49 BC, Caesar crossed the Rubicon at the head of his forces, plunging Rome into another civil war. The phrase "to cross the Rubicon" has remained a metaphor for a far-reaching and irrevocable action to the present day. Caesar's own comment at the time was *"Alea jacta est"* ("The dice are being thrown").

Pompey had two legions to Caesar's one, but they had both previously served under Caesar, and Pompey couldn't be sure of their loyalty in a civil war. Pompey was forced to spend time recruiting fresh troops, and Caesar took the initiative. Within months, Pompey's forces were forced to retreat across the Adriatic to Greece, and Caesar was the master of Italy. Through that winter, various negotiations were instigated by various parties, in the hope of averting civil war even at this late stage, but they all failed.

Caesar left subordinates named Marcus Antonius (Mark Anthony) and Marcus Aemilius Lepidus in charge of Italy and Rome respectively, and went to Spain to combat Pompey's sympathizers there. Caesar's deputy in Africa, Gaius Scribonius Curio, lost heavily to Pompeian forces there.

Pompey had the advantage in the east, and was building up his forces in Greece. Caesar had also raised troops, and forced a landing on the Greek coast in 48 BC. Pompey was defeated at the Battle of Pharsalus that year, and fled to Egypt. There the Pharaoh Ptolemy XIII wanted Caesar's support in the ongoing succession struggle with his half-sister Cleopatra VII; he had Pompey murdered as soon as he stepped ashore.

Caesar arrived three days later with 4,000 men, and decided to impose a settlement on Egypt; however, he alienated Ptolemy with his autocratic manner, and Caesar allied himself with Cleopatra, who became his mistress. The two were besieged in the palace at Alexandria through the winter of 48–47 BC by a hostile mob, and it was only with the arrival of another legion and the death of Ptolemy that peace was restored. Leaving three legions in Egypt to support Cleopatra and her new husband, her younger half-brother

Ptolemy XIV, Caesar put down another rebellion in Pontus, and returned to Rome in the summer of 47 BC. After a short time passing necessary legislation, he sailed for Africa, where Pompey's surviving followers had massed their forces, destroying them at the Battle of Thapsus and ending the Civil War.

CAESAR'S DEATH

Caesar had been given the office of *dictator* at various points in his career, but when he returned to Rome from Africa he was a dictator in the modern sense. His power was legitimized by successive elections to the consulship, but in February 44 BC he was made *dictator perpetuus* ("perpetual dictator") in addition to holding the consulship with Mark Anthony. This unprecedented office brought back memories of the kings the Romans had expelled centuries earlier, and on the Ides (15th) of March, 44 BC, Caesar was assassinated by a group of conspirators.

When Caesar died, he left Mark Anthony as the surviving consul, and Lepidus as the *magister equitum* ("master of horse," but a more powerful office than its name implies). The conspirators failed to ignite a popular uprising, and holed up in the Capitol. At Caesar's funeral, Anthony gave a speech that stirred the mob into rioting, Brutus and the other conspirators were forced to flee the city, leaving Anthony and Lepidus in control. However, Anthony must have been disappointed that Caesar's will did not name him as chief heir; instead, it favored Caesar's great-nephew, Gaius Octavius, who was not even 20.

OCTAVIUS' GAMBIT

What Octavius lacked in age, he made up for in political acumen, and he quickly crossed to Italy from Illyricum, where he had been training for a military campaign. He changed his name to Gaius Julius Caesar Octavianus, emphasizing his links to the murdered dictator, and was welcomed by Caesar's friends and, perhaps more importantly, by his veterans. Anthony delayed executing Caesar's will (perhaps jealous of the reception this previously obscure young man received) but Octavian paid several of Caesar's bequests out of his own pocket, further adding to his newfound popularity.

Anthony left Italy at the head of an army to chase down the surviving conspirators, and Octavian made good use of his rival's absence. He charmed the Senate. Cicero saw in him a useful tool who could be used against Anthony to strengthen the republic, and then be dropped when he'd served his purpose. Anthony was declared a public enemy: Lepidus supported him, and was also outlawed.

Octavian surprised the Senate by raising an army from Caesar's veterans, marching on Rome, and demanding to be elected consul for 42 BC. The Senate had clearly underestimated both his ambition and his ability. He outlawed Caesar's surviving murderers, and the Senate was persuaded to drop the decrees against Anthony and Lepidus. Octavian met with them on a small island near Bononia. All three brought their legions with them, and the fate of the Roman world hung in the balance once again.

THE SECOND TRIUMVIRATE

Like Caesar, Pompey, and Crassus before them, Octavian, Anthony, and Lepidus hammered out an agreement. They had themselves appointed *triumviri republicae constituendae* ("the three-man commission to restore the republic") and set about carving the Roman world up between them. Anthony received Cisalpine and Transalpine Gaul, strategically placed in the north of Italy, Lepidus took the rest of Gaul and Spain, while Octavian had Africa, Sicily, and Sardinia. To sanctify Caesar's memory, and further strengthen his own position, Octavian had Julius Caesar officially recognized as a god, and from this time on, deification was routine for Roman emperors upon their death.

The Triumvirate embarked on a series of proscriptions that eliminated political rivals and raised money; Cicero was one of the most prominent victims. Meanwhile, Brutus and Cassius, the last surviving conspirators against Caesar, had built up strength in the east. Brutus had seven legions in Macedonia, and Cassius another 12 in Syria. They joined forces in the late summer of 42 BC, but Octavian and Anthony took 28 legions to confront them, leaving Lepidus in charge of Italy. After three days of fighting at Philippi, both Brutus and Cassius were dead, and the republican cause effectively died with them.

DIVIDING THE SPOILS

The triumvirs rearranged the empire between them, in writing this time so that there would be no confusion. Anthony received the whole of Gaul (except Cisalpine Gaul which became part of Italy). Octavian received Spain, Sardinia and Africa, and Lepidus, who was falling out of favor, received no territory. Anthony was sent to the east to re-establish order, while Octavian consolidated the western empire. When Anthony's first wife died, he married Octavian's sister, Octavia.

Meanwhile, Sextus Pompeius, the son of Pompey the Great, had occupied Sicily and Sardinia, and had been joined by a number of exiles and refugees from the proscriptions. He wanted a slice of the empire, and forced the Triumvirate to deal with him by intercepting Italy's supply of imported grain. They concluded a treaty that included concessions for the surviving republicans. But the treaty didn't hold; the triumvirs invaded Sicily, and Sextus was defeated in a major sea battle at Naulochus in 36 BC. Octavian then secured Italy's eastern flank by conquering the far coast of the Adriatic, establishing an overland route to Greece.

ANTHONY AND CLEOPATRA

When Anthony went to the eastern provinces to raise money in 41 BC, he met Cleopatra again (having been with Caesar in Alexandria years before). While their relationship may in part have been a self-destructive infatuation, more importantly by allying himself with the last powerful independent monarch around the Mediterranean, Anthony hoped to use Egypt's wealth to form a stable base for an eastern empire to rival Octavian's territories in the west. He was away from Egypt campaigning in the east for four years, and in the interim, she bore him twins.

On his return, Anthony recognized Caesarion, Cleopatra's son by Caesar (implying that his heir and adopted son Octavian was not Caesar's legitimate successor), and gave him and his mother ruler of Cyprus in addition to Egypt. He further divided the eastern empire among his own children by Cleopatra.

This news did not go down well in Rome, where a propaganda war was fought between Anthony's supporters and Octavian. Octavian played on the Roman distrust of foreigners, painting Cleopatra as a scheming harpy and reminding the people that Anthony had rejected Octavian's own sister Octavia (a good Roman woman) for an eastern temptress.

A showdown was inevitable, and Anthony met Octavian's forces in a sea battle at Actium in 30 BC. Anthony and Cleopatra were forced to flee to Egypt, where they both committed suicide. Egypt was added to the Roman Empire, but instead of being just another province it became the personal domain of the emperor.

On January 11, 29 BC, Octavian ceremonially closed the doors of the Temple of Janus in Rome, indicating that peace had been restored. More than a century of strife had been brought to an end, but the price of peace was the death of the republic.

- THE EARLY EMPIRE (27 BC-69 AD) -

When Octavian took the name Augustus ("the majestic") and became the first emperor of Rome, the post of emperor did not yet officially exist. He held onto power using a package of republican offices, including both consul and tribune, and relied equally on force of personality. The Senate and people of Rome, none of whom had seen significant peace in their lives, didn't oppose him, not least because of the fear of yet another round of civil wars.

Although Augustus was unopposed after the defeat of Anthony at Actium, his reign as emperor is marked as starting three years later, in 27 BC. In that year, he entered the Senate, announced that the Republic had been restored, and humbly offered his resignation. The Senate responded by giving him the title *princeps* ("first citizen" -- the origin of the word "prince") and various offices that gave him almost absolute power.

AUGUSTUS

Augustus' reign was a period of rebuilding after the civil wars, and saw many public works funded by Augustus and by his former admiral Agrippa. Augustus is said to have boasted that he found a city of brick and left a city of marble. In addition to building works, Augustus carefully consolidated the whole of the empire, laying a solid foundation for his successors.

He also created a full-time civil service of talented freedmen (many of them Greek) within the imperial household, to deal with the day-to-day administration of the empire.

Previously this had been carried out by senators and holders of various offices, and the results had been inefficient at best and corrupt at worst.

Augustus continued the expansion of the empire with campaigns in Germany, but this ended in disaster in 9 AD when three legions under general Quinctilius Varus were utterly destroyed in the Teutoberg Forest by the German chieftain Arminius. From then on, the Rhine became the frontier of the Roman Empire in Germany.

When Augustus died in 14 AD, the fundamental administrative machinery of the Roman Empire was in

THE JULIO-CLAUDIAN EMPERORS

Rome's first imperial dynasty takes its name from the two families that spawned it: the Julian line of Augustus, and the Claudian line of Livia, his second wife and mother of his successor Tiberius. It lasted nearly a hundred years, and is probably the best-known of Rome's imperial families.

Augustus	27 BC-14 AD
Tiberius	14-37 AD
Gaius (Caligula)	37-41 AD
Claudius	41-54 AD
Nero	54-68 AD

place, but the question of the succession was a vexed one. The titles and offices he had held were elected, rather than hereditary. However, Augustus had given his stepson Tiberius, an accomplished general, various constitutional powers during his lifetime, and it was clear that Tiberius was his chosen successor. It remained only for the Senate to vote him the title of augustus.

Tiberius

Tiberius lacked the charm of Augustus. He was moody, morose, and fearful, and quickly gained a reputation for brutality in disposing of anyone he saw as a potential threat; he had only become Augustus's heir after the untimely deaths of two adopted sons and the exile of a third, and may have felt insecure in his position. However, the bureaucracy kept working throughout his reign, giving Rome and the Empire an efficient administration.

Tiberius did not like Rome, and spent the last 11 years of his reign at his villa on the isle of Capri, leaving Rome in the hands of his lieutenant Sejanus, who drew more and more power to himself until he overstepped his bounds and was arrested and put to death by a squad of vigiles (the Praetorian Guards being entirely loyal to Sejanus) acting on Tiberius's orders. As the years of his seclusion went by, rumors started to reach the city of Tiberius' dissolute lifestyle, and when he died in 37 AD, there was rejoicing in the city.

Gaius (Caligula)

Gaius was Tiberius' great-nephew, and the son of the war hero Germanicus (a descendant of both Julius Caesar

and Augustus). He had grown up with his father on his campaigns in Germany, and his nickname of Caligula ("little boots") came from his mother's habit of dressing him in a miniature uniform.

Caligula wasn't Tiberius's first heir, becoming heir-apparent after the deaths of four predecessors (including his two older brothers), but he was welcomed as a change from the moody and despotic Tiberius. He was young and handsome, and upon his accession, he took the popular steps of pardoning political offenders and reducing taxes. As his reign progressed, however, he became increasingly unstable. He emptied the imperial coffers with a fantastically lavish lifestyle, and started threatening prominent citizens with death unless they turned over their wealth to him. He had Incitatus, his favorite racehorse, appointed to the Senate and given a marble stall with hangings of imperial purple. He is even said to have declared himself a living god and slept with his sisters to conceive children in imitation of the Greek god Zeus.

Caligula's End

In 41 AD, a group of officers assassinated Caligula. Then only 30, he had not appointed a successor. While the Senate debated the problem, the Praetorian Guards rampaging through the palace found Claudius, the 50-year-old uncle of the murdered Caligula, cowering behind a curtain, and decided he should be the next emperor. The Senate was in no position to refuse.

Claudius

Claudius was an unlikely emperor. He had a limp and a heavy stammer, and was thought by many to be a fool; it may be that the Praetorians chose him at first as a joke. But he turned out to be just what Rome needed after Tiberius and Caligula. His administration was just, and he endeared himself to the people by his informal manner at games and other events.

Claudius's second wife, Agrippina the Younger, was mother to Nero, and actively promoted her son as his successor. Claudius already had a son, named Britannicus in honor of his father's conquest of southern Britain, but Agrippina is said to have plotted against him, and after Claudius died (poisoned by Agrippina, according to Suetonius) Britannicus himself was poisoned.

Britain

After the disaster in the Teutoberg Forest, Augustus hadn't added new territories to the Empire, and neither had Tiberius. Caligula had sent an expedition with the intent of conquering Britain, but this dissolved in farce at the edge of the English Channel when the troops were ordered to collect sea-shells that Caligula then displayed in Rome as tribute from his supposed conquest of the Ocean.

Claudius could have had several reasons for invading Britain. Adding a new province to the empire would increase his prestige and help counter any thoughts that he was an unfit emperor. Sending a force to garrison Britain would weaken the army by placing several legions there, out of striking distance of Rome in case they decided to promote another emperor. The official reason was that the Celtic tribes of southern Britain were offering support and encouragement to rebel elements in Gaul.

In 43 AD, four legions were sent to Britain. They quickly overcame resistance in the open country of the south and east, but ran into problems as they pressed into the areas that are now Wales and northern England. A frontier was established on a line between Gloucester and Lincoln, and legionary bases were built at key points. A Roman colony was established at Camulodunum (modern Colchester), to provide land for Roman veterans and to give the new province a Roman city as its capital.

NERO

Nero became emperor at the age of 16. He had an ambivalent relationship with his mother Agrippina; some sources claim that she tried to rule through him, and others that she embarked on an incestuous affair with him to safeguard her own position. In the end, he decided to have her killed.

In 64 AD, Rome was swept by a great fire that caused widespread destruction, especially in the poorer areas where buildings were predominantly of timber. Rumors started to spread that Nero was behind the fire: There were whisperings that he wanted to destroy Rome in order to rebuild it to his own plan, renaming it Neropolis, the city of Nero. Stories were told of gangs of men throwing torches into buildings as the fire spread, claiming they were acting on the Emperor's orders. The most famous tale said Nero played a lyre (not a fiddle, which had not been invented) and sang of the fall of Troy as he watched Rome being consumed by flames. Nero defended himself by foisting the blame on a little-known Jewish sect called the Christians, and centuries of persecution began.

Nero always had ambitions to be a singer and musician, and more than once he went to Greece to compete in various musical festivals, where terrified judges awarded him the top prize, adding to his vanity. No-one was allowed to leave while he was performing, for any reason. Stories are told of audience members who gave birth in mid-performance, and others who feigned death in order to escape by being carried out for burial.

EMPORER'S FOLLY

Discontent with Nero grew, both in the city and, more dangerously, in the army. In 65 AD, a plot against him was discovered in the Senate, and many prominent Romans were forced to commit suicide along with their families in order to avoid even worse fates at Nero's hand. Rebellions broke out in Britain (under Queen Boudicca), Judea (the Zealot revolt that resulted in the destruction of the Temple), and Armenia, and by 68 AD army commanders in Gaul, Africa, and Spain were taking control of their provinces and marching on Rome. Nero fled the city, and was condemned in absentia by the Senate. He took his own life with the words "What an artist dies here!"—vain to the last.

THE YEAR OF THE FOUR EMPERORS (69 AD)

With Nero's death, the Julio-Claudian dynasty ended. The rebellious governor of Hispania Tarraconensis, Galba, took control of Rome, and was made Emperor with the support of the Praetorian Guard. When Galba tried to cut spending, however, the Praetorians murdered him and transferred their allegiance to Otho, governor of Lusitania, who had marched from Spain with his troops. Then the army of the Rhine declared their commander, Vitellius, Emperor, marching on Rome and defeating Otho's force's north of the city. Not to be outdone, the army of the Danube came out in support of Titus Flavius Vespasian, another general, who was putting down the revolt in Judea. They marched on Rome and killed Vitellius, pillaging the city while they waited for Vespasian to arrive.

- THE MIDDLE EMPIRE (69–235 AD) -

The Flavian dynasty (from Vespasian's family name) began a new age for Rome. The emphasis was on stabilizing the frontiers and maintaining order, and the wealth and power of the city grew, inviting comparisons with the so-called Golden Age under Augustus. Emperors took the name Caesar among their various titles, even though they had no family ties to justify it: Caesar had become a title, and in later centuries would be the ancestor of titles such as Kaiser and Czar.

VESPASIAN

Unlike all his predecessors, Vespasian was not an aristocrat. He came from fairly humble origins (his father was a tax-collector and moneylender from a small town in the Sabine Hills), but Vespasian had joined the army and risen through the ranks. Upon reaching Rome, Vespasian took control of the city from the army and returned it to the Senate, which promptly voted him complete Imperial power.

A hard and efficient worker, Vespasian stabilized the Empire after the disruptive reigns of the later Julio-Claudians. He extended the qualifications for Roman citizenship to include the people of many provinces, giving the people of the Empire more of a stake in it. He refilled the Imperial coffers, depleted by excess and plunder, but was careful in imposing new taxes. He expanded the civil service created by Augustus, and linked it with the Senate rather than the Imperial household.

Throughout his reign, Vespasian never let power go to his head. He was known for being direct and down-to-earth, and his last words were reportedly "I think I feel deification setting in." Joke or not, it was an accurate prediction, and Vespasian was the first Emperor since Claudius to be made a god after his death.

TITUS

Vespasian's eldest son, Titus, showed promise of continuing the peace and prosperity his father had brought to the Empire. Handsome, charming and generous to a fault, he was immensely popular, although historians may have exaggerated his virtues to emphasize the contrast with his brother and successor, the gloomy and unpopular Domitian.

However, Titus never seemed to have much of a head for government; he enjoyed being Emperor too much to concern himself with actually ruling. The civil service ruled the Empire, and corrupt officials made fortunes behind his back. A second fire ravaged Rome during his reign, and in 79 AD the towns of Pompeii and Herculaneum were destroyed by a catastrophic eruption of Mount Vesuvius; on both occasions, Titus donated to relief efforts with characteristic generosity. When he died at the age of 41, he had run through much of the cash reserves that his father had built up.

DOMITIAN

Titus died without heirs, and was succeeded by his brother Domitian. At 29, he was much younger than Titus and had none of his brother's charm. Like his father Vespasian, Domitian was an able soldier, and seems to have been more comfortable among the troops on the Rhine and Danube frontiers than ruling in Rome. However, he lacked his father's sense of humor, and was suspicious and easily offended. He tried to rule firmly, but crossed the line and became a tyrant.

Domitian's major achievements were in securing the Empire's frontiers. He reorganized the army of the Rhine to make it more efficient, and coincidentally to reduce its numbers so that its commanders would be less confident about marching on Rome in a bid to become Emperor themselves. In his reign, the celebrated general Agricola pacified the north of Britain and established the northern frontier at the line where Hadrian's Wall would later be built.

Domitian ignored the Senate, placing his trust in nouveau riche equites and convening a Council of State to pass legislation and conduct treason trials. A network of paid informers assured a steady flow of trials, and the confiscated wealth of those condemned went to refill the Imperial treasury after the drains of Titus' short but lavish reign. His unpopularity grew, until at last he was murdered by a member of his own household. Where his father and brother had been declared gods upon their deaths, Domitian fared differently: The vengeful Senate ordered his name removed from all inscriptions in public places, stamping out his official memory.

NERVA

Although the Senate had always gone through the process of ratifying an Emperor's succession by voting him various legal powers, Nerva was the first Emperor to actually be appointed by the Senate. He was of good birth, elderly, and a lawyer by profession, and although he

only ruled for two years, he set the stage for a period of peace and prosperity that lasted for almost a century. He pardoned those who had been exiled by Domitian's courts, but in a bold move, he refused to give up the informers who had testified against them; this was to be a time of reconciliation and fresh starts, not a continuing spiral of vengeance and bloodshed.

As the Senate's appointee, Nerva made a show of deferring to them, but he did not relinquish any of the powers of the Emperor. Fortunately, they never came into conflict. He selected as his successor a commander on the Rhine frontier by the name of Trajan, adopting him as his son. Upon Nerva's death, the Senate accepted his choice.

TRAJAN

Trajan was another first: The first Emperor who was not Italian by birth. Although he was of Roman ancestry, he was born in Spain, where his father had been governor. Like Vespasian before him, Trajan was a professional soldier, and he threw himself into the task of governing with military zeal and efficiency.

It was under Trajan that the Roman Empire reached its greatest extent. Looking for a tenable frontier north of the Danube, he campaigned in Dacia (modern Hungary and Romania). The official account of the campaign can be seen in Rome carved on the monument known as Trajan's Column. Towards the end of his reign, he also led an expedition into Armenia and Mesopotamia.

Unlike Domitian, Trajan was a capable administrator as well as a soldier. His informal manner put people at ease, and he was well-liked. He took various measures to stamp out corruption and profiteering among provincial administrators. The provinces flourished, becoming as prosperous as Italy.

HADRIAN

Trajan chose his cousin and fellow Spaniard Hadrian as his successor. Like Trajan, he was a soldier, but he was more cautious by nature. At the time of Trajan's death, the frontiers were looking insecure. Rebellions in freshly conquered provinces and heavy losses in cross-border warfare in Britain convinced Hadrian that Rome had over-reached. One of his first acts as Emperor was to tour the frontier provinces and see to their security.

In Britain, Hadrian is most famous for the wall that bears his name, running for more than 80 miles from one side of the island to the other and still visible today despite centuries of stone-robbing for farms and other buildings. Initially, this fortification was built of earth, faced with turf, and topped with a wooden palisade; it was not until later, under Septimius Severus (see page 118), that the turf wall was rebuilt in stone. On the Rhine and Danube frontiers Hadrian set up a similar fortification, known as the *limes* ("boundary"). Armenia and Mesopotamia were abandoned.

Hadrian also codified Roman law, making it consistent across the whole Empire; previously, different cities and provinces had different laws, imposed by or negotiated with

Rome on an individual basis. Cities continued to grow in most of the provinces—a vital tool, to the Roman mind, for the spreading of *romanitas* ("Roman-ness," the word they gave to their own civilization and cultural values).

ANTONINUS PIUS

Titus Aurelius Antoninus was a middle-aged Senator when Hadrian adopted him and appointed him as his successor. Despite his age, he was to rule for 23 years; the longest rein since Augustus. He later gained the name Pius ("the dutiful") as a gift from the Senate, in recognition of his devotion to Hadrian. Like Nerva, he had made his reputation as a lawyer.

Unlike Hadrian, Antoninus had a philosophical and studious nature, and was content to stay in Rome and leave the frontier in the hands of his subordinates. During his reign, an adjustment was made to the frontier between the headwaters of the Rhine and the Danube, and the northern frontier in Britain was pushed back to a new turf fortification (the Antonine Wall) built in what is now Scotland; by the end of his reign, though, the legions had retreated to Hadrian's Wall.

Historical documents from the reign of Antoninus are comparatively rare, but there seems to have been trouble on the frontiers, especially in the north and east of the Empire from Dacia to Armenia, Judea, and Egypt. However, these were not on the scale that would be seen in future centuries.

MARCUS AURELIUS

When Marcus Aurelius became Emperor, many people thought that the dream of Plato's ideal philosopher-king had been realized. On the same day that Hadrian had adopted Antoninus as his heir, Antoninus had adopted Hadrian's 16-year-old nephew, Marcus; Antoninus's 23-year reign gave Marcus Aurelius ample time to learn the art of diplomacy from his adopted father, and to develop a rapport with the populace that assured a smooth transition when Antoninus died.

Marcus Aurelius is best known today for his *Meditations*, a philosophical work he wrote while Emperor. He believed in duty and charity, and his moral outlook made him a favorite among early Christian monks, who preserved much of what remains of Roman literature.

Although he had no military training, Marcus was forced to travel around the frontiers of the Empire shoring up the defenses as pressure from the north began to mount. His health was delicate, and the task was arduous for him. He repulsed an attack from Parthia, but worse was to come.

Troops returning from the wars brought a pestilence with them, a plague that raged from 164–180 AD, reaching Rome in 166 AD. According to chroniclers of the time, thousands died every day in Rome and whole areas of the countryside were depopulated. Marcus Aurelius himself died of the plague in 180 AD; the Christians were blamed for calling down the wrath of the gods on the Empire, and fresh rounds of persecutions followed.

THE FLAVIANS AND LATER EMPERORS

The Flavian dynasty consisted of Vespasian and his two sons, Titus and Domitian. They were followed by a dynasty known as the "five good Emperors," selected for their abilities and adopted in order to legally inherit the imperator. After this period, Rome returned to civil wars until the Severans settled the problem of the succession for a time, but not the problem of finding good Emperors.

THE FLAVIANS

Vespasian	69–79 AD
Titus	79–81 AD
Domitian	81–96 AD

THE FIVE GOOD EMPERORS

Nerva	96–98 AD
Trajan	98–117 AD
Hadrian	117–138 AD
Antoninus Pius	138–161 AD
Marcus Aurelius	161–180 AD

THE SEVERANS

Septimius Severus	193–211 AD
Caracalla	211–217 AD
Macrinus	217–218 AD
Elegabalus	218–222 AD
Alexander Severus	222–235 AD

The Antonine Plague wasn't the only problem facing Marcus Aurelius in the latter part of his reign. Constant campaigning was required on the northern frontier to keep German and Sarmatian tribes at bay. A false rumor of Aurelius's death in 175 AD led to a revolt in the east, with the military commander Avidius Cassius declaring himself Emperor with the support of the governor of Egypt. Although Cassius was murdered by one of his own officers before the revolt came to battle, Aurelius was obliged to pull troops away from the northern frontier in order to deal with the threat, and the barbarians were quick to take advantage.

Between the plague and the constant warfare, Rome was running out of manpower, both for the army and for agriculture. Several of Aurelius' predecessors had enlisted newly conquered and frontier-dwelling barbarians as auxiliaries, and others had been pacified by grants of land; the plan was that, once exposed to the civilizing influence of the Roman way of life, they would become productive members of the Empire rather than a threat. Aurelius carried this policy further than anyone before him and settled large populations of Germans in depopulated rural areas along the Danube frontier, and, briefly, in northeast Italy. Over time, this practice was to develop into a widespread policy of giving land within the Empire to barbarians, on the condition that they keep other barbarians out.

COMMODUS

Marcus Aurelius departed from the policy that had brought him and his immediate predecessors to the Imperial throne. Instead of appointing a successor on the basis of merit, he chose his son Commodus, who became Emperor upon Aurelius' death. Just 19 years old, Commodus was more interested in horseracing and the spectacles of the arena than in the task of governing an Empire that was falling steadily into crisis. He indulged the Praetorian Guard (perhaps to secure his own personal safety) and promoted his friends to high offices, regardless of their abilities or birth.

After a bungled attempt on his life, Commodus responded with great savagery, executing senators if he merely suspected them of disloyalty. This gave rise to fresh conspiracies, which resulted in more executions. Commodus took to dressing himself as Hercules, carrying a club with which he would lash out at anyone who displeased him. He insisted on driving his own team at the races, and even competed in the arena as a gladiator. Like Caligula before him, Commodus had become both a tyrant and an embarrassment to the office of Emperor; after his mistress failed to kill him with poison, a gladiator was brought in to murder him.

SEPTIMIUS SEVERUS

The conspirators who arranged for Commodus' death chose Pertinax, one of his more able lieutenants, as the next Emperor, and the Praetorian Guard agreed. However, the Praetorians changed their minds when Pertinax began to reimpose discipline and undo the indulgences they had enjoyed under Commodus. After just three months, the Praetorian Guard, in theory the Emperor's personal bodyguard, murdered Pertinax, and announced they would give the office of Emperor to the highest bidder.

That was a senator named Didius Julianus, but his reign was also brief. The army of the Danube frontier marched on Rome, and Lucius Septimius Severus, the governor of Pannonia, was installed as Emperor. Severus did not wait to see how the Praetorians reacted to his accession; he disbanded the Praetorian Guard and replaced them with a bodyguard chosen from among his own troops.

Severus was the first Emperor who was not of Roman descent. He came from North Africa, and spoke Punic (the language of the Carthaginians) as a first language, rather than Latin. He lacked the education and culture of most Roman citizens, but he was a decisive leader, which Rome desperately needed.

Among his first acts was to defeat a rival candidate for Emperor, Prescennius Niger, and the troops from the eastern frontier who backed him. He showed no mercy to those he defeated, and the city of Byzantium, which had held out for Prescennius, was razed. Albinus, the governor of Britain, had raised an army in Gaul with the intention of replacing Severus, and was dealt with equally firmly. After defeating the rebels, Severus turned over the city of Lyons, Albinus's stronghold, to the fury of his troops.

At home, Severus took steps to reduce the power of the Senate and the nobility. He took personal command of the treasury, and the Senate's role in government was reduced to that of a city council for Rome. He kept a legion of Parthians stationed within easy reach of Rome, and while he made a public display of venerating Marcus Aurelius and the noble Emperors of the past, it was no secret that he ruled by the sword.

On the other hand, Severus did much to improve the lot of provincials and the lower classes. Some historians attribute this to a sympathy based on his own humble origins, while others ascribe to him a more practical motive; it was, after all, from this pool of manpower that the army was recruited, and the army was the means by which he gained and held onto power.

The frontiers were comparatively peaceful during his reign. He undertook a major rebuilding of the northern frontier in Britain, replacing the old turf and timber wall with a stone one. So extensive was this project that up until the 19th century, scholars knew the wall as the Severan Wall rather than Hadrian's Wall.

Severus died at York in 211 AD; his final advice to his heirs was reportedly "Stick together. Enrich the troops; nothing else matters."

CARACALLA

Severus appointed his two sons, Caracalla and Geta, as joint Emperors. Bitter rivals, they ignored their father's advice to stick together, and after an attempted compromise of dividing the Empire between them, Caracalla had Geta murdered in his mother's arms. He followed this up, according to chroniclers, by a massacre of 20,000 people whom he suspected of favoring his brother.

Caracalla did take to heart his father's advice about enriching the troops—so much so that the treasury ran out of cash, and, with the silver mines becoming exhausted, he was obliged to debase the currency by mixing cheap alloys with the precious metal. He extended Roman citizenship to all freeborn inhabitants of the provinces, but this was a means of increasing tax revenues rather than an act of benevolence.

Fancying himself as a new Alexander the Great, Caracalla mounted an expedition to conquer Parthia. When this force reached Alexandria in Egypt and some of the city's inhabitants made fun of him, Caracalla had all the young men of the city paraded before him, and killed.

In 217 AD he was murdered by his own Praetorian Prefect, Macrinus.

ELEGABALUS AND ALEXANDER SEVERUS

Macrinus appointed himself Emperor, but his reign didn't last long. When he returned from the unsuccessful Parthian expedition, he was ambushed by a force whose loyalty had been bought by Julia Maesa, a sister-in-law of Septimius Severus and a longtime enemy of Macrinus. She installed her son Elegabalus as Emperor.

Elegabalus (sometimes spelled Heliogabalus) was a high priest of the Syrian cult of the sun god, and decided to use his status as Emperor to impose this religion on the whole Roman world. This and a luxurious lifestyle more like that of some decadent eastern potentate than an Emperor of Rome caused discontent to grow until he was murdered by the Praetorian Guard, who declared his younger brother, Alexander Severus, Emperor.

Alexander was only 13 when he came to power, and for at least the early part of his reign Rome was ruled by his mother's appointees. The Empire was facing economic ruin, both from increasing lawlessness and from the increasing debasement of the currency. Financial reforms pulled the Empire back from the brink of disaster, but a revolt in Parthia led to Sassanid princes threatening Asia Minor. In 231 AD, Alexander led a force to deal with them, and was badly defeated.

Meanwhile, as frequently happened, the withdrawal of troops from the other frontiers for this campaign led to trouble. Alexander rushed to the Rhine, but instead of mounting another expedition against the Germans, he offered to buy them off with gold. This offended the soldiers so deeply that they murdered both Alexander and his mother. This time, there were no Imperial candidates waiting in the wings, and the Empire was plunged into anarchy.

- THE ANARCHY -

In the 50 years that followed the death of Alexander Severus, no less than 26 Emperors came and went, each no more able than the last to restore order. Most came to power at the head of an army; their reigns lasted from a few months to a few years before another army came forward with another candidate. Only one of the whole number died of natural causes.

While the Empire was convulsed with revolts and civil wars, external threats arose on all sides. The Franks, expanding from their Baltic homelands, crossed the Rhine, driving other German tribes before them. Goths (from what is now Poland) descended on the Danube frontier and overran Thrace, Macedonia, and Dacia. Persia attacked the eastern frontier, and even captured one short-lived Emperor named Valerian, after defeating a Roman expedition. As

the Franks and Alemanni broke through on the Rhine, the commander of the Rhine garrison, Posthumus, proclaimed himself head of an "Empire of the Gauls" that maintained its independence for 14 years and four of its own Emperors.

The Goths were defeated by Claudius, who took the title Claudius Gothicus in recognition of his achievement. To add to Rome's difficulties, a plague (probably smallpox) ravaged the Empire from 251–266 AD, with Claudius Gothicus among its victims. His successor, Aurelian, repulsed the Alemanni in northern Italy, and began a major strengthening of Rome's defenses; a sign that nowhere in the Empire was safe.

Meanwhile, Egypt and a number of eastern provinces declared independence, and the governor of Egypt adopted the title

Augustus and started issuing his own currency. Britain joined the breakaway Empire of the Gauls. After some years, Aurelian was able to subdue them both and begin stabilizing the Empire, but he was murdered by a group of disaffected officers in 275 AD, and the chaos resumed.

Diocletian and Maximian

In 289 AD, the Praetorian Guard gave the office of Emperor to Diocletian, the son of a freed slave from the east. Realizing that the Empire was too large to control and its enemies too numerous for one man to face, Diocletian appointed the general Maximian co-ruler, making Maximian the Augustus of the West, and keeping the Eastern Empire for himself.

He also completely reorganized the army, creating a mobile force to back up the frontier garrisons in the event of barbarian attacks. Recruited from the wilder parts of the Empire, this force included barbarian mercenaries from beyond the frontiers, and was much more potent in battle than the settled garrison troops. Formerly under the command of the governor, troops within a province were now led by a career soldier, known as the Dux (originally meaning "leader," this word evolved over the centuries into the medieval title of duke).

Diocletian also reformed the civil service and provincial administration, and stabilized the freefalling currency. He even published an edict setting the prices for major commodities in an effort to slow the rampant inflation of previous decades.

Dicocletian's reforms relied upon a much expanded civil service, and one commentator of the time claimed, perhaps in jest, that half the population of the Empire worked for the state. This expansion of government slowed Rome's decline for a time, and the only serious problem during Diocletian's reign was the revolt of Britain under its fleet commanders, Carausius and Allectus, from 287 to 297 AD.

Because of failing health, Diocletian abdicated in 305 AD. For the sake of a peaceful succession, Maximian was persuaded to abdicate with him.

Constantine

A few years after Diocletian had appointed Maximian Augustus of the West, the two created a pair of junior Emperors (Caesars) to act as deputies: Constantius in the West and Galerius in the East. When the two Augusti stepped down, the two Caesars filled their roles.

This left the posts of Caesar vacant. They were to have been filled by Maximian's son Maxentius and Constantius' son Constantine, but Galerius had other ideas. He promoted two of his own followers, Maximinus Daia and Severus, and detained Constantine in Asia Minor. However, Constantine was able to escape, and stayed one step ahead of pursuers to reach his father, who was in Britain at the time. Constantius died in York the following year, and the troops hailed Constantine as Augustus of the West, the senior title Severus had been looking forward to. Galerius and Severus disputed Constantine's elevation in rank.

Meanwhile, Maxentius was proclaimed Augustus in Rome, with the help of his father Maximian (who returned from his retirement, claiming the title of Caesar of the East) which put him in direct conflict with Galerius. Galerius sent Severus to retake Rome, but Maxentius bribed Severus's troops to desert, and the Caesar of the East was killed. Maximian then tried to take his son's title, but failed, and fled to Gaul.

By 308 AD, the situation was confused: Constantine claimed to be Augustus of the West, Maxentius and Galerius Augustus of the East, Maximian Caesar of the West, Maximinus Daia Caesar of the East. Galerius considered Constantine to be merely Caesar of the West (which meant that the position of Augustus of the West was vacant to his mind), there were two Augusti of the East, and Maxentius was out for his father's blood. Attempts were made to persuade Diocletian to leave retirement to take over the vacant (as far as Galerius and Maximinus were concerned) position of Augustus of the West, but instead he brokered a new deal: Galerius and Maximinus Daia were confirmed in their Eastern titles, Constantine was officially demoted to Caesar in the West, Maximian and Maxentius lost their titles (although Maxentius still held onto power in Rome), and a friend of Galerius, Licinius became Augustus in the West.

Other pretenders arose in North Africa and the East, and in 310 AD Maximian attempted to take Constantine's Caesarship, but was soon captured and hanged himself. In 311 AD, Galerius died of natural causes, provoking a war between

THE LATE DYNASTIES

THE HOUSE OF CONSTANTINE

Constantius I	305–306 AD
Constantine the Great	307–337 AD
Constantine II	337–340 AD (West)
Constans I	337–350 AD (Central; later West and Central)
Constantius II	337–361 AD (East; later all)
Julian	360–363 AD

THE HOUSE OF VALENTINIAN

Valentinian I	364–375 AD (West)
Valens	364–378 AD (East)
Gratian	367–383 AD (West)
Valentinian II	375–392 AD (West)

THE HOUSE OF THEODOSIAN

Theodosius I	379–395 AD (East)
Arcadius	395–408 AD (East)
Theodosius II	408–450 AD (East)
Honorius	395–423 AD (West)
Valentinian III	425–455 AD (West)

THE POPES

The authority of the Popes (originally the bishop of Rome) in the early Empire was weak, and their situations were often precarious. Indeed, of the 32 Popes from the time of Peter (the first Pope; martyred between 64 and 68 AD) to Miltiades (the Pope at the time of Constantine's Edict of Toleration in 313 AD), three were martyred (and legend claims three more shared this fate), two died in prison, some were forced to abdicate, some served terms measured only in months, there were frequent periods of months or years when the church was prevented from electing a new Pope, and at times rival antipopes held sway over some portion of the Roman church.

In addition, the early Popes had to deal with the competing claims of the bishops of other major cities. In 380 AD, Emperor Theodosius I finally declared the bishop of Rome superior to his brethren. The Patriarch of Constantinople (the Eastern Capital of the Empire) never accepted his inferiority to the Patriarch of Rome (the Western Capital of the Empire) and this resulted in antagonism over the centuries and a permanent schism between the Roman Catholic Church and the Eastern Orthodox Churches in 1054 AD.

It must be remembered that, while they inserted themselves into Imperial politics in the Empire's waning years, and were advisers to the Christian Emperors, it wasn't until the 8th century that the Popes became secular rulers of Rome and the Papal States of central Italy.

Licinius and Maximinus Daia over his title. Meanwhile, in 312 AD, Constantine was finally strong enough able to march on Rome. He scattered the defensive forces, and Maxentius drowned in the Tiber while trying to escape.

Constantine's mother was a Christian, and according to legend, when he was marching to confront Maxentius, he had a vision of a cross in the sun, with the words *in hoc signo vincas* ("under this emblem you will conquer") He adopted the Christian chi-rho monogram as his banner, and after his victory published the Edict of Toleration, banning all persecution of Christians.

A year later, Maximinus Daia committed suicide, leaving only Constantine and Licinus in power. But Constantine believed that Rome's future lay under a single command rather than a divided rule, and after 11 years of biding his time and raising forces, in 323 AD he attacked Licinus with over 100,000 men. After a series of victories, Constantine was left in sole control of the Empire.

A dedicated Christian since 312 AD, Constantine attended (as a layman) a council of western bishops in 314 AD to settle the question of the Donatist heresy, outlawed pagan sacrifice in 324 AD, and convened the Council of Nicaea in 325 AD to deal with the heresy of Arianism. In 330 AD, Constantine moved the capital of the Empire from pagan Rome to the new Christian city of Constantinople (on the site of ancient Byzantium in Thrace).

- THE END OF EMPIRE -

Constantine died in 337 AD, and the Empire's unity did not survive him. His three sons, Constantine, Constans, and Constantius, divided the territory between them, and another 25 years passed in civil wars, murders, and usurpations. The last of Constantine's sons died in 361 AD, and his cousin Julian gained sole control of the Empire for a short time. He was devoted to the traditional gods, and worked to undo the influence of Christianity on the state; for this reason history knows him as Julian the Apostate. However, he was killed in battle against the Persians after

reigning for just two years, and Christianity returned, becoming increasingly influential in Rome.

The Valentinian and Theodosian Dynasties were moderately successful for a time, but both suffered from the practice of appointing children Emperor to keep the throne in the family. While some of these children would eventually grow into their positions, they had little authority to deal with crises while still young. And there were crises: Under pressure from the Asiatic Huns, Germanic and Russian tribes began crossing into the Empire in the late 4th

century AD. Hoping to end their raids, eastern Emperor Theodosius I allowed the Visigoths to settle in Thrace, but in 401 AD, they marched into northern Italy under their chieftain Alaric. In 408 AD they made for Rome, accepting a tribute in gold and spices to leave the city alone. The same thing happened in 409 AD. In 410 AD, when the Britons appealed for troops to protect them from the encroaching Saxons, western Emperor Honorius wrote back that Britain must look to its own defense; that same year, the Visigoths finally sacked Rome, massacring the inhabitants against Alaric's. Luckily, the Imperial court had moved to the more defensible Ravenna.

Meanwhile in the East, only Constantinople's strong defenses and regular payments of tribute kept the Huns at bay. In the West, the Huns were driven from Rome, but this victory was as much due to the now-settled Visigoths as to the Roman provincials who fought beside them. The Vandals rampaged through Spain, and seized the provinces

of North Africa, setting up their own kingdom. The Franks and Burgundians took Gaul, the Visigoths and Sueves divided Spain between them, and the barbarian kings set up largely irrelevant puppet-emperors with or without the approval of the Emperor in the east. In 474 AD, the Eastern Emperor tried to take control of the situation, declaring Julius Nepos Western Emperor, and sending him and a small army to Italy. Julian took Rome, but was then overthrown by his army's commander, who appointed his own 15-year-old son, Romulus Augustulus, Western Emperor. In 476 AD, Orestes was killed by the army and Romulus was forced to abdicate the throne. The Senate of Rome asked the Eastern Emperor to appoint a successor to Romulus, but none was ever declared; the Western Roman Empire was gone.

The Greek-speaking Eastern Roman Empire (eventually called the Byzantine Empire) was to last (in name at least) for another thousand years, slowly declining in extent and import.

- ROMAN TIMELINE -

THE AGE OF KINGS 753–509 BC

753	Rome founded; Romulus is its first king.
725	Carthage founded.
509	Tarquin the Proud, the last of the kings, is expelled.

THE EARLY REPUBLIC 509–133 BC

509	Republic established.
496	Tarquin and his Etruscan allies finally defeated at Lake Regillus.

453	Plague wipes out much of Rome's population.
390	Rome sacked by Gauls.
343–341	First Samnite War.
327–304	Second Samnite War.
298–290	Third Samnite War.
280–275	Pyrrhic War.
264–241	First Punic War.
237–219	Carthage conquers Spain.
226–222	Gallic invasions.

218–202	Second Punic War.
215	First Macedonian War.
200–196	Second Macedonian War; Rome declares Greece free.
196–118	Conquest of Cisalpine Gaul, Spain, Greece, and North Africa.
176–171	Third Macedonian War.
164	Smallpox from the eastern Mediterranean reaches Rome, spreading throughout Europe over the next decade.
149–146	Fourth Macedonian War; province of Macedonia created.
146	Corinth sacked as an example to other Greek cities; Carthage destroyed.

THE LATE REPUBLIC 133–31 BC

133–121	Gracchi brothers push various reforms through Senate; both are murdered.
112–105	Jugurthine War; rise of Sulla.
104–102	Marius reorganizes Roman army, defeats invading Gauls.
90	Social War.
88–85	Mithridates of Pontus conquers Roman territories in Asia Minor and Syria, orders the massacre of all 100,000 Romans there. Sulla leads Roman army against Mithridates.
87	Marius seizes control of Rome.
85	Sulla returns to Rome and purges the city of Marius' supporters; made dictator.
80	Sulla retires.
77–62	Pompey campaigns in Spain, Greece, Pontus, Armenia, Syria, and Judea.
73–71	Slaves revolt under Spartacus.
60	Caesar, Pompey, and Crassus form First Triumvirate.
58–49	Caesar conquers Gaul.
53	Crassus killed in battle with Parthians.
48	Pompey assassinated.
47	Caesar besieges Alexandria; the Great Library is damaged by fire.
44	Caesar assassinated.
43	Anthony, Octavian, and Lepidus form Second Triumvirate.
41	Anthony joins Cleopatra in Egypt.
31	Anthony and Cleopatra defeated; Octavian takes the name Augustus, allows Lepidus to retain position of pontifex maximus.
12	Lepidus dies of natural causes; Augustus adds pontifex maximus to his titles.

THE EARLY EMPIRE 31 BC–69 AD

31 BC–14 AD	Augustus establishes the foundations of Imperial rule.
27 BC	Thousands die in Fidenae, near Rome, when a poorly-built amphitheater collapses during gladiatorial games.

circa 30 AD	Jesus of Nazareth crucified.
43 AD	Invasion of Britain.
64 AD	Much of Rome destroyed by fire; Nero blames Christians. Organized persecution of Christians lasts until 313 AD.
61 AD	Revolt of Boudicca in Britain.
66 AD	Beginning of Zealot revolt in Judea.
69 AD	Year of the Four Emperors.

THE MIDDLE EMPIRE 69–180 AD

70	Titus captures Jerusalem and destroys Temple.
74	Last Zealots commit suicide at Masada.
79	Pompeii and Herculaneum destroyed by eruption of Mt. Vesuvius.
97–88	Outbreaks of plague ravage Empire.
132	Simon Bar-Kochba leads revolt in Judea.
135	After revolt put down, Hadrian bans Jews from Judea.
164–180	Epidemic (either plague or smallpox) breaks out in Syria, spreading throughout Empire.

THE LATE EMPIRE 180–476 AD

193	Two Emperors and two pretenders in first half of year before Septimius Severus made Emperor in June.
235–284	26 Emperors (including 4 of the independent Gallic Empire) in 49 years; shortest reign is 20 days.
250–265	Plague strikes Empire. Deaths in Rome reach 500 per day.
260	Seven contenders declared Emperor in different parts of Empire; all but one defeated by Emperor Galliensus
313	Edict of Toleration legalizes Christianity.
325	Council of Nicaea defines Christian orthodoxy.
365	Alexandria struck by an earthquake and tidal wave.
375	Visigoths and Ostrogoths cross the Danube into Roman territory.
400	Goths invade Italy.
406–439	Vandals, Alans, and Suevi invade Gaul and Hispania; Vandals continue on to North Africa.
409	Rome buys off Alaric the Goth to avoid invasion.
410	Alaric and the Goths sack Rome; Emperor Honorius abandons Britain.
451	Alliance of Romans and Goths repels Huns.
472	Mt. Vesuvius erupts. Athough not as destructive as the earthquake of 79 AD, thousands die.
472–476	5 Emperors in less than 5 years.
476	End of Western Roman Empire.

Chapter Ten: Roman Culture

Rome culture changed over the millennium of its history. The most significant changes were from a community of farmers to a local and then a regional power. But whatever the changes in practice, the theory of Roman society remained surprisingly resistant to change. Even in the waning days of the Empire, Romans still looked back to the days of the Kingdom and the Republic for examples of what it meant to be Roman.

- Roman Society -

Rome started as an egalitarian society. According to legend, Romulus encouraged settlers to his newly founded city by granting a blanket amnesty to all within its walls: everyone was welcome, regardless of their past, and Rome marked a new start for all its founding citizens.

Under the Etruscan kings, society was divided into Etruscan nobility and a Roman lower class, but with the founding of the Republic, equality was restored, at least in theory. As the Republic aged, three distinct classes emerged, which were to remain for the rest of Roman history.

Social Classes

The Patricians

The patricians were the upper class of Roman society, and held a near-monopoly on Senate seats, allowing some to refer to them as the senatorial class. Most patrician families could trace their descent back to the earliest days of Rome; some, like the Julii (of whom Julius Caesar was a member), went further and claimed descent from figures including the mythical Aeneas, local nymphs, and even gods.

Through most of the Republic, the patricians held the true power in Rome. In the later Republic, they were challenged by the Populares, and throughout most of the Empire they were an aristocracy with high status but little real power; they still made up the majority of the Senate, but the Senate had become an advisory body for the Emperor.

The Equites

As Rome became wealthier and more influential during the Republic period, a middle class emerged. These were people who had become wealthy, but lacked political power because they were not born patricians. They became known as equites ("horsemen"), because the cavalry at that time was composed of troopers who were wealthy enough to provide their own horses.

In the chaos of the late Republic, many equites became as rich as the patricians. Crassus, for example, made a fortune in real estate, and could afford to fund the dealings of the First Triumvirate while Caesar provided the political brains and Pompey the military muscle. Although it claimed to represent the common people, the reforming Populares party was mainly composed of equites who were looking for a share of the patricians' political power, and used the votes of the plebeians to get it.

THE PLEBEIANS

The plebeians were Rome's lower class. While they were poorer and less powerful than the patricians and the equites, they still had one thing that made them valuable: They were Roman citizens, and they had votes in the Popular Assembly. During the late Republic, reformers and opportunists from the Gracchus brothers to Octavian won their votes or bought them with lavish entertainments and free distributions of grain, and pitted the Assembly against the Senate in struggles for power.

In the Empire, the plebeians became less powerful politically, but Emperors still had to appease them with free grain rations and entertainments in order to avoid discontent and even riots. Although the plebeians could not make and unmake Emperors by themselves, they were ready to lend their support to ambitious generals if they were unhappy with their current Emperor.

Another important effect of the plebeians' Roman citizenship was that they were eligible to serve in the legions, whose ranks were open only to citizens. The citizenship requirement led to a shortage of military manpower in the middle and later Empire period, and various measures were taken extending the rights and duties of citizenship first to Italy, then piecemeal to various other provinces, and finally to the Empire as a whole.

PROVINCIALS AND FOREIGNERS

Although the plebeians were the lowest class of Roman citizens, they were still Roman citizens, and this placed them above the increasing numbers of provincials and foreigners who came to Rome as the city grew and prospered. The differences were more theoretical than practical in most cases, and many provincials and foreigners prospered both as merchants and as artisans. Provincials and foreigners were exempt from some taxes, but they were also prevented from

ANCIENT SLAVERY

While slavery was as cruel in Roman times as in the early United States, one major difference was the ease with which slaves could achieve freedom for themselves and/or their children. Opportunities for slaves to earn money to buy their freedom were common, and a master freeing at least his senior slaves in his will was seen as a sign of noble character, and was thus a common practice.

Moreover, since the majority of Roman slaves came from conquered European and Middle Eastern nations, there was nothing obvious in appearance to set a freed slave apart from a freeborn Roman citizen the way color did in the 19th century. Thus, freedmen blended into the greater Roman society: From the time of Augustus onward, the Roman civil service consisted largely of freedmen from the Imperial household, and by the 2nd century AD, it's thought that the majority of citizens had some slave ancestry.

running for public office and there were limitations on their rights in court.

SLAVES

As Rome conquered neighboring peoples, slaves became an increasing part of Roman society. Conquered peoples provided a ready source of slaves, and Romans could be stripped of their rights and sold into slavery as punishment for some crimes.

Slaves were the property of their owners, who had the power of life and death over them. Their testimony in a court of law was only legally admissible if it had been given under torture. For most, the best they could hope for was a fair and lenient master. Some were able to buy their freedom, or were granted it in recognition of outstanding service. These freedmen often became capable artisans and businessmen, and a freed slave was automatically the client of his former master. Children of an ex-slave who were born after he'd become a freedman had full Roman citizenship.

Slaves could be beaten, and even killed, by their masters for any reason or for no reason at all. Runaway slaves who were recaptured were branded on the forehead with the letters FUG (*fugitivus*, or "runaway"), while those caught stealing were branded FUR ("thief").

The majority of gladiators were slaves.

- WOMEN -

The rights of women in Roman society were limited, but the power was often greater than expected. A woman wasn't allowed to enter into contracts (including marriage) without the permission of her male guardian (her father, husband, son, or appointed legal guardian), she couldn't vote or hold public office, and she had no patron or clients. Until the last years of the Republic women couldn't inherit directly; their inheritance

was managed for them by their guardians. A woman could turn down a marriage contract, but once married she couldn't initiate a divorce. Husbands had a major restriction on their ability to divorce their wives: a woman brought a substantial dowry with her into a marriage; this money became her husband's, but if he ever decided to divorce her he had to return the money, even if he'd already spent it.

A woman was expected to run the household (including managing the slaves and often her husband's financial affairs), raise her children, and be capable of performing domestic activities (from weaving to throwing dinner parties).

Some women worked through their children to wield power in Roman politics (*e.g.*, Livia Drusilla, Augustus's third wife, was accused of engineering the deaths of three of the Emperor's heirs, and possibly Augustus himself, so that her own son, Tiberius, would become Emperor), while others were useful in marriage as links between powerful families (*e.g.*, Octavia, the sister of Octavian and fourth wife of Mark Anthony). And as a wife knew much of her husband's political and business dealings, she could be a useful source of information.

Sex

Before Christianity became the official religion of the Empire, Roman sexual attitudes were very open and the pleasure of sex was considered a gift from the gods. So long as one's sexual partner was of a lower social station, there were no social restrictions on the age or gender of one's partner. Adultery was legal. The use of prostitutes and slaves for pleasure were accepted and legal practices, and some prostitutes could become as rich as the elite Romans they served.

- Childhood -

When a child was born, its father acknowledged it as his own by picking it up; if he refused, the child could be abandoned in the wilderness to die of exposure (although this was infrequently practiced). Children were not given names until several days after the birth (nine for a boy, eight for a girl) because of the high death rate among newborns. At that time, a *bulla* amulet was placed around the child's neck to ward off evil and bad luck.

Until the age of 6, children stayed at home and were cared for by their parents (both directly and through slaves). Boys started school (if their parents could afford the modest fees) at the age of 6 or 7; wealthy families employed private tutors. A boy was also taught his father's profession. Girls remained at home and were taught domestic arts by their mothers and servants, preparing them for the day when they would run a household of their own. A basic education consisted of reading, writing, and arithmetic. Boys also learned wrestling, boxing, and the use of weapons.

Sons of families who could afford a further education were tutored in history, grammar, philosophy, and Greek, starting at the age of 10 or 11. A higher education, starting at the age of 13 or 14, consisted of law and rhetoric, which were important disciplines for the aspiring politician.

Girls came of age at 12, and boys at 14. From then on, they could marry (subject to parental approval) and had the legal status of adults.

Roman children had a full range of toys and games, from play weapons, to dolls, blocks, balls, *etc*. Many modern children's games (*e.g.*, hide-and-seek, blindman's bluff) had their Roman equivalents. Dogs were common pets; cat's didn't become popular until Rome conquered Egypt at the end of the Republic.

- Patrons and Clients -

The idea of patronage was central to Roman society, especially in the Republic period. Put simply, a wealthy and powerful patron would do favors for his clients in exchange for their votes and political support. It was a mark of status to have a string of clients at one's door at the start of the day, ready to pay their respects and discuss their problems.

A client can be a source of information, the provider of refuge, or even a participant in a plot (although average clients wouldn't be members of adventuring classes). One thing clients are highly unlikely to do is lend money to their patrons; that would be turning the patron-client relationship on its head, and if it was generally known that a patron was asking his clients for money, the patron's Fame score would be halved. A PCs' patron and any clients that have specific roles should be detailed NPCs, instead of just nameless money and flattery sources.

For more details on the mechanisms of patronage and clientele, see page 53.

Careers and Offices

In Roman society, law and rhetoric were two major elements of a higher education, along with Greek, philosophy, and other subjects upon which a lawyer (a respected profession in Rome) or budding politician could draw to make his speeches sound more erudite, cultured, and elegant.

Successful lawyers used their knowledge and talent to run for political office. The sons of wealthy families might skip a legal career (although an education in the law was still regarded as a vital preparation for public office, even if merely for self-defense), and run for an office straight away.

Public offices were unpaid positions; part of a citizen's voluntary service to the Republic or the Empire. Still, there were many ways to make money indirectly from public office.

A few offices are described as follows (see page 50 for Fame costs and benefits of each office):

Assemblyman

The *Comitia Curiata* (Popular Assembly; named for the tribes, or *curia*, that members were divided into) represented the voice of the people of Rome. The populace was divided into a number of tribes (originally along family lines, but later by neighborhoods in the city) representing all equites and plebeians. The size of the Popular Assembly varied greatly over time, numbering as little as 20 and as much as

200. Assemblymen were elected for life, but the Assembly could also vote them out of office.

In early Rome, the Assembly elected kings. Beginning in the Republic it appointed tribunes. While it could pass legislation, none was official until ratified by the Senate, which quite refused in order to protect its own independence and the prerogatives of the patricians it served.

SENATOR

Chosen as representatives of patrician families, during the Republic the 300 senators actually controlled Rome, but during the Empire (when their numbers had grown to 600) they were increasingly advisers to the Emperor and a rubber-stamp for his legislation. One power they did retain until the chaos before the end of the Empire was the power to declare the legitimacy of an Emperor; although their decision was sometimes ignored, an Emperor without Senatorial consent could lose the support of the people. Seats in the Senate were not only permanent, but hereditary. In addition, many high officers would be elected to the Senate following their terms as consuls, praetors, *etc.*

INTERREX

Election supervisor, a minor office only held on a temporary basis just before and during an election.

VIGINTIVIRATES

Literally, a vigintivirate is a committee of 20 men, but they could have 20, 10, or fewer members. Regardless of numbers, the term was applied to committees convened for a variety of purposes, from ensuring the fairness of the judicial system to making sure the roads were swept. Some vigintivirates were temporary; others permanent. A post on a vigintivirate was the first step in a political career.

QUAESTOR

In the early Republic, there were two quaestors; from the late Republic onwards there were 20. A quaestor was a treasury official, and quaestors could be deputized to assist higher officials. A candidate had to be at least 25 years old, and have served on at least one vigintivirate.

TRIBUNE

In the Republic, the tribunes were elected to look after the interests of the people. They could attend sessions of the Senate, and had the power to veto any measure. There were 10 tribunes, who were elected for one year by the Popular Assembly.

AEDILE

The aediles supervised the actions of vigintivirates, and performed administrative tasks such as supervising building codes. There were 16 aediles, elected annually.

CURATOR

These officials were in charge of the upkeep of public buildings and monuments, and the maintenance of public utilities (including aqueducts, fountains, grain distribution,

---

PATRONS, CLIENTS, AND ADVENTURERS

Just as a player character can make a request of his patron or one of his clients for some sort of aid, clients and patrons provide an easy hook for the GM to use to draw a PC into an adventure. Since it's expected that a Roman will *always* honor the requests of his patron, and that a patron will at least try to help his clients, the GM must take care not to abuse this power to compel the heroes into plots.

It's generally not a good idea, though, for one player character to choose another as a patron or client. While it presents some interesting plot possibilities, it also runs the risk of causing tension within the gaming group as one player's character will be expected to act subservient to another's at all times. In addition, having NPC patrons and clients provides the heroes with sources of money, advice, and aid they wouldn't have otherwise.

---

sewers, and non-military roads). Each curator was assigned a specific building or utility of concern, and the prestige of the position depended on the size and importance of the assignment. They supervised the activities of the aediles in their spheres of influence.

Former curators (procurators) served these same functions in the provinces.

PRAETOR

The praetors were senior magistrates. Sixteen were elected each year, divided into two classes: the *praetor urbanus* was responsible for administering the laws in the city of Rome, and the *praetor peregrinus* administered lawsuits concerning foreigners in Rome. During the later Republic, more praetors were created to administer certain provinces. Under the Empire, their main function was to oversee the staging of games.

A praetor could be from any class, but those who were not patricians were required to have served as aediles. Former praetors (propraetors) sometimes served as provincial governors.

AUGUR

While there were priests, fortunetellers, and soothsayers throughout the Empire (including at least one attached to each legion on campaign), there were only 15 official omen-readers charged with the most important auguries concerning Rome and its leaders, and with the custody and interpretation of the Sibylline Books (see page 146). Members of the College of Augurs were elected by the Senate and membership was for life or until retirement. While expertise with omens and magic were useful, as a political appointment more than a few non-soothsayers became augurs.

Consul

Under the Republic, this was the highest political office. Two consuls were elected annually. Consuls had to be from patrician families, be at least 42 years old, and have served as praetors. In order to limit the power of consuls, no-one could be elected to back-to-back consulships; with a gap of 10 years between consulships being the norm.

Former consuls (proconsuls) were usually awarded the governorship of provinces.

Censor

The censor maintained the electoral rolls and kept various other records. The English word "census" derives from this office. A censor had to be a former consul, and one was elected every five years, for a term lasting 18 months.

Prefect

In the Empire, various prefects were appointed by the Emperor to command units such as the Praetorian Guard, the Urban Cohorts, and the Cohorts Vigilum (see page 134). They were usually equites rather than patricians, ensuring that they owed all their power and position to the Emperor.

Pontifex Maximus

The chief priest of the Roman religion, this position was mostly administrative: he chose priests and priestesses for the temples, and dealt with breaches of law involving the temples (including vow-breaking among the Vestal Virgins). The pontifex officiated at a number of annual ceremonies and perform certain sacrifices for the good of Rome. A candidate for this office needn't have any cleric levels, but despite being appointed by the Popular Assembly he had to be a patrician. Pontifex maximus was a lifetime appointment usually granted to one who'd served in a number of other high offices.

Dictator

Not a regular Roman office, during emergencies a dictator could be appointed (usually with a six-month term of office) to wield the powers of a king and command all the legions. The office disappeared with the creation of the Empire.

Augustus

The official title of the Roman Emperor (although he usually held many others as well).

- The Calendar -

With only a few adjustments, the Roman calendar introduced by Julius Caesar is still in use today across most of the world.

Months

The 12 months of the Roman calendar are as follows.

The Roman Months

Month	Meaning
Martius (March)	Month of Mars
Aprilis (April)	Month of Aprilis, an ancient Etruscan goddess
Maius (May)	Month of Maia, a nature goddess
Iunius (June)	Month of Juno
Quinctilis/Iulius (July)	Fifth month, renamed for Julius Caesar
Sextilis/Augustus (August)	Sixth month, renamed for Augustus
September	Seventh month
October	Eighth month
November	Ninth month
December	Tenth month
Januarius (January)	Month of Janus
Februarius (February)	Month of Februus, an Etruscan name for Dis Pater

The numbers of days in each month are the same as in today's calendar, except that February always has 28 days. Before the time of Julius Caesar and Augustus, Quinctilis and Sextilis each had 30 days, as did Februarius.

The Roman year started in March, with the end of winter and the beginning of spring.

Dates

Each month had three special days: the *kalends* was the 1st of the month; the *nones* was the 5th of the month, except in March, May, July, and October when it was the 7th; the *ides* was the 13th of the month, except in March, May, July, and October when it was the 15th.

Dates were numbered by the number of days to the next special day. For example, March 31st was the day before the kalends of April, and was called *pridies kalends Aprilis*; March 30th was the second day before the kalends of April, and was called *ante dies* ("the day before") *II kalends Aprilis*.

Days of the Week

The Roman names of some days survive in Romance languages and English today, while others have had the names of Roman gods replaced with the names of their Anglo-Saxon or Viking equivalents.

Hours

Roman days began and ended at dawn. Each day always consisted of exactly 12 daytime hours and 12 nighttime hours, which means that the length of an hour had to vary with the seasons, ranging from about 44 minutes (daytime at winter solstice and nighttime at summer solstice) to 1 hour 16 minutes (daytime at summer solstice and nighttime at winter solstice). Only at the spring and autumn equinoxes were hours exactly 60 minutes long.

It's up to the individual GM if he wants to introduce this complication to his campaign in order to promote an authentic Roman feel.

HOLY DAYS AND FESTIVALS

The following list denotes the dates of the festivals of various gods throughout the Roman year.

MARTIUS

1st: Janus. The first day of the year and (to a lesser extent) the first day of every month were sacred to the god of new beginnings. These were considered propitious days for beginning new enterprises.

1st: Matronalia (Juno). Ceremony in the sacred grove of the Palatine. Mistress of the house received a gift from her husband, and served her slaves at the table.

17th: Liberalia (Liber Pater, a minor deity of fields). Coming-of-age ceremonies for boys.

19th–23rd, Spring Equinox: Quinquatrus (Minerva and Mars). No bloodshed was permitted on the first day (Minerva's birthday), but martial contests and gladiatorial games marked the others. The 20th was a good day to begin a military campaign.

APRILIS

1st: Janus.

21st: Palilia (Pales, a minor goddess of flocks and fertility). Livestock and stables sprinkled with holy water. Also the date of the founding of Rome.

28th–May 3rd: Floralia (Flora, Venus, and several minor goddesses). Theatrical performances (especially comedies) and gladiator games held.

MAIUS

28th April–3rd: Floralia (Flora, Venus and several minor goddesses).

1st: Janus.

A TYPICAL DAY

A Roman day started at dawn, and as a Roman proverb said, "The first six hours of the day are for working; the rest are for living."

The first and second hours of the day, for those not engaged in work or crafts, were spent visiting. This is the time when clients called upon their patrons, to discuss problems and to give and receive gifts. The lower a person's Fame, the earlier in the day he had to present himself to his patron.

The law courts opened at the third hour, and political activity also began at this time. The workday lasted until the end of the seventh hour.

The eighth and part of the ninth hour were spent at the baths, exercising, or at the games. Dinner was served during the ninth hour. All could be social activities, with people discussing business, politics, and other interests while they ate, bathed, or cheered on gladiators.

Night-time entertainment (*e.g.*, the theater) was followed by sleep.

DAYS OF THE WEEK

Day	Meaning	Italian	English
dies Solis	day of the Sun	Domenica (Lord's day)	Sunday
dies Lunae	day of the Moon	Lunedi	Monday
dies Martis	day of Mars	Martedi	Tuesday (Tiw's (Tyr's) day)
dies Mercuris	day of Mercury	Mercoledi	Wednesday (Woden's (Odin's) day)
dies Iovis	day of Jupiter	Giovedi	Thursday (Thor's day)
dies Veneris	day of Venus	Venerdi	Friday (Freya's day)
dies Saturni	day of Saturn	Sabato (Sabbath)	Saturday

9th, 11th, 13th: Lemuria (Lemures). The head of the house conducted a ritual to cleanse it of hostile ancestral spirits. He arose at midnight bare-footed, snapped his fingers to drive away the spirits, and washed his hands three times. Then he filled his mouth with black beans, threw them behind him, and said "I throw away these beans, and with them I redeem myself and mine." He repeated this invocation nine times, washed his hands and struck a gong, repeating nine times "Paternal manes, go."

29th: Ambarvalia (Mars). Burnt offering of a pig, a ram, and a bull.

Iunius

1st: Janus.

7th: Vestalia (Vesta). Mothers of families brought gifts of food to the temple of Vesta.

17th: Ludi Piscatori. Fishermen and divers sacrifice to Tibernius, god of the Tiber River.

Quinctilis/Iulius

1st: Janus.

23rd: Neptunalia (Neptune and other water gods). Outdoor feasts held in the countryside. And auspicious day to begin new irrigation works.

Sextilis/Augustus

1st: Janus.

17th: Portunalia (Tiber). Also known as Tibernalia. Incense burned at temples of Janus and Portunis (who was considered an aspect of both the Tiber and of Janus). Old keys through into temple fires for good luck.

19th: Vinalia Rustica (Venus). Lambs were sacrificed and the year's wine vintage was opened for drinking. Vineyard workers have day off.

21st: Consualia, first (Consus and Ops, minor deities of agriculture). Chariot and horse races, dancing and other entertainments.

23rd: Volcanalia (Vulcan). Bonfires were lit, and a live fish was thrown onto the fire at the temple of Vulcan.

24th: *Lapis manalis* ("Stone of the Shades"), a stone covering a symbolic portal to the underworld on the Palatine Hill, removed, allowing friendly spirits to return home and feast with the living, and the spirits of the newly dead to pass through to the underworld.

27th: Volturnalia (Vulcan). As Volturnus, a god of the Tiber River. Feasting, wine-drinking, and gladiatorial games held.

September

1st: Janus.

October

1st: Janus.

5th: *Lapis manalis* removed.

November

1st: Janus.

8th: *Lapis manalis* removed.

December

1st: Janus.

15th: Consualia, second. Chariot races with mules instead of horses.

17th–23rd: Saturnalia (Saturn). Seven days of feasting and celebration. All official activities (courts, schools, military campaigns) temporarily halted.

Januarius

1st: Janus.

11th: Juturnalia (Juturna, goddess of springs and rivers). Anniversary of founding of the temple of Juturna by Augustus. Sacrifices performed mainly by engineers who worked on aqueducts and fountains.

Februarius

1st: Janus.

13th–26th: Parentalia (spirits of deceased parents). Businesses and temples closed, marriages prohibited. Ancestral tombs decorated with violets, lilies, roses, and myrtle, and offerings of food placed on them. Families held reunions on the 22nd (called Carista), where disputes were settled and sacrifices were made to the family lares (household gods). The 26th (called Feralia) featured a feast to the powers of the underworld.

15th: Lupercalia (Silvanus). Burnt offering of goats left at the cave where Romulus and Remus were suckled and reared by the wolf. Priests of Silvanus, called Luperci, dressed only in the skins of the sacrificed goats, ran wildly through the streets, and used special goat-hide whips to touch the backs of women who wished to become pregnant.

- Housing -

Wealthy Romans owned large houses in the city. Rich Romans owned houses in the city and rambling villas in the countryside. These houses were all built around a central atrium (unroofed courtyard) where cooking was done, and included rooms for greeting and entertaining guests, a garden, household shrines, sleeping quarters for all the family (including slave quarters), and sometimes rooms fronting the street and small rooms on a second floor that were rented out as shops and as bachelor apartments respectively. These homes didn't typically include bathrooms; the public baths and latrines were used for those functions. Sometimes the kitchens were rudimentary, as precooked food could be readily bought at a variety of shops.

The poor lived in cramped tenements called insulae. These could be up to seven stories tall, and the higher up one went the lower the size and quality of the apartments: a first-floor apartment could resemble a wealthy man's house, while a top-floor apartment might be a single drafty room. As with wealthy homes, many functions were performed in public facilities, especially cooking, as an open fire in a wooden building could (and frequently did) have disastrous consequences.

Tombs and Catacombs

During the Republic and the early Empire, most Romans were cremated after death, with their ashes stored in a family tomb (or in one of many niches in a large, public tomb, for the modest of means). The tombs could be freestanding buildings, natural caves with elaborately carved entrances, in buildings along city streets, or in cemeteries (originally outside of the city limits, but as the city grew they'd be encompassed within its walls). Christians, on the other hand, were interred whole in accessible tombs similar to those of pagan Romans, or in underground tomb complexes (called catacombs) with hidden entrances during times of Imperial persecution. The underground caves also served as gathering places for Christians when meeting in private homes was too risky.

Occasionally, a disused cemetery would be covered with fill (either deliberately, or through natural erosion or the collapse of adjacent buildings in fires or earthquakes) and after a time new buildings would be erected on the "clear" land. One spectacular example is an entire cemetery street (clear of fill; as easy to walk today as 20 centuries ago) lined with tombs buried under St. Peter's Basilica. The current 16th century AD basilica was built on the site of the previous basilica, which was itself built atop an earlier church, each featuring a central altar immediately over the tomb of St. Peter, the first bishop of Rome.

Fashion

The most common item of clothing in Rome was the sleeveless belted tunic: men wore theirs knee-length, and women's tunics came to the floor. These could be made of wool or linen. In cold weather, a hooded cloak was worn over the tunic.

The more recognizable item of Roman clothing, the toga, was worn only by freeborn male citizens, and only on formal occasions (including sessions of the Senate, parades, funerals, religious ceremonies, and trials). Most togas were undyed whitish wool, but dark togas were worn in mourning, purple ones were worn by triumphators, the toga of a senator had a purple border, that of a child a red border, and candidates for political office would bleach their togas. The toga could be worn over a tunic, and with a cloak in cold weather.

Full-length trousers were a barbarian innovation, and weren't popular in Republican or early Imperial Rome. Knee-length breeches were sometimes worn, especially by legionaries in cold weather.

For everyday use, most Romans wore sandals; boots were reserved for long journeys or inclement weather.

Perfumes and makeup (including eye shadow, lip paint, and whitening face creams made from animal fat, starch, and tin oxide or toxic lead acetate) were used by women and sometimes men.

Women's hair was worn long, in curls or elaborately coiffed. Men's hair was usually short, with beards going in and out of fashion multiple times over the centuries; whatever style the Emperor sported quickly became popular throughout the city.

- MONEY -

Coins of different values came and went throughout Roman history, and the size, metal purity, and value of coinage varied throughout the Empire, as the coinage was exposed to inflation, devaluations, adulteration of metal content, the minting of coins by claimants to the throne, and widespread counterfeiting (with the counterfeit coins sometimes more widely accepted by the public than the official coins). The following values are a compromise between historical accuracy and the *d20 System* default.

ROMAN CURRENCY

Coin	Metal	Value
As	copper	1 cp
Sestertius	bronze	5 cp
Denarius	silver	1 sp
Aureus	gold	1 gp

Note: Ancient Rome had no equivalent to platinum pieces.

FOREIGN CURRENCY

Foreign coins were valued according to their weight in metal as opposed to their local value in their place or origin. Here are a few of the more common foreign coins brought to Rome by trade and conquest.

FOREIGN CURRENCY

Coin	Origin	Metal	Value
Speculum	Celtic	bronze	2 cp
Obol	Greek	silver	1.2 cp
Thaler	Celtic	silver	1.5 cp
Drachma	Greek	silver	8 cp
Greek stater	Greek	silver	1.5 sp
Gallic quarter-stater	Celtic	gold	2.5 sp
Gallic half-stater	Celtic	gold	5 sp
Gallic stater	Celtic	gold	1 gp

- ROMAN NAMES -

Most Romans had two names, a personal name (*praenomen*) and the name of their clan (*nomen*). Those from prominent families added a family name (*cognomen*). Thus, Gaius Julius is Gaius of the Julian clan. Gaius Julius Caesar is Gaius of the Caesar branch of the Julian clan. The praenomen was usually abbreviated, with the rest of the person's name being his public name; thus G. Julius Caesar.

A man's first-born son often had the same name as his father, using a nickname to differentiate between them. Later-born sons would have names borrowed from higher up in the family tree. Daughters had the same name as their father, with a feminizing "a" at the end; e.g., Julia would be the daughter of Julius. If a man had multiple daughters, he'd number them: Julia Prima, Julia Secunda, *etc.*

If a slave is freed, he takes his former master's praenomen and nomen, retaining his slave name as his cognomen.

MALE PRAENOMEN (PERSONAL NAMES)

Aemilius, Aulus, Decimus, Gaius, Gnaeus, Lucius, Manius, Marcus, Numerius, Publius, Quintus, Servius, Sextus, Spurius, Suetonius, Tiberius, Titus, Vibius

FEMALE PRAENOMEN (PERSONAL NAMES)

Agrippina, Antonia, Atia, Aurelia, Calpurnia, Drusilla, Flavia, Helvia, Julia, Livia, Messalina, Octavia, Portia, Scribonia, Terentia, Tullia, Viciria

NOMEN (CLAN NAMES)

Accius, Acilius, Aelius, Aemilius, Afranius, Annius, Antonius, Appuleius, Apustius, Aquillius, Atilius, Attius, Aufidius, Aurelius, Caecilius, Caedicius, Calpurnius, Carvilius, Cassius, Claudius, Clodius, Coelius, Cornelius, Cornificius, Coruncanius, Cremutius, Curius, Decius, Domitius, Duilius, Ennius, Fabius, Fabricius, Fannius, Flaminius, Flavius, Fufius, Fulvius, Fundanius, Furius, Gellius, Genucius, Hirtius, Hortensius, Hostilius, Iulius, Iunius, Iuventius, Labienus, Licinius, Livius, Lutatius, Maccius, Mamilius, Manlius, Marcius, Marius, Minucius, Mummius, Munatius, Nautius, Norbanus, Octavius, Ogulnius, Opimius, Otacilius, Papirius, Paulus, Paulinus, Petillius, Pompeius, Pompilius, Popillius, Pomponius, Porcius, Postumius, Pupius, Quinctius, Rupilius, Rutilius, Scribonius, Sempronius, Sergius, Servilius, Sosius, Sulpicius, Tarquinius, Terentius, Tullius, Valerius, Vatinius, Vibius, Vipsanius, Volcacius, Volumnius

COGNOMEN (FAMILY NAMES)

Achaicus, Aemilianus, Afer, Agrippa, Ahenobarbus, Albinus, Allobrigicus, Arvina, Asina, Barbula, Blaesus, Blasio, Brutus, Buteo, Caecus, Caepio, Caesar, Caesoninus, Caiatinus, Calvus, Calvus, Canina, Carbo, Catalina, Cato, Catulus, Caudex, Caudinus, Celer, Censorinus, Centumalus, Cerco, Cethegus, Cicero, Cinna, Clepsina, Clodianus, Corculum, Corvus, Cotta, Crassus, Creticus, Crispinus, Crus, Curio, Cursor, Decula, Dentatus, Diadematus, Dives, Dolabella, Drusus, Eburnus, Etruscus, Falto, Fimbria, Flaccus, Flaminius, Florus, Frugi, Fundulus, Gallus, Geminus, Germanicus, Geta, Glabrio, Gracchus, Gurges, Hispallus, Hypsaeus, Isauricus, Labeo, Laenas, Laevinus, Lentulus, Lepidus, Libo, Licinius, Ligus, Livianus, Longinus, Longus, Lucullus, Lupus, Luscinus, Magnus, Malleolus, Mancinus, Marcellus, Maso, Matho, Maximus, Megellus, Merula, Messalla, Metellus, Murena, Mus, Nasica, Niger, Nobilior, Noctua, Octavianus, Orestes, Pacilus, Paetinus, Paetus, Pansa, Papus, Papus, Paterculus, Paullus, Pennus, Pera, Philippus, Philo, Pictor, Piso, Pius, Plautus, Pollio, Porcina, Pulcher, Pullus, Purpurio, Ravilla, Regulus, Rufinus, Rufus, Rullianus, Russus, Sabinus, Salinator, Saverrio, Scaevola, Scipio, Serapio, Serranus, Servilianus, Silanus, Sophus, Spurinus, Strabo, Sulla, Sura, Tamphilus, Tappulus, Thalna, Thermus, Torquatus, Tremulus, Tuditanus, Tullus, Turrinus, Varro, Varus, Verrucosus, Vitulus, Vulso

- THE ARMY -

The Roman army consisted of the legions and the auxiliaries. The legions were heavy infantry (with a small number of supporting cavalry; generally no more than 120 cavalry to a legion), trained to fight in close order. The auxiliaries provided every other troop type.

THE LEGIONS

The legions attained their final structure in the late Republic period, but a legion always consisted of about 5,000 men. A legion was divided into the following units:

Unit	Made up of	Number of Men
Contubernium	8 men	8
Century	10 contubernia	80
Maniple	2 centuries	160
Cohort	3 maniples	480
Legion	10 cohorts	4,800

In camps, members of a contubernium (the Roman equivalent of the modern infantry squad) shared a tent. The figures for a legion are based only on combat troops, and don't include carters, muleteers, and other logistical staff, which were hired by the legion commander for a specific campaign. Officers (especially the high-ranking ones) generally had small staffs of slaves and freedmen.

RANKS

CENTURION

Each century was commanded by a centurion (the equivalent of a modern NCO), who carried a vinewood stick as a sign of his rank.

MILITARY TRIBUNE

Not to be confused with the political office of tribune (see page 133), a military tribune was a senior officer. Each legion had six tribunes.

LEGATE

Each legion was commanded by a legate.

COMMANDER

An army composed of more than one legion could be commanded by a consul, a general, a provincial governor or (after the reforms of Diocletian) a dux. Some emperors even led their armies in person.

TERMS OF SERVICE

Throughout most of the Roman period, the legions were open only to Roman citizens. Instead of being called up in time of trouble like the soldiers of many other countries, the Roman legions were a standing force. Each legionary signed up for a term of 25 years, making army service a career commitment.

Retired legionaries were granted pensions and land. In troublesome provinces, it was a common practice to establish colonies of Roman citizens, which consisted largely of retired legionaries and their families. As well as offering the unruly provincials a good example of what Roman civilization was all about, the colonies provided a source of trained reserves.

AUXILIARIES

The auxiliaries were recruited from the provinces, and auxiliary units were made up of men from the same home province. The officers were largely Roman (or at least Italian) but some elite units and others who had proved their loyalty were allowed to have officers from among their own countrymen.

The most common auxiliary types were infantry, cavalry, archers, slingers, and peltasts (skirmishers armed with three or four javelins whose main job was to disrupt the enemy front ranks before the legionaries engaged them). The equipment of various auxiliary types is described in **Chapter Two: Character Classes**.

Auxiliary cavalry was organized into units called *alae* ("wings"). A typical cavalry *ala* was made up of 500 men, but a few were 1,000 strong. Auxiliary infantry (including archers, slingers, and other types) was organized into cohorts of 500 or 1,000 men. There was also a mixed cavalry and infantry unit called a *cohors equitata*.

Finishing a 25-year term in the auxiliaries would earn a foreigner Roman citizenship.

ORDER OF BATTLE

A typical Roman army consisted of two legions of regular infantry plus an equivalent number of auxiliaries (which could be cavalry, ranged-weapon users, or regular infantry), for a total of up to 20,000 troops. If the auxiliaries were missile-users, they'd typically be deployed in front of the legionaries to make initial disrupting attacks. They'd then fall back to allow the legion infantry to press the main assault. The auxiliaries would take station on either side of the legionaries to protect the flanks (often with the auxiliary legions splitting in half, so, for example, half a peltast and half a cavalry auxiliary legion could be deployed on each flank). Cavalry (except for cataphracts) was rarely used as a shock weapon; generally they were scouts, messengers, or a force to pursue retreating enemies.

The Romans typically didn't employ a strategic reserve, although individual commanders had flexibility in how they conducted battles, and many showed great tactical initiative.

THE FLEET

The formidable Roman fleet was always under a separate command from the army, although certain legions (distinguished by the title *adiutrix*) were marines. The bulk of Roman warships were biremes and triremes, with two and three banks of oars respectively; larger ships were built, but most proved impractical. A trireme could be 150 feet long and 20 feet wide, with 250 rowers and crew and up to 600 troops.

Roman warships used sails as well as oars, but relied on oar power alone for battle. They mounted a bronze beak for ramming, and some were also equipped with catapults. The rowers were slaves, or convicts who had been sentenced to a certain time in the galleys.

From the Punic Wars of the middle Republic onward, Roman warships were always equipped with the *corvus*, a moveable gangplank with an iron spike at the end used for boarding enemy ships.

LAW ENFORCEMENT

Rome lacked effective law enforcement during the Republic, which is one reason why criminal gangs were able to disrupt elections so easily. Augustus introduced a number of reforms when he became Emperor, including the organization of three forces to protect the city and the Emperor's person.

THE PRAETORIAN GUARD

The Praetorian Guard originated in the practice of Roman generals of keeping a hand-picked unit as a personal bodyguard. As the Emperors took over power, the Praetorian Guard became the Emperor's personal bodyguard. The Guard consisted of from three to nine 1,000-man cohorts. They operated in the city and sometimes took part in military campaigns as an elite force. The Guard was commanded by the Praetorian Prefect, who was appointed by the Emperor. Their pay was up to three times that of ordinary legionaries, and their duties were usually much lighter, including parades and guard duty.

The Praetorian Guard was a double-edged weapon. They could—and did—replace Emperors by force if they felt they were bad rulers, or if their own demands for pay and conditions were not met. A wise Emperor kept the Praetorian Guard happy.

THE URBAN COHORTS

The Urban Cohorts were instituted by Augustus as a police force for the city, after the rampant lawlessness that had accompanied the end of the Republic. Originally, there were nine cohorts, but Caligula increased the number to 12. They were based in the *castra praetoria* in Rome, alongside the Praetorian Guard, and were commanded by the Urban Prefect, who was appointed by the Emperor. Outstanding service in the Urban Cohorts could lead to a post in the Praetorian Guard.

THE COHORTS VIGILUM

Fire was a huge threat to any urban settlement in the ancient world. During the Republic, firefighting was performed by private groups of firefighters (usually slaves) who would arrive at the scene of a fire and negotiate the price of their services as the buildings burned; if a price wasn't agreed to in time, the captain of the team would instead negotiate to buy the property at a discounted rate.

After a devastating fire in 6 AD, Emperor Augustus instituted a professional force of firefighters and night-watchmen, the Cohorts Vigilum. At first only charged with protecting Rome, the Vigilum quickly proved its value. In later centuries similar forces were organized in other cities throughout the Empire.

The vigiles were organized along military lines, but while only Roman citizens could join the legions, the vigiles were freedmen, who were promised citizenship after six years in the Cohorts Vigilum (which would be followed by another 20 years of service). Theoretically, the force numbered 7,000 men. Commanded by a prefect, they were divided into seven cohorts, each led by a tribune and responsible for two of the 14 city districts.

Protecting the city from fire was the primary duty of the vigiles. During the day time, most of them would remain in barracks scattered throughout Rome ready to respond to a fire call. Some also performed minor security functions, such as watching over personal belongings of those in the baths, but during the day the primary policing in Rome was performed by the Urban Cohorts.

At night the vigiles actively patrolled the streets looking for fires while the citizenry was asleep. Vigiles were equipped with axes, buckets, and firehooks (see page 56), and had ladders, crude pumps and hoses, and even mobile ballistae (to launch hooked climbing ropes onto the roofs of buildings, or to knock down crumbling walls in a safe manner) in their barracks that were brought to fires as needed. As they were already on the streets, they also took over the policing duties of the Urban Cohorts.

- BREAD AND CIRCUSES -

Decimus Junius Junevalis ("Juneval") was a critic of the early Empire, complaining in one of his satires that with almost all power vested in the Emperor and almost none in the Assembly and the Senate, the Roman people had lost interest in everything except bread and circuses. To some extent, this was part of the Emperors' plans: If the populace was kept fed and entertained, there'd be less incentive for them to meddle or rebel.

FOOD

Bread (or wheat porridge for the poor), cheese, fish of all sorts, vegetables (beans, cabbage, onions, garlic), fruits (apples, figs, plums), and a variety of meats (pork, chicken, goose—goat for the poor) were eaten by all classes of Romans. The wealthy added imported fruits and vegetables, as well as exotic and expensive spices, to their diet; a diverse menu at supper (the most important meal of the day) was a sign of status, and the frequent dinner parties were an important occasion to do business and for people to ingratiate themselves with those higher up on the social ladder.

Olives were an important staple: eaten raw; their oil used as a sauce or spread, in recipes; and as a source of cooking oil. They were so important to the Roman diet, that a man who planted a large enough grove or olive trees was excused military service.

Wine was the universal drink of those who could afford it. Water was only drunk on its own by the poor, although it was used by everyone to dilute wine. Milk was drunk more in the countryside than in Rome itself.

To spice up the sometimes bland diet of the poor (and to cover up the taste of foods starting to go bad in an age before refrigeration), pungent sauces were popular. The best known is *garum*, a salty sauce made from spices and fish allowed to ferment in the sun for a period of months. The rich had their own sauces, including a more expensive variety of garum that substituted shrimp for the fish. Herbs and spices from the nearby countryside and from as far away as China, Madagascar, and Indonesia were available in the markets from mid-Republic times, imported overland via the Silk Route or by sea by way of Arab traders. Pepper from India was once listed as one of the most important foreign imports (along with ivory, amber, silk. and incense) of the Empire.

For the rich, food preparation was elaborate, with presentation of each of the many courses of a dinner being almost as important as the contents. The poor tended to cook little in their apartments, in part because of the risk of fire. City streets abounded in take-out cookshops and tiny stalls selling cooked meat by the slice, fruit and vegetables ready to eat, and wine of every quality.

Knives and spoons were rarely used at the table and the fork hadn't been invented. Instead, most Roman foods were prepared to be eaten with the fingers, sometimes with bowls of dipping sauce on the side. Hard, flat bread could also be used as a trencher (an edible plate), and soft bread could sop up juices and sauces.

THE ANNONA

Partly as a welfare program and partly as a means to gain votes in the Popular Assembly, during a famine in 123 BC, Gaius Gracchus put a cap on the price of grain, allowing ordinary Romans to buy that staple at less than market price. In 70 BC, Marcus Licinius Crassus, in order to distract attention from a less-than-successful consulship, gave 40,000 adult male citizens three months of free grain. Soon afterward, the *annona* (distribution of free bread) became permanent for the city's poorest, and the number of recipients grew: at the time of Julius Caesar it was over 200,000, and in the early Empire it swelled to 300,000—a third of Rome's population.

At the beginning of the 3rd century AD, Emperor Septimius Severus added free olive oil to the annona. His grand-nephew Alexander Severus replaced the free grain with baked loaves of bread 30 years later, and 40 years after that Aurelian added free wine. But as the Empire declined, this accelerating welfare couldn't go on, and eventually the annona was eliminated (although price subsidies on staple foods were kept).

THE GAMES

According to Roman tradition, it had been customary to perform human sacrifices as part of a funeral, but in the early Republic period, turning this into a fight to the death between slaves was seen as a more civilized alternative.

The first recorded gladiatorial contest was staged in 264 BC by Decimus Junius Brutus, in honor of his deceased father: Three pairs of slaves fought in a market square. Traditionally, these spectacles began on the ninth day after the funeral, which marked the end of the official period of mourning, and were repeated every five years.

Over time, the religious connotations of gladiatorial games faded, and they became spectacles staged by candidates for office and anyone else seeking popularity. They became elaborate and fantastically expensive as the individuals staging the games tried to outdo each other, often borrowing heavily against the income they expected to make from the office if they were elected.

In the Empire period, the Emperor reserved the sole right to stage games, although exceptions were made. This was probably to stop other individuals from using games to gain enough popularity to threaten Imperial power. Different Emperors had different attitudes towards the games, and some even fought as gladiators themselves.

SOCIAL ATTITUDES

For many people, the idea of gladiatorial games (which often included public executions, including the throwing of Christians to lions) is difficult to reconcile with the aspects of Roman culture that are regarded as civilized.

The Romans justified their love of the bloody spectacle of the games as a means of hardening themselves for war;

A DAY AT THE GAMES

A day at the games generally followed a set pattern, with the gladiators as the highlight of the show.

The first event, beginning in mid-morning, was usually the *venatio* ("hunt"). Animals of various kinds were let loose in the arena and hunted down by venatores (see page 29), or particularly fierce animals were set against each other. As time went on, presenters strove to outdo each other with new and exotic animals. Julius Caesar, for example, is said to have been the first to exhibit a giraffe in the arena, which must have been brought from sub-Saharan Africa at considerable expense. Some hunts were conducted with trees and bushes set up in the arena to represent a forest; as shows became more and more spectacular, sometimes trees of gold were pushed up through the floor of the arena by hidden machinery.

At lunchtime, the executions began. Criminals could be sentenced *ad bestias* (to be thrown to the beasts) by the courts, but other kinds of executions were also practiced. Some criminals were forced to kill each other with a dagger, handing it over to the next convict who would kill him and be killed in his turn. Those who were reluctant were "encouraged" with whips and branding irons. The last man was killed by a *confector*, who was also responsible for finishing off wounded animals in the hunt.

After the executions, the arena was cleared and the gladiatorial portion of the show began. It started with a parade, in which the gladiators made a circuit of the arena, dressed in colorful costumes. Then lots were drawn to decide who would fight whom, and their armor and weapons were checked to make sure that they conformed to regulations.

The games frequently concluded with the distribution of gifts; the Emperor Commodus, who liked to fight as a gladiator himself, even used a catapult to throw tokens into the crowd, each one representing anything from a brace of game birds to a country estate. Members of the audience were frequently killed in the scuffles to recover as many of these tokens as possible.

hand-to-hand combat with swords is a nasty business, and potential soldiers had to be used to the sight of blood and the sounds of battle from childhood. And the attitudes of individuals to gladiatorial games seems to have been much like those of present-day fans of professional sports and action movies. The blood was real, of course, but since it belonged to slaves and convicted criminals, its spilling was somehow justified.

CHARIOT RACES

Chariot races may have been less bloody than gladiatorial games, but they often drew bigger crowds. In Rome, races were held in the Circus Maximus, which could seat 260,000 spectators compared to the 50,000 of the Colosseum (where the gladiatorial bouts were held). The track was long and straight, with a sharp turn at each end.

There were four teams in Rome, each known by its color: the Blues, the Greens, the Whites, and the Reds. Each team had its staunch supporters, and violence was not uncommon when groups of rival supporters met. Each team fielded two, three, or four chariots in a race, with equal numbers from each team making the field range from eight to 16 chariots.

Naval Battles

A popular form of entertainment in the arena was the recreation of historical battles and of more recent victories using teams of gladiators. Some presenters went further, and staged events called *naumachiae*, which recreated naval battles in an arena that was specially flooded for the purpose. These events ranked among the most expensive and technically complex spectacles of their time.

Literature and the Arts

Romans, especially the wealthier and more cultured, also enjoyed gentler entertainments.

Theater

Most Roman cities and towns had a theater, where plays ranging from Greek tragedies to broad farces were staged. Shakespeare wasn't above stealing the plot of *The Comedy of Errors* from the Roman farce *The Brothers Menaechmus* by the playwright Plautus, who probably stole it from the Greek playwright Menander, most of whose work is now lost.

Literature

Literature, especially poetry (in both Greek and Latin), was held in high regard, and popular poets enjoyed the same kind of status as popular musicians do today. Greek myth was a favorite subject for poetry, but contemporary subjects, especially social satire, were also popular. Orators, especially Greeks, reciting poetry were a popular form of entertainment for dinner parties.

Music

The Romans had a range of musical instruments, including flutes, lyres, horns, and an early form of organ. Music often accompanied plays and dancing. There were even musicians hired to provide suitably dramatic music for gladiatorial games.

Art and Sculpture

The walls of a well-to-do Roman home were almost always painted. False windows or whole walls showing rustic or mythical scenes were

Letters and Numbers

The Roman alphabet is largely the same one that we use today. The Romans didn't have the letters J, W, and Y (they used I instead of J, and did without the others altogether). On inscriptions, at least, they normally used V instead of U.

The Romans also used letters to represent numbers. I, II, III, IV, V, VI, VII, VIII, IX, and X represented the numbers from 1-10 respectively, and larger numbers were made by adding more letters. A smaller digit preceding a larger one was subtracted from the larger; *e.g.*, IX is X minus I, or 10−1=9.

There could be more than one correct way to write a large number. For example, 1,999 could be written MDCCCCLXXXXVIIII (1,000 plus 500 plus 100 plus 100, *etc.*) or, more elegantly, MIM (1,000 plus 1 less than 1,000).

Roman Numerals

Roman Numeral	Arabic Equivalent
I	1
V	5
X	10
L	50
C	100
D	500
M	1,000

especially popular. Mosaic floors were a favorite status symbol, often depicting scenes or characters from mythology, surrounded by borders of intricate knot designs. Battles and gladiatorial scenes were also popular.

Roman sculptures are famous throughout the world, and Rome carried on the Greek tradition of realism. Sculptures were commissioned by the wealthy to decorate their homes and gardens, and it was customary to keep busts of one's ancestors in the home, which were used in certain religious observances.

In upper-class homes, it was also common to have a number of paintings either hung on the wall or actually painted as frescoes directly on the plaster. Subjects could include scenes from mythology (Greek and Roman), family portraits, and erotic subjects that ranged from restrained to what would be pornographic today.

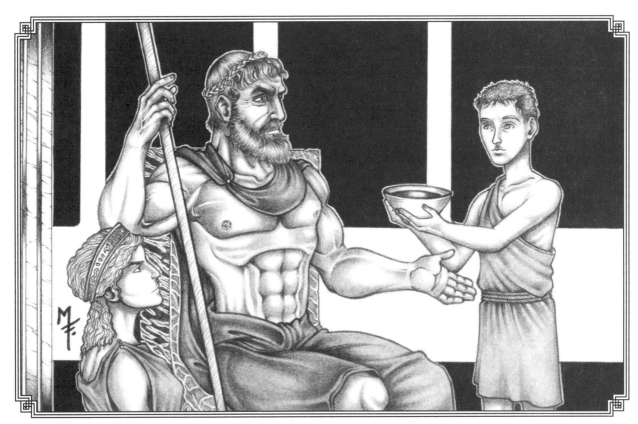

Chapter Eleven: Roman Religion

The Roman gods are often regarded as identical to the Greek gods, with different names that correspond to the planets of the solar system. But while Roman culture, literature, and mythology were greatly affected by Greek influences from the time of the Kingdom, Roman religion never entirely lost touch with its origins in Etruscan and other early Italian religions. Deities like Janus and Vesta (and, to a lesser extent, Silvanus) are uniquely Roman, and were not equated with incoming Greek gods.

And the Roman gods reflected the Roman national character as much as the Greek gods reflected their own.

The amorous Zeus of Greek myth had many affairs with nymphs and mortal women, fathering a whole line of heroes in the process; many of his illegitimate offspring were mercilessly persecuted by his vengeful wife Hera, giving rise to many heroic sagas.

By contrast, the Roman Jupiter was a stern and dutiful paterfamilias, the head of the Olympian family. Juno had far less to complain about than her Greek counterpart Hera, and the Romans regarded her as a more benevolent deity, guiding and protecting Roman women and their households.

- Cosmology -

In the Roman cosmos, the living inhabit the material world, and the dead (and certain demons and spirits) inhabit the underworld. As in Greek mythology, the gods live in Olympus, a realm in the sky that can be reached from the mortal world by climbing Mount Olympus.

Olympus

There is little information in Roman sources about the realm of Olympus. It is sometimes depicted as an idealized palace complex of dazzling white marble, where the gods live when they aren't active in the mortal world.

The Underworld

The underworld (sometimes called Hades after the Greek name of its ruling god, who was equated by the Romans with Saturn) can be entered from the living world through a limited number of portals. These often take the form of deep caves or pools. Some sources state that there is only one entrance to the underworld, through the secret Grove of Persephone. The souls of mortals automatically go to the underworld upon death, unless they are prevented from doing so by a curse, magic, or some overriding duty or

COSMOLOGY AND OUTSIDERS

In the *Eternal Rome* setting, with its simple cosmology, there is little scope for the wide range of outsiders from a multitude of planes found in other fantasy settings. Some (as noted in **Chapter Seven**) are native to Tartarus, while others are servants of the gods, dispatched from Olympus to do their bidding.

The GM must decide whether to use outsiders in an *Eternal Rome* campaign, and assign them to realms of origin as desired.

obsession that causes the soul to be trapped in the living world as a ghost.

The entrance to the underworld is guarded by Cerberus, a massive three-headed dog whose jaws drip deadly venom. In myth, various heroes got by him in different ways: Orpheus charmed him with music, Aeneas (acting on the advice of Venus) bribed him with a honey cake, and Hercules simply overpowered him. For ordinary mortals, however, entering the underworld is much more difficult.

THE STYX

Those entering the underworld, by whatever means, find themselves on the near bank of the Styx (generally regarded as a river, but sometimes described as a lake or swamp). The only way to cross the Styx (whose water is a deadly poison capable of destroying both the living and the dead) is to ride Charon's ferry. It is customary to put a coin in the mouth of the deceased as part of the funeral rites in order to ensure they could pay the fare to ride the ferry. The near bank of the Styx is crowded with the stranded souls of those who did not receive proper funerals and cannot pay the ferryman; they crowd pitifully around each new arrival, begging for help and in some cases trying to snatch away any money they have.

The living are not allowed on the ferry—Charon had enough trouble with Orpheus trying to rescue Eurydice—but in exceptional circumstances, with the permission of the gods, a mortal is granted a trip across the Styx.

On the far bank, another crowd of souls waits for judgment by a tribunal composed of the legendary King Minos of Crete, keeper of the Minotaur, his brother Rhadamanthys, and King Aeacus of Aegina in Greece, the grandfather of Achilles. Those found worthy are sent to the Elysian Fields, while those burdened with guilt are sent to Tartarus, to be punished until their souls are purified.

THE ELYSIAN FIELDS

The Elysian Fields (or simply Elysium) consists of bright, sunlight meadows and groves, where the souls of the deserving live a pleasant afterlife. Through Elysium flows the River Lethe, whose waters cause forgetfulness; a soul drinks the waters to erase memories of its past life before being sent back into the mortal world as a newborn.

TARTARUS

Tartarus is a dark and violent place, filled with demons punishing the souls of the guilty. Much of the Roman image of Tartarus is derived from previous Greek myth and literature: Sisyphus is condemned to spend eternity rolling a rock to the top of a hill only to see it roll down the other side; Tantalus is racked with thirst and hunger, within sight of fruit and water that both draw back when he approaches; and so on.

The most complete image of the Roman conception of the underworld is Book VI of Virgil's *Aeneid*, where the Roman ancestor-hero Aeneas visits Tartarus with the help of Venus, to meet the shade of his dead father and be shown the souls of the great waiting to be reborn (including that of Virgil's patron Augustus).

- THE GODS -

While clerics served particular gods, and many people venerated members of the Roman pantheon with interests close to their own (Mars, for example, was always a patron of soldiers), the bulk of the Roman population worshiped "the gods" rather than "a god." Rather than following one god above all others, the Romans went to specific gods (or their temples) for specific reasons.

In the late Republic period and afterward, the gods of Rome were equated very closely with the Greek gods of the Olympian pantheon. As a result, the interests of some deities changed over time.

APOLLO (INTERMEDIATE GOD)

Apollo was originally a Greek god. His worship was taken up by the Romans, and he became a part of the Roman pantheon. He took over the role of sun god from various earlier Italian deities, and was also a patron of the arts, music, and poetry. He also was the deity of oracles; the famous Oracle of Delphi was a priestess of Apollo.

His symbol was a sun disk, and his favored weapon was the shortbow.

CASTOR AND POLLUX (DEMIGODS)

These Greek heroes were twins, who sailed with Jason and the Argonauts and had several other adventures. During the wars that spread Rome's influence across Italy in the early Republic period, a Roman general vowed to build a temple to Castor and Pollux in exchange for victory. He won the battle, and it was even said that Castor and Pollux themselves led the Roman cavalry to victory. A temple was built in the Forum, and they became part of Rome's religion. Castor was said to be a horseman without equal, and Pollux was an invincible boxer. They could also calm storms and ensure the safety of ships.

Castor and Pollux were always worshiped together. Their symbol was twin men (they later became the Gemini twins of the Zodiac), and their favored weapon was the cestus.

CHARUN (LESSER GOD)

In Greek mythology, Charon was the boatman who ferried the souls of the dead across the Styx into the realm of Hades. He was stern, but not especially threatening. In Rome (and with a slightly different name), Charun was a murderous spirit whose job was to carry the souls of the dead to the underworld. In the *Eternal Rome* setting, he is an evil deity, the bringer of bloodshed, appearing as a powerfully-built, bearded man dressed in a tunic and sandals and carrying a huge hammer he uses to kill his victims.

Charun's symbol and favored weapon was the warhammer.

DIANA (LESSER GOD)

Originally, Diana was a goddess of mountains and forests, but even by the founding of Rome, she had become equated with the Greek goddess Artemis, patron of hunters, wild places, and women. She was not a major deity in the Roman pantheon, and was best known as the patron goddess of the Amazons (see page 9).

Diana's symbol and favored weapon was the shortbow.

DIS PATER (GREATER GOD)

Dis Pater (literally "rich father," because as long as mortals continue to die his realm will increase) was thought by some to be an aspect of Hades as ruler of the underworld, and by others to be a powerful demon or devil associated with death.

He was also called Orcus in some sources. In the *Eternal Rome* setting, he is an independent deity who rules Tartarus, the plane where the evil dead are punished throughout eternity.

Dis Pater appeared as a tall, dark man with a pointed beard. His symbol was a skull, and his favored weapon was the scythe.

HERCULES (DEMIGOD)

A son of Zeus, Hercules was one of the most celebrated of the Greek heroes. Famed for his superhuman strength, Hercules became a god revered by those who rely on strength and combat ability.

Hercules's symbol was a lion skin (commemorating one of his famous Twelve Labors), and his favored weapon was the greatclub.

JANUS (LESSER GOD)

Janus was rare among the Roman gods in that he was never equated with any of the Greek gods. Portrayed with two faces, one looking forward and the other backward, he was the god who watched over gates and doorways, and by extension over travel and the beginning of new enterprises. According to ancient Roman tradition, Janus was older even than Jupiter, and took part in the creation of the universe.

Janus's symbol was a key, and his favored weapon was the club.

JUNO (GREATER GODDESS)

Juno was the wife of Jupiter, and also his sister. She was worshiped all over Italy from the earliest times, and represented the female essence while Jupiter represented the male. She was a goddess of fertility and childbirth, and protected the Roman people just as Jupiter protected the Roman state. After she became equated with the Greek goddess Hera, Juno took on Hera's role as the wronged wife of the philandering Jupiter/Zeus, and the punisher of unfaithful husbands. Hera was often called on to right wrongs done to women, both as individuals and as a gender.

Juno's favored weapon was the longspear, and her symbol was the scepter she carried in her role as queen of the gods.

JUPITER (GREATER GOD)

Also known as Jove, Jupiter was the patriarch of the Roman pantheon. He originated as an Etruscan god of weather (very important to a farming community) and used his thunderbolts to warn mortals when they were displeasing the gods, and, as a last resort, to punish them. After the end of the Kingdom, Jupiter became the great protector of Rome, and the supreme deity. As Greek influences entered Roman culture, Jupiter became identified with the Greek god Zeus.

Jupiter was worshiped by all Romans, regardless of class or profession.

Jupiter's favored weapon was the javelin, symbolizing the thunderbolt that was his symbol.

MARS (LESSER GOD/INTERMEDIATE GOD)

According to myth, Mars was the father of Romulus, the legendary founder of Rome, and his brother Remus. Like Jupiter, he was originally a god of agriculture, but lost this aspect as Rome's influence grew, and became the god of war. The wolf was always sacred to him, and its image appears

Table 11-1: Roman Deities

Deity	Alignment	Domains	Typical Worshippers
Kingdom/Early Republic			
Castor and Pollux, Gods of Adventure	NG	Good, War, Weather	adventurers, soldiers (especially cavalrymen), sailors, boxers
Charun, Underworld Ferryman	NE	Death, Destruction, Evil	murderers
Diana, Goddess of the Wild	CN	Animal, Chaos, Healing, Plant	Amazons, barbarians, druids, rangers, slaves
Dis Pater, Lord of Tarterus	LE	Death, Evil, Law	thieves, necromancers, the rich
Janus, God of Beginnings	LN	Knowledge, Law, Protection, Travel	vigiles, doorkeepers, homeowners, people undertaking journeys or beginning new enterprises
Juno, Goddess of Families	LG	Animal, Healing, Law, Protection	women (especially matriarchs), paladins
Jupiter, God of Weather	LN	Air, Animal, Law, Plant, Weather	farmers, sailors
Lares and Penates	N	—	all Romans
Mars, God of Agriculture and War	LN	Animal, Plant, Law, Strength, War	farmers
Mercury, God of Trade	LN	Air, Knowledge, Law, Magic	merchants
Minerva, Goddess of Learning	LG	Knowledge, Law	teachers, wizards, seekers after knowledge, traders
Neptune, God of Rivers	LN	Water, Weather	fishermen, sailors, merchants
Saturn, God of Fertility	LN	Earth, Law, Plant, Protection	farmers, miners
Silvanus, God of Forests	N	Animal, Healing, Knowledge, Plant	druids, rangers, those who rely on the wilderness for their living
Venus, Goddess of Fertility	CG	Animal, Chaos, Good, Plant	farmers
Vesta, Goddess of the Hearth	LG	Good, Hearth, Law, Protection	all Romans
Vulcan, God of Fire	LN	Earth, Fire, Law, Strength	all Romans
Late Republic/Empire			
Apollo, Sun God	NG	Charm, Good, Knowledge, Sun	bards, soothsayers, healers, those seeking oracles
Castor and Pollux, Gods of Adventure	NG	Good, War, Weather	soldiers (especially cavalrymen), sailors, boxers
Charun, Underworld Ferryman	NE	Death, Destruction, Evil	murderers
Deified Emperors	LN	Law, War	all Romans
Diana, Goddess of the Wild	CN	Animal, Chaos, Healing, Plant	Amazons, barbarians, druids, rangers, slaves
Dis Pater, Lord of Tarterus	LE	Death, Evil, Law	thieves, necromancers, the rich
Hercules, Demigod of Strength	NG	Destruction, Good, Strength	fighters, gladiators, barbarians
Janus, God of Beginnings	LN	Knowledge, Law, Protection, Travel	vigiles, doorkeepers, homeowners, people undertaking journeys or beginning new enterprises
Juno, Goddess of Families	LG	Animal, Healing, Law, Protection	women (especially matriarchs), paladins
Jupiter, Father of the Gods	LN	Law, Protection, War, Weather	all Romans
Lares and Penates	N	—	all Romans
Mars, God of War	LE	Death, Destruction, Evil, Strength, War	fighters
Mercury, Messenger of the Gods	CG	Chaos, Good, Knowledge, Magic	merchants, rogues, sorcerers, illusionists, wizards
Minerva, Goddess of Martial Knowledge	LG	Knowledge, Law, Strength, War	teachers, wizards, fighters, paladins, gladiators, vigiles
Neptune, God of the Seas	LN	Animal, Law, Water, Weather	fishermen, sailors, merchants
Orpheus, Demigod of Music	NG	Animal, Charm, Good	bards, orators, poets
Saturn, God of Death	LN	Death, Earth, Law, Protection	necromancers, miners
Silvanus, God of Forests	N	Animal, Healing, Knowledge, Plant	druids, rangers, those who rely on the wilderness for their living
Venus, Goddess of Love	CG	Chaos, Charm, Good, Trickery	lovers, bards, poets, orators, wizards, thieves
Vesta, Goddess of the Hearth	LG	Good, Hearth, Law, Protection	all Romans
Vulcan, God of Crafts	LN	Fire, Law, Magic, Strength	metalworkers, craftsmen
Imported Deities			
Cybele, Goddess of Wild Passion	CN	Animal, Chaos, Fertility, War	warriors, those with links to wild nature
Isis, Goddess of Magic	NG	Death, Good, Healing, Magic	wizards, women
Mithras, God of Valor	LG	Good, Law, Sun, War	warriors

on many of his temples. After becoming associated with the Greek god Ares, Mars took on a more destructive nature: he was still the god of war, but came to symbolize its horrors as well as its glory.

It was customary to make offerings at the temple of Mars before setting out on a military campaign. Offerings were also made before battle, and a part of the spoils of a victorious campaign was dedicated to Mars.

In all periods, his favored weapon was the shortspear, and his symbol was a sword or a wolf's head.

Mercury (Lesser God)

Mercury was a relatively late addition to the Roman pantheon. He was first recorded as a god of merchants in the

5th century BC. He became equated with the Greek god Hermes, who was a god of communications and trickery as well as trade.

His symbol was a staff with two snakes winding round it, sometimes shown with wings. His favored weapon was the shortspear.

Minerva (Intermediate Goddess)

Originally an Etruscan deity, Minerva became equated with the Greek goddess Athena even before the founding of Rome. She was a patroness of learning, commerce, and industry, and during the later Republic she also became a war goddess, representing military science and the controlled application of force instead of the blind ferocity of Mars.

Minerva's symbol was a Greek-style full-face helmet, and her favored weapon was the longspear.

Neptune (Lesser God/Intermediate God)

Originally a god of rivers and streams, Neptune became identified with the Greek Poseidon, and became god of the seas. The tritons were his special servants, and he was sometimes depicted riding in a chariot made of a giant seashell pulled by a team of hippocampi (see page 84). He was revered by those who made their living from the sea.

His symbol, and his favored weapon, was the three-pronged trident.

Orpheus (Demigod)

The Greek hero Orpheus was the son of a Muse and a mortal—or according to other myths, a son of Apollo himself. He was given a lyre by Apollo, and his music could charm wild beasts and make rocks and trees dance. After his death, he became a patron of musicians.

His symbol was a lyre, and his favored weapon was the short sword.

Saturn (Intermediate God)

Saturn was originally another agricultural deity, who ensured the fertility of the soil and helped crops to grow abundantly. In early Italian myths, he was supposed to have been king of Italy during a long-lost golden age. Because of his association with the earth and its riches, he was worshiped by miners as well as farmers, and he became associated with the dead, ruling the gloomy realm of Hades, eventually being equated with the Greek god of that name. He was propitiated rather than worshiped, but all those who hoped to gain riches from the earth had to reckon with him. The temple of Saturn, near the Capitol, housed the state treasury.

Saturn's symbol and favored weapons was a sickle.

Silvanus (Lesser God)

His name derived from the Latin word for forest, Silvanus was a god of wild places. In Greece, he was called Pan. He was often depicted as a tall and handsome satyr.

Silvanus's symbol was a satyr, and his favored weapon was a falcata (equivalent to a scimitar), a traditional forester's weapon.

Venus (Lesser Goddess/Intermediate Goddess)

Venus was originally a comparatively minor fertility goddess, one of three goddesses who oversaw the return of fruitfulness to the earth each spring. She became equated with the Greek goddess Aphrodite at an early stage, and became the goddess of love and the inspiration of poets. Her followers included bards and orators, and those hoping for good luck in love or the ability to charm others.

Her symbol was a scallop shell, and her favored weapon was the shortbow.

Vesta (Intermediate Goddess)

Vesta was never equated with a Greek deity. The goddess of the hearth, she protected the home, and every Roman home had an image of her in the family shrine, where she was worshiped along with the lares and penates (see below). Her temple in Rome was attended by the Vestal Virgins, who looked after her sacred fire and made sure that it never went out; while they could easily have used magic to maintain the fire, for religious reasons the fed it normal fuel.

Vesta's symbol was a flame, and her favored weapon was a torch (treat as a club, with an additional 1d6 fire damage).

Vulcan (Lesser God)

Vulcan was originally a god of earth and fire, and volcanoes (especially the volcanic Island of Vulcan, off the northern coast of Sicily) were sacred to him. He became equated with the Greek smith god Hephaestus, who forged the thunderbolts of Zeus/Jupiter and many other magical treasures. In the Kingdom period, he was worshiped as a god of natural forces, especially fires; later on, he became the patron of craftspeople, especially metalworkers.

Vulcan's symbol and favored weapon was the warhammer.

Minor Gods and Spirits

Lares and Penates (Quasi-deities)

A very ancient cult, the ancestor spirits called lares and penates were worshiped in household shrines, along with Vesta, and often the patron deity of the householder's trade or profession.

Lares familiaris ("family spirits") had shrines in houses, and protected their living descendants. So long as their rites were properly observed by the head of the household (including the observances of Parentalia, Lemuria, and the lapis manalis festivals, as well as daily libations to their statues), the lares provided +2 to the saves of all family members within the confines of the house.

Lares comptiales (attended by the Vestal Virgins as part of the cult of Vesta) protected the city of Rome, providing a +2 to the saves of all citizens within the confines of the city, but only against threats to the entire city (e.g., raging fires, barbarian hordes).

The penates watched over the physical property of the family (including the house itself) especially the stores of food and drink. Their statues were offered the first helping of food at every meal. Depicted as wingless pixies, they invisibly attended all inanimate objects in the house, allowing the objects saving throws (Fort +0, Ref +0, Will +0) normally not permitted to unattended objects (see **Chapter Nine: Adventuring** in the *PHB*). The *penates populi romani* granted the same saving throws to public buildings (including granaries).

Lares and penates didn't grant spells, nor did they have symbols or favored weapons.

Genii (Quasi-deities)

The genii (singular genius) were patron spirits of a particular place, trade, or organization of people. They were similar to lares and penates, in that they didn't have an organized priesthood, and didn't grant spells to their followers, but they looked after their interests just as the lares and penates looked after the interests of their mortal charges.

The Romans would regard a dryad as the *genius loci* (spirit of place) of the tree with which she was linked, and similar beings were linked to caves, mountains, waterfalls, and other natural features. Sometimes they could be summoned and persuaded to give oracles and prophecies, and sometimes they simply had to be propitiated to avoid accidents befalling travelers on their territory. A mountain genius, for example, might cause a rockslide or and avalanche to sweep down over a road if travelers neglect to make the proper offerings.

In addition to spirits of place, there are the *genius publicus populi Romani*, who takes the Roman people under his protection. Each city ward has its own presiding genius, as do trade and craft guilds and other groups of people.

Genii are less than deities, akin to the guardian angels (mazzalim; see *Testament*, page 118) of the Jews.

Tutelary Deities (Lesser Deities)

There were a vast array of deities of places who were regarded as more powerful than genii loci. Every city had its tutelary deity, who was normally female and shared its name; Roma, for example, was the goddess of the city of Rome. Rivers usually had masculine deities; Father Tiber, also known as Volturnus, was associated with Saturn.

There were also deities associated with ideas, values, and principles. Fortuna, the goddess of fortune, Pecunia, the goddess of wealth, Flora, the goddess of flowers, Terminus, the god of property boundaries, and Victoria, the goddess of victory, are a few examples. The Bona Dea ("Good Goddess") was a deity of the earth, whose cult was open only to women.

Tutelary deities didn't grant spells to their worshipers, but could intervene in their areas of interest, especially if induced to do so by offerings.

The Emperors (Demigods)

Augustus declared that his predecessor Julius Caesar had become a god after his assassination, and set up a temple to *divus Iulius* ("the divine Julius"). In his turn, Augustus became a god after his death and (with the exception of unpopular Emperors like Tiberius, Caligula, and Nero) the practice continued. The divine Emperors were worshiped together as a group alongside the Roman pantheon, and were acknowledged to be less powerful than gods like Jupiter, Venus, and Mars;

however, it was believed that they kept a fatherly eye on the Empire, and would take action to protect it.

Imported Gods

As the Roman Empire grew and spread, a few gods from other cultures became popular. Of these, the Egyptian Isis and the Persian Mithras were the most prominent.

Cybele (Lesser Goddess)

Worship of Cybele, a fertility goddess from Phrygia (modern-day Turkey), spread to Greece before it reached Rome. She was depicted wearing a crown, seated on a throne flanked by two lions, or driving a chariot drawn by two lions. Her followers often whipped themselves into a frenzy, clashing their swords against their shields as they danced or beating themselves with whips. Among her ceremonies was a ritual cleansing bath in the blood of a sacrificed bull.

Cybele's symbol, and her favored weapon, was the whip.

Isis (Intermediate Goddess)

In Egyptian mythology, Isis was the sister and wife of Osiris and the mother of Horus, who learned the secret name of Ra and became unrivaled in her magical power. Her cult was first introduced to Rome in the 2nd century BC, but became more popular after the Emperor Caligula dedicated a temple to Isis in Rome. She remained a popular deity until the fall of the Empire, even after Christianity was made the state religion.

Isis invented the process of mummification while trying to revive Osiris, who had been slain by his jealous brother Set. Her wifely devotion made her a patroness of women as well as a goddess of magic.

Judaism and Christianity

Judaism and Christianity were both significant religions in the Roman world. The Roman Empire saw the beginning of Christianity, as well as a number of Jewish wars and revolts and the start of the Jewish diaspora.

Any treatment of living religions in the context of historical roleplaying is bound to be controversial. No matter how respectfully it is done, it is almost certain that someone will be genuinely offended at the thought of their spiritual beliefs being reduced to a set of game rules. Therefore, no definite guidelines are given here for dealing with Judaism or Christianity in an *Eternal Rome* campaign.

That isn't to say, however, that these two religions should be ignored; from the early Empire period onward, they both played a significant role in the Roman world, and as several books and movies have proven, the conflicts between these religions and the Roman establishment are fertile ground for adventure and heroism. Early Christians in Rome, trying to practice their faith under the threat of state persecution, would make for a very challenging roleplaying campaign, as would Jewish Zealots trying to throw off the Roman yoke and regain freedom for their people.

The GM is encouraged to develop an approach to Judaism and Christianity according to the period, the desired tone of the campaign, and the tastes and beliefs of the gaming group. Green Ronin's *Testament* sourcebook contains information and ideas for roleplaying Israelite characters in the pre-Roman period, and provides a great deal of inspiration and information for both Jewish and Christian characters in the Roman world. More information, of course, can be found in the Bible.

Gnosticism

Gnosticism was an offshoot of Christianity, incorporating elements of several other religions that flourished among the more academically-inclined members of the Roman world in the middle Empire period. It derived its name from the Greek word *gnosis* ("knowledge"), and Gnostics believed that spiritual knowledge was the key to spiritual truth. According to Gnostic belief, achieving *agape* ("spiritual love") by a process of learning and study brings the individual into the true knowledge of God.

Gnosticism was a dualist faith, holding that every person was composed of both the spiritual and the material, and that only by rising above the material could true spirituality be achieved. Some Gnostics were ascetics who fasted and used other techniques to purge themselves of material concerns.

There was considerable animosity towards Gnostics by Christians, in part because of the Gnostic teaching that all of the imperfect physical world and the evil god who'd created it (*i.e.*, the god of the Jews and Christians) were inferior to the spiritual world and the supreme god who ruled there.

conquered peoples, he retained his own identity and wasn't regarded as a local interpretation of Apollo. Sculptures showed him sacrificing a bull to ensure the fertility of the earth and initiates to his cult were given a ritual cleansing bath in the blood of a sacrificed bull.

His symbol was the Phrygian cap, and his favored weapon was the short sword.

Other Imported Gods

The Romans were extremely tolerant of foreign religions, and at one time or another, from the late Republic onwards, temples of just about every deity from the lands Rome had conquered might be found in Roman cities, attracting Roman worshipers as well as those from the deities' native areas. It wasn't Roman religious intolerance that led to the persecution of Jews and Christians; instead it was the religious isolationism of the Jews and Christians, especially their refusal to recognize the deified Emperors, whose worship as required across the Empire as a form of submission to Rome.

In a large Roman city (and especially in Rome itself) followers of Egyptian deities like Horus and Bast rub shoulders with followers of Celtic deities like Epona and Middle Eastern deities like Ishtar and Baal. While the Roman deities generally had larger temples and were worshiped by the bulk of the population, the atmosphere of religious toleration allowed just about any religion to establish itself, so long as its teachings were not anti-Roman and its religious observances were not contrary to any law.

Isis's symbol was a magical knot called *tet* in Egyptian. Her favored weapon was the dagger.

Mithras (Greater God)

The cult of Mithras first appeared in Rome during the 1st century BC. It became popular in the early and middle Empire periods, especially in the army; small temples to Mithras have been found within several legionary fortresses. Mithraism also spread throughout the upper classes of Roman society, and in the 3rd and 4th centuries AD it was the only serious rival to Christianity.

Mithras was a god of strength, valor, and sacrifice. He was generally depicted as an athletic young man with dark, curly hair, dressed in a simple tunic and cloak and wearing a Phrygian cap. Originally he was a sun god, and Roman inscriptions referred to him as *Sol Invictus* ("The Unconquered Sun"), but unlike the sun gods of other

THE SOOTHSAYER

AN ETERNAL ROME ADVENTURE FOR 4-6 1ST-LEVEL CHARACTERS

The Soothsayer is an introductory adventure for the *Eternal Rome* setting. Gathered together to repay old debts to a wealthy Roman merchant, the would-be heroes are sent on a journey to a soothsayer who is said to live in the caverns beneath Lake Avernus. Although they do not know it, the journey is actually a test to gauge the worthiness of young Romans; as they navigate the encounters and obstacles under the watchful eye of the soothsayer, the choices they make guide them to their destinies.

Soothsayer is designed to take place early in the reign of the Emperor Claudius (between 41 and 45 AD; well before the downfall of the Empress Messalina in 48 AD).

LEGEND OF THE SIBYL OF CUMAE

Sometime before 510 BC, during the reign of Tarquin, the last king, the Sibylline oracle left her home in a grotto under Lake Avernus and made the journey to the city of Rome. There she offered to sell nine books of her matchless prophecies to the king. But Tarquin, being a venal and greedy man, refused to meet her price. Each time the king

Thus, from the dark recess, the Sibyl spoke,
And the resisting air the thunder broke;
The cave rebellow'd, and the temple shook.
Th' ambiguous god, who rul'd her lab'ring breast,
In these mysterious words his mind express'd;
Some truths reveal'd, in terms involv'd the rest.
At length her fury fell, her foaming ceas'd,
And, ebbing in her soul, the god decreas'd.

– Virgil, *The Aeneid*,
Book VI (ed. John Dryden)

refused her offer, the Sibyl burnt three of her books and doubled the price. When only three books of prophecy remained, the king finally relented, and the remaining prophecies of the oracle of Cumae were taken to the great temple of Jupiter, where they remained until Rome's fall. The Sibyl returned to her grotto home.

The gods granted the oracle the gift of immortality, but not eternal youth. Over the centuries, she shrunk until nothing was left but her voice. Her voice resided in a magical stone urn that lay at the bottom of the grotto, hung in an alcove by the priests. Those who wished to hear her words descended into the grotto of the Sibyl, and opened the urn so she could speak.

When Augustus became Emperor, his first act was to seize the books of prophecy and remove any references that might be interpreted as predicting the return of the Republic. The entrance to the grotto of the Cumaean Sibyl was sealed under a pile of rubble, so men could never again consult the oracle, and she could never issue a prophecy that would challenge the authority of the Emperor.

JUNIUS SERVILIUS STRABO

Outside of Rome is the villa of a wealthy merchant named Junius Servilius Strabo. He is one of the richest men in the Empire, and helped finance many of Emperor Claudius's building projects. He has the reputation of being an extremely clever man (having survived both the bloodshed of Tiberius's reign and the perversions of Caligula intact) but honorable by the standards of a less than honorable profession. A stout hedonist, Junius Strabo enjoys parties, wine, and wantons of all persuasions. He is also highly influential and the sort of man that most Roman families court as a friend to advance their social station.

Of course Strabo knows this, and usually treats anyone who seeks his influence with contempt; however Strabo also has a very good eye for spotting young Romans with potential. He's kept his eye on the PCs' families, military regiments, and patrons, and has determined that the PCs are worthy of his patronage. And so, having a great need of servants, he has sent messengers to the PCs' families, commanders, and masters, bidding them to come to his villa on an errand of undisclosed importance.

THE ERRAND

Recently, Strabo hired an astrologer to write his horoscope. To everyone's amazement and horror, it revealed that the great merchant was destined to die sometime during the next six weeks. Like many powerful Romans, Strabo is a superstitious man and utterly afraid of death. He wants to negate the prophecy by appealing to a higher authority— specifically the highest prophetic source imaginable: the legendary Sibyl of Cumae. While the Sibyl's grotto was

buried by Augustus, rumor has it that the mad Caligula (who wasn't known for respecting any of his great-grandfather's wishes) secretly opened the passage so he could descend to the oracle and hear her predict the greatness of his destiny.

Strabo wants the party to travel (in secret) to the city of Cumae, ascend the volcanic slopes to the crater, walk to the shores of Lake Avernus, and find the oracle's grotto. Once they've found the entrance, they are to descend into the caves and beg the oracle for a prophecy regarding Strabo's fate.

To ensure that they bring back a genuine prophecy, they're to take a special scroll with them; when the scroll makes physical contact with the Sibyl's ampulla, the scroll will turn into a color that only Strabo knows.

The adventurers are also asked to invent an explanation for their journey that does not connect them to Strabo. While Strabo believes that the Emperor would not object to his expedition, the memory of Augustus is strong, and his wishes (even three decades after his death) carry a weight beyond words.

Strabo tells them that if they need information or assistance while in Cumae, the temple of Apollo should be able to provide it; unfortunately, he can't give them a letter of introduction to the temple's priests, since his involvement must be kept secret.

STRABO'S ESTATE

Strabo's villa is an extravagant place, sprawling over six acres, with gardens and elaborate paintings (one of Rome's finest artists, Cabriabanus Pictor, is currently working on a fresco in the atrium), baths, a hypocaust (central heating system), and mosaics in the floor from Roman mythology; the unfaithfulness of Jupiter is a common theme, as are

HISTORICAL MATTERS

The reign of Claudius has been chosen for this adventure because it stands as an island of relative calm between the tumultuous reigns of Caligula and Nero, allowing the heroes to have tragic backgrounds from Caligula's reign and become embroiled in the problems of Nero when they reach higher levels. Additionally, the accessibility of the popular television series *I, Claudius* makes it more likely that the politics and personalities of the era will be known to the players and the GM, making it an accessible introduction point. (Although many historians believe Claudius was neither as kindly nor as wise as author Robert Graves portrays him.)

To alter this scenario for pre-Augustan times, the grotto is not sealed. Later eras can use the scenario virtually unchanged; if set in Augustus' or Tiberius's reigns, the consequences of being caught disturbing the Cumaean Sibyl will probably be much higher.

One possibility is to set the adventure during the reign of Claudius II (268–270 AD), over two centuries later. Legend has it that this Claudius consulted the Sibylline Books (still a source of useful prophecy eight centuries after being sold to Rome) when the Empire was threatened by various barbarian invaders. The Sibyl's predictions gave Claudius a choice: he could enjoy a long but troubled reign by staying in Rome, or he could defeat Rome's enemies at the price of his own life. As a dutiful Roman, Claudius went on campaign against the barbarians, winning victories against the Alemanni and the Goths (and winning the title Gothicus for himself), but dying in the second year of his reign.

But what if a fresher prophecy could be procured that took precedence over the original Sibylline one; a prophecy that could show Claudius II how to defeat the barbarians and survive? Such an oracle could only come from a source able to overrule the Sibylline Books: the Sibyl of Cumae herself.

Many of the details, like the sealing of the grotto, are matters of historical dispute. Also the grotto's layout was not even remotely like the one described in the scenario, and Strabo is a completely fictional personage.

depictions of Mercury (god of commerce) and symbols to ward off the evil eye.

Strabo has no sons. His heir is an Athenian Greek named Antenor, who was taken as a slave by Strabo's now deceased brother (a military tribune) and who gradually rose to favor.

ANTENOR

Male (Greek) human fighter 6, pankretiast 4; CR 10; Medium humanoid; HD 6d10+6 plus 4d10+4; hp 63; Init +4; Spd 30 ft.; AC 14, touch 14, flat-footed 10; Base Atk +10; Grap +18; Atk +15 melee (1d8+4, unarmed) or +14 melee (1d4+4/19–20, dagger) or +14 ranged (1d4+4/19–20, dagger); Full Atk +13/+13/+10 (1d8+4, unarmed) or +14/+9 melee (1d4+4/19–20, dagger) or +14 ranged (1d4+4/19–20, dagger); SA throw; SV Fort +10, Ref +10, Will +4; AL CG; Fame –14; Str 19, Dex 18, Con 12, Int 12, Wis 12, Cha 15.

Skills and Feats: Climb +11, Drive (chariot) +8, Diplomacy +4, Escape Artist +7, Handle Animal +11, Hide +4, Intimidate +10, Listen +3, Move Silently +4, Ride +6, Sense Motive +3, Spot +3, Tumble +7; Blind-Fight, Canny Charge, Cleave, Dodge, Improved Grapple, Improved Unarmed Strike, Mobility, Power Attack, Stunning Fist, Weapon Focus (unarmed strike).

Languages: Greek, Latin

Possessions: Dagger.

Antenor, a surly Greek was a champion pankretiast (winner of the Ellis Games 11 years ago) then joined in a revolt against Rome and was enslaved as his punishment. Now a man in his mid-30s, neither time nor kind treatment have softened him. He blames Strabo's family for his fall from grace, and has been plotting his master's death for years. It was Antenor who urged Strabo to commission his horoscope, and it was he who planted the idea to send adventurers to consult the Cumaean Sibyl (if his plans to poison Strabo fall through, sending visitors to the forbidden Sibyl in Cumae will be his fallback plan; in this event, Strabo can be arrested on suspicion of treason). Antenor's also secretly working with someone else in Rome who's eager to seize possession of Strabo's holdings.

When Antenor meets the heroes he's rude and dismissive. If he gets a chance to spar with a PC and display his fighting skills, he gladly "puts the pup in his place." He won't kill a PC or be rude enough to convince them not to run the errand; he just wants to visibly distance himself from their mission.

THE ROAD TO CUMAE

There are many roads from Rome to the southern port city of Cumae, In Claudian times, these roads are secure from bandits and travel shouldn't be a problem. It's 100 miles as the crow flies from Rome to Cumae, or approximately a five-day trip on foot.

During the journey, the player characters will have four encounters. These events provide opportunities for favorable prophecies that may provide minor benefits for them. The GM should feel free to change the location, situations, and rewards as needed.

ENCOUNTER 1: THE SERPENT AND THE CHARIOT (EL 3)

Suggested Location: A day south of Rome

On the road to Cumae, in an area of bush and thin forests, one of the heroes notices an overturned chariot rusting on the side of the road. It obviously belongs to the Roman army, and bears the emblem of the II Augusta legion (which is currently assigned to Claudius's invasion of Britain).

Within the wreckage of the chariot is a fallen legionary's shield. Under the shield is a nest of adders; they can be noticed with a DC 18 Spot check. The adders attack anyone who comes within 5 feet.

Small Viper Snake (5): hp 4 each; see the *MM* for statistics.

If someone checks the area around the chariot, a DC 15 Spot check reveals the body of Tiberius Paulus, a soldier from the II Augusta legion. He carries a message addressed to one Lucius Flavius, bearing the news of his son's death; Julius Flavius, another soldier in the legion, was killed in battle in Britain.

If someone takes the message to Lucius Flavius, consult the Sibylline prophecies on page 146 for the consequences.

ENCOUNTER TWO: THE EMPTY HOUSE (EL 3)

Suggested Location: Three days south of Rome, near Tarracina.

A sudden storm whips up, and it's obvious the party needs to take shelter. On a nearby hill stands an apparently abandoned house. As the heroes decide what to do, they hear over the noise of the storm a chilling wail coming from the house.

The grounds of the villa look like they haven't been tended for weeks or months, and the door to the house is open. If the PCs enter the *vestibulum* ("entry hall"), they hear the harsh sound of a crone's voice (a voice distinctly different from the moan heard earlier, but no more pleasant), railing against her husband, accusing him of drunkenness. Walking into the *atrium* ("courtyard"), they behold an incredible sight: the semi-transparent shade of an old man, wearing dated legionary's armor and a golden laurel wreath, hate brimming in its eyes, recoiling under the sharp tongue of an old woman.

If the heroes make any attempt at diplomacy, they can avoid conflict. The woman begrudgingly retires to find food and drink for her guests (the servants and slaves fled long ago), leaving the PCs alone with the shade.

The shade is Linus Paterculus and the old woman is his wife, Julia. Once they were wildly in love, but in her old age Julia became such a nag that her husband tried to poison her. Unfortunately, he botched the job, poisoned himself, and died. As punishment for his attempted crime, his shade remains on Earth, clothed in ethereal copies of prized possessions from his heroic days in the legions. He's tried to attack Julia, but every time he does, she goes into a fit, and even as a ghost he's no match for her sharp tongue.

LINUS PATERCULUS

Male ghost warrior 1, commoner 1; CR 3; Medium undead (incorporeal): HD 2d12; hp 11; Init +0; Spd 30 ft., fly 30 ft. (perfect); AC 11, touch 11, flat-footed 11; or AC 17, touch 10, flat-footed 17; Base Atk +1; Grap +1; Atk +2 melee (draining touch) or against ethereal opponents +2 melee (1d6/19–20, gladius); Atk +2 melee (draining touch) or against ethereal opponents +2 melee (1d6/19–20, gladius); SA draining touch, frightful moan, manifestation; SQ darkvision 60 ft., incorporeal traits, rejuvenation, +4 turn resistance, undead traits; AL NE; Fame +2; SV Fort +2, Ref +1, Will +0; Str — (10), Dex 12, Con —, Int 11, Wis 11, Cha 13

Skills and Feats: Hide +9, Intimidate +3, Listen +8, Profession (farmer) +2, Search +8, Spot +9, Survival +2 (+4 follow tracks); Close Order Fighting, Weapon Finesse.

Languages: Latin.

Possessions: Ethereal gladius, lorica segmentata, scutum, corona aurea.

Being unable to kill his wife, the ghost wants the PCs to kill her for him. She's a 1st-level commoner, and easily killed; however, if she is slain, she becomes a ghost herself and torments her husband for eternity.

The heroes may elect to destroy Linus instead. If that happens, Julia assumes her husband's gone wandering off to get drunk, and goes about her business. Aside from normal XP awards, this solution confers no special benefits on the PCs.

The way to bring peace to Linus's shade without murdering an innocent woman is to convince Julia that he's dead. His body, several months old, still lies in the garden under a fig tree. If it's pointed out to her, Julia starts complaining about how

her husband never cleans up messes about the house. If the characters persist and are willing to be cruel in forcing her to realize the truth (especially if she's shown the body and Linus's shade at the same time), she breaks down, realizes that her husband's dead, and she begins to wildly mourn his death—like many nagging wives, she really does love him.

When Linus touches her in sympathy, his shade changes to a much younger version of himself (when he and Julia first fell in love). She falls dead, and their shades pass to the underworld. If this happens, the Sibyl provides a benefit to the adventurers later in the scenario.

ENCOUNTER THREE: THE MAN ON THE CROSS (EL VARIES)

Suggested Location: Four days south of Rome, near the crossing of the Voltumus River.

When the PCs cross the Voltumus River, they come upon a grisly sight: a field of crucifixion. Twenty slaves who revolted against their masters and murdered them were captured and have been crucified to set an example. Their bodies have been maimed and defaced; over one of them (presumably the leader), there's a sign in Latin that reads: "Labellius, Master of No Man; Slave of Crows."

Two Roman soldiers guard them. The soldiers really don't care what people do to the bodies, as long as no one removes the sign or tries to take the slaves down from the crosses.

MARCUS AND LUCIUS (AUXILIARY INFANTRY)

Male human fighter 3; CR 3; Medium humanoid; HD 3d10; hp 18; Init +6; Spd 20 ft.; AC 19, touch 12, flat-footed 17; Base Atk +3; Grap +6; Atk +7 melee (1d6+3/19–20, gladius) or +5 ranged (1d6+3, pilum); Full Atk +7 melee (1d6+3/19–20, gladius) or +5 ranged (1d6+3, pilum); AL N; Fame +2; SV Fort +3, Ref +3, Will +1; Str 16, Dex 14, Con 11, Int 10, Wis 10, Cha 14

Skills and Feats: Balance +3, Climb +1, Hide +5, Jump +3, Listen +3, Move Silently +3, Spot +1; Close Order Fighting, Improved Initiative, Track, Weapon Finesse, Weapon Focus.

Languages: Latin.

Possessions: Lorica segmentata, heavy metal shield, gladius, pilum.

If the heroes act differently than previous passers-by (who either jeered or ignored the crucified slaves), Marcus and Lucius become suspicious and urge the PCs to leave the area and avoid trouble. If pressed with questions, they simply say that Labellius led a slave revolt that was easily crushed by the Italian auxiliaries. Lucius, the more gregarious of the two soldiers, adds that there've been a number of recent slave revolts in southern Italy, and the local administrators are quite concerned.

The rebels have been crucified for three days; Labellius is the only one who's still alive. If the PCs approach, he begs for mercy: a quick death, an herb that reduces pain, or a drink of water—anything to ease his suffering. The guards don't care what the PCs do to him, as long as nothing happens that would get them in trouble.

Labellius tells the PCs that he was encouraged by Draco, an alleged soothsayer of Celtic blood who's been stirring up trouble in the region. Labellius curses the day he ever listened to Draco, claiming he was ensorcelled by the soothsayer's words. He warns the adventurers to "Beware the dragon's voice."

If mercy is granted, the Sibyl provides a benefit to the heroes later in the scenario.

ENCOUNTER FOUR: THE BIRDS (EL VARIES)

Suggested Location: On a rise near the lake the heroes spot a sight as unusual as it is cruel. Lake Avernus means "The Lake Without Birds," but on the slopes of this hill an injured giant eagle is being attacked by a small flock of metallic birds. The bodies of many dead birds are scattered about the area, but the wounded eagle is weakening, forced to merely hold the remainder at bay with shrill cries from its snapping beak, and the flapping of its single unbroken wing.

Stymphalian Birds (9): hp 6 each; see page 85 for details.
Giant Eagle: hp 30 (currently 9); see the *MM* for statistics.

The heroes likely won't be able to kill the entire flock of birds, but they may be able to drive the birds away or hold them off long enough for the eagle to be healed and to escape (or join them in the fight). It's well known that eagles are the symbol of Rome. If the eagle is healed, the heroes are rewarded when they encounter the Sibyl.

To heal the eagle, a character must succeed on a DC 15 Diplomacy check. If the character is a Roman citizen, he gains a +3 circumstance bonus to the check and if there is a Roman soldier present in the party, the character gains an additional +2 circumstance bonus. Assuming the characters calm the noble creature, the healer needs to succeed on a DC 15 Heal check to set the broken wing. Once healed, the eagle gives an appraising look at whoever healed it, and flies away (or rejoins the fight if the Stymphalian birds are still present). The PCs should take note of this, since healing of this sort would normally take weeks, not seconds.

If the PCs attack the eagle, every Roman citizen who dealt it damage it is subject to a *bestow curse* spell (with effects determined randomly; caster level 10th; no save).

CUMAE

The city of Cumae is a port on the Mediterranean, in the shadow of several volcanoes.

A moderate-sized city, Cumae is quiet (by Roman standards), known for its oracle, amphitheater, and hot baths. It's also quite ancient, dating back to well before the founding of Rome. Its conquest in the 6th century BC by the Greeks gave it some of the most pronounced Grecian influences of any city in Italy, although its influence waned long ago. Near the end of the Republic, other ports took its place in the Roman sphere, and for the last century Cumae has been in decline. Parts of the city have been abandoned, particularly the sections east of Lake Avernus.

The PCs receive a cold greeting in Cumae. They're referred to the temple of Apollo for information ("as that is where

ILL OMENS IN CUMAE

Recently, three events have occurred that have raised concerns among the populace of this backwater.

SMOKE

Two weeks ago, smoke began appearing out of the mountain east of Lake Avernus. The hot baths have been getting scalding hot, and vapors have issued from the vents around the mountain. These vapors are beginning to subside (and the baths are beginning to cool), but people are nervous. If there's an eruption, it will be seen as a bad omen; something to blame on newly-arrived strangers.

THE REPUBLICAN

A man who came to the temple of Apollo as an initiate turned out to be a Republican agitator. Six days ago, Roman soldiers, led by Centurion Gallo, came, ignored the protests of the priests, and dragged the man from the temple. The agitator was brought to Rome for judgment. The locals are under a cloud of suspicion, and they're suspicious that strangers will turn out to be agents of the emperor sent to spy on the temple.

It's also rumored that several auxiliaries vanished while searching the lands around Avernus. The foolish say that they were carried down into the underworld.

REVOLT

A Celtic soothsayer named Draco has been inciting slaves on several of the wealthiest and most influential villas to revolt. There's rumor that Draco is being sheltered by the temple of Apollo, a claim the priests furiously deny. The gladiator Marcus Maximus (see page 153) is serving as his bodyguard, although its rumored he prefers to consort with evil spirits.

the fate of Cumae has always been decided"). The people of Cumae heard nothing about Caligula unsealing the grotto and believe it's a lie, however (as people quietly note) Caligula is the one man in the history of Rome for whom the reality is stranger than the myth.

If the locals aren't panicked (*i.e.*, the volcano hasn't blown or the PCs have antagonized the temple of Apollo), it would be possible to pay a local to act as a guide to the area around the lake.

LAKE AVERNUS

This circular lake, described in the *Aeneid* as "black Avernus," stretches for over a mile across an ancient volcanic crater. It's surrounded by gloomy groves of trees, but no birds (except for those in **Encounter 4**). Noxious vapors issue out of vents on the side of the lake, the waters are hot and lifeless, and

CUMAE AND ENVIRONS

1. CAVE OF THE SIBYL
2. TEMPLE TO APPOLO
3. NORTHERN CAVERN
4. AMPITHEATER
5. ACROPOLIS

LAKE AVERNUS

VOLCANO

0   1

SCALE IN MILES

inventor Daedalus, a large staircase on the south side leads up to an artificially raised terrace on which it sits. Once it was bustling with priests, prophets, and soothsayers, but now it has largely fallen from favor. The high priest, Aulus Laevinus (12th-level cleric) is a capable politician as well as a priest, who wields the historical importance of the temple as a fine instrument in his struggle to keep Rome from completely destroying the temple or driving out the priests.

However, Aulus has grander designs. He would like to restore the Sibyl (and Cumae) to the prestige it possessed in the days of the Republic. As soon as the PCs arrive, he recognizes them as potential tools to that end.

If the adventurers are polite to Aulus, he reciprocates. The wounded are healed, the famished are fed, and the weary are given soft beds. He'll give them further assistance with their errand, but he has a price: the death of Draco.

After the Roman army invaded the temple in search of a Republican agitator, that Celtic sorcerer came to the temple and tried to recruit their help in manufacturing a prophecy that would proclaim the success of his slave rebellions against Rome. Draco hoped they would be so angry with the Empire that they'd become his willing dupes, but Aulus knew he was being manipulated, and refused him with contempt. Draco threatened to return with an army of dark spirits and raze the temple. He also tried to seize some of the temple's most sacred relics, but was driven away before he could lay hands on them.

For three days afterward, the sacred statue of Apollo in the temple courtyard radiated such fiery heat that any who touched it singed their fingers. One of the soothsayers prophesied that heroes would soon come who would swear to kill Draco, and that he was to provide them with comfort, aid, and shelter. Although the other priests are suspicious of strangers, Aulus believes that the PCs are the answer to prophecy, and thus deserving of his support. His only stipulation is that they swear an oath before the statue of Apollo to hunt down and kill Draco.

If the PCs refuse to swear the oath, they're politely escorted away from the temple. No further help is offered to them.

However, if they swear the oath, the ground rumbles slightly, and any sheathed weapons begin to rattle, which Aulus takes as a good omen. He is then extremely helpful. First, he provides the party with a flask containing 10 doses of *potion of cure moderate wounds*. He gives them with a flask containing three doses of a medicine against the effects of the sulfurous vents surrounding the lake (*potion of neutralize poison*, but limited to neutralizing the effects of volcanic vapors). Finally, he provides them with healing kits, climbing kits, and provisions. He also allows them to touch the relics of the temple (see below), which temporarily bestows powers upon them.

there's a general sense of desolation in the air. It is easy to believe this could be the gateway to the Underworld.

If the PCs have no guide and are exploring the lands surrounding the lake, once per day each member of the party must make a DC 13 Survival check. On a failed check, the character gets too close to a poisonous vent and must succeed on a DC 12 Fortitude save or take 1d3 points of Constitution damage. Ten rounds later, the character must succeed on another DC 12 Fortitude save or take 1d2 points of Wisdom damage.

There are three noteworthy areas around Lake Avernus: the entrance to the cave of the Cumaean Sibyl, the temple of Apollo, and the entrance to the Grotto of Cocceio.

ENTRANCE TO THE SIBYL'S CAVE

When the PCs arrive here, they discover the entrance was indeed sealed by Augustus—and the seal has not been breached. Strabo was wrong. The story that Caligula reopened the cave is a lie. No force of the party can remove the tons of rubble covering the entrance to the grotto.

If a guide is accompanying the PCs, he says there are rumors of secret entrances to the Sibyl's grotto still known to the priests of Apollo, and that they should consider consulting them.

THE TEMPLE OF APOLLO

This large temple complex stands on the eastern shore of the lake. Allegedly constructed by the ancient Greek

APOLLO'S CURSE

If the PCs swear the oath, each loses 1 hit point for every month that Draco remains alive. This curse can only be broken by the death of Draco, or the use of a *limited wish*, *miracle*, or *wish* spell, or a *remove curse* cast by a 14th-level caster.

If Aulus is questioned about the cave of the Sibyl, he tells them it was sealed by Augustus and hasn't been reopened—the Caligula rumor was a lie that Strabo foolishly believed. All hope is not lost, however, for there is a second passage to the Sibyl that can be found in the Grotto of Cocceio, a tunnel dug in the days when Augustus was still Octavian, to connect Avernus with the sea that connects with the Sibyl's grotto. On Apollo's holy days, Aulus still visits it in secret.

Features of the temple include:

THE VENTS OF PROPHECY

There are still numerous soothsaying women in the temple who venture to the volcanic vents and breathe the vapors of prophecy. They dance in the vapors, go into a trance, and prophesy in their delirium. Any female PC may do the same. She has to inhale enough poison that she takes 1d4 points of Constitution damage, but if she succeeds on a DC 20 Wisdom check (any levels in the soothsayer prestige class are added to the roll as a circumstance bonus), she receives a prophetic vision.

The vision shows: (1) Strabo, in his Roman villa, holding a cup; (2) the volcano east of Lake Avernus erupting; (3) Strabo drinking from his cup and choking; (4) Strabo being choked by Antenor; (5) an ashen rain falling on Cumae; (6) a tall man with thick golden hair standing over Roman corpses and carving the word "Arverni" on their bodies with a sword; (7) Strabo slumping dead to the ground, Antenor walking away from him and washing his hands in a bowl.

THE GREAT STATUE

There's a statue of Apollo in the temple that has a legend associated with it: Once, when Apollo disapproved of a war between Greek states, the statue cried for four days, and the warring parties were accursed.

If the heroes swear the oath to kill Draco, blood begins to flow from the statue's feet, and when it's noticed a junior priest rushes to find Aulus who then brings the PCs to its presence. If the PCs' weapons are dipped in the blood, they steam and receive a +2 damage bonus for the next 24 hours.

THE REMAINS OF THE WILD BOAR OF ERYMANTUS

This relic is the body of a boar killed by Hercules during his labors. The first person who lays hands on the boar each day receives a *bull's strength* spell that lasts for 24 hours.

THE BLACK STONE OF CYBELE

This is a relic brought from Asia to Cumae in 217 BC, to calm the hysterical populace that had been panicked by the approach of Hannibal. The first time anyone touches this relic, he receives a *bless* spell that lasts for 24 hours.

THE GROTTO OF COCCEIO

This grotto is a collection of artificial tunnels linking natural caves, designed by the famed architect Cocceio in the days of Octavian to provide sea access for Lake Avernus. An impressive feat of engineering, the grotto was abandoned when ships began to circumvent Cumae for other ports.

Now, however, it is being used as a temporary base for the rebel sorcerer Draco, who's gathering ghastly shades and other followers. Using the vapors of the vents as a narcotic, the charismatic (and deluded) sorcerer is becoming increasingly convinced that he's a god, and that it's his destiny to lead a revolution against Rome, whereby he'll burn the capital, topple every statue of Jupiter in the empire, and replace them with his own image.

The cavern is composed of a mix of limestone and volcanic rock: white in sunlight, red in torchlight. The grotto stretches over a large distance, so the map is *not* drawn to scale.

1. ENTRANCE

The grotto entrance is a large tunnel, 10 feet high and 10 feet wide, carved into a limestone cavern at a 20-degree downward angle. Unlit torches in sconces line the walls.

In one part, there's steep stone step that leads to a 15-foot drop. To descend it without injury, a climber must succeed on a DC 8 Climb check. Falling characters take 1d6 points of damage.

2. REMINDERS OF DEFEATS (EL 1)

In this large chamber, four skeletal warriors stand guard. If the password "Arverni" (the name of Draco's Gallic tribe) is spoken in the room, the skeletons remain immobile. If the adventures try to cross the chamber without saying the password, the skeletons attack. These skeletons are the remains of Gallic warriors, but not members of Draco's tribe.

Human Warrior Skeletons (4): hp 6 each; see *MM* for statistics.

3. THE TORTURED SOLDIER (EL 4)

As the PCs approach this cavern, they hear a man's voice, groaning in pain, and two high-pitched voices getting into a heated argument about whether Romans are more stoic than Spartans. One argues Romans are much more stoic than Spartans, while the other asserts that the Spartans had no choice but to be stoic, whereas Rome manages to be "a fascinating blend of Athenian decadence and Spartan brutality that makes stoicism merely an interesting lifestyle choice." If they're not interrupted, they compare the brutality of the empires they've seen: Assyrians, Babylonians, Persians, and Seleucids, and come to the conclusion that Rome's the most effective tyranny of them all ("Maybe we should be working for those guys!").

The two voices belong to imps, creatures attracted by Draco's activities. In an attempt to convince them to fight for him, Draco handed over some captured Roman soldiers to the imps. Six soldiers have been bound and tortured, and five are dead (two others died in the initial fight with Draco). The last is still alive and moaning in pain.

The soldier is a 1st-level Italian auxiliary named Quintius Cassius Pacilus. Eight days ago, his contubernium was searching for the republican agitator in Cumae, and an informant told them he was camped near Avernus; this was a trap, and he and the others were captured by Draco. Quintius is a loyal soldier of Rome, but when it becomes apparent that the PCs are in the grotto without Roman permission, he agrees to tell no one that he saw them there. (*Note:* If the GM needs to introduce a new player character to the adventure in progress, this would be a good opportunity to do so.)

Imps (2): hp 13 each; see *MM* for statistics.

The heroes likely won't be able to kill the imps, but if they rescue Quintius by any means (*e.g.*, playing on the imps' innate cowardice), they receive full XP for meeting the challenge.

4. PASSAGE TO THE COAST

This long limestone tunnel eventually leads to the coast.

5. THE ANIMATED TABLE (EL 1)

There's a small armory here: 20 neatly stacked swords and iron shields are leaning against a wall, along with five short bows and 200 arrows. There's also a small metal chest set on a side table. If the chest is touched by anyone who is not of Celtic blood, the table animates and attacks.

Small Animated Object (1): hp 15; Spd 50 ft.; see *MM* for statistics.

Inside the chest are 300 denarius, 40 aureus, and 200 Gallic half-staters (170 gp total).

6. THE MAD PRECIPICE

This tunnel leads over a vent that's issuing poisonous vapors. Across the precipice is a narrow, 60-foot-long beam of natural stone, requiring a DC 8 Balance check to cross. The vapors from the chasm disorient those who cross, forcing PCs to succeed on a DC 12 Fort save or take 1d6 points of

Dexterity damage and be forced to make another Balance check (affected by the loss of Dexterity). Those who fail the second Balance check fall 100 feet before they hit the bottom taking 10d6 points of damage and likely ending their careers.

7. BEWARE OF FALLING STONE

As the tunnels open up into an area of worked stone, the earth begins to rumble. Pieces of masonry rain down from the ceiling. Fifty feet from the cavern mouth, the heroes take 1d2 points of damage from the falling debris unless they succeed on a DC 10 Reflex save. If they do not immediately sprint for the cave, they must succeed on a DC 13 Reflex save (in addition to the first) or take 1d6 additional points of damage.

8. THE SIBYL'S CAVE (EL 4)

This large cave is the home of the Cumaean Sibyl. A black, dead tree sits in the center of the room, and the Sibyl's ampulla hangs from a string over one of the branches.

Beneath the ampulla, the sorcerer Draco sits naked (except for a pouch hanging from a thong around his neck and a golden torc) with a dagger lying at his feet inside a square with a burning oil lamp at each corner, apparently in a trance. Next to him, the gladiator Marcus Maximus stands, sword drawn. Draco foresaw that he would be attacked, thus Marcus won't wait to negotiate—he attacks immediately.

MARCUS MAXIMUS

Male human (Roman) gladiator 4; CR 4; Medium humanoid; HD 4d10+4; hp 34; Init +3; Spd 30 ft.; AC 23 (22 on left side and from behind), touch 14, flat-footed 19 (18 on left and from behind); Base Atk +3; Grap +7; Atk +9 melee (1d6+4/19–20, gladius) or +6 ranged (1d4+4/19–20, dagger); Full Atk +9 melee (1d6+4/19–20, gladius) or +6 ranged (1d4+4/19–20, dagger); SA +2 damage against Thracian-style gladiators, dirty fighting +1d4, dramatic attack +1, Samnite style (+1 melee, +1 AC); SQ reputation (gladiator), SV Fort +5, Ref +7, Will +3; AL NE; Fame –10; Str 18, Dex 16, Con 13, Int 14, Wis 14, Cha 15

Skills and Feats: Balance +4, Bluff +6, Climb +8, Diplomacy +4, Disguise +2 (+4 acting), Hide +3, Intimidate +11, Jump +5, Knowledge (the games) +3, Listen +2, Move Silently +3, Perform (gladiatorial combat) +7, Spot +2, Swim +5, Tumble +4; Combat Expertise, Improved Disarm, Weapon Focus (short sword).

Languages: Latin, Greek.

Possessions: Manicus on sword arm, cingulum, 2 ocreae, enclosed helmet, heavy metal shield, gladius, dagger.

Draco awakens in three rounds. As long as the lamps burn, he has damage reduction 5/magic per lamp with cumulative effects; thus while all four lamps are lit, he has DR 20/magic. The slightest damage will break a lamp, dealing 1d4 points damage to the sorcerer and ending that lamp's contribution to his DR. Overturning a lamp creates a burning pool of oil (see Adventuring Gear in the *PHB*) and ends Draco's DR from that lamp, but doesn't cause him damage unless he touches the flames.

When Draco awakens, he's in a near trance state. He wildly proclaims that he can "smell the filth of Rome in the wind" and attacks in the name of lost Arverni. If he's killed, his last act is to cast a *dying curse* spell (see page 67) on whoever slew him.

DRACO

Male (Gallic) human sorcerer 6; CR 6; Medium humanoid; HD 6d4; hp 18; Init +1; Spd 30 ft.; AC 11, touch 11, flat-footed 10; Base Atk +3; Grap +4; Atk +4 melee (1d4+1/19–20, dagger) or +4 ranged (1d4+1/19–20, dagger); Full Atk +4 melee (1d4+1/19–20, dagger) or +4 ranged (1d4+1/19–20, dagger); SQ familiar; AL LE; Fame –5; SV Fort +2, Ref +4, Will +6; Str 13, Dex 13, Con 11, Int 13, Wis 13, Cha 16

Skills and Feats: Bluff +11, Concentration +5, Diplomacy +5, Disguise +3 (+5 acting), Hide +1, Intimidate +5, Knowledge (arcana) +9, Listen +1 (+3 with familiar), Move Silently +1, Sense Motive +2, Spot +2 (+4 with familiar); Brew Potion, Run, Spell Focus (enchantment).

Languages: Celtic, Latin.

Possessions: Dagger, *potion of cat's grace, potion of resistance, torc of shielding* (equivalent of *brooch of shielding*, 15 charges)

Sorcerer Spells Known (*Cast per Day* 6/7/6/4; DC 13 + spell level): 0—daze, detect poison, ghost sound, light, mage hand, read magic, resistance; 1st—cause fear, charm person, dying curse, magic missile; 2nd—cat's grace, touch of idiocy; 3rd—false omen

FALX

Male raven familiar; CR —; Tiny magical beast; HD 6; hp 9; Init +2; Spd 10 ft., fly 40 ft. (average); AC 17, touch 14, flat-footed 15; Base Atk +3; Grap –10; Atk +5 melee (1d2–5, claws); Full Atk +5 melee (1d2–5, claws); Space/Reach 2-1/2 ft./0 ft.; SA deliver touch spells; SQ empathic link, improved evasion, low-light vision, share spells, speak with master; AL LE; SV Fort +2, Ref +4, Will +6; Str 1, Dex 15, Con 10, Int 9, Wis 14, Cha 6

Skills and Feats: Concentration +0, Hide +2, Listen +3, Move Silently +2, Spot +5; Weapon Finesse (claws)

If the sorcerer and the gladiator die, the Sibyl's ampulla may be safely opened. When it's opened a voice as loud as thunder shouts: "I WANT TO DIE!" The Sibyl doesn't know how to achieve this; she might speculate that the gods are forgotten, she may be allowed to quietly slip away to the underworld.

If she's asked about Strabo's fate, the cavern shakes as the volcano to the east suddenly erupts, requiring all PCs to succeed on a DC 16 Reflex save or fall prone (no damage). When the fury and smoke die down, the Sibyl's voice says: "You have your answer." Anyone who makes a DC 20 Spot check sees Strabo's shade briefly appearing in the passage to the underworld and then passing down the passage to the River Styx.

The Sibyl tells the adventurers that they've done well. At some point, when their heroic reputations are established (*i.e.*, when every PC's Fame is double what it is at the end of this adventure), they may ask to be guided down the passage to the underworld.

If any Christian is in the party, golden leaves waft from the dead tree's branches and settle on his feet. The words "He will be crowned again" are written on the leaves.

THE SIBYL AND CHRISTIANITY

The Sibyl of Cumae was respected by Christians because one of her most famous prophecies was easily interpreted to refer to the coming of Jesus: "Come soon, dear child of the gods, Jupiter's great viceroy! Come soon the time is near to begin your life illustrious!" St. Augustan considered the words divinely inspired.

CONCLUDING PROPHECIES

In addition to any gifts listed earlier, the Sibyl rewards the player characters with a number of benefits, depending on their actions earlier in the adventure.

If they found the message of the dead legionary, the Sibyl gives the prophecy:

> *Below the House of the Huntress stands a decayed home,*
> *Where grim men refuse their tears.*
> *If Hermes bears a landless champion to its door*
> *Then Mars shall embrace him, and elevate his station.*
> *And the house shall decay no more.*

Benefit: The run-down house of Lucius Flavius is at the foot of the Aventine Hill, a crowded residential area marked by the Temple of Diana on the hill's lower slopes. If a strong young man without noble blood bears the message to the father, the son-less father offers to adopt the PC and elevate him to the position of his heir. This won't make the PC rich, but it will give him the noble nomen "Flavius," and allow him to seek a new patrician destiny.

If the heroes managed to bring peace to the shade in the Empty House, the Sibyl issues the following prophecy:

> *Life is Lethe and Lethe is life, a silent ambrosia.*
> *Death is life and life is death, a still preeminence*
> *As one shade knelt, so shall all shades bend*
> *Before the emissary of life and death.*
> *As long as the price is paid.*

Benefit: Once per day, any of the heroes who can turn undead gain a +2 bonus to one of his turning attempts. The character must make a sacrifice worth at least 50 gp/month to Jupiter or Apollo to maintain this ability, or he loses it permanently.

If the party showed mercy to the crucified man, the Sibyl issues the following prophecy:

> *The shattered man is a human standard*
> *In his punishment, the strength of Mars displayed.*
> *Yet Mars wins not all battles*
> *And the hand of Asclepius has its place.*

Benefit: Once per day, the hero gains +2 sacred bonus a Heal check, or +2 to the total number of hit points healed by a *cure* spell.

If the eagle was healed, the Sibyl issues the following prophecy:

*This is the day of the rising eagle
When the battlefield becomes an eyrie for honor
When Mars smiles upon his boldest captains
And the enemies of the eagle are torn to pieces.*

Benefit: If fighting against an acknowledged enemy of the Empire, the heroes may smite him, as per a paladin's smite evil ability (level equal to his character level). This benefit may be used once per day, but is lost if the character ever retreats from a fight or is arrested or outlawed by Rome (the player should not be aware that his PC can lose the power).

If Draco was slain, the Sibyl gives the following prophecy:

*The Dragon is dead, yet greater dragons remain.
Protect Britannicus, or Rome will burn.*

Britannicus is the young son (born 39 AD) of the Emperor Claudius and his third wife, Messalina. If the future follows real-world history's course, Nero, the son of Claudius's fourth wife, Agrippina, will succeed Claudius (who is murdered by Agrippina) as Emperor, and then quickly murder his popular step-brother and potential rival, Britannicus. Less than a decade later, Nero will be blamed for the Great Fire of 64 AD.

No power that the PCs possess can move the ampulla from the tree or damage hurt the tree. Likewise, the Cumaean Sibyl ranks as a demigoddess and cannot be affected by mortals. When she finishes issuing the last of her prophecies, the lid flies back on the Sibyl's jar and the cavern falls as silent as a tomb. If the ampulla is reopened, she screams "I want to die!" but has nothing else to say.

Strabo's scroll turns purple when it touches the ampulla, but if the heroes reopen it outside the cave, it appears smeared with blood.

9. Passage to the Underworld

This passage leads down to the Underworld. After the Sibyl's blessing has been won, if the heroes want to descend to the underworld they may take the passage, present a golden bough to Charun (a practice an educated Roman would know from the story of Aeneas), and visit the lands beside the Styx. GMs who do not wish to expand this adventure should play up the dangers of the Underworld, perhaps using Cerebus as a deterent.

Consequences

If the volcano erupts, Cumae is largely deserted as the locals flee in panic. The exception is the few wealthy villas near the sea, which are too rich to be abandoned (or left undefended).

The temple of Apollo isn't deserted—the oracles said that no one was too leave the temple until those who sought the Sibyl had returned. If Draco was slain, Aulus pledges himself to help the PCs in the future; of course, he hopes that when they win influence at Rome, they'll try to advance the cause of the priesthood of Apollo, revitalize the Sibylline cult, and restore Cumae's importance in the empire.

If the adventurers return to Rome, they find Strabo dead. He died mysteriously while they were away, and rumors have it that he was poisoned by the emperor or the emperor's wife Messalina (like half the men in Rome, Strabo is said to have been the empress's lover). Antenor quietly left Rome shortly after Strabo's death. Strabo's body has already been burned, and the funeral rites were performed; the cremation was conducted three days after Strabo's death, instead of a week, which would have been customary for a man of his station.

A day after their return to Rome, the PCs are ordered to meet with Pallas, the Emperor's finance minister (who, most curiously, picked up many of Strabo's holdings after his death at quite a cheap price). The heroes are asked to explain Strabo's dealings with them. Once the interrogation is concluded, they're asked to remain as a band and deliver a message to one of the distant provinces of the empire.

This keeps the party together and establishes Pallas (who was one of Emperor Claudius's most despised councilors) as a long-term villain in the campaign. The implication should be that Pallas was behind Strabo's murder (although Antenor actually committed the deed). Pallas keeps silent about the visit to Cumae; after all, with Strabo dead, Antenor gone, and his most valuable holdings safely under Pallas's control, there's no need to draw further attention to the dying merchant's "last desperate actions." After a few months, Strabo's death is a distant memory as new scandals emerge, and Antenor and the PCs are long forgotten by the great Pallas as he wrestles with the affairs of state.

If he wishes, the GM can set up his campaign so the PCs become a powerful opposing force to the corrupt influence of bureaucrats like Pallas, Pallas's brother Felix (the conniving governor of Samaria and Judea), Narcissus, Empress Agrippina (Messalina's successor) and Agrippina's loathsome son Nero. It looks like the heroes of *Eternal Rome* have some work to do.

BIBLIOGRAPHY

This bibliography is intended as a starting point for additional reference and research.

ANCIENT SOURCES

Most of these sources are available in translation. Penguin Classics and Loeb's Classical Library are two of the biggest publishers, but they are by no means the only ones.

Caesar, *The Civil War*

Caesar, *The Gallic War*

Josephus, *The Jewish War*

Livy, *History of Rome*

Plautus, *The Comedies*

Pliny the Elder, *Natural History*

Sallust, *The Jugurthine War*

Suetonius, *Lives of the Caesars* (also published as *The Twelve Caesars*)

Tacitus, *Agricola*

Tacitus, *Germania*

Tacitus, *The Histories*

Terence, *The Comedies*

Virgil, *The Aeneid*

Various authors, *The Augustan History* (also published as *Lives of the Later Caesars*)

MODERN SOURCES

Airne, C.W., *The Story of Prehistoric and Roman Britain Told in Pictures*, Thomas Hope, undated

Allen, Steven, *Celtic Warrior, 300 BC–AD 100*, Osprey Warrior #30, 2001

Asimov, Isaac, *Asimov's Chronology of the World*, HarperCollins Publishers, 1991

Bagnall, Nigel, *The Punic Wars, 264–146 BC*, Osprey Essential Histories #16, 2002

Baker, Alan, *The Gladiator: The Secret History of Rome's Warrior Slaves*, Thomas Dunne, 2000

Bray, R.S., *Armies of Pestilence: The Impact of Disease on History*, Barnes & Noble, 1996

Campbell, Duncan B., *Greek and Roman Siege Machinery, 399 BC–AD 363*, Osprey New Vanguard #78, 2003

Campbell, Duncan B., *Greek and Roman Artillery, 399 BC–AD 363*, Osprey New Vanguard #89, 2003

Champion, Craig B., *Roman Imperialism: Readings and Sources*, Blackwell, 2004

Cowan, Ross, *Roman Legionary, 58 BC–AD 69*, Osprey Warrior #71, 2003

Cowan, Ross, *Imperial Roman Legionary, AD 161–284*, Osprey Warrior #72, 2003

Edwards, Mike, "Siberia's Scythians: Masters of Gold," National Geographic Magazine, June 2003

Fields, Nic, *Hadrian's Wall, AD 122–410*, Osprey Fortress #2, 2003

Flexner, Stuart and Doris, *The Pessimist's Guide to History*, Avon, 1992

Frere, Sheppard, *Britannia: A History of Roman Britain*, Routledge and Kegan Paul, 1978

Gilliver, Kate, *Caesar's Gallic Wars*, Osprey Essential Histories #43, 2002

Goldsworthy, Adrian, *Caesar's Civil War*, Osprey Essential Histories #42, 2002

Goodman, Martin, *The Roman World: 44BC–AD 180*, Routledge, 1997

Goscinny and Uderzo, *Asterix the Gaul* series, Hodder, various dates

Guiley, Rosemary Ellen, *Encyclopedia of Mystical and Paranormal Experience*, Grange Books, 1991

Hadas, Moses, *Great Ages of Man: Imperial Rome*, Time-Life Books, 1966

Healey, Mark, *Cannae 216 BC*, Osprey Campaign #36, 1994

Hodge, Peter, *Roman Family Life*, Longman, 1974

Hodge, Peter, *The Roman House*, Longman, 1976

Jiménez, Ramon L., *Caesar Against the Celts*, Barnes & Noble, 1996

Macdonald, Fiona, *Inside Story: A Roman Fort*, Peter Bedrick Books, 1993

MacDowall, Simon, *Adrianople AD 378*, Osprey Campaign #84, 2001

Malam, John, *You Wouldn't Want to be a Roman Gladiator!* Franklin Watts, 2001

Martinez, R. Trevino et al, *Rome's Enemies 4: Spanish Armies 219–218 BC*, Osprey Men-at-Arms #180, 1986

Matyszak, Philip, *Chronicle of the Roman Republic*, Thames & Hudson, 2003

Maxwell-Stuart, P.G., *Chronicle of the Popes*, Thames & Hudson, 1997

Newark, Tim, *Women Warlords*, Blandford, 1989

Nicolle, David, *Rome's Enemies 5: The Desert Frontier*, Osprey Men-at-Arms #243, 1992

Nicolle, David, *Romano-Byzantine Armies, 4th–9th centuries*, Osprey Men-at-Arms #247, 1992

Pallottino, M., *The Etruscans*, Pelican, 1955

Radice, Betty, *Who's Who in the Ancient World*, Penguin, 1977

Rankov, Boris, *The Praetorian Guard*, Osprey Elite #50, 1994

Richmond, I.A., *Roman Britain*, Pelican, 1973

Robinson, Cyril E., *A History of Rome*, Methuen, 1971

Roebuck, Carl, *The World of Ancient Times*, Macmillan, 1974

Scarre, Chris, *Chronicle of the Roman Emperors*, Thames & Hudson, 1995

Scullard, H.H., *From the Gracchi to Nero*, Methuen, 1976

Sekunda, Nicholas, *Republican Roman Army, 200-104 BC*, Osprey Men-at-Arms #291, 1996

Sekunda, Nicholas and Northwood, Michael, *Early Roman Armies*, Osprey Men-at-Arms #283, 1995

Simkins, Michael, *The Roman Army from Caesar to Trajan*, Osprey Men at Arms #46, 1984

Simkins, Michael, *The Roman Army from Hadrian to Constantine*, Osprey Men at Arms #93, 1979

Sumner, Graham, *Roman Military Clothing 1, 100 BC-AD 200*, Osprey Men-at-Arms #374, 2002

Sumner, Graham, *Roman Military Clothing 2, AD 200-400*, Osprey Men-at-Arms #390, 2003

Tannahill, Reay, *Food in History*, Three Rivers Press, 1998

Trehearne, R.F., and Hullard, Harold (eds), *Muir's Historical Atlas*, George Philip and Son, 1976

Various Authors, *The Larousse Encyclopedia of Mythology*, Paul Hamlyn, 1964

Watkins, Richard, *Gladiator*, Houghton Mifflin, 1997

Whitby, Michael, *Rome at War, AD 293-696*, Osprey Essential Histories #21, 2002

Wilcox, Peter, *Rome's Enemies 1: Germanics and Dacians*, Osprey Men-at-Arms #129, 1984

Wilcox, Peter, *Rome's Enemies 2: Gallic and British Celts*, Osprey Men-at-Arms #158, 1988

Wilcox, Peter, *Rome's Enemies 3: Parthians and Sassanid Persians*, Osprey Men-at-Arms #175, 1986

Wisdom, Stephen, *Gladiators, 100 BC-AD 200*, Osprey Warrior #39, 2001

Wise, Terence, *Armies of the Carthaginian Wars, 265-146 BC*, Osprey Men-at Arms #121, 1982

GAMES

Deities and Demigods, Jim Ward and Robert Kunz, TSR, 1980

Deities and Demigods, Rich Redman, Skip Williams, and James Wyatt, Wizards of the Coast, 2002

Fulminata: Armed With Lightning, Jason E. Roberts and Michael S. Miller, Thyrsus Games, 2001

The Glory of Rome campaign sourcebook, David L. Pulver, TSR, 1993

GURPS Imperial Rome, C.J. Carella, Steve Jackson Games, 2000

Ram Speed, Colin Keizer, Metagaming Microgames, 1980

Roma Imperious, William Corrie III, HinterWelt Enterprises, 2004

Rome: Total War, Creative Assembly, Activision, 2004

WEB RESOURCES

The Complete Petra, http://www.isidore-of-seville.com/petra/

Pankration: Martial Art of Ancient Greece, http://www.fightingarts.com/content01/panktration.shtml

RedRampant.com: Illustrated Ancient History, http://www.redrampant.com/

The Roman Army, http://www.romanarmy.com

Roman Calendar, http://www.clubs.psu.edu/up/aegsa/rome/romec.html

Roman Calendar, http://www.roman-britain.org/calendar.htm

Roman Government Officials, http://www.bol.ucla.edu/~smartin/rome/gloss/govt.html

Extensive glossary of Roman terminology, http://myweb.tiscali.co.uk/temetfutue/glossary

Index

A

Achaea 95
Aedile 127
Aeneas 101
Africa 9, 77, 91
Agrippa 113
Agrippina 114
Alexander Severus 119
Alexander the Great 10, 13, 91, 93–95
Alignment 52
Amazon 28
Amazonia 9
Ancus Martius 101
Andabate 29
Antoninus Pius 117
Arabia 77, 91
Arcane Archer 29
Arcane Trickster 29
Archer 21
Archmage 29
Arimaspi 86
Armenia 94
Ascanius 101
Asia 9, 77, 93
Assassin 29
Assemblyman 127
Augur 127
Augustus 7, 90, 101, 113
Auxiliaries 133

B

Barbarian 15
Bard 16
Belgica 98
Bithynia 94
Blackguard 30
Brennus 102
Britain 114, 116
Britannia 99
Britannicus 114
Brutus 112
Burial 131
Byzantine Empire 10, 95
Byzantium 95

C

Calendar 128
Caligula 90, 114
Campus Martius 101
Cappadocia 94
Caracalla 119
Careers 126
Carthage 7, 90, 91, 92, 104–106
Cataphract 22
Cavalry 19, 20
Celt 90, 94
Censor 128
Centaurs 86
Centurion 133
Cernunnos 17
Chariot 41, 43, 63, 136
Childhood 126
Christianity 8, 9, 115, 117, 121, 144
Cicero 110
Cicilia 94
Claudius 114
Cleopatra Selene 90
Cleopatra VII 10, 90, 111, 112
Cleric 17
Clients 126

Clodius 23
Cohorts Vigilum 134
Commander 133
Commodus 118
Constantine 120
Consul 128
Corsica 90
Crassus 7, 89
Crete 95, 96
Curator 127
Cyclopes 86
Cyprus 94
Cyrenaica 91

D

Dacia 97
Daedalus 96
Dictator 128
Didius Julianus 118
Dimachaerius 28
Diocletian 9, 120
Divination 52
Domitian 116
Druid 17
Duelist 30
Dwarven Defender 30
Dwarves 87

E

Egypt 10, 91
Eldritch Knight 30
Election 52
Elegabalus 119
Elves 88
Elysian Fields 139
Ephesus 93
Epirus 95
Equites 124
Essedarius 28
Etruria 6, 7, 100, 101, 103
Europe 77, 78

F

Fame 49
Fashion 131
Festivals 129
Fighter 19
First Triumvirate 7
Food 135

G

Gaius Gracchus 107
Gaius Marius 108, 109, 110
Galatia 94
Galba 115
Gallienus 19
Games 135
Gaul 7, 10, 89. 98, 102, 103, 108–109
Germania 10, 97
Gladiator 40, 56, 59
Gnomes 87
Gnosticism 144
Gods
  Apollo 139
  Castor 139
  Charun 140

Cybele 143
Diana 19, 93, 102
Dis Pater 140
Genii 143
Hercules 140
Isis 143
Janus 140
Juno 140
Jupiter 102, 140
Lares 142
Mars 100, 140
Mercury 141
Minerva 142
Mithras 144
Neptune 142
Orpheus 142
Penates 142
Pollux 139
Saturn 142
Silvanus 142
Venus 142
Vesta 142
Vulcan 142
Greece 7, 10, 95

H

Hadrian 93, 116
Half-orcs 88
Halflings 88
Hannibal 7, 89, 90, 105–106
Han Empire 7
Hierophant 30
Hispania 11
Honorius 122
Hoplite 22
Hoplomachus 28
Horizon Walker 30
Housing 131
Huns 12
Hyperboreans 87

I

Illyria 12
Illyricum 97
Incitatus 114
Infantry 19, 20
Interrex 127
Italy 12, 89

J

Jesus of Nazareth 92
John the Baptist 92
Judaism 144
Judea 8, 12, 91, 92
Jugurthine War 108
Julian 121
Julius Caesar 7, 23, 107, 110–112

L

Laestrygonians 87
Laquearius 29
Latin League 102, 103
Legate 133
Legionary 19, 61, 103
Legions 133
Library of Alexandria 91
Licinius 9
Literature 137
Loremaster 30
Lucius Sergius Cataline 110

Lucius Tarquinius Priscus 101
Lucius Tarquinius Superbus 102
Lycia 94

M

Macedonia 13, 95
Macrinus 119
Magic 64
Marcus Aemilius Lepidus 7, 111–112, 117
Mark Anthony 7, 111–113
Mauretania 90
Maxentius 9
Maximian 9, 120
Maximinus 9
Maximinus Daia 9
Mesopotamia 93
Military Tribune 133
Milo 23
Minos 96
Mirmillo 28
Moesia 97
Money 132
Music 137
Mystic Theurge 30

N

Naples 103
Nereids 87
Nero 114, 115
Nerva 116
Noricum 97
Numitor 101
Nymphs 88

O

Octavia 112
Octavian 7, 112. *See Also* Augustus
Octavius 107
Offices 126
Olympus 138
Optimates 7
Orator 32
Otho 115

P

Paladin 23
Pamphylia 94
Pankretiast 35
Pannonia 97
Parthia 7, 13
Parthian Empire 93
Patricians 124
Patron 53, 55

Patrons 126
Peltast 22
Pertinax 118
Phoenicia 13, 92
Picts 13
Plebeians 125
Pompey 7, 10, 23, 94–95, 110–111
Pontifex Maximus 128
Pontus 94
Populares 7
Praetor 127
Praetorian Guard 134
Prefect 128
Prescennius Niger 118
Provincials 125
Ptolemy 90
Ptolemy II 104
Ptolemy XIII 111
Punic Wars 90–92, 104
Pyrrhic War 103
Pyrrhus 96, 104

Q

Quaestor 127
Quinctilius Varus 113
Quintus Fabius 105

R

Ranger 23
Remus 101
Retiarius 28
Rhaetia 97
Rhodes 95, 96
Rogue 23
Roman Empire 7–8, 89–92, 100, 113–121
Roman Republic 7, 102–113
Rome 6, 100
Romulus 100–101

S

Sagittarius 29
Samnite War 103
Sardinia 90
Satyrs 88
Saxons 13
Scots 14
Sculpture 137
Scythia 14
Secutor 28
Sejanus 114
Seleucid Empire 92
Senator 127
Septimius Severus 93, 116, 118

Servius Tullius 102
Sextus Pompeius 112
Shadowdancer 30
Shaman 19
Sicily 90
Silvanus 17, 19
Slavery 106, 107, 125
Slinger 21
Social War 109
Soothsayer 36
Sorcerer 23
Spain 90
Spartacus 89, 110
Spells 64
Styx 139
Sulla 109–110
Syria 14, 92

T

Tarentum 103, 104
Tartarus 139
Taurarius 29
Thaumaturgist 30
Theater 137
Theodosius I 122
Thrace 14, 28, 95
Tiberius 8, 114
Tiberius Gracchus 107
Titus 116
Trajan 8, 90–93, 116
Tribune 127
Triumph 53
Troy 101
Tullus Hostilius 101

U

Urban Cohorts 134

V

Venator 29
Vespasian 115
Vigil 38
Vigintivirates 127
Virgil 101
Visigoths 89
Vitellius 115

W

Wizard 23
Women 125

X

Xanthippus 105